An Affluent Society?

Modern Economic and Social History Series

General Editor: Derek H. Aldcroft

Titles in this series include:

Studies in the Interwar European Economy
Derek H. Aldcroft

Arms and the State
Sir William Armstrong and the Remaking of British Naval Power,
1854–1914
Marshall J. Bastable

Whatever Happened to Monetarism?
Economic Policy Making and Social Learning in the United Kingdom
Since 1979
Michael J. Oliver

Disillusionment or New Opportunites?
The Changing Nature of Work in Offices, Glasgow 1880–1914
R. Guerriero Wilson

Raleigh and the British Bicycle Industry
An Economic and Business History, 1870–1960
Roger Lloyd-Jones and M.J. Lewis

Battles for the Standard
Bimetallism and the Spread of the Gold Standard in the
Nineteenth Century
Ted Wilson

The British Footwear Industry
Peter R. Mounfield

Trade Unions and the Economy: 1870–2000
Derek H. Aldcroft and Michael J. Oliver

The British Electronics Industry
Technical Promise and Market Failure, 1930–2000
John F. Wilson

DATE OF RETURN
UNLESS RECALLED BY LIBRARY

PLEASE TAKE GOOD CARE OF THIS BOOK

An Affluent Society?

Britain's Post-War 'Golden Age' Revisited

Edited by

LAWRENCE BLACK

HUGH PEMBERTON

ASHGATE

Published by

Ashgate Publishing Limited
Gower House
Croft Road
Aldershot
Hampshire GU11 3HR
England

Ashgate Publishing Company
Suite 420
101 Cherry Street
Burlington, VT 05401-4405
USA

Ashgate website: http://www.ashgate.com

British Library Cataloguing in Publication Data
An affluent society? : Britain's post-war 'golden age' revisited. – (Modern economic and social history)
1. Great Britain – Social conditions – 1945- 2. Great Britain – Economic conditions – 20th century 3. Great Britain – Politics and government – 1945-
I. Black, Lawrence, 1971- II. Pemberton, Hugh
941'.085

Library of Congress Cataloging-in-Publication Data
An affluent society? : Britain's post-war 'Golden Age' revisited / edited by Lawrence Black and Hugh Pemberton.
    p. cm. – (Modern economic and social history)
    Includes bibliographical references and index.
    ISBN 0-7546-3528-7 (alk. paper)
    1. Wealth–Great Britain–History–20th century. 2. Great Britain–Economic conditions–1945-1946. 3. Great Britain–Social conditions–1945- I. Black, Lawrence, 1971- II. Pemberton, Hugh. II. Modern economic and social history series

HC260.W4A38 2003
330.941'085–dc22

2003063712

ISBN 0 7546 3528 7

Printed and bound by TJ International Ltd, Padstow, Cornwall

Contents

List of Figures, Tables and Plates   *vii*
General Editor's Preface   *viii*
Acknowledgements   *ix*
List of Contributors   *x*

1   Introduction – The Uses (and Abuses) of Affluence
    Lawrence Black and Hugh Pemberton   1

2   Affluence, Conservatism and Political Competition in Britain
    and the United States, 1945–1964
    Brian Girvin   15

3   Modernizing Britain's Welfare State: The Influence of
    Affluence, 1957–1964
    Rodney Lowe   35

4   The Forgotten Revisionist: Douglas Jay and Britain's Transition
    to Affluence, 1951–1964
    Richard Toye   53

5   Total Abstinence and a Good Filing-System? Anthony Crosland
    and the Affluent Society
    Catherine Ellis   69

6   The Impression of Affluence: Political Culture in the 1950s and
    1960s
    Lawrence Black   85

7   Affluence, Relative Decline and the Treasury
    Hugh Pemberton   107

8   Economists and Economic Growth in Britain, c.1955–65
    Roger Middleton   129

9   The Polyester–Flannelled Philanthropists: The Birmingham
     Consumers' Group and Affluent Britain
     Mathew Hilton   149

10   Anticipating Affluence: Skill, Judgement and the Problems of
     Aesthetic Tutelage
     Lesley Whitworth   167

11   'Selling Youth in the Age of Affluence': Marketing to Youth in
     Britain since 1959
     Christian Bugge   185

12   Losing the Peace: Germany, Japan, America and the Shaping of
     British National Identity in the Age of Affluence
     Richard Weight   203

Bibliography   223
Index   245

List of Figures, Tables and Plates

List of Figures

7.1 UK growth indices, 1950–60 (at 1995 market prices, 1950=100)   108
7.2 Real consumer spending (selected items), 1948–60 (1948=100)   109
7.3 Indices of industrial production, selected countries, 1950–8   110
7.4 Britain's export performance in the 1950s   111
8.1 Real GDP at 1995 market prices (1958=100): actual and trend,   130
    NEDC 1961–6 projections and National Plan 1964–70 projections

List of Tables

7.1 Productivity growth (GNP per employee year), 1950–9   111
7.2 Top seven countries by GDP, selected years   112

List of Plates

1. Lawrence Harvey as Joe Lampton in the film version of John
   Braine's *Room at the Top*, produced by John and James Woolf and
   directed by Jack Clayton. Here Joe visits the scene of his childhood
   in the northern industrial town of 'Dufton' © 2003 London Features
   International Ltd.

2. The (anonymous) 500,000th visitor to the Britain Can Make It
   exhibition receives a radio set from the Deputy Director of the
   Council of Industrial Design, N.E. Kearley, 1946

3. The Industrial Designer; detail of the exhibit 'What Industrial
   Design Means' at Britain Can Make It, 1946

4. The Figure of 'Mr Designer' directed visitors at the Britain Can
   Make It exhibition and brilliantly embodied the Council of
   Industrial Design's core message to consumers

   Plates 2–4 © Design Council/Design History Research Centre,
   University of Brighton. http://ww.brighton.ac.uk/descoarchive/

Modern Economic and Social History Series
General Editor's Preface

Economic and social history has been a flourishing subject of scholarly study during recent decades. Not only has the volume of literature increased enormously but the range of interest in time, space and subject matter has broadened considerably so that today there are many sub-branches of the subject which have developed considerable status in their own right.

One of the aims of this new series is to encourage the publication of scholarly monographs on any aspect of modern economic and social history. The geographical coverage is world-wide and contributions on the non-British themes will be especially welcome. While emphasis will be placed on works embodying original research, it is also intended that the series should provide the opportunity to publish studies of a more general thematic nature which offer a reappraisal or critical analysis of major issues of debate.

Derek H. Aldcroft
University of Leicester

Acknowledgements

The editors would like to thank the Economic History Society, the Royal Historical Society and the University of Bristol Alumni Fund for funding a two–day conference at the University of Bristol in May 2002 at which the ideas for the book took shape. We would also like to thank all those who attended and participated in the discussions that took place, in particular: Antoine Capet, Steven Fielding, John Goldthorpe, Martin Hunt, Harriet Jones, Ruth Levitas, Gregg McClymont, Marc Stears, Richard Sheldon, Nick Thomas, Andrew Thorpe, Jim Tomlinson and, of course, those who have contributed to this volume. We are also very grateful to those who helped us to organize the conference: Paula Warburton, Karen Williams and Sarah Britton.

We would also particularly like to express our gratitude to Rodney Lowe and our thanks go to both to Derek Aldcroft as series editor and to Tom Gray, our editor at Ashgate, for their assistance.

In addition, we owe much to the institutions that have funded and hosted our respective postdoctoral studies, during which the book has been edited: the University of Bristol, Westminster College, Fulbright Commission and Council for the International Exchange of Scholars, in the case of Lawrence Black; and the Economic and Social Research Council (award number T026271086), British Academy, University of Bristol and London School of Economics in the case of Hugh Pemberton.

List of Contributors

Lawrence Black is author of *The Political Culture of the Left in Affluent Britain, 1951–64: Old Labour, New Britain?* (Palgrave, 2003) and was Fulbright–Robertson Visiting Professor of British History at Westminster College, Missouri, USA in 2002–3. Lecturer in History at the University of Durham, he is researching consumer and cultural politics and political marketing in postwar Britain.

Christian Bugge received his Ph.D., 'The End of Youth Subculture? Dance Culture and Youth Marketing 1988–2000', in 2002. The research for this was undertaken at Kingston University's Centre for the Understanding of Society and Politics, where he also organized an international conference on youth marketing. He now works in Brussels as a market research consultant.

Catherine Ellis is Assistant Professor of History at Ryerson University, Toronto, Canada. She is currently working on a book manuscript entitled 'Between Two Worlds: The British Labour Party in Opposition, 1951–1964' and has also published in the *Journal of British Studies* and the *Historical Journal*.

Brian Girvin is Professor of Comparative Politics at the University of Glasgow and was Visiting Professor of Political Science at Iowa State University, USA, 2002–3. His most recent books are *From Union to Union: Nationalism, Democracy and Religion in Ireland, Act of Union to EU* (Gill and Macmillan, 2002) and co–edited (with Geoffrey Roberts), *Ireland and the Second World War: Politics Society and Remembrance* (Four Courts Press, 2000) Other research interests include the US presidency and Conservatism and national identity in Britain. He is currently completing a comparative study of nationalism in the twentieth–century (forthcoming, Routledge) and a study of Irish neutrality during the Second World War.

Matthew Hilton is Senior Lecturer in History at the University of Birmingham. He is the author of *Smoking in British Popular Culture 1800–2000* (Manchester University Press, 2000) and *Consumerism in Twentieth–Century Britain: The Search for a Historical Movement* (Cambridge University Press, 2003) and editor, with Martin Daunton, of *The Politics of Consumption: Material Culture and Citizenship in Europe and America* (Berg, 2001). He is a Phillip Leverhulme Prizewinner (2002) and is working on a project on consumption and globalization.

Rodney Lowe is Professor of Contemporary History at the University of Bristol. He is currently on long–term secondment to the Cabinet Office to write the official history of the British civil service since 1968. He has written widely on welfare policy and policy–making in Britain and abroad during the twentieth century. Amongst his recent works are *The Welfare State in Britain Since 1945* (Macmillan,

3rd edition, in press); with Margaret Jones, *From Beveridge to Blair: The First Fifty Years of Britain's Welfare State* (Manchester University Press, 2002) and 'Riches, poverty and progress' in Keith Robbins (ed.), *The British Isles, 1901– 1951 (Short Oxford History of the British Isles)*, Oxford University Press, 2002).

Roger Middleton is Reader in the History of Political Economy at the University of Bristol. He is the author of *The British Economy since 1945: Engaging with the Debate* (Palgrave, 2000), a forthcoming chapter in the Cambridge Economic History of Modern Britain and is currently working on a book about 'Stop–Go' and the British economy.

Hugh Pemberton is British Academy Postdoctoral Research Fellow at the London School of Economics and Political Science. He is the author of *Policy Learning and British Governance in the 1960s* (Palgrave Macmillan, 2004) and has published in *Public Administration, Twentieth Century British History,* the *British Journal of Political Science and International Relations,* and *Governance.*

Richard Toye is Lecturer in History at Homerton College, Cambridge. He is the author of *The Labour Party and the Planned Economy, 1931–1951* (Royal Historical Society, 2003) and co–author (with Jamie Miller) of *Cripps Versus Clayton* (forthcoming, Ashgate, 2004) and (with John Toye) of *The North–South Encounter* (forthcoming, Indiana University Press, 2004).

Richard Weight is the author of *Patriots: National Identity in Britain 1940–2000* (Macmillan, 2002) and co–editor (with Abigail Beach) of *The Right to Belong: Citizenship and National Identity in Britain, 1930–1960* (I.B. Tauris, 1998). He currently teaches at the University of London, is a regular broadcaster and is a Fellow of the Royal Society of Arts.

Lesley Whitworth researched shopping processes and practices in the inter–war Midlands for her doctorate at Warwick University. She is currently an ESRC/AHRB 'Cultures of Consumption' Research Fellow at the Design History Research Centre, University of Brighton, where she is investigating the relationship between retailers, the Council of Industrial Design and the British buying public in the post–war period.

CHAPTER 1

Introduction – The Uses (and Abuses) of Affluence

Lawrence Black and Hugh Pemberton

> And so the Britons were gradually led on to the amenities that make vice agreeable – arcades, baths and sumptuous banquets. They spoke of such novelties as 'civilization', when really they were only a feature of enslavement. (Tacitus, 'Agricola', 21)[1]

Analyses of post-war Britain have mainly adopted (sometimes explicitly but often implicitly) an international or comparative perspective that has centred on discussions of national decline: economic, military, diplomatic, imperial or cultural. Recently, contemporary historians such as Jim Tomlinson have begun to argue for a focus on 'declinism' rather than 'decline'. Ironically, however, such scholars continue to work within the parameters of decline as the core concept for the study of post-war British history. The core premise of this collection is that attention to affluence can enrich historians' understanding of post-war Britain. This requires a shift in focus to the domestic rather than the international. Such a shift radically alters the analytical perspective: emphasizing absolute growth over relative decline; highlighting the enormous improvement in British living standards that took place in the post-war years; and emphasizing the widespread cultural consequences associated with the growth of post-war consumerism.[2]

The paradox of absolute growth versus relative decline

That the post-war 'golden age' of British economic development and the concomitant advent of the 'affluent society' should have coincided with the publication of new comparative data revealing both Britain's relative economic decline and an acceleration in that decline is the great paradox of modern British social and economic history. This paradox lies at the heart of this book. A number of its chapters highlight the existence and the profound economic, social and political significance of rising popular consumerism, improving health and life expectancy, and rising living standards and expectations. Shifting the focus towards affluence in this way questions the usefulness of a language of decline, even of relative decline, to characterize a period that saw unprecedented economic growth. Nevertheless, the collection does not seek to supplant entirely a narrative of 'relative decline' with one of 'affluence', since the fact of relative decline remains; instead it sets out to use affluence to unpack and explore the nuances of this debate, the complexities of the post-war period, and the paradox of affluence in the face of relative decline.

This paradox is well personified by Harold Macmillan in the latter half of the 1950s. The Prime Minister profited politically from association with the phrase 'most of our people have never had it so good', coined in a 1957 speech to the electors of Bedford. The remark, plucked out of context, seemed to many to be simply a justified acknowledgement of Britain's new 'affluent society' and it became the leitmotif of the Conservatives' 1959 election campaign; exemplified by the slogan 'Life's better with the Conservatives. Don't let Labour ruin it'. What has too often been forgotten, however, and what was sometimes overlooked at the time was that Macmillan went on to say '... what is beginning to worry some of us is "Is it too good to be true?" or perhaps I should say "Is it too good to last?"'.[3]

The paradox of rising affluence coincident with growing pessimism might be understood as the product of different experiences: of elites and the people, or in terms of the differing history of Britain and of Britons. In comparative economic and imperial terms Britain might have been in decline, but the full employment, the availability of consumer durables, and the benefits of the post-war welfare state were palpable. This inconsistency did not escape contemporaries. As early as 1950, Michigan University economist, Clare Griffin, noted: 'the worker is told Britain is poor ... but the worker doesn't feel poor. He has more money than before and his job is more secure'. Official 'propaganda appeals are being applied in one direction while his personal interests point in the opposite direction.' The spending and leisure that full employment and the welfare state allowed created an anxiety, expressed by Griffin, that workers might opt for relaxation over output, threatening economic competitiveness; and that anxiety that grew as the 1950s progressed.[4]

Declinism

The fear expressed by Macmillan that there was something rotten at the heart of the British economy in the 1950s, that economic success contained within it the seed of its own destruction, was a common one at the time. A growing fixation with decline (particularly economic, but military, colonial and cultural too), what Tomlinson has termed the 'new declinism', is a remarkable feature of the period.[5] It can be found in the records of government, employers associations and trade unions, and permeated contemporary broadsheets and 'quality' periodicals. The mood was one of, 'What's wrong with Britain?', as an influential early-1960s Penguin series was entitled.[6] The crescendo of anxieties about relative decline prompted Macmillan to complain in his diary for 1962: 'If only all the people who write, lecture, broadcast and even preach about economic growth did some useful work, the increase in manpower would perhaps enable us to achieve it.'[7] So pervasive was the 'declinist' narrative, both at the time and subsequently that it has tended to dominate analysis of developments in the 1950s and 1960s.

As Tomlinson has pointed out, the declinist narrative constructed during the 1970s and 1980s owed a great deal to the Thatcherite backlash against the post-war political settlement.[8] Historical works, notably Martin Wiener's account of the lack of entrepreneurial instincts and the rural nostalgia endemic in English culture; Rubinstein's case that commerce and finance out-ranked manufacture (differing from Wiener's emphasis, but fitting Thatcherite prejudices nonetheless) and Corelli Barnett's audit of Britain's loss of economic, military and imperial power, were prominent in this narrative. National decline was taken as read in this analysis – though there was less of a consensus about its precise causes or chronology. The political agenda of much of this work was transparent, targeting 'one nation' Conservatism as much as social democracy. As Paul Addison argues, 'used in this context the "decline of Britain" is not a historical fact, but a highly partisan interpretation in which the loss of social and imperial ascendancies is equated with the decline of Britain both at home and abroad.'[9] However, the Thatcherite or New Right context alone cannot explain why decline has retained such currency.

Since the late 1950s, the declinist narrative has also had a purchase on the left. From popular works in the 1960s and 1970s (such as the writings of Anthony Hartley, Michael Shanks, and Anthony Sampson) to Will Hutton in the 1990s, left intellectuals have not only subscribed to, but been key sponsors of the decline concept.[10] Perry Anderson, in his 1964 *New Left Review* essay 'Origins of the Present Crisis', shared Shonfield, Shanks and Hartley's identification of the 'secular decline of the British economy', but felt they described symptoms more than explained causes. Rejoining the debate in the 1980s, Anderson approvingly cited the explanations forwarded by Barnett, Wiener and Rubinstein. Anderson, echoing Barnett's *Audit of War*, located the roots of decline in the legacy of the industrial revolution.

In explaining decline, therefore, both camps have stressed the specific development of industrial capitalism in Britain – fashioned by class structure, empire, the balance of finance and manufacturing, culturally skewed against modernity and prone to nostalgia for a lost (and largely mythical) rural idyll. Its causes peculiar to British culture, this was a 'very British' decline and also one partially blamed on Britons in both versions. Anderson's 'supine proletariat' were Barnett's 'segregated, subliterate … proletariat.' In this sense both New Left and New Right shared a working assumption of post-war British 'decline'. Whatever else, this demonstrates the eclectic sources and force of declin*ism*.[11]

That decline has been so embroiled in political debates should make historians wary of accepting it at face value, to be proved or rejected. The idea and fear of decline has been rife in Western culture and historical writing for a long time, certainly long before British de-colonization and relative economic decline. Declin*ism* then was, on the one hand, a state of mind, disclosing much about the assumptions through which the meanings of this period were constructed. As Dintenfass argues, when discussing the language of the decline debate, 'the narrative constructions to which pessimists and optimists [about Britain's economic performance] alike necessarily resorted … indicate that the parties to this dispute unknowingly occupied a good deal of common ground'.[12] On the other hand, historians should be interested in how declin*ism* (the assumption of national decline as the problematic) underpins a host of political projects, from Macmillan's modernization of Britain and Wilson's 'white heat' scientific and technological revolution, to Thatcher's economic rationalization.

Affluence – an alternative narrative?

The concept of 'declinism' is a welcome attempt to break out of the sterile 'decline' debate. Yet, because that debate is its starting point, the declinism thesis is itself rooted in arguments about Britain's performance relative to other countries.[13] The problem is that the analysis remains focused too much on international comparisons and too little on the domestic experience. Shifting to a domestic (and simultaneously less elitist, less economic) perspective might cast post-war Britain in a much more positive light than that which characterizes both the 'declinist' literature and the literature of 'declinism'.

Richard Weight, for instance, has made a case for a British cultural renaissance in the 1960s, centred around popular culture and crafting a post-imperial focus for national identity.[14] This foreshadowed the Blair government's promotion of 'Cool Britannia' in the late-1990s, and its focus on the 'creative economy' of information technology, the arts, design and culture. Less decline and fall, in this analysis what was being witnessed was Britain's transition from an industrial to post-industrial, more democratic, even post-modern economy.[15] This is not to deny the fact of Britain's relative decline but to point out that on the domestic front relative decline manifested itself as a rather pleasing decay, accompanied as it was by unprecedented popular wealth and health. Though not, it has to be said, by much if any increase in the happiness of the average British citizen since affluence bred a new range of discontents and entailed a new set of social costs.[16] This was less decline than a shift to post-industrial consumption patterns. It is on this that historians should perhaps focus rather than continuing to be transfixed (like contemporaries) by decline – for which social change could all too easily be mistaken.

Of course, as a number of chapters in this book show, affluence was not evenly distributed around Britain or amongst Britons: patterned as it was by region, gender, generation, class and a host of other variables. It was itself a relative concept – referring not to the experience of a wealthy elite, but to that of the mass of Britons. It was not that the rich were extinct, although it seemed that way to some, but that affluence had a quite demotic, democratic emphasis. Affluence did little to erase quantitative inequalities, but the absolute shift in spending power extended the ownership of luxuries from the elite to the mass. As US management guru Peter Drucker saw it (cold war-style) in 1960, 'Automobiles and traffic jams are mightier levellers than Karl Marx'.[17]

Affluence, then, is at once potentially an alternative to the dominant historical narrative about post-war Britain and a refinement of the 'declinism' thesis. But it can be more than this, for the phenomenon of affluence was the source of contemporary debates traversing political, economic, social and cultural spheres. It has the potential to allow historians to do likewise, to a much greater extent than historical writing on post-war Britain in either of these two schools of thought. Using affluence as an 'organizing perspective' can therefore allow historians to respond to the recent and increasingly loud calls for a more integrated approach to contemporary history.[18] To this end, this volume consciously brings together social, cultural, welfare, political and economic historians to reconsider our understanding of Britain's post-war 'golden age'.[19]

Another use of 'affluence' is its potential to confront a further charge sometimes made against contemporary history – that it has too easily adopted the dominant terminology of its subject matter.[20] Contemporary historians, of course, face particular difficulties in achieving a critical distance from their subject. The concern of contemporaries (or at least of contemporary elites) with decline has tended to be translated uncritically into historical writing, whereas affluence, which was largely taken for granted at the time, has featured much less. We need to historicize the terms 'affluence' and 'decline', recognizing that they impute rather than embody or reflect the meaning of certain characteristics of the period.

Although affluence has not been subject to much investigation by contemporary historians, it was the subject of contemporary analysis by sociologists (and to a lesser extent by political scientists).[21] Such contemporary social science readings have set the parameters of the debate. We have not yet sufficiently recognized the consequences for historians of the post-war rise of the social scientist. If journalists write the first draft of history, as the old saw has it, then increasingly social scientists have come to write the second. The ways in which political science, economics, sociology and cultural studies have fashioned interpretations of the meanings of this period ought to be of at least as much interest to historians as the veracity of their interpretations themselves. Thus the questions posed by seminal accounts in the 'required reading' on post-war Britain – for example, the 'affluent worker' sociological studies; the writings of cultural commentators like Raymond Williams and Richard Hoggart; the work of political psephologists like Mark Abrams; popular sociological accounts by the likes of Wilmott, Young and Zweig; or the comparative data accorded importance by economists – can better inform our understanding of how affluence was conceived in particular ways. With access to the records now obtained under the thirty-year rule, historians must consider how valid these analyses really were. One thing is certain: Britain's 'decline' is as moot as its rise and surely as receptive to historical cross-examination.

When was 'affluent Britain'?

'Affluent Britain' is rather easier to periodize than British 'decline' (which is variously dated as far back as the 1870s). The long boom or 'golden age' is conventionally dated from 1945 to 1973. Most of the chapters in this volume focus on debates about an 'Age of Affluence' that began in 1951 with the end of the immediate post-war 'Age of Austerity' and ended with the OPEC oil crisis of 1973 and the economic downturn and return to mass unemployment.[22] However, it is apparent that the chronology of 'affluence' is subject to debate.

From the point of view of social as well as political history, for example, the ending of food rationing (instituted in 1940) in July 1954 might be seen as a decisive moment, and Zweiniger-Bargielowska contends 1955 was the general election that marked the end of austerity. This did not, however, mean that affluence had arrived for all.[23] Another moment might be the establishment of the Consumers' Association in 1957 and its rapid growth which signified the salience of consumer concerns with abundance, choice and quality not with scarcity. Macmillan's 'never had it so good' speech the same year drew few doubters, though plenty who deplored its vulgar materialism and the speaker himself was cautionary about inflation and wondered 'can it last?' As another popular commentator, John Montgomery, mused, 'if conditions were really so good, why was hire-purchase so popular?' J.K. Galbraith's influential, *The Affluent Society*, primarily about the USA, but with wider implications and readership, was published in the UK in 1958 and offered a more sophisticated language for articulating the significance of popular spending power than Macmillan's (if one that was as uncertain). If affluence marked a qualitative as much as quantitative shift then the signs were legion. The shift to privatism impressed many commentators. For instance, the 1950s housing boom was underpinned by a massive rise in private home ownership; or 1961 being the first year since the 1880s that the number of off-licences (supplying drink for the home not pub) grew; or the threefold decline in cinema audiences and closure of almost 1000 cinemas between 1954 and 1961 as TV viewers stayed at home.[24]

To some extent 'affluence' was a product of comparing the better years of the 1950s with the preceding 'age of austerity'; an illusion produced by below trend growth in living standards during the 1930s and 1940s. Parts of the Midlands and South-East England in the 1930s witnessed the sort of consumer culture and middle-class suburban lifestyles that would become more common in the 1950s. Likewise, Fowler has made a case for an emerging modern youth culture in the 1930s.[25] By the 1960s, however affluence was far more pervasive and was often purported to be having a homogenizing, standardizing effect – it was the norm, encroaching even into traditional communities like South Wales. What was uniquely Welsh was 'gradually disappearing as the television sets, the neat bungalows, the Ford Cortinas and the age of affluence advance into the valleys.'[26]

The relationship between affluence and the cold war is also touched upon by several contributors to this volume. As the Nixon-Khrushchev 'kitchen' debate at the American National Exhibition in Moscow in 1959 showed, domestic consumer durables were contested commodities, the kitchen a Cold War terrain.[27] Although there was some debate as to exactly how resilient a defence affluence provided against Soviet military and technological advances. In these respects affluence linked the domestic and everyday with global politics.

Paradoxically, however, in the historiographical sense it might be argued that affluence began at the very moment it ended. As Eric Hobsbawm put it, 'I cannot say that we recognized it as what I have called "The Golden Age" in my *Age of Extremes*. That became possible only after 1973 when it was over.'[28] Similarly, looking back in 1974, Mary Proudfoot found the period from 1951 to 1970 to be 'the two happiest and most affluent decades yet in British history'. This highlights a tension between affluence as perceived at the time and as perceived after the event. Bogdanor and Skidelsky, writing in 1970, designated 1951–64 the *Age of Affluence*, arguing that after 1964 the (Labour) view that there was rather less to celebrate about the Conservative administration and economic achievements in this period prevailed.[29] Had they written the book after 1973 they might have reassessed this end date. Affluence, as a useful contemporary shorthand to describe Britain and Britons, slipped from the zeitgeist or lost its hegemony during the 1960s. Permissiveness and the counter-culture seemed a more novel and appealing rhetoric – though at the same time, shared with affluence a range of moral-cultural concerns and emphases, such as the individualism and the 'self'. The 'rediscovery of poverty' by social policy experts like Townsend and Abel-Smith in 1965 had also eroded the perspicacity of the term, by emphasizing that not all were sharing in affluence.[30] Yet these important shifts in culture and perception were, in a sense, only made possible by affluence.

One might also argue that in so much as affluence meant a rising standard of living for the mass of the population and greater access to consumer durables, affluence did not go away at all – even in the 1970s – and that it is still with us. Indeed recent anti-globalization protests echo the concerns about cultural homogenization, the power of business, advertising and the market, voiced about affluence in the 'golden age'.[31] Nevertheless, as a state of mind or 'feel good factor', affluence clearly dissipated during the 1970s. Inflation, unemployment, industrial and nationalist discontent, all made a context in which arguments that Britain was culturally backward or weighed down by its own heritage, and that this partly explained its 'decline', resonated more strongly. Although again, historians are now beginning to stress how partial, even mythic, the popular, declinist image of the 1970s is.[32] Even heritage culture has won historical advocates – who rather than baiting it as evidence of a backward-looking nation in decline, have celebrated it as (not only good business) but evidence of a healthy, popular historical consciousness.[33]

As Lowe and Ellis show in their chapters in this volume, both political parties selectively used aspects of affluence to suit their vision of a Conservative or democratic socialist Britain. But their visions worked on premises, perhaps most notably full employment, that were highly specific. The 'Golden Age' was a phase of rather than a permanent change in capitalism, at the close of which Keynesianism lost its appeal to business, workers and both political parties. Thus, as Toye's chapter argues, New Labour's vision cannot simply be related to post-war revisionism.[34]

Although one can debate its exact dates, therefore, in the domestic context Britain's 'Golden Age' was a period of notable progress and political, economic, social and cultural change. Using affluence to frame our analysis of post-war Britain thus dramatically shifts the terms of the debate and has the potential to throw new light on Britain's post-war history.

The uses of affluence

In a sense affluence was as much an aspiration as a reality, yet one whose prospect of attainment was far more likely in the 'golden age' than ever before, with Britons liberated from inter-war poverty and from post-war controls and austerity. Affluence's distribution also remained sharply regional: for example, one in three homes in London and the South-East had a telephone in 1964 compared with one in ten in Northern Ireland, Wales and Northern England.[35]

Still, the economic individualism and consumer choice celebrated from the later 1950s (and the consumer skills Whitworth dates to earlier in her chapter) points to this underpinning rather than resulting from the 'cultural revolution' or hedonism of the 1960s, something which is at odds with the accounts of Arthur Marwick or Jose Harris.[36] If this was so then it was the developments of the 1950s rather than the 1960s that fed the shift to neo-liberalism and free market ideology in the 1980s. Frank Mort's cultural history of 1980s advertising and marketing and consumer identities, similarly plots this story from the 1950s.[37] As Raymond Williams, the leading left-wing cultural commentator, echoing Galbraith, put it in 1961: 'The popularity of 'consumer' as a contemporary term ... is significant, because ... it materializes the individual ... who has not heard that impassioned cry of the modern barricade: 'but it's my money you're spending on all this; leave my money alone'.[38] In this critique of affluence can be seen the later mantra of neo-liberalism.

America was seen as the source of many of the changes overrunning British society; signifier of Britain's declining world standing and post-war economic dependency or elite fears at the malaise in British culture (as Weight discusses in his chapter). Affluence was commonly bound up with Americanization and, in turn, equated with British 'decline'. Francis Williams' biography of Attlee, *Twilight of Empire* was soon followed by *The American Invasion* and its contention that 'What British families should be taught to feel and think in order to persuade them to spend has more and more become the prerogative of American advertising men.'[39] Thus the significance of the British cultural revival of the 1960s – shedding US dominance such that by the close of the 1960s the UK was swinging whilst the USA was bogged down in imperial conflict.

Alongside debates over affluence, the 1950s saw an intense debate amongst economic historians about the impact of the industrial revolution on living standards in Britain. In discussing the merits and iniquities of the development of industrial capitalism this debate had obvious Cold War analogies, but also with affluence in addressing whether changes in the standard of living were worth it in terms of the quality of life.[40] And whilst Galbraith's 'public squalor' was not quite Blake's 'dark satanic mills', it begged the same question of whether economic change was bringing social and cultural benefit. Indeed history (the discipline) felt the consequences of affluence just as keenly as other parts of British society. Cannadine has argued, 'the period from the late 1940s to the early 1970s was ... a Golden Age for professional British historians ... when academe in general was an affluent society, and when Clio in particular had never had it so good.'[41] Perhaps refocusing the debate on affluence could yet prove as productive and rewarding for historians today.

Chapter summaries

In the next chapter, Brian Girvin notes that in both Britain and the USA affluence followed a process of political change initiated by the left: in the United States the

New Deal and in Britain the introduction of the Welfare State. He suggests that the Republican Party in the United States and the Conservative Party in Britain were both able to benefit from the politics of affluence. Both understood that affluence and its cultivation could provide an electoral edge in a highly competitive party system and that it also offered an important counter to the class-based politics of both the Labour Party and the Democratic Party.

In Chapter 3, Rodney Lowe shifts the focus to the modernization of Britain's welfare state between 1957 and 1964. He argues that rising affluence challenged the very existence of the post-war welfare state – which had been essentially designed as a response to the mass unemployment and poverty of the 1930s. In reaction to this, argues Lowe, the Conservatives developed proposals which sought to roll back the welfare state – prefiguring the policies of the Thatcher era. These proposals, however, were rejected on grounds of both principle and pragmatism. Instead both ministers and officials committed themselves to an unparalleled peacetime expansion of government in all areas of welfare policy (economic and social).

Two chapters then follow that consider the ways in which the Labour Party attempted to come to terms with the changed political environment that affluence produced. In Chapter 4, Richard Toye assesses the reaction of Douglas Jay to affluence – in particular, his opposition to Nicholas Kaldor's proposal for an expenditure tax, his attitude to advertising, and the furore over his advocacy in 1959 of a change in the Labour Party's name. He argues that, whilst it is tempting to suggest that Labour was 'alienated from popular affluence', the problem was more that it was only after 1959 that the party found the language or the occasion to mobilize popular concern about the consequences of an unregulated economy.

In Chapter 5, Catherine Ellis looks at the way in which Anthony Crosland's political philosophy was shaped by the affluence of the 1950s. Crosland, argues Ellis, believed that it was necessary for socialists to approach the affluent society from a practical point of view, to analyse and resolve its shortcomings, but not to condemn the achievement of higher standards of living and material equality. Ellis concludes that Crosland's enduring accomplishment was to demonstrate the continued relevance of socialism in the 'affluent society'.

The following two chapters consider the development of economic policy in the 'age of affluence'. In Chapter 6, Hugh Pemberton outlines economic developments in the 1950s and the ways in which, coupled with fears of relative decline, these shaped the development of economic policy. He argues that too little importance has been attached to increasing affluence and that relative economic decline was overstated. Nevertheless, he suggests that superior economic performance on the Continent had the potential to become more than simple 'catch-up and convergence', that real shortcomings in the prevailing Keynesian policy making framework were already apparent by the beginning of the 1960s, and that the (so often maligned) Treasury recognized both these problems and made a serious attempt to address them.

In Chapter 7, Roger Middleton considers the degree to which academic economists and economists within government might be held responsible for the patent failure of Britain's attempt further to raise its rate of economic growth during the 1960s. Middleton largely exonerates them. He argues that the economic ideas that emerged after 1955, and which dominated policy during much of the 1960s, had good academic provenance and that Britain's economics establishment tried hard to contribute positively to policy needs. Instead, Middleton pins much of the blame for the failure of 1960s 'planning' on 'ersatz economists' in politics and the media.

In the following three chapters, the focus is shifted towards the social and cultural impact of affluence. In Chapter 8, Lawrence Black considers the impact of affluence on post-war political culture and civil society – the fortunes of Britain's main political parties and their understanding of affluence, but also its impact on political styles and communication and how organizations in civil society articulated it. The Consumers' Association, Co-Operative movement and Young Conservatives who dealt with affluence socially and politically, provide useful examples. Notwithstanding the political uses made of it, Black argues affluence was received uneasily – with many commentators stressing the moral and cultural abuses they saw in it, tallying it with narratives of decline. The resulting elite-popular divide was quite characteristic of this period.

In Chapter 9, Lesley Whitworth examines the ways in which rising affluence contributed to a growth in sophistication of the discriminatory abilities of ordinary consumers. Using sources from a city that was enjoying dynamic growth even before the Second World War, Whitworth problematizes the periodization of affluence whilst also arguing that attempts better to inform the British buying public via the creation of the Design Council largely failed to connect with its target audience.

In Chapter 10, Christian Bugge traces how marketers and business have played an important role in constructing the category and subcultures of youth in post-war Britain. He argues this was a process that developed in important ways from the later 1950s as the spending power of youth grew and dawned upon business, but was uneven and refined in subsequent years. Bugge effectively counters the assumption in cultural studies that youth was a site for resisting market forces, but instead plots the commercialising and globalizing forces in society and their operation via advertising and commercial strategies aimed at recruiting young people.

Then in Chapter 11, Mathew Hilton examines the development of the active consumer and the consumer movement in Britain, via a study of the Birmingham Consumers' Group. He argues that whilst most of its members were middle class, politically their interests were not class specific and their allegiances did not neatly coalesce with the divisions within formal party politics. Rather, suggests Hilton, they were a distinct social group with a set of shared dispositions structured by their social and economic capital but with the ability to participate in the developments of their own tastes, beliefs and preferences. Such consumer activists aimed not to oppose the developing market society but to redirect its developments to suit the concerns of consumers.

Finally, in Chapter 12, Richard Weight discusses how affluence impacted on British national identity. Whilst the values imagined in Britain's performance in the Second World War were those subscribed and aspired to by most Britons, they also defined themselves in various ways against their former adversaries, Germany, and Japan, and against both Americanization and European integration. Affluence seemed to symbolize how Britain had lost the peace to its competitors. Trapped in a widespread notion that Britain's finest hour was in World War Two, jealous of Japan and Germany's economic resurgence, and concern amongst elites about Americanization meant Britain struggled to cope with its new post-imperial status.

Notes

1. Mattingly, H.: *Tacitus on Britain and Germany. A New Translation of the 'Agricola' and the 'Germania'*, Penguin, Harmondsworth, 1948.
2. Tomlinson, Jim: *The Politics of Decline: Understanding Post-War Britain*, Longman, London, 2001; English, Richard and Kenny, Michael, (eds): *Rethinking British Decline*, Macmillan, Basingstoke, 1999; Cannadine, David: *Britain in 'Decline'?*, Markham Press Fund, Waco TX, 1998.
3. 20 July 1957, quoted by Horne, Alistair: *Macmillan, 1957–1986*, Macmillan, London, 1989, pp. 64–65.
4. Griffin, Clare E.: 'Britain: A Case Study for Americans', *Michigan Business Studies*, vol. 10, no. 3 (June 1950), p. 39.
5. Tomlinson, Jim: 'Inventing "Decline": The Falling behind of the British Economy in the Post–war Years', *Economic History Review*, vol. 49, no. 4 (1996).
6. See Malik, Rex: *What's Wrong with British Industry?*, Penguin, Harmondsworth, 1964; Wigham, Eric L.: *What's Wrong With the Unions?*, Penguin, Harmondsworth, 1961. Other titles in the series dealt with institutions such as the Church and Parliament. For a review of this literature see Grant, Matthew: '"What Sort of Island?" Historians, the Penguin Specials and the State-of-the-Nation Literature, 1958–64', *Contemporary British History*, vol. 17, no. 3 (2003).
7. Macmillan Diary, 16 February 1962, quoted in Catterall, Peter: 'Roles and Relationships: Dean Acheson, "British Decline" and Post-War Anglo-American Relations' in Capet, Antoine and Sy-Wonyu, Aissatou (eds): *The "Special Relationship"*, University of Rouen Press, Rouen, 2003.
8. Tomlinson, *The Politics of Decline:* op. cit., ch. 4.
9. Addison, Paul: 'Churchill and the Price of Victory: 1939–45' in Tiratsoo, Nick (ed): *From Blitz to Blair: A New History of Britain Since 1939*, Weidenfeld and Nicholson, London, 1997 , p. 75. Wiener, Martin J.: *English Culture and the Decline of the Industrial Spirit, 1850–1980*, Cambridge University Press, Cambridge, 1981. Rubinstein, W.D.: *The Very Wealthy in Britain Since the Industrial Revolution*, Croom Helm, London, 1981.
10. Tomlinson, *Politics of Decline*, ch. 3. Hartley, Anthony: *A State of England*, Hutchinson, London, 1963. Sampson, Anthony: *Anatomy of Britain*, Hodder and Stoughton, London, 1962; Shanks, Michael: *The Stagnant Society,* Penguin, Harmondsworth, 1961; Hutton, Will: *The State We're In*, Jonathan Cape, London, 1995. For the 1970s see Nairn, Tom: *The Break-Up of Britain: Crisis and Neo-Nationalism*, New Left Books, London, 1977 and see also Kramnick, Issac (ed): *Is Britain Dying? Perspectives on the Current Crisis*, Cornell University Press, Ithaca, NY, 1978.
11. Anderson, Perry: 'Origins of the Present Crisis' (1964) and 'The Figures of Descent' (1987) in Anderson, Perry: *English Questions*, Verso, London, 1992, pp. 15, 139–40, 148, 154–5. Barnett, Corelli: *The Audit of War: The Illusion and Reality of Britain as a*

Great Nation, Macmillan, London, 1986, pp. 187, 304. The New Left and right are also linked by Stapleton, Julia: *Political Intellectuals and Public Identities in Britain Since 1850*, Manchester University Press, Manchester, 2001, pp. 183–4.

[12] Dintenfass, Michael: 'Converging Accounts, Misleading Metaphors and Persistent Doubts: Reflections on the Historiography of Britain's "Decline"' in Dintenfass, Michael and Dormois, Jean-Pierre (eds): *The British Industrial Decline*, Routledge, London, 1999, p. 22.

[13] For example, even when scholars such as Brian Brivati argue that New Labour's most significant success since 1997 has been to transcend and escape the debate over relative decline, by accepting the cultural vibrancy and multiculturalism of a more fragmented nation, the context for this discussion remains that of declinism (Brivati, Brian: 'The End of Decline: The Blair-Brown Governments and Contemporary British History', inaugural lecture, Kingston University, March 2003).

[14] Weight, Richard: *Patriots: British National Identity, 1940–2000*, Macmillan, London, 2002.

[15] Mandler, Peter: 'Two Cultures – One – Or Many?' in Burk, Katherine (ed): *The British Isles Since 1945*, Oxford University Press, Oxford, 2003. See also Bewes, Timothy and Gilbert, Jeremy (eds): *Cultural Capitalism: Politics After New Labour*, Lawrence and Wishart, London, 2000. Offering more upbeat accounts than Robert Hewison's treatment of post-war culture.

[16] See Offer, Avner (ed): *In Pursuit of the Quality of Life*, Oxford University Press, Oxford, 1996; Oswald, Andrew: 'Happiness and Economic Performance', *Economic Journal*, vol. 107, no. 445 (1997), pp. 1815–31; Zweiniger-Bargielowska, Ina: 'Living standards and consumption' in Addison, Paul and Jones, Harriet: *The Blackwell Companion to Contemporary Britain, 1939–2000*, Blackwell, Oxford, in press.

[17] Drucker, Peter: 'Politics for a New Generation', *Harper's* (June 1960), p. 30.

[18] Gamble, Andrew: 'Theories of British politics', *Political Studies*, vol. 38, no. 3 (1990), p. 405.

[19] See Conekin, Becky E. : *'The Autobiography of a Nation': The 1951 Festival of Britain*, Manchester University Press, Manchester, 2003; Brooke, Stephen: 'Memory and Modernity', *Journal of British Studies* vol. 42, no. 1 (2003), pp. 135–6.

[20] See 'Introduction' in Conekin, Becky: *Autobiography of a Nation*, op. cit. ; Mort, Frank and Waters, Chris (eds): *Moments of Modernity: Reconstructing Britain 1945–64*, Rivers Oram, London, 1999.

[21] Notably, Galbraith, John Kenneth: *The Affluent Society*, Penguin, Harmondsworth, 1958 and Goldthorpe, John et al: *The Affluent Worker,* 3 vols., Cambridge University Press, Cambridge, 1968–69. See also Zweig, Ferdynand: *The Worker in an Affluent Society*, Heinemann, London, 1961.

[22] Sissons, Michael and French, Phillip (eds): *Age of Austerity, 1945–51*, Penguin, Harmondsworth, 1964.

[23] Zweiniger-Bargielowska, Ina: *Austerity in Britain: Rationing, Controls and Consumption, 1939–55*, Oxford University Press, Oxford 2000, pp. 16, 234.

[24] Montgomery, John: *The Fifties*, Allen and Unwin, London, 1966, pp. 275, 277 Hopkins, Harry, *The New Look*, Secker and Warburg, London, 1963, p. 331.

[25] Vinen, Richard: *A History in Fragments: Europe in the Twentieth Century*, Little, Brown, London, 2000, pp. 202–3, 354. Fowler, David: *The First Teenagers: Young Wage-earners in Inter-War Britain*, Woburn Press, London, 1995.

[26] 'How Welsh is Wales?', *Sunday Times* 17 November 1963 in Weight, *Patriots,* op. cit., p. 413.

[27] Discussed in May, Elaine Tyler: *Homeward Bound: American Families in the Cold War Era*, Basic Books, New York, 1988.

[28] Hobsbawm, Eric: *Interesting Times: A Twentieth Century Life*, Allen Lane, London, 2002, p. 222.

[29] Proudfoot, Mary: *British Politics and Government, 1951–70: A Study of an Affluent Society*, Faber and Faber, London, 1970, p. 9. Bogdanor, Vernon and Skidelsky, Robert (eds): *The Age of Affluence, 1951–64*, Macmillan, London, 1970.

[30] Abel-Smith, Brian and Townsend, Peter: *The Poor and the Poorest*, Bell, London, 1965. See also George, Vic and Howards, Irving: *Poverty Amidst Affluence: Britain and the United States*, Edward Elgar, Aldershot, 1991.

[31] 'Introduction: Luxury's Shadow' in Hilton, Matthew: *Consumerism in Twentieth-Century Britain: The Search for a Historical Movement*, Cambridge University Press, Cambridge, 2003.

[32] Tiratsoo, Nick: 'You've never had it so bad'?: Britain in the 1970s' in Tiratsoo, *From Blitz to Blair,* op. cit..

[33] Samuel, Raphael: *Theatres of Memory: Past and Present in Contemporary Culture*, Verso, London, 1994.

[34] An argument also made in Fielding, Steven: *The Labour Party: Continuity and Change in the Making of 'New' Labour*, Palgrave, Basingstoke, 2003, pp. 12–13.

[35] Dunne, M.: *Telephones and the Private Subscriber*, International Organisation of Consumer Unions, London, 1967, pp. 4–5.

[36] Marwick, Arthur: *British Society Since 1945*, Penguin, Harmondsworth, 1996. See also comments in the conclusion to Harris, Jose: *Private Lives, Public Spirits*, Oxford University Press, Oxford, 1993.

[37] Mort, Frank: *Cultures of Consumption: Masculinities and Social Space in Late Twentieth-Century Britain*, Routledge, London, 1996.

[38] Williams, Raymond: *The Long Revolution*, Columbia University Press, New York, 1961, p. 296.

[39] Williams, Lord Francis: *The Twilight of Empire*, Barnes, New York, 1961 and *The American Invasion*, Anthony Blond, London,1962.

[40] For an overview, Taylor, A.J. (ed): *The Standard of Living in Britain in the Industrial Revolution*, Methuen, London, 1975.

[41] David Cannadine: 'The State of British History', *Times Literary Supplement*, 10 October 1986.

CHAPTER 2

Affluence, Conservatism and Political Competition in Britain and the United States, 1945–1964

Brian Girvin

Uncertainty and affluence

At the end of the Second World War, many people were cautiously optimistic that there would be no return to the instability that had characterized world politics from 1929 to 1945. However, in a UNESCO sponsored poll in 1948 most respondents recalled that they had expected post-war conditions to be better than turned out to be the case. In France, Germany, Italy and the Netherlands a majority of those interviewed concluded that they were not secure enough to plan ahead at this time (in France only 14 per cent agreed that they had enough security to plan). In Britain the respondents were evenly divided on this question, while in the United States 57 per cent considered themselves to be in a position to plan ahead. In addition there was widespread unease that it would not be possible to live in peace, though opinion was fairly closely divided on this issue. Uncertainty had returned to world politics by this time, reflected in the onset of the Cold War, the continuation of rationing in most countries and political conflict in a number of European states.[1] Successful post-war recovery removed some of this pessimism, though French opinion remained sceptical. Ellwood suggests that despite clear signs of recovery, 'the sense of well being was fragile' until the mid-1950s. A Foreign Office memorandum in 1953 confirmed this unease among the policy elite:

> Economists are almost unanimous in agreeing that the current relative prosperity is largely superficial, attributable to temporary factors – in particular, the American supported defence expenditure and the movement of commodity prices – and that the countries of Western Europe, having more or less recovered from the direct effects of the war upon their economies, are now faced with the task of redressing the serious structural defects which were already inherent in those economies before the war, and which certain indirect effects of the war have only served to aggravate.[2]

One of President Eisenhower's advisors warned him in late-1952 that the buoyancy of the economy could not be guaranteed, 'This boom isn't going to last forever, of course. America hasn't found the secret of perpetual economic motion'. A similar concern is evident at the British Treasury around this time and among leading Conservative Ministers when they returned to government late in 1951.[3] If opinion in the United States, Britain and Europe was no longer pessimistic, there is little evidence by 1953 that the public was aware that they were living in a golden age of capitalism or affluence.

Yet, within a few years most observers were offering a much more optimistic assessment of the 1950s and of the future of liberal democratic capitalist societies in general. It seemed as if some magic formula had been found to secure full employment, economic growth and extensive welfare provision, though disagreement continued on how this had been achieved.[4] The economic trends for the United States, Europe and Japan highlighted the major changes that had taken place. Per capita GDP growth was particularly impressive during the 1950s, while an increasing proportion of the population shared in the new prosperity. Most households now owned consumer goods such as televisions, washing machines and motor-cars, but increasingly house ownership itself became a realistic goal for the majority. Overall, real income increased appreciably and this fuelled the consumption boom that followed. Although secured in different ways in individual states, the United States, Europe and Japan had passed an important threshold between 1955 and 1965, moving from a period of scarcity to one that can be characterized as affluence.[5]

Affluence and contemporary history

The emergence of the affluent society is connected with a major social transformation initiated by the industrial revolution, but only fully delivered to the majority of citizens during the 1950s and 1960s. The main features of this transformation are fairly widely known and need only be summarized briefly here. They include the completion of European industrialization, the decline of agrarian Europe and the emergence of a 'post industrial' society a little later. During the 1950s, economic success was based on industrial expansion and export driven growth, even for those states (such as Denmark and the Netherlands) that had previously based their prosperity on agricultural exports. Closely related to this was a general commitment to full employment, government intervention to regulate the economy and enhanced spending on welfare. A commitment to full employment and a welfare state were closely linked to industrial expansion and export growth, as it was widely recognized that only thus could the temporary instabilities caused by econofmic change be accommodated. Accompanying this was the transition to mass consumption of an ever-increasing number of products, including motor-cars, televisions and kitchen appliances. This shift is qualitative, not merely quantitative. Perhaps for the first time in history a majority of the population of most liberal democratic states actually shared in prosperity and this was maintained despite changed circumstances during the 1970s.[6] Other factors which distinguish this period from previous ones include the emergence of a new wave of feminism, which created the conditions a little later for the incorporation of women more fully into society and offered for the first time a sustained challenge to patriarchy. In addition, we can also see the final secularization of public life in European political culture, a process also evident in the United States, despite its unusually high church attendance rates.[7]

Moreover, it is the adoption by Europe and Japan (whether consciously or not) of American attitudes towards prosperity and consumption that distinguished the 1950s from previous periods. There is a democratic consciousness at the heart of American political culture which was absent in much of Europe until the post-war decades as the legacy of feudalism and authoritarianism restricted European democratization. Central to this new consciousness is the view that everyone should share in prosperity in much the same way as everyone should have the vote. One group or other may not have the vote or be prosperous, but in theory they have a right to it even if in practise it is denied to them. The pursuit of happiness invoked at the origin of the American republic could in time include the pursuit of prosperity as the main avenue of achieving this happiness. This equation of happiness with prosperity had been resisted more frequently in Europe than the US, but its attainment became a political reality as well as an economic possibility only after the Second World War. It is during the 1950s that the political and economic conditions for this achievement were put in place.[8]

In his innovative study of contemporary history, Geoffrey Barraclough made an appeal for a distinctive methodology in analysing the nature of the contemporary world. Forty years after publication some aspects may be dated, but his insights continue to enhance the understanding of the present (or contemporary). Barraclough suggests that two features are critical to any appreciation of contemporary history. The first of these is that in theory (if not always in practice) history has to be written in a global context, rather than in a narrowly European fashion. The distinction between the modern and the contemporary is the second important feature. This involves the recognition that contemporary history does not refer simply to the present generation or its concerns, but focuses on events and processes that continue to influence the lives, politics and culture of that present-day generation. For example, the Russian Revolution continued to be contemporary in this sense up to 1991 (when the Soviet Union imploded) but since then it is a matter of modern historical analysis in much the same way that study of Nazi Germany is. Clearly the boundary between the modern and the contemporary can be blurred and there will be grounds for dispute as to what may be placed in one or the other category, but it is an important distinction to make.[9]

In the sense briefly outlined here, affluence is a process that continues to have an impact on the present, though this can be both negative and positive. For those living in the OECD (or stable liberal democratic states) affluence remains a central feature of everyday life. The rise in house ownership is one indication of this process. In the 1950s the majority of families lived in rented accommodation, whereas by 2000 over 60 per cent of families now owned their own homes. In the United Kingdom, approximately 70 per cent of families owned their own home by 2000, whereas less than one-third had done so prior to the Second World War. Another indicator of affluence can be found in data released by the Office of National Statistics in the United Kingdom, which reported that between 1998 and 2000 the percentage of households with satellite, digital and cable television had increased from 29 per cent to 40 per cent, which the increase for home ownership of computers jumped from 34 per cent to 45 per cent.[10] Not all consequences of affluence are positive of course. There is considerable evidence of indebtedness in the United States and the United Kingdom caused by individuals using home equity to fund their life style, a situation that may have serious consequences in the future.[11]

Luxury has always been available for the few, but affluence (mass consumption for the majority) has eluded mankind for most of its history. Goods can be considered luxurious when they are available only to an elite within the society, they become mass consumption goods when the majority can and do acquire them. Berry has suggested that a luxury good is one that is currently enjoyed or owned by a select few, but that 'many others would also like to enjoy it'.[12] At one time owning a book, effective transportation or communication media were luxuries and restricted to an elite, and as such luxuries, but due to mass production, technology and rising income it becomes possible for most if not all to own these items (it is a decision that can be made, whether one decides to own this or that item is a personal choice for most). If luxury is about elite ownership, then affluence is about democratic ownership or the possibility that the majority can own a particular product. But there is an additional factor, which distinguishes affluence from previous social contexts, and this involves the acceleration of consumption. Not only are existing desires satisfied, but also new desires appear (or are created?) while older products become obsolete and are replaced by newer versions. Obsolescence is driven by both desire and technology, as the replacement of black and white televisions with colour demonstrates. Only in the 1950s do conditions exist where it is possible to claim that a genuinely mass consumption and affluent society appears in some OECD states.[13]

The breakthrough to affluence

Democratic mass consumption appeared first in the United States.[14] Since the nineteenth century Americans had been generally better paid and better fed than their European counterparts and white male Americans had the vote. This however did not mean that the United States was an affluent society in the nineteenth or early twentieth century. The political conditions for affluence were generated during the New Deal period and consolidated in the decade immediately after the Second World War.[15] While the United States was the first affluent society, it is necessary to distinguish affluence from one that is prosperous but where the majority does not share in this prosperity. The United States was prosperous but not affluent during the 1920s since a significant proportion of Americans were excluded from the prosperity that surrounded them. While many families were able to purchase cars and radios, there is little evidence of sustained growth in mass consumption, even before the depression cut off what prosperity there was. Some estimates suggest that approximately 60 per cent of American families received less than the $2,000 per annum considered necessary to sustain a minimum standard of living. This does not mean that these families did not own a car or a radio, but it usually implied that any setback in the economy significantly weakened their ability to purchase new consumption goods. The position was even worse for the one-third of the population whose incomes was estimated at $1,200 or less per annum.[16] It is evident that while many working class Americans succeeded in buying a car or a new electrical appliance during the 1920s and 1930s, this did not entail consumption levels that can be considered affluent. Scarcity rather than affluence was the experience of the majority of American families during these two decades. Affluence was restricted to middle class families, a section of society with high income and long-term employment security. For working class families, the availability of credit for the new consumer products was a mixed blessing as loss of employment or other mishaps led to the loss of the product due to repossession resulting from non-repayment.[17]

The three decades after the Second World War are a stark contrast to the 1920s and 1930s. Post-war recovery was followed by sustained expansion and this contributed to the significant rise in the standard of living for most Americans. The most important change is that real income for most families increased dramatically (nearly doubling between 1949 and 1959). In addition, the per centage of those in poverty fell by nearly a third while transfers from government to individuals increased by 40 per cent. The tax burden increased only slightly, but income distribution remained highly unequal. There are four interacting elements that secured the affluent society during this decade. The first of these was full employment and the recognition that high levels of economic growth would be maintained. This was accompanied by rising real income throughout the decade for the majority. There was considerable confidence that these conditions would be sustained, if need be by government action. The welfare state provided a cushion for most citizens while access to credit allowed low-income families to increase consumption, especially of household appliances.[18]

However, affluence was never inevitable, but was dependent on the mix of policies adopted by individual governments. Social democratic governments in Scandinavia pursued a mix that gave priority to full employment and welfare, whereas conservative and Christian Democratic governments paid closer attention to inflation and private consumption.[19] That most OECD states became affluent should not disguise the differences among these states in respect of income, welfare provision and employment levels. It also helps to account for the timing of affluence. While most states made the transition between 1950 and 1970, it was achieved at different speeds and times. Thus, there is a complex relationship between external factors that all states were exposed to (including the Cold War, trends in world trade and the commitment to industrialization) and internal factors (the nature of the political system or the composition of the government for example). It is the blend of these factors that produces a specific outcome.[20] One way to demonstrate this is to focus on those states that did not become affluent during the period under review. The failure of Greece, Spain and Portugal to achieve income, consumption and employment levels anywhere close to those of the United States or northern Europe can be attributed to their continuing dependence on agriculture, lack of industrial development and economic nationalism. But it is more difficult to explain the failure of the Republic of Ireland to do so. Ireland had been a moderately prosperous country by European standards between 1900 and 1945, but between 1945 and 1970, despite some economic modernization, fell well behind its European neighbours. By 1973, when Ireland joined the EEC, it was the poorest member state and was not an affluent society in terms of income, consumption or employment. Indeed, it was only in the 1990s that Ireland achieved this status, essentially by-passing the period of affluence most other states experienced between the 1950s and 1970s. It is not the purpose of this chapter to discuss the Irish case, but it does provide a useful counterpoint to the claim that affluence was an inevitable product of powerful social processes. These social processes were indeed powerful, but unless a state adopted policies to reflect them, it would not receive the benefits of the changes.[21]

The Irish case suggests that the transition to affluence was not inevitable. Achieving affluence was contingent on governments adopting a policy regime that facilitated this transition, and some states did not do so. Nor was the policy regime associated with a specific political ideology. Though it is possible that the specific form affluence took in the 1950s can be associated with conservative or centre-right incumbency, this neglects the earlier contribution of centre-left governments in establishing the new post-war policy arena.[22] Social democratic policy success legitimized state intervention, the welfare state and a high employment policy in Europe and the United States. The mixed economy that resulted was a compromise between socialism and the market, but it was one that could be managed by either left or right.[23] Moreover, when conservatives did come to power they were constrained by this social democratic legacy and by the expectations of the electorate that there would be no return to the depression of the 1930s. Conservatives were widely identified with deflation and depression and these concerns contributed to the election of Harry Truman as President in 1948 and denied the Conservatives victory in the British general election in 1950. Harold Macmillan warned the Conservative Party in 1949 that victory in the forthcoming election was not a foregone conclusion. He believed it was necessary to 'socialise' Conservative party policy to take account of the reforms introduced by Labour and asked 'can we develop a more inspiring and more moral theme, different from Cripps? Have we an answer to the problem? How to make Britain solvent at a reasonable level of life?' While Macmillan urged the party to give renewed consideration to ethical issues and anti-communism he also firmly endorsed the reality of what had been achieved by Labour:

> While bias should always be towards private initiative, we should take account of what has been done – rightly or wrongly – and we should recognise more formally certain changes in relations between government and industry which have taken place during recent years.

Macmillan's prescription reflected the opinion of those who believed it was necessary to engage in a new departure if the Conservatives were to return to office.[24] The difficulties for the party were highlighted in an analysis of by-elections between 1945 and 1949. While the party won 15 out of 42 elections, all of them were in safe Conservative or Liberal constituencies. The Conservatives did not win a single seat from Labour throughout this period, despite the often severe economic conditions that prevailed. This indicated to Macmillan, Rab Butler and others that the policy environment for Britain had been dramatically changed by the Labour Party's victory in 1945.[25]

Eisenhower and the politics of prosperity in the United States

American politics had realigned as a consequence of the New Deal and the Republican Party took much longer to recover than was the case with its British counterpart. The party lost five consecutive presidential elections and only controlled Congress for a brief period in 1947 and 1948.[26] The Republicans became the minority party in Congress and struggled for much of the 1930s and 1940s to extend its political appeal beyond its traditional support base in the mid-west and among the white Anglo-Saxon protestant (WASP) population. The majority of Republicans continued to oppose the New Deal on principle, considering it to be socialistic and anti-American. Eisenhower concluded that this form of conservatism was short sighted and would continue to damage the Republican Party. He recognized that some accommodation with the New Deal was necessary to preserve what he believed to be the fundamentals of American capitalism. One of the reasons he accepted the Republican Presidential nomination in 1952 was that he concluded that anyone associated with traditional republicanism would find it difficult to build a new electoral coalition for the right.[27]

It was only after the defeat of Thomas Dewey by Truman in the 1948 presidential election that the Republicans recognized that the New Deal was not going to be dismantled and that they had to persuade the electorate that it would not roll back the reforms once in office. Even earlier, Senator George Aiken of Vermont emphasized the need for the Republican Party to redefine its message to take account of the changed political and social landscape:

> True conservatism consists of maintaining the best in our institutions without obstructing progress. We must not confuse conservatism with obstructionism for the latter may lead to rifts in our social structure with undesirable consequences.

For Senator Arthur Vandeberg, the onset of the Cold war and his opposition to Federal encroachment on the private sector motivated his support for a more moderate programme.[28] Indeed Dewey himself appealed to Eisenhower after the 1948 defeat to consider running in the next presidential election:

> We must look around for someone of great popularity and [sic] who has not frittered away his political assets by taking positive stands against national planning, etc., etc., ... Elect such a man to Presidency, after which he must lead us back to safe channels and paths.[29]

Eisenhower was the ideal 'non-partisan' candidate, but this disguised his conservative nature and his commitment to Republican policies. His main interest was in foreign policy but he also recognized, perhaps more than many of his colleagues, that American politics had changed since 1932 and that a Republican President would have to accommodate these changes. This did not entail a rejection of party policy but it did mean adapting it to take account of these changes.[30]

Eisenhower was comfortably elected President in November 1952. Gabriel Hauge, one of his economic advisors, remarked in a memorandum that his electoral success was remarkable as it occurred while the economy was still expanding. Conventional wisdom held that the incumbent party would benefit from a buoyant economy. Hauge further emphasized the need for both stability and growth in Eisenhower's economic policy. This emphasis on stability and growth reflected Eisenhower's view that stability without growth would lead to deflation and this in turn would undercut his support base.[31] This support base was a finely balanced one, as it depended on former Democratic voters supporting Eisenhower. In September 1952 approximately 25 per cent of those who had voted for the Democrats in 1948 said they would switch to a Republican in 1952. On this basis Eisenhower could build a coalition of the centre, albeit one tilted to the right. In fact Eisenhower had a self-conscious sense of what he called a 'middle of the road Republicanism', one that:

> Preserves the greatest initiative, freedom and independence of soul to the individual, but that did not hesitate to use government to combat cataclysmic economic disasters which can, in some instances, be even more terrible than convulsions of nature.

When the United States faced an economic downturn at the end of the Korean War, Eisenhower asserted that he was not another Hoover arguing that, 'now is the time to liberalize everything we can, because the fear in America is not the fear of inflation; it is the fear of deflation, of going down, not up.'[32] This is not to suggest that Eisenhower was merely a Republican New Dealer, though Senator Barry Goldwater certainly considered him to be so, but that he acknowledged a more interventionist role for the Federal government than had been the case with this Republican predecessors. The political reality was that if Eisenhower were associated with economic decline or high levels of unemployment he and the Republican Party would suffer for it.

That affluence and political success were linked was brought home to Eisenhower on a number of occasions between the end of the Korean War and his 1956 re-election bid. In early 1954, unemployment more than doubled and it was this situation that prompted him to say he would not be another Hoover. Yet, despite urgings from Vice-President Nixon and Henry Cabot Lodge very little in the way of counter cyclical initiatives were introduced. Opinion polls reported that while the public was concerned about unemployment, nearly three-quarters of those interviewed in January 1954 believed that the United States would not experience a depression on the scale of the 1930s. More important was the finding that only 28 per cent believed that the Democratic Party would handle the economy better than the Republicans at this time.[33] While this gave Eisenhower some political leverage, his reluctance to act decisively contributed to the Republican losses at the November 1954 mid-term elections, when the party lost control of Congress. This was certainly the conclusion drawn after the election by the Republican Party.[34] Vice-President Nixon endorsed this view during a presentation on the election to the Cabinet, a discussion that led the President to comment that 'He thought the next two years extremely critical because the Republican theory of moderation remained to be proved sufficiently to wean the people back from ideas dependent on wartime emergencies.'[35] During the previous month, Hauge insisted that the 'economy is operating at high levels but we must do better. We must move forward to find more jobs and to improve living standards.' He added that this could not be achieved by more government intervention and if this proved to be necessary then 'we had better turn in our suits right now.'[36]

For the Eisenhower administration, the key to success was maintaining high employment and increased consumption without increasing Federal intervention or introducing higher taxes. The danger for the Administration was that it would alienate middle-class voters who had a stake in a high consumption economy, especially those elements of it supported by Federal programmes. Likewise, organized labour could mount a formidable challenge to Republicans if its resources were mobilized, as proved to the case in 1954.[37] Though the Democrats won control of Congress at the 1954 mid-term elections, at the 1956 Presidential election Eisenhower benefited from a general belief that his administration had indeed sustained prosperity. In a note to Eisenhower immediately after he was re-elected Arthur Burns, the Chairman of the CEA, concluded that 'a grateful nation went to the polls yesterday.' This, he added, 'is the true and whole meaning of your tremendous victory.' In August Burns had produced a memorandum for Eisenhower emphasizing the 'three years of prosperity' under a Republican President. In October he provided consumption and economic details to sustain this view. Burns showed that the average family had improved its after tax income by nearly $400 in real terms between 1952 and 1955. The evidence from the previous three years suggested to Burns that the administration had been effective in maintaining the economic welfare of Americans. He added that expenditure on university education had increased and that over 25 per cent of non-farm families now owned their own home. There had also been a dramatic shift in consumption patterns among Americans, with over two-thirds of homes now owning a motorcar, television and washing machine. The trends in consumption confirmed that more and more families were sharing in the prosperity secured by affluence.[38]

While there were certainly other factors that contributed to Eisenhower's success in 1956 (such as foreign policy), it would be mistaken to ignore the widespread belief that the Administration had secured prosperity and maintained high levels of consumption. The Gallup Poll recorded that 75 per cent of Americans believed that the country was prosperous in 1955 and a further 55 per cent considered that a depression was not inevitable after a period of prosperity. One important feature of this process was the increasing dependence on credit to purchase the new consumer products. During the late-1940s less than a third of those purchasing a motor car did so by using credit, by 1960 the figure had jumped to over two-thirds. This was a reflection of higher income, full employment and the ability of working and lower class families to use credit facilities and to plan for the future in a stable environment. The spectre of uncertainly that had prevailed in the past had diminished if not disappeared and this provided the basis for the expansion of credit. Furthermore, access to credit was now viewed positively, whereas in the past there was a stigma attached to it. This change placed added pressure on the administration to maintain high levels of employment, as a fall could have disastrous consequences for those who had used credit to purchase these new consumer items. There was a political need to maintain high levels of employment and income if a credit driven economy and consumption patterns were to be continued.[39] This was recognized by the Administration, though the policy conclusions did not necessarily involve further Federal intervention. It is no accident that Galbraith published his *Affluent Society* in 1958, a book that identified the phenomenon of affluence although it did not celebrate it and worried about the role of credit in contemporary society. Galbraith was criticized by various members of the administration but the book's popularity further confirmed the subtle shift that had taken place in the public consciousness in respect of prosperity and affluence. The Republican Party was defeated at the 1958 mid-term elections, due in large part to the perception that the Administration had not acted decisively in the face of a further downturn in 1957 and early 1958. Likewise, Nixon blamed his 1960 defeat at the hands of Kennedy to a failure on the part of Eisenhower to use Federal resources to counter economic difficulties in 1960.[40]

Conservatism and affluence in Britain

Many of the same considerations affected the Conservative party in Britain during the 1940s and 1950s. The Conservatives had been out of office since 1945 and had been replaced by a reforming Labour government, one whose policies proved to be quite popular. Despite the Conservative Party's weakness in the face of this success for the left, Churchill found it difficult to come to terms with the new reality of the welfare state. When he returned to office at the end of 1951 he worried that Keynesianism had become dominant in the Treasury and at times indulged in nostalgia of what might have been if the Conservatives had won the 1945 election. He seemed at times to be arguing for a return to the deflationary policies of the 1930s. The Chancellor of the Exchequer, Rab Butler recognized the difficulties facing the economy, but he also sought to divert the new Prime Minister from advocating policies that would alienate sections of the electorate necessary for Conservative electoral success.[41] Reformers within the party were fortunate that Churchill was prepared to listen to Butler and to others who advocated a cautious policy in respect of the welfare state and government intervention. While nationalization was not particularly popular, the welfare state and full employment were. In a similar fashion to the United States, British conservatives had to demonstrate a capacity to operate a system that they had not created and with which they were often ideologically uncomfortable. Prior to the 1950 election the party leadership was warned to avoid alienating the so-called floating voter, on whom victory depended. Drawing on the experience of the 1948 United States presidential election it was noted that this floating vote 'reversed the whole tide in the last few days of the Presidential Election'. The party's research department concluded that while these voters were disenchanted with the Labour Government, Conservative proposals to improve the situation would have to be more persuasive. The 1950 election demonstrated the accuracy of this analysis. There was a swing to the Conservative party amongst former Liberal voters and floating voters who had previously voted for Labour, though this was not enough to give the Conservatives a majority.[42]

By 1950 the party had reluctantly accepted full employment as a feature of its programme, something the Republicans never did in the United States. But it also sought to emphasize some distinctive features that would appeal to traditional supporters and attract others. Although approximately 30 per cent of the working class voted Conservative between 1945 and 1960, this support could never be guaranteed. One way of bolstering such support was to emphasize both security and opportunity:

> Conservatives do not believe in equality of wealth, but in the greater equality of opportunity. We believe that it is for the individual to make the best use of his talents, and that harder work and higher skill should receive a higher reward. The wage differential between the skilled and unskilled worker is fundamental to this belief. The Social Services would provide a minimum standard below which no one through adversity or misfortune should fall. They should not be used to stifle initiative by bringing down the enterprise to the level of the idle and shiftless.[43]

Moreover, it added a commitment to remove 'unnecessary' regulation and to improve both consumption and choice after the austerity of the post-war years. Of considerable importance was the commitment to build at least 300,000 new houses per year and to shift housing to the private sector. This was a policy that could appeal not only to middle class voters, but also to some sections of the working class who valued private home ownership. As both the 1950 and 1951 general elections were very close run affairs, Conservatives had to be especially sensitive to every section of its electoral coalition. In 1951 the Conservatives actually received fewer votes than Labour, yet enough seats to form a government. In 1955 the Conservatives had approximately 900,000 more votes than the Labour party. The Conservative vote was more secure in 1959, but even in 1964 Labour's vote was only 200,000 in excess of the Conservatives. The nature of political competition reinforced the pressure on governments to deliver both security and affluence.[44]

Nor were concerns about the volatility of the electorate misjudged. Support for the new government fell appreciably between October 1951 and June 1952 and opinion polls recorded a shift to Labour. The most significant defections came from working class voters who had supported the party in 1951.[45] The new government was faced with multiple problems in respect of its need to remain in power. It had to maintain confidence in the economy and the pound. It had simultaneously to sustain full employment and low inflation, while increasing consumption and delivering on its election promises. By the end of 1953, however,

Michael Fraser at the Conservative Research Department felt able to circulate a very positive assessment of the first two years of a Conservative government in a welfare state. He highlighted the continuing levels of employment (in effect full employment), but also emphasized that taxation had not been increased and inflation had been controlled. He noted that 'any government in the modern world must try to ensure that general demand is strong enough to provide full employment but not so strong that inflation develops', insisting that the government had achieved this. Nor was this simply self-congratulatory on Fraser's part; in June 1954 the *Economist* proclaimed 'The miracle has happened ... full employment without inflation'.[46]

Although Conservative governments during the 1950s focused closely on the need to strengthen the pound, maintain full employment and promote further economic growth, there was a strong consumptionist message at the heart of its programme. The Conservative appeal was particularly successful in 1950 and 1951 with middle class and women voters who had become disillusioned with the austerity they now associated with the Labour government. An emphasis on affluence (and its accompanying consumption) could maintain that vote for the party (as proved to be the case in 1955 and again in 1959).[47] While not always fully appreciated in the early days of the new government, affluence came to play a central role in attracting Conservative majorities during the 1950s, as also proved to be the case in the United States and Germany. The government assumed that consumption would be based on private expenditure, but recognized that the state provided much of the social infrastructure to facilitate this. As a consequence there is a shift in priorities on the part of the government, with a new emphasis on private consumption to accompany public provision. The decision to introduce a commercial television station is one reflection of this, but perhaps the most successful policy during the Churchill premiership was the new housing programme. Macmillan, who was responsible for the programme, insisted that not only would the provision of additional housing be popular but that most of the new housing could be built by private companies for individual families to own. The government met its targets as a result of Macmillan's determination but also because he persuaded Churchill of its positive political impact for the party.[48] Butler reluctantly accepted this after an exchange with Macmillan in 1953:

> It appears that we shall do the Housing Grand Design. This means longer for me to re-establish the finances fundamentally, (i.e., no election for some time). I have decided that I must face this duty. I cannot go on putting things off unto the Budget of 1955 and hoping things won't be too bad in '54.

As Chancellor of the Exchequer, Butler was uncomfortably aware of the economic problems that Britain faced in the 1950s (including a weakening pound and an increasing lack of competitiveness on export markets), but he also had to recognize the constraints that were imposed by both Conservative voters and the general political environment at the time. As a consequence Butler was not prepared to recommend deflationary policies to control wage or price increases, as these could be 'so severe as to destroy the state of full employment'. He had been persuaded that 'if price stability were made the over-riding objective the policy of high and stable employment would have to be abandoned' and this was not a policy departure he was prepared to advocate.[49]

A further constraint on deflation was the growing influence of the trade union movement and the reluctance of Churchill, Eden or Macmillan to confront them on the issues of wages. The TUC defended free collective bargaining vigorously in discussions with the government and refused to accept a link between inflation and wage increases. One of the great fears expressed by trade union leaders was that the government would use unemployment to control earnings, though the government went to considerable lengths to demonstrate that this was not part of its policy package. Indeed on occasions it appeared that the TUC had an informal veto on policy. One discussion concluded by admitting that without trade union cooperation, 'it would not be possible to take the proposals further, [and] every effort should be made to get them to cooperate'. Lord Woolton persistently insisted on a moderate approach to the unions arguing that a Conservative government could not be associated with a decline in the standard of living for the majority of the population:

> We will find ourselves in politically difficult waters if we begin by making serious cuts in the social services or in the standard of living of the general public and leave ourselves open to the charge that what we have saved by this means we have later spent in the reduction of taxation.

But he also highlighted the persistent demand among the working class for more food and consumption goods. He argued that controls over these products should be removed to allow the working class to purchase them in increased quantities.[50] He also worried that an increase in unemployment would lead to a 'serious defeat at the next election.'[51]

Such concerns were widespread during the first Conservative government but continued in the second half of the 1950s even when full employment, affluence and high levels of consumption had been achieved. The Treasury declared (echoing Butler) that full employment was 'second to none among the objectives of post-war economic policy'.[52] There were those, such as Peter Thorneycroft, who believed that an increase in unemployment was a price worth paying to achieve fiscal and economic stability. This was not an option that either Macmillan or the party leadership were prepared to risk at this time.[53] Macmillan, who became Prime Minister in 1957, thus confirming the reformist tendency in the party, self-consciously promoted this view: 'I intend to run it ... as a *centre* party. I was not prepared to run it on an extreme right wing basis.' More significantly, Macmillan accepted the resignation of his Treasury team in 1958, including Thorneycroft, precisely because he concluded that their proposed policies would break the reformist consensus that had prevailed since 1951.[54] Macmillan went further than this in 1958 when unemployment increased and there was fear of a depression. Within the government he actively promoted expansion and criticized the policy proposals coming from the Treasury, dismissing one as 'absurd' and another as disgraceful, adding that 'It might have been written by Mr Neville Chamberlain's government'. Thus, Macmillan remained sensitive to charges that the Conservative party intended to introduce policies similar to those of the 1930s and acted to prevent any hint of such policies from emerging.[55]

Pressure from the trade unions, women, and the Conservative middle class, as well as the recognition that prosperity helped the party win elections, reinforced the government's willingness to pursue expansionist policies. This was the case with Butler's April 1953 Budget as it was during Macmillan's premiership, but especially between 1957 and 1959. Macmillan was rewarded with a 100-seat majority at the 1959 general election. In 1961 Butler reflected that the Conservative party at the 1959 election effectively committed the party to 'increasing the standard of living – if not year by year then election by election'. At the same time Iain Macleod observed that the British electorate was in expansionist mood and seemed to have little patience with regulations or obstacles to progress.[56]

Conclusion

By the early 1960s the uncertainties that had been associated with the inter-war decades and the immediate post-war years had disappeared. In a relatively short period, most liberal democratic states had been transformed. The 'age of affluence' had dawned and the majority were now sharing in the new prosperity. Conservative parties had been the most successful managers of affluence and prosperity and were most closely associated with the accompanying consumer boom. The 1956 presidential election in the United States, the West German Bundestag election in 1957 and the 1959 British general election reinforced this association between the centre right and affluence. Conservatives had promised prosperity and security to the electorate and had in large part delivered it. However, there were unintended consequences of affluence that challenged conservative dominance. Eisenhower warned Macmillan in 1958 that the electorate had an appetite for further government intervention. This was confirmed in the United States by Republican setbacks in the 1958 mid-term elections and by Kennedy's successful bid for the presidency in 1960. By July 1960 Gallup could report that 46 per cent of those interviewed now considered that the Democrats would do a better job than the Republicans at keeping the country prosperous.[57] In Germany and Britain the social democratic opposition had absorbed the lessons of affluence and were challenging conservative governments on their own political territory. The British Labour party remade its image as the party of prosperity and technological innovation at the 1964 and 1966 general elections, while the SPD demonstrated its economic competence during the Grand Coalition government with the Christian Democrats. Beyond electoral competition, the 1960s proved to be less favourable for conservatives than had the 1950s. The Cold War abated and left wing politics entered a new phase of confidence. Progressive politics became more attractive and gained widespread support in most advanced capitalist states. Furthermore, social change generated new cleavages in society (around race, gender and life style) that provided increased political support for the left. Conservatives had benefited from the economic changes associated with affluence during the 1950s, but were uneasy with its social consequences. At first, conservatives sought to meet this challenge by moving in a more progressive direction, but in time most conservative parties began to resist the politics of the new left. A new phase of affluence began in the 1960s (often associated with the concept of permissiveness), which was to have long-term consequences for the realignment of politics in the liberal democratic states. New questions in respect of political authority, life style and culture emerged as a consequence of the success of affluence. What had begun as a consumption boom in the 1950s became a far more complex social transformation during the 1960s. The debate over affluence widened during the 1960s, dividing communities everywhere on issues such as inclusion, tolerance and multiculturalism. These debates continue to affect political positions in the new century, evidence of the continuing importance of affluence in understanding contemporary society and history.

Notes

[1] Buchanan, William and Cantril, Hadley: *How Nations See Each Other: A Study in Public Opinion*, Greenwood Press, Westport, CT, (1953) 1972, pp. 121–216.

[2] Ellwood, David: *Rebuilding Europe: Western Europe, America and Post–war Reconstruction*, Longman, London, 1992, pp. 206–07; Public Records Office, London (hereafter PRO): FO/1059975/M1037/1, 'Economic Problems of Western Europe' (May 1953).

[3] Eisenhower Presidential Library, Abilene Kansas (hereafter EPL): Ann Whitman, Administrative Series: Gabriel Hauge to Dwight D. Eisenhower, 13 November 1952; TNA: PRO CAB. 128: CC57(52), 29 May 1952 and CC75(52), 31 July 1952.

[4] Strachey, John: *Contemporary Capitalism*, Victor Gollancz, London, 1956; Shonfield, Andrew: *Modern Capitalism: The Changing Balance of Public and Private Power*, Oxford University Press, Oxford, 1965; Bell, Daniel: *The End of Ideology: On the Exhaustion of Political Ideas in the Fifties*, Free Press, New York, 1962.

[5] The United States made this transition earlier than Europe while Japan did so a little later, but the trends were in the same direction, see Griffiths, Richard T and Tachibanaki, Toshiaki: 'From Austerity to Affluence: The Turning-Point in Modern Societies' in Griffiths, R.T. and Tachibanaki, T. (eds): *From Austerity to Affluence: The Transformation of the Socio-Economic Structure of Western Europe and Japan*, Macmillan, London, 2000, pp. 1–24.

[6] The second half of the 1970s was much harsher for some sections of the population than had been the case between 1955 and 1974. Despite this, governments remained committed to delivering affluence for the majority if not for everyone.

[7] Rowbotham, Sheila: *A Century of Women: The History of Women in Britain and the United States*, Penguin, London, 1999, pp. 280–397; Girvin, Brian: 'The Political Culture of Secularisation: European Trends and Comparative Perspectives' in Broughton, David and Napel, Hans-Martien ten: (eds): *Religion and Mass Electoral Behaviour in Europe*, Routledge, London, 2000, pp. 7–27.

[8] Zakaria, Fareed: *The Future of Freedom: Illiberal Democracy at Home and Abroad*, W. W. Norton, New York, 2003, pp. 13–24; Pommerin, Reiner (ed): *The American Impact on Post–war Germany* Berghahn, Providence RI, 1993; Berghahn, Volker, R.: 'Recasting Bourgeois Germany' in Schissler, Hanna (ed): *The Miracle Years: A*

Cultural History of West Germany 1949–1968, Princeton University Press, Princeton NJ, 2001, pp. 326–40.

[9] Barraclough, Geoffrey: *An Introduction to Contemporary History*, Penguin, Harmondsworth, (1964) 1967, pp. 9–42 for the methodological case.

[10] *The Economist*, 30 March 2002 for the data on this. Germany is the only major OECD state where house ownership falls below 50 per cent; *Living in Britain – The 2001 General Household Survey*, Office for National Statistics, London, 2002 (accessed at www.statistics.gov.uk/lib).

[11] *Financial Times*, 24–25 May 2003 noted significant increases in remortgaging in the United Kingdom during 2002.

[12] Berry, Christopher J: *The Idea of Luxury*, Cambridge University Press, Cambridge, 1994; Berg, Maxine and Clifford, Helen (eds): *Consumers and Luxury: Consumer Culture in Europe 1650–1850*, Manchester University Press, Manchester, 1999.

[13] Cohen, Lizabeth: 'The New Deal State and the Making of Citizen Consumers' in Strasser, Susan, McGovern, Charles and Judt, Matthias (eds): *Getting and Spending: European and American Consumer Societies in the Twentieth Century*, Cambridge University Press, Cambridge, 1998, pp. 111–26. Cohen's timing is somewhat different from mine, but I find her argument that the state provided the stimulus during the New Deal period for the emergence of a mass consumption society a persuasive one. See also her *A Consumers' Republic: The Politics of Mass Consumption in Post–war America*, Knopf, New York, 2002.

[14] Lipset, Seymour Martin and Marks, Gary: *It Didn't Happen Here: Why Socialism Failed in the United States*, W.W. Norton, New York, 1999; Halpern, Rick and Morris, Jonathan (eds): *American Exceptionalism? US Working-Class Formation in an International Context*, Macmillan, London, 1997.

[15] Cohen, *A Consumers' Republic*, op. cit., makes this link explicit; more generally see Daunton, Martin and Hilton, Matthew (eds): *The Politics of Consumption: Material Culture and Citizenship in Europe and America*, Berg, Oxford, 2001.

[16] National Bureau of Economic Research, *Recent Economic Changes in the United States*, Vol. 2 (New York, 1929), pp. 625–6; Leven, Maurice, Moulton, Harold G, and Warburton, Clark: *America's Capacity to Consume*, Brookings Institution, Washington DC, 1936; Cross, Gary: *Time and Money: The Making of Consumer Culture*, Routledge, London, 1993.

[17] Benson, Susan Porter: 'Gender, Generation, and Consumption in the United States: Working Class Families in the Interwar Period' in Strasser, McGovern and Judt, *Getting and Spending* op. cit., pp. 223–40.

[18] For a more detailed discussion see Girvin, Brian: 'A New Sensibility? Affluence, Disposable Income and the Politics of Private Consumption, 1955–1975', in R.T. Griffiths and T. Tachibanki, (eds): *From Austerity to Affluence: The Transformation of the Socio-Economic Structure of Western Europe and Japan*, Macmillan, London, 2000, pp. 99–119; for American data see Levy, Frank: *Dollars and Dreams: The Changing American Income Distribution*, Norton, New York, 1988, pp. 45–9.

[19] Hibbs, Jr. Douglas A: 'Political Parties and Macroeconomic Policy', *American Political Science Review*, vol. 71, no. 4 (1977), pp. 1467–87.

[20] This chapter challenges the claim made by Marwick 'that it is a mistake to concentrate on politics and change of government', Marwick, Arthur: *The Sixties: Cultural Revolution in Britain, France, Italy and the United States c.1958–c.1974* Oxford University Press, Oxford, 1998, p. 9. This is partly a matter of focus. Marwick is primarily concerned with cultural and social change and consequently diminishes the importance of the political. However, to ignore the political, even in the narrow sense of

party politics, is in my opinion to exclude a crucial dimension of both change and continuity in this period.

[21]   I have discussed some of the reasons for Ireland's failure in Girvin, Brian: *From Union to Union: Democracy, Religion and Nationalism from the Act of Union to the European Union*, Gill and Macmillan, Dublin, 2002. See also Fitzgerald, Rona and Girvin, Brian: 'Political Culture, Growth and the Conditions for Success in the Irish Economy' in Nolan, Brian, O'Connell, Philip J, and Whelan, Christopher T. (eds): *Bust to Boom? The Irish Experience of Growth and Inequality*, Institute for Public Administration, Dublin, 2000, pp. 268–85. Nor should such a focus be limited to Ireland. Denmark, also prosperous, had a particularly difficult decade during the 1950s due to policy differences among the political parties. These were not resolved until the very end of the decade. I am grateful to Johnny Larsen at the University of Aarhus for discussion on the Danish case.

[22]   Nau, Henry R.: *The Myth of American Decline*, Oxford University Press, New York, 1990, pp. 9, 41–9; Sloan, John W.: *Eisenhower and the Management of Prosperity*, University of Kansas Press, Lawrence KS, 1991, makes much the same claim for the United States.

[23]   Girvin, Brian: *The Right in the Twentieth Century: Conservatism and Democracy*, Pinter, London, 1994; Harris, Howell John: *The Right to Manage: Industrial Relations Policies of American Business in the 1940s*, University of Wisconsin Press, Madison WI.,1982; Kersbergen, Kaas van: *Social Capitalism: A Study of Christian Democracy and the Welfare State*, Routledge, London, 1995; Baldwin, Peter: *Politics of Social Solidarity*, Cambridge University Press, Cambridge, 1990. For a discussion of the mixed economy model see Shonfield, *Modern Capitalism* op. cit.

[24]   Conservative Party Archives (hereafter CPA): CCO 20/1/1, Macmillan to Lord Woolton, 18 January 1949.

[25]   CPA: CCO 180/1/3 Public Opinion Research Department (PORD), 14 June 1949.

[26]   Sundquist, James L: *The Dynamics of the Party System*, Brookings Institution, Washington, DC, 1983, pp. 196–203; Girvin, *The Right in the Twentieth* Century, op. cit., pp. 159–69.

[27]   Miles, Michael W: *The Odyssey of the American Right*, Oxford University Press, New York, 1980, p. viii; Griffith, Robert: 'Why They Liked Ike', *Reviews in American History*, vol. 7, no. 4 (1979), pp. 577–83; For recent discussion on American Conservatism see Brinkly, Alan: 'The Problem of American Conservatism', *American Historical Review*, vol. 99, no. 2 (April 1994), pp. 409–29.

[28]   Malsberger, John W.: 'The Transformation of Republican Conservatism: The U.S. Senate, 1938–1952', *Congress and the Presidency*, vol. 14, no. 1 (Spring 1987), pp. 17–31, p. 22 for quote; Vandeberg, Jr., Arthur H: *The Private Papers of Senator Vandeberg* Greenwood Press, Westport, CT, 1974 (reprint of 1952 original), pp. 425, 464–7 for details.

[29]   Cited in Griffith, 'Why They Liked Ike', op. cit., p. 583.

[30]   For discussion of Eisenhower as President and his impact on the party see Ambrose, Stephen: *Eisenhower: The President*, Simon and Schuster, New York, 1984; Greenstein, Fred I.: *The Hidden-Hand Presidency*, Basic Books, New York, 1982.

[31]   EPL: Administration Series, Box 18, Hauge to Eisenhower, 13 November 1952.

[32]   EPL: Presidential papers, Name Series, Box 5, Eisenhower to Chynewith, 20 July 1954; loc. cit., Administrative Series, Box 9, Eisenhower to Arthur Burns, 2 February 1954.

[33]   EPL: Burns papers, Box 99, minutes of the Advisory Board on Economic Growth and Stability, 1 April 1954; EPL: Presidential papers, Name Series, Burns notes for Cabinet 2 April 1954; Gallup, George (ed): *The Gallup Poll: Public Opinion 1935–1971*,

Random House, New York, 1972: 3 volumes: pp. 1207–23; 1257, all references are in volume 2 of the series.

[34] EPL: Campaign series, Box 2, 'Public Opinion Survey on Political Issues, 1954'.

[35] EPL: Cabinet series, Box 4, 5 November 1954 for both Nixon and Eisenhower contributions.

[36] EPL: Hauge papers, Box 1, Hauge to Humphrey, 16 October 1954.

[37] Cohen, *A Consumers' Republic*, op. cit., who suggests that the GI Bill, the expansion of higher education and the availability of housing disproportionately subsidized the middle classes after 1945.

[38] EPL: Administration series, Box 9, Arthur F. Burns to Eisenhower, '3 Years of Prosperity', 17 August 1956; loc. cit., 'Some facts on the current economic situation' 22 October 1956; loc. cit., Burns to Eisenhower, 7 November 1956.

[39] EPL: Administration series, Burns to Eisenhower, 17 August 1956, 22 October 1956 and 7 November 1956. Data from Wattenberg, Ben J.: *The Statistical History of the United States: From Colonial Times to the Present*, Basic Books, New York, 1976; Gallup, *The Gallup Poll*, op. cit., 2: pp. 1949–58 for details.

[40] A detailed assessment of the policy advice available to Eisenhower and some of the policy initiatives taken can be found in Sloan: *Eisenhower and the Management of Prosperity*, op. cit., pp. 12–68.

[41] TNA: PRO PREM 11/129, draft minute Churchill to Butler, September 1952, Butler to Churchill, 8 October 1952; Churchill to Butler, 13 October 1952.

[42] CPA: CCO4/3/250 'The approach to the Ex-Socialist Floating Voter', 30 December 1949.

[43] CPA: CRD2/7/6, 'Report of the working party on the approach to the industrial worker', 20 July 1950; Conservative Party, *This is the Road*, Conservative Party, London, 1950, p. 8; Conservative Party, *The Election Manifesto*, Conservative Party, London, 1951, p. 3; Abrams, Mark and Rose, Richard: *Must Labour Lose?*, Penguin, Harmondsworth, 1960, p. 76.

[44] Zweiniger-Bargielowska, Ina: *Austerity in Britain: Rationing, Controls, and Consumption 1939–1955*, Oxford University Press, Oxford, 2000, pp. 243–55 which discusses the Conservative party's successful appeal in the elections of 1951 and 1955 in terms of consumption; Pinto-Duchinsky, Michael: 'Bread and Circuses? The Conservatives in Office, 1951–1964' in Bogdanor, Vernon and Skidelski, Robert (eds): *The Age of Affluence 1951–1964*, Macmillan, London, 1970, pp. 55–77.

[45] CPA: CCO180/2/2, Public Opinion Summary no. 37, June 1952.

[46] Butler papers: H. 36, Michael Fraser to John Boyd-Carpenter, 4 December 1953.

[47] Zweiniger-Bargielowska, *Austerity in Britain*, op. cit., pp. 202–55; Abrams and Rose, *Must Labour Lose?*, op. cit., pp. 64–98.

[48] The internal discussion on priorities can be followed in TNA: PRO T. 229/402, 'Urgent Economic Problems', 21 November 1951; CAB 130/72, GEN 388, 'The Economic Position', 30 October 1951; 31 October 1951; 2 November 1951; see also Seldon, Anthony: *Churchill's Indian Summer: The Conservative Government 1951–1955*, Hodder and Stoughton, London, 1981, pp. 254–55.

[49] Butler papers: G.26, Butler to Bridges, 3 September 1953; Butler to Macmillan 2 May 1953; TNA: PRO T.229/747, Churchill to Butler, 9 July 1952; Butler to Churchill, 11 July 1952.

[50] TNA: PRO CAB 134/936, Home Affairs Committee, HA (WC), 4 July 1952; 9 July 1952; 30 July 1952; 12 September 1952. Woolton Papers: Ms. 25, Woolton to Churchill, 18 March 1952; Churchill to Woolton 19 March 1952; Woolton to Churchill, 19 March 1952. Woolton's remarks on working class income can be found in TNA: PRO CAB

130/72, GEN 388, 'The Economic Position' 30 October 1951; 31 October 1951; 2 November 1951.

51 Woolton Papers: Ms 26, Woolton to Churchill, 24 April 1953.

52 TNA: PRO T 230/299, 'Full employment and priced stability', 18 June 1954. An earlier memorandum by Butler expressed very similar views in TNA: PRO T 230/298 memorandum by the Chancellor, 18 April 1952.

53 TNA: PRO PREM 11/1824 C (57) 195, 7 September 1957; Macmillan response, 16 September 1957.

54 Horne, Alistair: *Macmillan: 1957–1986*, Macmillan, London, 1989, pp. 17, 37; for details of the dispute between Thorneycroft and Macmillan on expenditure see TNA: PRO CAB 128/31, CC(57)77th Cabinet Conclusions, 31 October 1957; CC. (57) 86, 31 December 1957; CAB 128/32, CC. (58) 3 January 1958, 11AM; CC. (58) 3 January 1958, 4.30 PM; CC. (58) 5 January 1958.

55 TNA: PRO PREM 11/2311, 'Future Employment prospects following recession', 23 October 1958; Directive by Prime Minister, 27 October 1958; CAB 134/1734, Cabinet Committee on Employment, for Macmillan's interventions.

56 Butler papers: H.46, 'Pride of Country' (no date but probably 1961); Macleod is cited in Horne: *Macmillan,* op. cit., p. 76.

57 EPL: Presidential Papers: Diary Series, Box 10, Eisenhower and Macmillan meeting, 11 November 1958; Name Series, Box 26, 'Memo for the record', 9 December 1958; Gallup, *The Gallup Report,* op. cit., 3, p. 1676.

CHAPTER 3

Modernizing Britain's Welfare State: The Influence of Affluence, 1957–1964

Rodney Lowe[1]

Welfare policy is not a subject noted for setting either the blood pulsing or the mind racing. This is somewhat strange because it has been at the heart both of all post-war elections and of social scientists' explanations of one of the key phenomena of the twentieth century: the growth of central government. On the one hand, for instance, Iain Macleod as Conservative Party chairman commenced preparations for the 1964 election by advising colleagues that it was 'important to make contact ... with Ministers who are going to be key to us: the Social Service Ministers ... These are the most relevant to a Manifesto'.[2] On the other, a plethora of theories has been developed to explain the growth of welfare states.[3] Were they, as functionalists have argued, the inevitable consequence of 'modernization'? Did they represent a series of concessions from above designed to maintain the power of the ruling elite (the 'Bonapartist' or Bismarckian premise)? Alternatively, did they represent a genuine victory from below (the 'labourist' explanation)? Welfare policy, in short, can provide a key to an understanding of political conflict in both the short and long-term.

Peter Baldwin is the historian who has best succeeded in marrying detailed empirical research to welfare theory; and he has consistently maintained that 'the nuts and bolts of social policy testify to the heated struggles of classes and interests. The battles behind the welfare state lay bare the structure and conflicts of modern society'.[4] This observation, however, suggests a reason why welfare history – as opposed to welfare theory – has never fully caught fire. The devil is all too often in the detail. Only when welfare policy has been heroic, as with the pre-1914 Liberal Reforms, or presented in apocalyptic language, as in the 1942 Beveridge Report, have political reputations been made and has conventional historical interest been consequently aroused.

Welfare policy in the late 1950s and early 1960s has rarely been portrayed as heroic. Rather, historians have joined with most contemporary observers in condemning any change in policy – in so far as it has been noticed – as either a cynical attempt to win votes or a reprehensible betrayal of principle. The first option has proved the more popular, with the majority of historians echoing Gaitskell's dismissal of Macmillan's ambitious attempt to 'modernize Britain' in 1962 as the typical product of 'a Government of gimmicks, an Administration of admen'. The second option has been largely adopted by Thatcherite historians, endorsing Powell's verdict that Macmillan's actions were 'semi-socialist'.[5] Given Baldwin's claims, however, cannot welfare policy be used more imaginatively to 'lay bare' the nature of affluent Britain? The challenge appears all the more attractive because in 1958 the Conservative government commissioned the Party's in-house think tank, the Conservative Research Department (CRD), to undertake an enquiry entitled, The Social Services in an Affluent Society.[6] This was proof, if proof were needed, that affluence was – and was then perceived to be – a significant new social and political phenomenon.

The purpose of this chapter is, therefore, to examine the interrelationship between welfare policy and affluence. Affluence is defined here as the release of the majority of people from both the interwar fear of poverty and the restrictions of post-war austerity; and the sense of economic, social and political liberation uniquely felt when they enjoyed, or could realistically hope to enjoy, for the first time a novel range of consumer goods capable of transforming the material quality of their lives. Such a sense of liberation inevitably affected government and the services it provided; and the subsequent response of policy-makers in Westminster and Whitehall will be traced through the activities of two representative bodies, the Conservative Research Department and the Treasury. Contrary to received opinion this response will be shown to have been, on the whole, not opportunist but both principled and, to a degree, heroic. This is, admittedly, not a wholly novel conclusion. It was sensed at the time by two particularly well-informed observers. In relation to the political response Christopher Booker noted:

> It was one of the paradoxes of the period ... that halfway through 1962, when it was almost daily being castigated for its 'complacency' and 'inertia', the Macmillan government was in fact in the thick of the greatest burst of radical activity since the years immediately after the war.[7]

In relation to the administrative response, Samuel Brittan similarly remarked:

> Many of the new policies which Labour was later to proclaim its own had already emerged in the far-reaching reappraisal which went on inside the Treasury and other government departments around 1960–1.[8]

It is the intention of this chapter to confirm these two, rather unfashionable, observations; but it will go further. Welfare policy, as has been argued, is not something insulated from wider social forces but an expression of them. It thus embodies the disparate elements of affluence identified elsewhere in this book as well as providing a focus for their integration. In the mid-1950s, for example, growing dissatisfaction with the range and quality of welfare was a principal expression of the liberating influence of relative wealth and of the greater sophistication of consumer demand. This dissatisfaction led to a questioning of the values on which the services were based; and, by contributing to a suspicion of authority, helped to translate a generally benign attitude towards government (inherited from the Second World War) into one of distrust. This growing divergence of popular and official values underlay the transformation of assumptions on which political rhetoric and administrative action were based. The initial reaction of the Conservative Party may have appeared – and may continue to appear to historians – the more effective. For two reasons, however, this was not necessarily true. First, the reaction was frequently prompted by and even dependent on opposition initiatives. R.A. Butler's characteristic response to the Labour Party's plans for pension reform in 1957, for instance, was that the government should 'not only steal the Whig's clothes but also dye them a more attractive shade'.[9] This suggests that Labour perhaps responded more constructively than has sometimes been suggested to the substantive need for change. Secondly, the Conservatives' response was highly contested – as well illustrated by the resignation in October 1963 of the two leading modernizers, Macleod and Powell, when Home succeeded Macmillan as prime minister. Welfare policy, nevertheless, does illustrate one continuing area of agreement across Westminster and Whitehall: an antipathy in public policy to American influence, as reflected in the isolation of the free market Institute of Economic Affairs (founded in 1956).

Challenge and response

Increasing prosperity in the mid-1950s awakened instincts within both the Conservative Party and the Treasury to 'roll back the state'. The welfare state was perceived in Enoch Powell's words as 'a delayed reaction to Victorian poverty'[10] and thus increasingly outdated. As an early statement of principle to the CRD enquiry into The Social Services in an Affluent Society explained:

> In our increasingly affluent society, many people can manifestly now afford to provide for themselves. It would seem sensible to ask them either to do so or to contribute more towards the cost of the social services. This should encourage self-reliance and independence, relieve the Exchequer, and [is] thoroughly in line with Conservative philosophy.[11]

The Treasury, needless to say, had long been seeking ways to 'relieve the Exchequer' and in December 1955 succeeded in persuading Cabinet to convene a Social Services Committee 'to examine the issues which would arise' if increases in welfare expenditure over the next five years 'were to be avoided or substantially reduced'.[12] The state, however, was not rolled back. Rather than being avoided or substantially reduced, expenditure on the social services in fact rose between 1955 and 1964 from 13.9 per cent to 16.5 per cent of GDP. Moreover, when the full range of the Conservative's welfare commitments was spelt out in December 1963 in the first white paper on public expenditure – itself a symbol of the new professionalism in public policy – the reaction of Callaghan, Labour's shadow chancellor of the exchequer, was instructive. 'The programmes', he concluded, 'could not be exceeded by any party with any degree of responsibility'.[13]

Callaghan's comment was confirmation that, whereas they had previously advanced singly, the five core areas of welfare policy – social security, education, health, the personal social services and housing – were now expanding in unison. In social security policy, a fundamental principle of the Beveridge Report, that state action should be limited to the provision of flat rate subsistence benefits, had been breached. Graduated pensions were introduced in 1961 and the detailed plans for earnings-related unemployment and sickness pay were prepared for implementation in 1964. Even in that final bastion of poor law 'less eligibility', the National Assistance Board, officials had come to accept that the level of means-tested benefit should enable recipients to participate, and not just survive, in society.[14] This was recognition, as successive Conservative manifestos made clear, that in an affluent society people sought a guarantee not against destitution but against the loss of their newly acquired life-styles; and that the poverty line should rise in line with average living standards (the acceptance of a 'relative' as opposed to an 'absolute' definition of poverty).

In both education and health care ambitious programmes of capital expenditure were being implemented or planned. In 1958, £300m was assigned to the rebuilding of secondary schools over five years and in 1962 a further £500m over ten years was committed to the modernization of the hospital system. The commitment to educational advance was epitomized by the 1963 Robbins Report, accepted by the government within 24 hours, which committed government to increasing students in higher education by 50 per cent in four years and by 250 per cent by 1980. The broader ambition of the Hospital Plan was also underlined in 1963 by the first attempt to draft a comprehensive programme of community care (to enable the infirm to be cared for in their own homes). In the same year, the personal social services also witnessed another major change of principle when the state was empowered by the Children and Young Persons Act to intervene in family life to prevent, rather than just halt, child neglect. Such policy changes reflected the higher standard of service which an affluent society required and the lifting of the tight restrictions on 'the private' which were fundamental to a poverty culture.

Housing was the one policy area where the Conservatives did try to 'roll back' the state. As in the interwar period building subsidies to local authorities were restricted in 1956 to slum clearance schemes and rent controls were relaxed by the 1957 Rent Act to encourage tenants in the private and then the public sector to pay 'economic' (i.e. unsubsidized) rents. However, ironically under Sir Keith Joseph as housing minister, interventionism came fully back into vogue. To counter the failings of the market, general building subsidies were reintroduced in 1963, a building target of 400,000 new homes announced in the 1964 manifesto and a full range of regional plans commissioned to provide a framework for urban development over the following 20 years. This emphasis on planning accorded with the thrust of Macmillan's modernization programme, which he had recommended to Cabinet in October 1962 in the following terms:

> Do we, or do we not, set out to control the pattern of events, to direct development, to plan growth, to use instruments of Government to influence or determine private decisions. Believe that this is inevitable. Forces at work now too complicated, risks of set back too great to leave to market forces and laissez faire. Dirigisme. But it must be creative dirigisme.[15]

Macmillan's concerns were primarily economic – the location, structural balance and productive efficiency of industry. They were built on three earlier initiatives. The first was an unusually wide-ranging and imaginative Treasury report, submitted to Cabinet in July 1961, outlining the economic, social and fiscal means by which economic growth – the precondition for continuing affluence – could be sustained.[16] The second was the establishment of the National Economic Development Council as a forum in which government, employers and trade unions could discuss such a programme. The third was the creation of the National Economic Development Office, an *independent* secretariat (a significant departure from Whitehall practice), one of whose first responsibilities was to consider the Treasury report. The subsequent debate, which culminated with the publication by NEDO of *Conditions Favourable to Economic Growth* in 1963, provided the stimulus for a range of 'active labour policies' directly targeting welfare reform on improved economic performance. They included the Contracts of Employment Act (to enhance job security), the Industrial Training Act (to widen the skills base) and the Redundancy Payments Bill (to encourage job mobility). Such legislation, extending far beyond the traditional five core areas of social policy, was far more in keeping with the concept of welfare as practised in continental Europe. It thus marked a radical policy departure for the British welfare state. How were the initial instincts of the CRD and Treasury so frustrated?

Modernization within the Party

The CRD, for its part, thoroughly examined the interrelationship between affluence and welfare policy. After preliminary discussions in 1958, its officials were formally reconstituted as the Committee on the Future of the Social Services in January 1960. This committee held 40 meetings before producing an interim report on the financing of the social services in April 1961 and then a further 25 meetings before issuing a final report in August 1963. It concentrated initially on proposals designed to 'roll back the state' by making people pay more directly and fully for their welfare provision. For example, pensions were to be placed on an actuarial basis so that, over their working life, everyone invested an amount appropriate to the pension that they would receive. Lower paid workers, whose contributions would not actuarially justify a subsistence pension, would be guaranteed a minimum retirement income. Various methods to fund this guarantee were advanced of which the most radical was a graduated social security tax. This would not entitle contributors, whose income in retirement exceeded subsistence, to a state pension. Rather, it was designed to make transparent the redistribution of resources which would otherwise have remained hidden by the tax system. The clear expectation was that, above the minimum guaranteed by the state, affluent life-styles should be financed in retirement by earnings-related occupational pensions. In education, it was argued, the cost of schooling was forseeable by parents and therefore should be met, at least in part, by the payment of fees. As one official reasoned: 'the most important aim of social policy, the promotion of family responsibility and individual self-reliance, will not be served in the case of education until part payment of school fees up to the age of 15 is introduced'.[17] The state's contribution to the rest of the cost should not take the form of a subsidized place in a state school but of an educational voucher, which might also be used in the private sector. Likewise in health care, patients should pay the full cost of all services, other than those provided by hospitals, through an insurance scheme; and, in order to encourage non-state provision, private patients should be reimbursed for all their expenditure on any items, such as drugs or basic hospital care, that was funded by the taxpayer.

The clear conviction of CRD officials was that, with rising incomes and expectations, everyone could and *should* pay fully for the welfare services they required. Their primary object was to ensure that welfare provision encouraged rather than undermined self-reliance and independence. There were, however, several other motivations which were later to be termed 'Thatcherite'. First, there was the desire to make people aware of the full cost of services, so that unrealistic demands (and thereby undue pressures on Parties at elections) would be curtailed. The purpose of actuarial pension contributions, for example, was 'to get the public to think of the rate of pension that can be paid by the scheme as inflexibly determined by the rate of contribution'.[18] Second, there was a desire to empower the consumer in relation to the professional provider, and thereby make the service more responsive. 'There would be', it was concluded, 'a great improvement in parent–teacher relationships if teachers knew that if the parents were not satisfied with the education their children were getting ... there was a danger that their pupils would be taken away'.[19] Thirdly, there would be a widening of choice, with people encouraged to look beyond state services to the private sector. A revival of independent schools was envisaged as state education was 'whittled away'.[20] Finally such competition, it was assumed, would reduce costs and thereby reduce, or at least limit further increases in, taxation. This would in turn stimulate the economic growth upon which everyone's welfare ultimately depended.[21]

By the time that the Committee's interim and the final reports were compiled, however, much of the confidence behind this radicalism had been eroded. As was admitted in the former:

> We began our examination ... with a bias in favour of radical change [but] our general conclusion is that ... existing or planned provision for finance are broadly on the right lines and we do not at this stage suggest any major changes.

When submitting the final report, the chair of the Committee and director of the CRD, Michael Fraser, also admitted to Butler that 'it was not dramatic – as the closer we looked at the more dramatic proposals the less we liked them'.[22]

Existing policy was adjudged to be on the 'right lines' because it provided an optimum compromise between the competing principles which dominated post-war welfare policy, universalism and selectivity. Universalism, the inclusion of all citizens within the same welfare scheme as an expression of community, was seen by most Conservatives as an embodiment of 'One Nationism' – a key concept since the days of Disraeli and one which epitomized the Conservative belief that theirs was a national, rather than a class-based, party. Any increase in privatization, or even the privileged treatment of private patients in the NHS, risked the reintroduction of a two-tier system and would consequently be 'retrograde'.[23] On the other hand greater selectivity, or the targeting of resources on those in genuine need, was required if the twin aims of relieving the Exchequer and encouraging self-reliance amongst the increasingly affluent was to be achieved. The graduated pension scheme, introduced in 1961, demonstrated how an effective compromise could be achieved. Middle income earners were required to make earnings-related contributions towards a second pension, which would ensure them a higher retirement income. Unlike the original flat-rate scheme, there was no direct government contribution, and so beneficiaries paid the full cost. They could, if they wished, opt out into a private occupational scheme but some of their contributions was retained by the state to subsidize low paid workers. In this way both self-reliance and the community spirit of universalism were reinforced. In health care and housing policy a similar compromise was reached. Patients were required to pay directly for a higher proportion of their treatment through sharply increased insurance contributions (which generated 17 per cent of NHS income in 1964, compared to 6 per cent in 1956) and charges. The needy were exempted from charges. Similarly in housing, tenants were required to pay increasingly economic rents in the public and private sector with the withdrawal of both general building subsidies and rent control. The introduction of rent rebates was designed to alleviate genuine hardship.

Under close scrutiny, therefore, existing policy increasingly appeared to offer an effective and principled compromise. In contrast, most of the initial radical proposals increasingly appeared to be impractical and impolitic. As Fraser acknowledged, 'the nation had originally wanted universality and appeared still to want it'. Any attack upon it, such as the withdrawal of the state pension, would be 'politically disastrous' – the more so because the payment of insurance contributions since the war were believed to have earned rights, the withdrawal of which would be viewed as a 'major attack on people's expectations'.[24] An official underlined this point with a powerful historical allusion. 'It is one thing to give something to people', he argued

> but it is politically quite another thing to take it away from them once they have been given it. This was the bitter lesson learnt by the Whigs. They saw that the poor were being given the wrong thing when they got lavish Speenhamland relief but the Whigs only earned howls of political opprobrium when they took it away in 1834 and gave the poor what their political economists said was the right thing in the shape of the New Poor Law.

Any similar dogmatic attack on welfare policy, he was sure, would be as popular electorally and as administratively impractical as the workhouse in 1834.[25]

The proposed reintroduction of school fees illustrated this very point. 'There is no developed country in the world where compulsory education is not free', the interim report confirmed, and 'it is not easy to contemplate being the first country in the world to reverse the modern practice'.[26] Further electoral damage would be sustained as a result of parents' anger. Not only would their expectations be disappointed but they would also see (in a country where the family was relatively poorly supported) a redistribution of resources away from parents and their necessary subjection to a means test. What would happen if they refused to comply? This highlighted an additional problem: the role of education as a 'public good', advancing both sociability and employability (thereby minimizing civil unrest whilst maximizing economic growth). It was, in short, the community as much as the individual that suffered from any disaffection with, and shortfall in, education.

Butler recognized the force of these arguments when he recommended the interim report to the Party's Advisory Committee on Policy. As he concluded:

> While in general there was a feeling in the Party that something should be done about the financing of the social services because of the increase in wages and in the general standard of life, he felt that this report was thoroughly sensible in approach. He did not think that people who advocated radical changes in fields such as education realised either the political implications or that any possible sum would be minimal in relation to teachers' salaries.[27]

Such reasoned reservations blunted the earlier philosophical animosity towards state welfare and, within government, enabled it to win greater resources and legitimacy. The Party at large, however, remained to be fully convinced and the 1964 manifesto contained the following pledge:

> The existing social security system ... was framed twenty years ago, and in the light of pre-war experience. Since then there have been dramatic changes in economic and social needs. We therefore propose to institute a full review of social security arrangements so that their subsequent development may be suited to modern circumstances.[28]

The response to affluence was still contested, as the resignations of Macleod and Powell demonstrated.

Modernization within Whitehall

Within the Civil Service the initial radical attacks mounted by Treasury officials on state welfare were similarly blunted. The Treasury's departmental interest, unlike those of 'spending' ministries, was to reduce rather than increase public expenditure – given its responsibility for maintaining the value of sterling (at a time when international financiers strongly disapproved of public spending) and officials' conviction that high taxation thwarted economic growth by restricting private risk-taking and investment. Affluence built upon inflation rather than increased production was, in their judgement, dangerously illusory – mere fizz. These views were of vital importance in Whitehall since Treasury officials controlled both the highly secretive budget process (through which levels of public expenditure were determined) and the careers of other officials (through the

Treasury's responsibility for the management of the civil service). Any change to them, therefore, significantly affected policy making.

The Treasury's first open attack on welfare policy at the Cabinet Social Services Committee between 1955 and 1957, as has been seen, preceded that by the CSD. It was repeated on the Plowden Committee on the Control of Public Expenditure between 1959–61. On both occasions, its essential purpose was to contain welfare expenditure within a given planning target. Such an objective could be – and later was – presented as part of the modernization process. Firm estimates of future policy commitments were to be matched against forecasts of national resources. This would provide a solid base on which ministers could exercise collective responsibility in determining priorities; and, in an early manifestation of 'joined-up government', officials whilst implementing the resulting policies could experience 'joint working in a common enterprise'.[29] Behind such a laudable objective, however, lay a hidden agenda as is revealed by the papers of the leading official behind each exercise, Otto Clarke. Pre-eminently interested in reducing taxation, he dismissed most social policies as wasteful and orchestrated, for example, a campaign to collect examples of 'waste' to present to the Plowden Committee. The list was long and included the long-standing Treasury conviction that family allowances, were used not to meet the additional costs of parenthood but to 'supplement the purchase of frills and inessentials'.[30] The real objective behind the proposed planning exercises, therefore, was not to rationalize public expenditure but either to cut it (as in 1955) or to cap it at its existing level (as in 1961).

This agenda was sensed by spending ministers with the result that both exercises rebounded on the Treasury. On the Social Services Committee, fundamental inconsistencies were exposed both in the Treasury's statistics (which exaggerated the costs of social expenditure whilst minimizing the future rate of economic growth) and in the logic justifying its preferred balance between levels of taxation and expenditure. The Plowden Report led to the establishment of the Public Expenditure Survey Committee (PESC) to draft the five-year expenditure plan. It was overseen by a ministerial committee, on which Macleod similarly exposed the Treasury's underlying assumption that public expenditure was 'inherently undesirable'. It was forced to retreat. This was frankly admitted by the Chancellor when he brought the first PESC report to Cabinet in July 1961. 'When I originally put in hand a review of expenditure and resources', he confessed, 'I was thinking mainly about taxation – about what we might achieve in tax reductions during the life of this Parliament.' As a result of heated debate provoked by Macleod, however, 'increasing weight has been placed on the role of public expenditure both as an obstacle and as *an instrument for bringing about* competitiveness, growth and solvency.'[31]

These two reverses represented critical points in the gradual evolution of Treasury policy. In relation to *public investment*, officials in 1958 – partly in acknowledgement of public demand for higher quality of services – condoned increases at twice the rate of economic growth; and by 1962 they acknowledged that investment in infrastructure, such as roads, could directly benefit economic growth. In relation to *current expenditure*, the search for real cuts ended with

Thorneycroft's resignation in 1958. By the IMF crisis of 1961, officials accepted that it should at least rise in line with GDP; and even they conceded that expenditure on certain social services such as education and health had 'a potential contribution to make to growth', albeit in the long run.[32] In part these changes had been forced on the Treasury but they were also the product of the major internal review, prompted by perception of relative economic decline, which led to the report on *Economic Growth and National Efficiency* in July 1961. Cumulatively they represented a remarkable change. For example, in 1963, Maudling as chancellor could even argue that it was 'right and desirable to plan deliberately to devote a higher proportion on GNP to public expenditure'. The following year, a determination to heed Galbraith and to prevent private affluence being matched by public squalor was evident in the advice tendered by the Cabinet Secretary to the Prime Minister. He minuted:

(a) An increase in public expenditure – and therefore in tax – is not necessarily a bad thing, in so far as it provides better social benefits for the less fortunate members of the community and eliminates the grosser disparities of wealth.

(b) By any reliable criterion of value for money, it is not always public expenditure that needs to be reduced. The private sector, particularly private consumption, may be the villain of the piece; and in so far as an increase on 'luxuries' is unavoidable, it may be preferable to an arbitrary cut in programmes of e.g. new housing and new schools.[33]

Treasury advice, admittedly, was not unambiguous. For example, under Clarke's influence, officials on a later PESC exercise disinterred the belief that 'it was rarely possible to argue that greater public investment was a prerequisite to growth'. Clarke himself also welcomed the IEA's pamphlet *Choice in Welfare*, which purported to show public support for private welfare provision, as a means for halting his colleagues' mounting support for a comprehensive scheme of earnings-related insurance.[34] Such reservations, however, did not mean that there had not been a radical change in Treasury thinking. It simply meant that, as within the Conservative Party, radicalism remained contested.

The influence of affluence

The onset of affluence, as earlier defined, prompted a fundamental reappraisal of welfare policy. Then, political awareness that increasing numbers of people were enjoying a sense of liberation heavily influenced the nature of that reappraisal. Affluence both facilitated and required reform, eliciting a response from Westminster and Whitehall that was both pragmatic and principled.

Economic growth, upon which continuing affluence depended, facilitated reform by increasing revenue from existing levels of taxes. It thereby enabled welfare services to expand without ministers having to face the political opprobrium of raising or introducing new taxes. Hard decisions, therefore, did not have to be made and they were not. This is a principal reason why modernization could remain contested. As Treasury ministers, in a certain degree of panic over escalating expenditure in March 1964, argued: 'we sometimes say that people are ready to accept higher rates of taxation to pay for public expenditure but so far they have not had to make this choice'.[35]

Opinion polls, which the Conservatives increasingly commissioned after 1960, certainly appeared to confirm a popular preference for higher taxes over welfare cuts; and this preference was significantly expressed not just by trade unionists and women but also by the 'new middle-class', whom their electoral strategy was targeting. This finding transformed thinking within the CRD. Tax cuts were dropped as a policy priority for the first time in 1960 and replaced a year later by 'adequacy of services'. It also underlay the confidence with which Macleod attacked the Treasury over the first PESC report. It even permeated the Treasury itself. 'We and ministers will get in a mess', Clarke was warned, 'if we do not accept that the public want some services to expand if the economy expands and does not mind paying'.[36] Peter Baldwin has argued that the NHS was welcomed by the middle-classes because, aware of increasing longevity and medical bills, they abandoned self-reliance in favour of a 'pooling' of risk in a tax-funded service. Calculations of individual self-interest rather than altruistic social solidarity, he concluded, became the principal motive for collective action. Little evidence for this 'rational' behaviour, and of the mechanism by which it was realized, is available for the 1940s; but by the early 1960s opinion polls provided the proof and CRD the calculations to explain why the 'middle class in the full sense' welcomed the NHS. It 'benefited more' from it than any other class.[37] Other tax-funded services were equally appreciated so long as they provided better value for money and a greater sense of security than their market equivalent. State welfare, in short, was required as reassurance that higher living standards could and would be maintained. Public services had become a vital prop of private affluence.

The increased sophistication of consumer demand also required a higher standard of state services in both kind and cash. A major reason for the Treasury's acceptance of a higher level of public investment in 1958, for example, was an awareness of the poor physical condition of many state services and the electoral embarrassment this was likely to cause. 'Our deficiencies as regards both schools and hospitals are notorious', as one official minuted, 'and we cannot postpone dealing with them for ever'. The same reasoning, so it was argued, lay behind the readiness of Enoch Powell – an economic liberal who maintained that private medicine was superior to the NHS – to launch the Hospital Plan whilst minister of health. If the NHS existed, then its facilities had to be of an acceptable standard.[38] Definitions of 'acceptability', moreover, were constantly changing as consumers became more demanding. As one CRD official cynically reacted to the findings of the opinion polls: 'having had the best tv [the electorate] will now want the best mental hospitals'.[39]

Rising aspirations similarly affected cash benefits. As average living standards and expectations rose, so insurance benefits appeared increasingly inadequate and caused public disquiet. This also concerned CRD officials, one of whom admitted:

> At a time of unprecedented national prosperity, at a time when too marked a
> disparity between the income levels of the most and the least well off is
> recognized to militate against the reality of One Nation, 25 per cent is too
> high a proportion of the aged on National Assistance to be accepted with
> equanimity.[40]

It was, however, national assistance – the official means-tested poverty line –
which aroused the most political and academic controversy. Should its payments
reflect a minimum subsistence or a minimum participatory level of need? In other
words, was the purpose of national assistance to prevent a state of destitution (by
providing for an essential static range of physical requirements) or a sense of
deprivation (by providing a wider range of goods which would allow recipients to
participate in normal communal activities)? The former reflected the historical
definition of poverty and that still prevalent in underdeveloped countries. The latter
was essentially a measure of inequality and meant that the 'poverty' level would
rise in line with average living standards. Poverty could only be eradicated by a
major distribution of wealth. Nevertheless, as has been seen, it was the new
concept of 'relative' poverty that NAB officials accepted. So too did the
Conservative Party – in advance of the 'rediscovery of poverty' by Labour's two
policy advisers, Abel-Smith and Townsend. Its 1959 manifesto promised that
pensioners would 'share in the good things which a steadily expanding economy
will bring' and this commitment was extended to all social security claimants in
1964.[41] Affluence, in short, afforded society the luxury of redefining poverty. It
thereby permanently changed, in industrialized countries at least, the terms of the
welfare debate.

    Such changes to the quality of services and the value of cash benefits might
appear pragmatic, and even cynical, responses to real or anticipated challenges
from the electorate. However, as the regular references to 'One Nationism'
suggest, reform was also driven by principle. Two major demonstrations of
political principle were the commitments to compensate the 'victims' of economic
growth and to temper materialism by idealism. The former permeated CRD
thinking and was most eloquently expressed by Macleod at the 1966 Party
conference. 'Let us remember', he proclaimed

> that we are not all pace-setters, we are not all competitors, and let us
> remember that change when it comes as it must is often a very cruel thing to
> an individual or to a township or to a community. So competition needs
> compassion.

Such an awareness of the 'diswelfare' of economic growth was strikingly similar to
– and may even have been prompted by – one of Richard Titmuss' major defences
of state welfare.[42] It was nonetheless genuinely felt and fitted naturally into the
Conservatives' paternalist traditions. It also underlines how, from very different
ideological perspectives, problems associated with affluence could elicit similar
concerns and responses.

    Conservative tradition, however, was offended by the materialism associated
with the 1959 election because, as Lord Hailsham volubly stressed whenever he

was able, that tradition was based on the promotion of 'spiritual values'. The reinstatement of these values in 1962 catapulted, rather incongruously, Reginald Maudling into contention for the Party's leadership. He wrote to his constituents:

> the real needs of the 1960s are not the needs of a country haunted by Jarrow and the Rhondda, nor any longer the needs solely of a country breaking away from the austerity of war and the meshes of socialism. They are the needs of a people conscious of the greatness of their past, enjoying the affluence and the freedom of the present, but feeling in their hearts the lack of a sense of this freedom and affluence. National purpose and national pride; prosperity based on enterprise and self-discipline, used as a means of enhancing the dignity and value of human life everywhere – this must be our message.[43]

Domestically, these values were expressed in the principled compromise between universalism and selectivity which, as has been seen, both promoted self-reliance and effected a redistribution of resources in favour of the poor. The strong were thus enlisted to help the weak. Abroad, they were expressed in the establishment of Voluntary Service Overseas and of a Department of Technical Co-operation (which was the forerunner to the Department of Overseas Development). By 1964, so Edward Boyle could argue, government had struck the right balance. Materialism in itself was not bad because rising standards of living throughout the world increased freedom. National wealth, however, had to be 'widely shared and wisely used'. 'No government', he then contended, 'had done more to strengthen the social fabric in so short a time'.[44] An optimum mix of materialism and idealism had, therefore, been achieved: private affluence had not, as it opponents claimed, been matched by public squalor.

At both a political and administrative level, however, principle was applied to policy most intensively in an attempt to legitimize a new balance between the state and the market. The market was deemed to have failed in two ways. First, as in the interwar years, it undersupplied services essential to the achievement of both social equity and economic efficiency. Thus before the CRD Committee, David Eccles (as minister for education) could dismiss any notion of a return to market provision and justify heavy state investment in secondary and higher education on the grounds that it would make good a system in which, in his opinion, only 10 per cent of children had been adequately educated. Market provision was also frequently less cost-effective than state welfare. This was the argument used by the Treasury to resist the IEA's suggestion that pensions should be privatized. The transactions costs would consume economic resources to the benefit of neither the consumer nor the economy as a whole.[45] It was also acknowledged that a centralized NHS was able to deliver a comparable standard of health care more cost-effectively than the systems of private and social insurance practised in the USA and continental Europe. Policy makers, in short, had grasped the later economic wisdom that governments could do things 'which private markets for technical reasons either would not do at all, or would do inefficiently'.[46] Contrary to the initial instincts of the CRD and Treasury officials, some form of state welfare was required for reasons of efficiency.

The second way in which the market was perceived to have failed was in the maximization of economic growth. The simplistic reaction to Britain's apparent relative economic decline was to blame government; but, as the Treasury's report on *Economic Growth and National Efficiency* convincingly argued in 1961, it was the market that was actually failing. The government action had to energize it. A key passage read :

> If this country is to improve its position against competitors, the modernisation of our market economy needs to be accelerated by a revolution in attitudes parallel to the revolutionary achievement of full employment and social services. In this revolution the Government has a part to play by striving to remove obstacles to the effective operations of a market economy in the production of goods and services. This does not imply re-examining the ideas which have come to be generally accepted in the last 10 years about the proper role of Government in education, health and national insurance.[47]

In other words, whilst government had adapted to post-war conditions, the market had not; and government action was needed, not to reduce public expenditure (as the market and traditionally the Treasury had demanded) but to remove other obstacles to greater economic efficiency. This was the objective behind the many measures to increase competitiveness, such as attempted entry into the EEC and the abolition of Resale Price Maintenance (which, in an election year, greatly benefited the consumer at the expense of core Conservative voters, the small shop-keeper). Were the stimulus of competition to fail, the government's duty was better to inform and co-ordinate industrial opinion, as on the NEDC; to encourage, and even insist upon, best industrial practice through active labour market policies; and, where necessary, to exercise – in Macmillan's words – 'creative dirigisme'. Examples of such dirigisme were the introduction of 'special deposits' (to counteract the self-interest of banks) and regional policy (to employ under-utilized resources and to reduce the regional 'diswelfare' identified by Macleod). Economic growth, it was acknowledged, was vital to the continuation of both affluence and the tax revenue which funded state welfare. Consequently, just as state social services had become essential to private affluence, so state economic intervention had become essential to private enterprise.

Conclusion

The 'total' history of any period requires an overarching theme through which the disparate histories of its component parts can be integrated. For post-war British history, 'consensus' and 'economic' decline have been tried as such a theme and have been adjudged wanting.[48] 'Affluence' is a compelling alternative. This is because it was the conflicts over economic, social and political values spawned by a combination of sustained economic growth and a popular sense of liberation that shaped the whole of society and therefore, by definition, government. As Baldwin has argued and this chapter has sought to demonstrate, welfare policy can 'lay bare' these conflicts. From above, the initial response to affluence in the Conservative government and the Treasury was to 'roll back the state'. Public demand for improved social services and higher cash benefits, however, forced a fundamental reappraisal. The CRD enquiry and the Treasury's report on *Economic Growth and National Efficiency* demonstrate just how fundamental this reappraisal was. Rather than being rolled back, the state rolled forward. This did not, as commonly assumed, represent a pragmatic concession or a cynical manoeuvre. It was a principled move based on the belief that state welfare and economic intervention were not a threat to, but an essential support for, private affluence and private enterprise. *Economic Growth and National Efficiency* described this change as revolutionary; and, as Booker and Brittan suggested at the time, it certainly established the early 1960s as an heroic period of welfare reform.

The potential for change, however, was not fully realized. Conflicts within society may have been addressed, but conflicts within both the Conservative Party and the Treasury were not resolved. Modernization remained contested. Britain's response to affluence, therefore, diverged from that in continental Europe where a new accommodation between government and the market was reached not just in social democratic Sweden but also, of more relevance to the Conservatives, in Christian Democratic West Germany. In Britain there were, for example, experiments in earnings-related benefits and in active labour market policy which tentatively sought to introduce market inequalities into social benefits and public interest into private enterprise. Their logic, however, was never fully followed through and conflicting class interests remained unreconciled. In consequence interventionist social and economic policy was not fully legitimated and by the 1970s, despite increasing affluence, the cost of state welfare appeared unsupportable. Britain was amongst the first countries to experience a taxpayers' revolt. The policy initiatives of the early 1960s, however, should not be retrospectively overshadowed or biased by events in the 1970s, let alone the actions of the Conservative Party under Mrs Thatcher or a Treasury influenced by monetarism. In the early 1960s, in reaction to the onset of affluence, the basis was laid for a radically new accommodation between government, private affluence and private enterprise. This modernization of the welfare state testifies to both the extent of the 'heated struggles and interests' which affluence unleashed and to the richness of the response.

Notes

[1] I should like to acknowledge the AHRB for funding some of the research on which this chapter is based (award number: APN13217/AN7270).
[2] CPA: CRD 2/52/9, Chairman's Committee, 2nd meeting, 12 February 1962.
[3] One of the best introductions to these theories is Baldwin, Peter: *The Politics of Social Solidarity*, Cambridge University Press, Cambridge, 1990, ch. 1.
[4] Ibid., p. 1.
[5] *Parl. Deb.* (Commons), vol. 663, col. 1750, 26 July 1962; see, for example, Heffer, Simon: *Like the Roman*, Phoenix, London, 1999, p. 299. Powell, of course, remained as

minister of health from 1960 until Macmillan's resignation in October 1963. 'Modernization' was a term used as frequently by the Conservative government in the early 1960s as by New Labour after 1997 and, at root, was equally nebulous. It denoted a frustration with the inability of current policy, and the assumptions underlying it, to meet changing economic and social needs; but, as this chapter is designed to show, the broad new principles to guide reform were contested and, to avoid short-term embarrassments, were too often left undeveloped and therefore unreconciled.

6   The papers of this committee are in CPA: CRD 2/29/4.

7   Booker, Christopher: *The Neophiliacs*, Fontana, London, 1970, p. 177.

8   Brittan, Samuel: *Steering the Economy*, Pelican, Harmondsworth, 1971, p. 227.

9   CPA: CRD 2/53/28, Policy Study Group, 5th meeting, 6 May 1957.

10   CPA: CRD 2/53/25, PSG(57)2, E. Powell to I. Macleod, 13 February 1957.

11   CPA: CRD 2/29/8, PCFSS/61/79, 'Social Services and the Distribution of Income', B. Sewill, 28 March 1961. This was the so-called 'Goldman line', after Peter Goldman – the principal draftsman of the highly successful 1959 manifesto, the defeated candidate at the Orpington bye-election in March 1962 which galvanized Macmillan into launching his campaign to 'modernize Britain', and later the guiding light with Michael Young (the draftsman of Labour's 1945 manifesto) behind that emblematic institution of the affluent society, the Consumers' Association.

12   For the Committee's papers, see TNA: PRO CAB 134/1327. For an analysis, see Lowe, Rodney: 'Resignation at the Treasury', *Journal of Social Policy*, vol. 18 (1989), pp. 505–26.

13   *Parl. Deb.* (Commons), vol. 691, col. 477, 11 March 1964.

14   Veit-Wilson, John: 'The National Assistance Board and the "Rediscovery" of Poverty', in H. Fawcett and R. Lowe (eds): *Welfare Policy in Britain*, Macmillan, Basingstoke, 1999, pp. 116–57.

15   TNA: PRO PREM 11/4520, 'Modernising Britain', 25 October 1962.

16   TNA: PRO CAB 129/105, C(61)94, 10 July 1961.

17   CPA: CRD 2/29/4, Polcoss/10, 'Aims and Implementation of Social Policy', J. Udal, 12 September 1958.

18   CPA: CRD 2/29/6, 'Future of National Insurance Pensions', J. Douglas, 1 April 1960.

19   CPA: CRD 2/29/8, PCFSS/61/65, 'Philosophy of the Social Services', J. Douglas, 3 February 1961.

20   CPA: CRD 2/29/4, Polcoss/11, 'Social Service Principles', B. Sewill, 22 September 1958.

21   Not all the CRD's proposals were 'Thatcherite' even in the early stages. International comparisons convinced officials that Britain's welfare expenditure was not excessive; benefit claimants were not demonized; the 'guaranteed minimum' was pitched well above Beveridge's subsistence level to make means-testing less demeaning; and the need to target proven areas of poverty was acknowledged – such as increased family allowances for the fourth and subsequent child to relieve child poverty.

22   CPA: CRD 2/29/9, PCFSS/61/88, p. 40, April 1961; Trinity College, Cambridge, Butler Papers: H50, ff. 76, 17 September 1963.

23   CPA: ACP 3/11, ACP(64)114, Women's Policy Group on the Future of the Social Services.

24   CPA: ACP 2/1, ACP(61) 46th and ACP 2/2, ACP (63) 57th, meetings of the Advisory Council on Policy, 3 May 1961 and 6 November 1963.

25   CPA: CRD 2/52/7, document 45, 'Paper on Social Policy', G. Block, 16 March 1962.

26   CPA: CRD 2/29/9, PCFSS 61/88, p. 37, April 1961.

27   CPA: CRD 2/1, ACP(61) 46th, 3 May 1961.

[28] Craig, F.W.S.: *British General Election Manifestos, 1959–1987*, Dartmouth, Aldershot, 1990, p. 38.

[29] For a summary of the Plowden Committee, and the relevant documentation, see Lowe, Rodney: 'Milestone or Millstone? The 1959–1961 Plowden Committee and its Impact on British Welfare Policy', *The Historical Journal*, vol. 40 (1997), pp. 463–91 and Lowe, Rodney: 'The Core Executive, Modernization and the Creation of PESC, 1960–64', *Public Administration*, vol. 75 (1997), pp. 601–15.

[30] TNA: PRO T 291/10, 'Sources of Waste', J. E. Hansford, 11 May 1961.

[31] TNA: PRO CAB 129/105,C(61)88, 'The Five Year Plan for Public Expenditure', 28 June 1961. Italics added.

[32] TNA: PRO T 298/65, MGPE(62)6, memorandum to Ad Hoc Group on Public Expenditure, 12 July 1962. Given the conventional fixation on annual budgets, the reservation was significant.

[33] TNA: PRO CAB 134/1697, EA(63) 20th, meeting of the Economic Policy Committee, minute 3, 9 July 1963; PREM 11/4778, B. Trend to A.D. Home, 8 April 1964.

[34] TNA: PRO T 320/495, PESC(63) 6th minutes of PESC, 22/5/1963; TNA: PRO T 227/1437, minute of 2 August 1963.

[35] TNA: PRO CAB 129/117,CP(64)65, 'The Prospects for Taxation', R. Maudling and J. Boyd-Carpenter, 31 March 1964.

[36] CPA: CRD 3/7/26/1–3, minutes of the Taxation Policy Committee; TNA: PRO CAB 128/36, CC(62) 75th Cabinet Conclusions, 20 December 1962; TNA: PRO T 298/65, D. Butt to R. Clarke, 12 January 1961.

[37] Baldwin, *Politics of Social Solidarity*, op. cit., p. 48; CPA: CRD 2/52/7, M. Fraser to I. Macleod, 29 March 1962.

[38] TNA: PRO PREM 11/3741, B. Trend minute, 22 December 1958; Utley, T.E.: *Enoch Powell: The Man and His Thinking*, William Kimber, London, 1968, p. 78. It has been convincingly argued recently, however, that Powell's unrealistic expectation was that increased capital expenditure would not just improve care but, through efficiency gains, reduce current expenditure. See Mohan, John: *Planning, Markets and Hospitals*, Routledge, London, 2002.

[39] CPA: CRD 2/21/6, 'Can Labour Win?', J. Udal, 17 May 1960.

[40] CPA: CRD 2/29/8, Draft interim report, 8 November 1960.

[41] Craig, *British General Election Manifestos*, op. cit., pp. 7, 37. *The Poor and the Poorest* in which Abel-Smith and Townsend firmly established the concept of relative poverty was published in 1965.

[42] Shepherd, Robert: *Iain Macleod*, Hutchinson, London, 1994, p. 438. For a succinct summary of Titmuss' philosophy, see Paul Wilding's chapter in V. George and R. Page (eds): *Modern Thinkers on Welfare*, Prentice Hall, London, 1995.

[43] *The Times*, 20 June 1962.

[44] University of Leeds: Boyle papers 47047, election address, 12 September 1964.

[45] CPA: CRD 2/29/8, Minutes of the Committee on the Future of the Social Services, 30th meeting, 1 March 1961; TNA: PRO T 227/1437.

[46] Barr, Nicholas: *The Economics of the Welfare State*, Oxford University Press, Oxford, 1993, p. 433.

[47] TNA: PRO CAB 129/105, C(61)94, para. 33, 10 June 1961.

[48] See, for example, Jones, Harriet and Kandiah, Michael (eds): *The Myth of Consensus: New Views on British History,1945–1964*, Macmillan, Basingstoke, 1996 and Tomlinson, Jim: *The Politics of Decline: Understanding Post-war Britain*, Longman, Harlow, 2001.

CHAPTER 4

The Forgotten Revisionist: Douglas Jay and Britain's Transition to Affluence, 1951–1964

Richard Toye

In the aftermath of Labour's 1959 general election defeat, Douglas Jay, one of its frontbench spokesmen, generated a furore by suggesting, in an article in *Forward*, that the party should rethink its nationalization proposals, and should consider changing the party name to 'Labour and Radical' or 'Labour and Reform'.[1] Responding to his critics in a further article the following month, he emphasized that he was by no means opposed to further public ownership, but that this should not take the form of the extension of public monopoly into manufacturing industry and the distributive trades. Rather, he argued, in a world of full employment and long-run capital gains, expanding ownership of industrial shares and other property by the community could supply the revenue for better pensions and public services without high rates of personal taxation. He declared: 'This is a form of socialism which the public will both understand and desire, in the more affluent society into which we are now moving – a fairer sharing of the nation's growing wealth at home and abroad.'[2]

Jay's explicit attempts to evolve a socialist response to the phenomenon of affluence marked him out as a key figure in Labour revisionism, albeit one whose contributions during the 'thirteen years of Tory misrule' have largely been forgotten. Admittedly, he is often mentioned in the same breath as Hugh Gaitskell, Tony Crosland and Evan Durbin, the group often being credited with providing (posthumously, in Durbin's case) an important intellectual influence on the party between 1951 and 1964.[3] Jay is also invoked by supporters of Tony Blair as one of the 'first voices of modernizing dissent' within the Labour Party.[4] Yet, unlike his fellow revisionists, Jay has received little serious scholarly attention – perhaps partly because he did not have the glamorizing advantage of an early death! However, a detailed examination of his thinking during the long years of opposition suggests important lessons about Labour's ideological adjustment from the era of rationing to that of rock and roll.

This chapter will draw on a range of Jay's speeches and writings in order to test the powerful argument that during these years Labour failed to come to terms with working-class affluence. According to Lawrence Black, the consumerist values of the 'affluent society' were seen as overwhelmingly negative by socialists, whom, he argues, 'can be seen to have to a large extent brought upon themselves their alienation from popular affluence.'[5] This argument – essentially that Labour was a victim of its own cultural snobbery – still has a strong political relevance today.

Philip Gould (Tony Blair's pollster) has used it to support New Labour's modernizing agenda. In contrast to the Blair years, he suggests, in the 1951–64 era and beyond Labour ignored and betrayed 'the hard-working majority as they moved from austerity to aspiration and demanded a new politics to match their new ambition.'[6] Was this true in Jay's case? It is certainly true that Jay had important doubts about affluence (although that was not a term he used until after the publication of J.K. Galbraith's *The Affluent Society* in 1958). Yet it would be wrong to suggest that these doubts were wholly spurious, or that they were exclusively the product of cultural or moral panic. Moreover, his desire to widen Labour's appeal was based on an acknowledgement that 'The better-off wage earners and numerous salary-earners are tending to regard the Labour Party as associated with a class to which they themselves don't belong.'[7] All the same, his brand of revisionism was one from which advocates of New Labour will be able to draw only limited comfort in the search for respectable Old Labour lineage for their own ideas.

The life of Douglas Jay

Douglas Jay was born on 23 March 1907. He was educated at Winchester College. In 1926, the year he went up to New College, Oxford to read Greats, the long miners' strike 'aroused my political feelings and left me by the autumn an ardently convinced supporter of the Labour Movement.' In October 1929 he joined *The Times*. Concurrently, he began to study economics, and in 1930 was elected a fellow of All Souls, Oxford. In 1933, he joined *The Economist*.[8] He was attracted by Hugh Gaitskell's ideas on the inefficiency and injustice of the financial system, and in particular by his contribution to G.D.H. Cole's edited collection *What Everybody Wants to Know About Money* (1933).[9] The contacts with Gaitskell that followed helped bring Jay into the Labour movement in an active role, as did the patronage of Hugh Dalton.[10]

In January 1937, Jay started work as City editor of the *Daily Herald*. His book *The Socialist Case* was published later the same year, and was generally well received, albeit with some important reservations from fellow socialists. It contained, however, a remark which would later be used as a stick to beat him: 'in the case of nutrition and health, just as in the case of education, the gentleman in Whitehall really does know better what is good for people than the people know themselves.'[11] After the outbreak of war in 1939, Jay remained at the *Herald* until he was recruited into the Ministry of Supply in December 1940. In September 1943 he became personal assistant to Dalton, now President of the Board of Trade. After Labour's 1945 election victory he became personal assistant and adviser on economic policy to Clement Attlee. In July 1946 he was elected MP for Battersea North. In October 1947, he became Parliamentary Private Secretary to Dalton as Chancellor. Shortly after Dalton resigned the following month, Jay was appointed to the new post of Economic Secretary to the Treasury. He became Financial Secretary to the Treasury after the election of February 1950, and after Labour's 1951 defeat he became a front bench opposition spokesman.

During the 'thirteen years of Tory misrule', along with Roy Jenkins, he acquired a generally undeserved reputation in left-wing Labour circles as one of the 'implacable extremists' in Hugh Gaitskell's coterie.[12] (Gaitskell became the leader of the Labour Party in 1955). This was due in part to his 1959 *Forward* article, but also to his role as a founder member of the anti-Tribunite Campaign for Democratic Socialism (CDS). After Labour's 1964 election victory, Harold Wilson appointed Jay President of the Board of Trade. In August 1967 he was dismissed, in part because of his opposition to British membership of the EEC. He took a prominent role in the 'No' campaign during the referendum of 1975, and remained an MP until 1983. He entered the House of Lords in 1987, and died on 6 March 1996.

Jay's significance

The episode of the *Forward* article aside, Jay's career in opposition in the 1951–64 era has received virtually no attention – in marked contrast to the huge interest in Crosland, who, if a more fertile thinker, was a more negligible political figure at the time, and who was out of parliament between 1955 and 1959. (As Kevin Jefferys has written, Crosland's *The Future of Socialism*, after its publication in 1956, was in many respects 'a slow burner, its influence growing steadily over the course of the next decade. What it did not do ... was to transform Crosland's career overnight.')[13] Admittedly, Jay was never a serious candidate for the leadership, or even for the great offices of state. In 1950, Attlee and Dalton had agreed that he would not be suitable as a replacement for Cripps as Chancellor, for, 'though very able, [he] had not always good judgement, and wasn't very personable.'[14] In the words of the financial journalist Nicholas Davenport, Jay was 'an extraordinary mixture of serious political thinker and economist, and a frivolous-minded eccentric.' (He had a pathological hatred of draughts, and was so suspicious of foreign food that he took packets of cereal abroad for breakfast.)[15] Jay was close to Gaitskell personally – but not to all of the Gaitskellites (Bill Rodgers, although respecting his 'obvious cleverness', thought him 'mean, anti-semitic and an intellectual snob').[16] Naturally enough, he did not much endear himself to the left. According to Richard Crossman, 'Douglas Jay regards himself as a middle-of-the-road man but he talks to me with pained surprise about the undemocratic character of the "party within the party" and said what a pity it was that Nye [Bevan] was not on the Parliamentary Committee. ... Like Christopher Mayhew, Hugh Gaitskell and a good many others, Douglas has had no experience of the backbenches and has grown accustomed to being part of the Government or official Opposition machine, with plenty of room for self-expression. To him it seems real wickedness that other people should set themselves up to challenge the policies he has worked out.'[17]

Unlike *The Socialist Case*, his 1962 book *Socialism in the New Society* has not generally been considered a seminal text. Nevertheless, without exaggerating either the originality of his thinking or his centrality to events, Jay's influence during the opposition was by no means negligible. His impact on policy could be decisive. For example, in 1955, the economist Nicholas Kaldor published a proposal for an expenditure tax, an issue that provoked 'violent disagreement' within Labour's working party on taxation. One of the group, David Worswick, recalled that:

> the decisive moment came when Douglas Jay made a powerful statement to the effect that ordinary people liked to have their tax payments behind them when they thought of spending, not still ahead of them. When an MP invokes the British working man or the people, the professional economist has no comeback, or did not in those days before polls on everything. My recollection is that after Jay's powerful intervention we might as well all go home.[18]

Moreover, in the early fifties at least, Jay's economic views were not those of a maverick, but were in line with mainstream Labour opinion – and, to a limited and temporary degree, his expression of them helped promote party unity. In a Fabian lecture given in November 1952, he advocated greater public ownership in the chemicals and engineering industries, and heavier industrial investment, twinned with continued physical controls over the economy, as a means of bridging the dollar gap.[19] Richard Crossman noted: 'Douglas Jay and Harold Wilson really want the same economic policy'; as did Gaitskell.[20] As a consequence, Jay received overtures from Wilson and from *Tribune*.[21] In addition to this influence within the party, his position as a part-time leader writer on the *Daily Herald* gave him an enviable direct link to the voters.

From austerity to affluence

The question of consumption lay at the heart of Jay's economic vision. He argued in 1962 that 'one of the fundamental flaws in the system of unregulated exchange is the persistent under-valuation of the need of the poorer consumer. Owing to this, the method of free pricing (*laissez-faire* in the consumer markets) often works badly in allocating resources according to needs. But in so far as initial incomes are redistributed by the social democratic States according to principles of social justice, the price process ... becomes at least a rather better though still imperfect guide to real needs.'[22] Since the 1930s, Jay had made this point consistently.[23] What had varied was the degree to which he felt it necessary for the government to intervene directly in the workings of the price system.

In the 1930s, as I have shown elsewhere, Jay was a rare Labour planning-sceptic. However, the experience of the Second World War and the immediate post-war era converted him to the virtues of planning.[24] As he put it in an election speech in 1950:

> The unemployment, high prices, poverty, hunger and deplorable housing conditions to be found in the unplanned countries in Europe today are ... largely the consequences of deliberate policy. It is, of course, delightfully easy to throw away controls. It is indeed a very pleasant surrender to mental cowardice and administrative incompetence. How easy to deprive the mass of the people of anything but low wages or a miserable unemployment dole,

let prices raise to scarcity heights, and then brutally announce that one is 'de-rationing' the necessities of life and restoring a 'free economy'.[25]

Ilaria Favretto has written of the 'hostility to planning displayed by centre-right revisionists' in the 1952–64 period.[26] But Jay, for one, at this time retained a firm belief in economic planning based partly on physical controls.[27]

Nevertheless, he did adapt his thinking in response to the improved economic conditions that contributed to affluence. During the initial period of opposition, his emphasis remained strongly Crippsian. He repeatedly praised, in fulsome terms, Cripps's record as Chancellor: 'how right he was; and how small-minded and myopic his critics look today.'[28] Moreover, he described the objective of long-term economic planning as being to secure Britain's economic survival – a reflection of the priorities of the years when he himself had been a Treasury minister under Cripps.[29] By 1958, though, the world dollar shortage, which Jay had believed would probably be a lifetime problem, had turned into a dollar glut.[30] At the same time, the governments of Churchill, Eden, and Macmillan demonstrated that the Conservatives were able to maintain full employment and rising real incomes, which, in turn, were translated into dramatically increased spending on consumption. As austerity receded, it became politically necessary for Jay and his colleagues to find grounds for attacking the Tories other than the somewhat implausible one that total economic catastrophe was imminent (the latter view having also been held by many on the left of the party).

This helps explain Jay's criticisms of decontrol and 'Conservative freedom' – criticisms which, it should be emphasized, were by no means wholly, or even mainly, a result of hostility to the cultural trappings of affluence. Jay believed – as did many other Labour thinkers – that decontrol was likely to jeopardize the possibility of *higher* national income. He believed that the result of reducing restrictions on consumption, via the relaxation of import controls, was recurrent balance of payment problems, which the government then solved by curtailing economic activity. This was the classic pattern of 'stop-go': 'As soon as things get better, people want to relax, and as soon as they relax, things get worse.'[31] It could, moreover, be manipulated for electoral reasons: 'the economy is held stagnant for three years, so that a six months' spurt may be engineered just before the next general election.'[32]

In fact, this view, that growth in Britain was slow because it was peculiarly unstable, although widespread, was open to doubt even at the time.[33] But concerns about British economic performance were accentuated in many people's minds by the apparently impressive growth rate of the Soviet Union. In April 1956, Jay – who had visited the USSR the previous year – argued as follows:

> Just because we rightly detest Russian methods, and rightly suspect her statistics, we should be extremely foolish to underrate her economic challenge. The evidence strongly suggests that Russian production is increasing at about 10 per cent a year. ... At that rate, the real standard of living in Russia may equal ours in perhaps fifteen years, and even that of North America in a period probably twice as long.[34]

With the benefit of hindsight, such claims may appear almost wildly improbable. But, as Jim Tomlinson has noted, other right-wing Labour figures expressed similar views.[35] (Such views were, of course, also common on the left of the party, which implies that on some substantive issues the Bevanites were often far closer to the Gaitskellites than many historical accounts suggest.)[36] Nor was the anxiety merely an economic one: if the Soviets could outpace the democracies in terms of growth, so much greater would be the attraction of communism in the 'uncommitted' areas of the world.[37] Therefore, it could be argued, by distributing the fruits of economic progress to the voters too freely, the Conservatives were not only risking future performance, but, in so doing, were damaging the West's prospects in the Cold War struggle of 'competitive coexistence'. The doubts of Jay and others about Tory economic policies were not, then, caused purely by cultural snobbery about the fruits of affluence, but were heightened by fears about relative British decline and the impact that this might have on East–West conflict.[38]

Moreover, Cold War anxieties were a major contribution to the success in America of Galbraith's *The Affluent Society*. This was the book that crystallized the concept of affluence for many in Britain, including Jay, who had previously not had a specific word to describe the phenomenon with which they were confronted. As Galbraith recalled, the questioning and anxiety that followed the launch of the first Sputnik in October 1957 made him certain that his attack on affluence would be heard: it now appeared that the USSR was able to make a much more purposeful use than the USA of a much less productive economy.[39] In Britain, where the element of hurt pride was perhaps less, reaction to the Sputnik itself was not quite so hysterical as in America. In Labour circles, at least, it did not provoke a frenzied desire to 'catch-up'. Jay subsequently suggested that the Russians should have spent the money on housing rather than on photographing the other side of the moon.[40] But Galbraith's book nevertheless struck a chord with British socialists. Jay found it 'powerful and eloquent': 'His [i.e. Galbraith's] conclusion – and no intelligent person can deny it, is that the modern community ought to expand greatly its allocation of resources to public services – education above all – and consequently take a more adequate share of the national income through the budget and tax systems.'[41] He reiterated the point in November 1959: 'We [the Labour Party] stand, in an increasingly affluent society, for the collective devotion of a far greater part of our national resources to those services which must be provided by public effort, and the electorate want.'[42] This was a logic that Jay would follow in *Socialism in the New Society*.

New policies for the age of affluence

Before he began to write that book, and even before the 1959 election defeat, Jay attempted to devise new policies appropriate for the post-Attlee era. He developed a proposal for small savers to be enabled to invest small amounts in a wide spread of shares through the Post Office Savings Bank and the Trustee Savings Bank. (Nicholas Davenport believed that Jay had got the idea from his own proposal for a State Participation Unit Trust (SPUT).)[43] The economic justification for such a scheme, he suggested, was that 'there is no reason or justice in the benefits of capital appreciation or rising income being confined to the present charmed circle of about 1,500,000 individuals who own equity shares.' Moreover, in political terms, because of the growth of private unit trusts, 'we are faced with a situation in which a movement shown by American experience to be inevitable, will, unless, we act, be distorted into a politically successful attempt to make an increasing section of wage-earners and salary-earners Tory-minded.'[44] Jay revived the idea, which he originally proposed to Labour's finance and economic policy committee in January 1959, in articles in 1962–3.[45] Nothing came of the plan when Labour came to power; but the episode demonstrates that Jay was willing to tackle the political challenge of affluence, even if not all his colleagues had the same degree of enthusiasm.

Much more controversial, of course, was the issue of public ownership, the case for which he consistently emphasized. 'The truth is that private "enterprise" can't be justified at all, unless there is free *competition*', he argued in 1957. 'If ... firms and the Government simply ignore the Monopoly Commission's Reports, yet another unanswerable case for public ownership will have been proved.'[46] However, in line with the principle of 'competitive socialism', which he had been advocating since at least 1950, he argued for state participation in private industry through the ownership of ordinary shares rather than the extension of public monopoly.[47] This was to a substantial degree in line with official Labour Party policy statements, and was a theme that he would follow up in the famous *Forward* article.[48]

In his memoirs Jay argued, justifiably, that the idea that the article had its origins in a Gaitskellite conspiracy, launched within hours of the election defeat, to remove public ownership from Labour's future programme, sever the link with the unions, and alter the wording of Clause 4 of the party's constitution, was a myth. He conceded, however, that he had made a mistake in putting his name to the piece, 'because my close association with Gaitskell led people to believe he had some responsibility for it'.[49] But even if criticisms of the article were exaggerated, it is easy to see why its hard-hitting phrases caused upset:

> The better-off wage earners and numerous salary-earners are tending to regard the Labour Party as associated with a class to which they themselves don't belong.
> Few of them – least of all the women – felt themselves to be members of a 'working class'. We are in danger of fighting under the label of a class which no longer exists.
> ...too many wage-earning families, with TV and second-hand car, did not see (unless they were coal miners) so much wrong with Tory Britain.[50]

In the short term, at least, the article proved counter-productive. Tony Benn noted a few days after it was published the collective left-wing opinion that 'Hugh Gaitskell had cooked his goose', or rather that 'Douglas Jay had cooked it for him by raising the Clause 4 issue.'[51] It may, however, have had a somewhat more constructive longer-term impact. As Jay later pointed out, his belief in 'social ownership', but not in the further extension of public monopoly, was a precursor of the National Enterprise Board (NEB) established by the 1974 Labour government.[52] The NEB was no great success, which, perhaps, has led to the revisionist thought which contributed to its birth being overlooked. It is easy, in the search for proto-Blairite attitudes amongst 'Old Labour' thinkers, to forget the extent to which revisionists still had a genuine faith in 'public enterprise'; and Jay's belief in its virtues has perhaps contributed to his eclipse by other figures whom it is easier – if not necessarily accurate – to view as prophets of New Labour.

Socialism in the New Society

In the wake of the row, Jay gave a short speech at the November party conference in Blackpool. He did not specifically endorse Gaitskell's plan to revise Clause 4 – he thought it was a mistake to raise the issue – but stressed once more the need to develop non-monopoly rather than monopoly forms of public ownership.[53] Jay recalled that his words were met 'with incomprehension rather than assent or dissent.' During the mid-winter weeks of 1959–60, he reflected on the controversies of the previous months, 'and wondered whether it was worthwhile re-thinking the whole basic issue of the meaning of socialism and the relevance of public ownership.' By Easter he had decided to write the book that would be published as *Socialism in the New Society*. He wrote in his memoirs: 'My aim in the book was to write something rather more philosophical and less purely economic, than Tony Crosland's illuminating *The Future of Socialism* ... Crosland had touched only lightly on the basic question whether any moral virtue resides in the economic consequences of *laissez-faire* and the distribution of incomes generated by a free market.'[54]

When it was published, in January 1962, the book got a mixed reception. Raymond Fletcher, in *Tribune*, wrote that 'Mr. Jay, one of *Tribune*'s favourite sparring partners, deserves the thanks of all Socialists for documenting a view that unites most socialists', i.e. that modern capitalism was characterized by increasingly functionless ownership and increasingly concentrated control. However, he disagreed with Jay's comparatively diminuendo approach to public ownership.[55] In a *New Statesman* review Richard Crossman (of whom Jay had been fairly critical in the book) noted 'the shattering impact of the Affluent Society' on the Labour Party. It was not an impact he felt Jay's ideas were likely to overcome. Although the book's exposition was clear and its polemic vigorous, *Socialism in the New Society* was no more than 'a brave attempt to explain in some detail how Attleeism can be applied once again in the 1960s.'[56] *The Times* devoted a leader column to the book, which it found 'substantial and persuasive', although it did not accept Jay's arguments for economic equality.[57] Disappointing reviews appeared in *The Economist* and *The Listener*.[58] Graham Hutton, in the *Times Literary Supplement*, felt that Jay's value judgements had 'lamentably weakened his case and turned what might have been a seminal work into a tract for the converted.' Moreover, 'Of those three most recent apologists for socialism only the youngest,

Mr. Crosland, sides with Aristotle. Like Mr. Galbraith, Mr. Jay comes down heavily on the side of Plato, the governing few, and the gentleman in Whitehall.'[59]

Hutton's comment, if true, would seem to imply that Jay did indeed fit into the alleged general Labour pattern of 'alienation from affluence'. He was certainly not wildly enthusiastic about many modern trends. As he commented in the Commons 1962, 'It is rather pathetic sometimes to remember that ten years ago some people were talking about a new Elizabethan age in this country. What we have had, in fact, is a new Edwardian age. We have had a decade of Premium Bonds, take-over bids, betting shops, hire-purchase frauds and all the rest. Under the party opposite, capital gains have almost become the national sport, and [the multi-millionaire takeover king] Mr. Charles Clore almost our national hero.'[60] However, in *Socialism in the New Society*, he drew back from endorsing the more extreme anti-consumerist arguments made, for example, by Dennis Potter in *The Glittering Coffin* (1960). He characterized (or caricatured) these arguments as follows:

> The avaricious profit-seekers have got hold of so many of the weapons of persuasion ('mass media' if you prefer the jargon) that the ordinary man has no longer a genuinely free choice as voter, reader, viewer, thinker, or indeed human being. We are so belaboured and bemused (the argument runs on) by commercial TV inanities and venalities, by sordid newspaper circulation-seeking, by advertising persuaders – loud, silent and secret – and all sorts of other hideous nightmares and horrors of modern life, that we are really dancing about like puppets controlled by hidden hands behind it all and cherishing only an illusion of free choice. Our tastes and standards are thus debased; our political, cultural and even shopping preferences, made for us without knowing it; and most of our freedom and dignity, as free individuals in an allegedly free society, cunningly filched away.[61]

Jay conceded that there was, indeed, some truth to this picture. 'Much, though not all, of our commercial advertising is an insult to the public's intelligence ... Much (but not all) of our commercial TV programmes, even between advertisements, can only be described as an expense of spirit in a waste of shame. Worst of all, the present state of the British Press, with its daily papers declining into little more than entertainment sheets, its women's weeklies compounded so often of little but snobbery and greed, its mass Sunday papers delving with a cunning almost worthy of Goebbels into the murkiest depths of human nature, can only fill anybody who has known thirty years of British journalism with distaste bordering on despair.'[62]

Nevertheless, Jay argued that this picture, left by itself, was neither fair nor in perspective: 'Though millions may expend their spirit in the arid wastes of TV entertainment, tens of thousands hear broadcast classical music who would never have heard it fifty years ago. Sales of books, good and indifferent as well as bad, mount and mount'. Moreover, he pointed out, attendance at concerts providing 'serious' music was far greater than before 1939, and more than twice as many people visited London's Tate Gallery in 1960 as in 1952. Furthermore, 'Many times more people (though still too few) go to universities than before the War ...

Even at the despised levels of political argument ... it cannot be denied that the normal level of discussion is markedly higher.'[63]

The truth, he concluded, was that 'in Britain and other open societies a battle is being fought ... between corrupting forces on the one hand, and civilizing forces on the other for the public mind.' Surely, he suggested, 'it should be the major purpose of the democratic State to join in on the side of enlightenment, and not to confess defeat and conclude that the only solution is authoritarian control of all the persuaders, hidden and otherwise.' Public authorities, therefore, should support and enrich all the cultural activities that unbridled market forces would tend to drown.[64] As Jay commented to Gaitskell in 1956, 'people cannot very well choose themselves between the football match and the art gallery if they have never been given the chance to appreciate one of them at all.'[65] (It remains unclear whether Jay himself had ever attended a football match.)

Overall, Jay's views do offer a certain amount of support for the view that Labour thinkers were suspicious of many of the trappings of affluence; but this was not, perhaps, the most important factor in determining his attitudes. As he had written in May 1957:

> Some M.P.s in last week's Press debate seemed to think the chief fault of the newspapers was the appearance of too many photos of Brigitte Bardot, Marilyn Monroe and Jayne Mansfield. I don't share this view at all. I am all in favour of these pictures. ...
> The real danger is different. Communists have always argued – it is to me one of their few strong points – that Parliamentary elections in a capitalist democracy would be, sooner or later, turned into a farce by concentration of newspaper ownership in the hands of a few millionaires.[66]

Jay was not a complete cultural pessimist, nor did he think it advisable to restrict people's freedom of cultural choice. Therefore Hutton's comment about 'the governing few, and the gentleman in Whitehall' does not seem wholly fair. This does not, of course, mean that Jay did not in some ways lay himself open to misrepresentation, and thus contribute to the *perception* that Labour was hostile to affluence, even if close reading of his opinions indicates that in his case it was not true.

Neither is Black's comment that 'Disregard for personal issues was characteristic of the socialist condition' fair in regard to Jay.[67] For example, in 1958 he strongly supported the proposal of the Wolfenden commission to decriminalize homosexual acts between adult males in private. The law as it existed, he believed, infringed a basic principle of personal freedom:

> I do not believe that the State or the criminal law has any right to interfere with the conduct of the individual, unless that conduct has some effect on other people. ... Once we depart from that principle ... we are on a very slippery slope. This seems to me to be the beginning of all intolerance. It is a road which leads – much further on, but going in the same direction – eventually to concentration camps and to the persecution of heretics.[68]

He also wrote in his *Forward* article, 'we should urge radical reforms of the betting, licensing and Sunday Observance laws – perhaps abolition of hanging and votes at eighteen also.'[69] Jay was not, apparently, totally consistent in his attitudes – see his 1962 remarks on betting shops, above – but he cannot be accused of *disregarding* personal issues. As he put it in the subsequent article in which he responded to attacks on him, 'the emphasis must be even more on personal liberty, if the new generation are to respond' (and, interestingly, this was an area in which he believed his critics agreed with him).[70] He did, however, put a great emphasis on the divisibility of 'personal' and 'economic' freedom, and was far keener on the former than the latter.[71] It may be argued, of course, that the distinction was ultimately unsustainable; but this is not the same as saying that Jay was uninterested in personal freedom.

Conclusion

Jay largely figures in the historiography in four caricatured guises: (a) a farsighted 'incipient Gaitskellite' in the 1930s, embracing Keynes and laying the groundwork for 1950s revisionism, (b) the arrogant and elitist author of the 'gentleman in Whitehall' remark, (c) the Gaitskellite extremist author of the 1959 *Forward* article, (d) a violent anti-European. With the possible exception of (d), these images are all misleading.[72] Moreover, (a) and (b) seem to contradict one another to some degree; the view of Jay as a man obsessed with controlling the lives of others sits at odds with the image of him as a farsighted revisionist who eschewed traditional socialist remedies. As regards (c), Jay appears to have been justified in defending himself against charges of conspiracy, and his arguments were scarcely extreme. Indeed, his revisionism had many things in common with what Favretto has identified as 'Wilsonism' – an emphasis on planning, efficiency, and reluctance to engage in moral condemnation of consumerism.[73]

Jay can thus be defended against the broad charge – which has been levelled at Labour in general rather than at him personally – that socialist suspicion of the cultural trappings of affluence led to voters' alienation from the party. His doubts about the era of affluence arose from genuine economic concerns, not purely from socialist snobbery. He did not want the state to *prevent* people from reading *The News of the World* if they chose to do so, but rather he wanted to enhance public provision of the arts. He did care about personal freedom, even if he was not enthusiastic about economic freedom. This was also true, at least to some degree, of other mainstream socialists at the time, even those who did not fall into the 'centre-right revisionist camp'. For example, the pages of *Tribune,* and the *New Statesman*, as well as those of *Forward*, regularly featured, on the one hand, articles opposing capital punishment, and on the other, attacks on untaxed capital gains and the extension of private monopoly.

One should not, of course, fall into the trap of imagining that all the extensions to personal freedom that Jay and others advocated would have been electorally popular. In other words, voters may have become alienated from Labour as much because its general disapproval of hanging and the willingness of some figures, such as Jay, to advocate homosexual law reform, as because of its attitude to affluence. Indeed, it is in general very difficult to assess how far 'alienation from popular affluence', was responsible for Labour's electoral troubles. Furthermore, was it not largely inevitable that those voters who were enthusiastic about affluence would, in 1955 and 1959, reward the party that had *delivered* it (or at least presided over its delivery)?

For, if Labour was to be elected, it needed the voters to lose confidence in the government. In the USA, after the launch of the Sputnik, the Democrats were able to successfully exploit concern about the consequences of the 'Affluent Society', by pointing to its implications for national security. Doubts about 'The Stagnant Society', by contrast, only caught the popular mood in Britain after the 1959 election. After this point, there was a general loss of confidence in British economic performance, which episodes such as De Gaulle's veto and the Profumo affair only served to accentuate. 'Amateurism' was blamed, and the scene was set for Wilson's 'white heat of technology' speech.[74] (Indeed, post-1962 Conservative 'modernization' policies also reflected unease about unregulated affluence.) Thus, Labour's doubts about affluence were in the long run not wholly harmful. It is tempting to suggest, then, that the problem was not so much that Labour was 'alienated from popular affluence', but that, it was only after 1959 that the party found the language or the occasion to mobilize popular concern about the consequences of an unregulated economy. Douglas Jay's contribution to this discourse may have been largely forgotten, but the concerns he articulated were neither marginal, nor hostile to all aspects of affluence, nor a form of incipient Blairism.

Notes

[1] Jay, Douglas: 'Are We Downhearted? Yes! But We'll Win Back', *Forward*, 16 October 1959. See also Jay, Douglas: *Change and Fortune: A Political Record*, London, Hutchinson, 1980, pp. 271–6, where Jay quoted from the article at length and gave an account of its origins.

[2] Jay, Douglas: 'Too Smug!', *Forward*, 20 November 1959.

[3] See, for example, Durbin, Elizabeth: in Ben Pimlott (ed): *Fabian Essays in Socialist Thought*, Heinemann, London, 1984, p. 40.

[4] Gould, Philip: *The Unfinished Revolution: How the Modernisers Saved the Labour Party*, Little, Brown and Company, London, 1998, p. 30.

[5] Black, Lawrence: 'Coming to Terms with Affluence? Socialism and Social Change in 1950s Britain', paper given at 'Consensus or Coercion? The state, the people and social cohesion in post-war Britain' conference, University College London, 13 March 1999. See also Tiratsoo, Nick: in Anthony Gorst, Lewis Johnman and W. Scott Lucas (eds): *Contemporary British History 1931–61: Politics and the Limits of Policy*, Pinter Publishers, London, 1991, pp. 44–61; and Zweiniger-Bargielowska, Ina: *Austerity in Britain: Rationing, Controls and Consumption, 1939–1955*, Oxford University Press, Oxford, 2000, p. 238.

[6] Gould: *Unfinished Revolution*, op. cit., p. 16.

[7] Jay, Douglas: 'Are We Downhearted?', *Forward*, 16 October 1959.

8   Jay: *Change and Fortune*, op. cit. pp. 15–49, quotation at p. 22. For a bibliography on Jay, see Toye, Richard, 'The "gentleman in Whitehall" reconsidered: the evolution of Douglas Jay's views on economic planning and consumer choice, 1937–1947', *Labour History Review*, vol. 67, no. 2, (2002), pp. 187–204, n. 14.

9   Jay, Douglas: in W.T. Rodgers (ed): *Hugh Gaitskell*, Thames and Hudson, London, 1964, pp. 77–8.

10 Jay: *Change and Fortune*, op. cit. pp. 61–2; Dalton, Hugh: *The Fateful Years: Memoirs 1931–1945*, Frederick Muller Ltd., London, 1957, p. 417n; Davenport, Nicholas: *Memoirs of a City Radical*, Weidenfeld and Nicolson, London, 1974, pp. 103–4.

11 Jay, Douglas: *The Socialist Case*, Faber and Faber, London, 1937, p. 317; Toye, 'The "gentleman in Whitehall"', op. cit.

12 Mikardo, Ian: *Back-Bencher*, Weidenfeld and Nicolson, London, 1988, p. 152.

13 Jefferys, Kevin: *Anthony Crosland: A New Biography*, Richard Cohen Books, London, 1999, p. 63.

14 Pimlott, Ben (ed): *The Political Diary of Hugh Dalton, 1918–40, 1945–60*, Jonathan Cape, London, 1986, p. 466 (entry for 27 January 1950).

15 Davenport: *Memoirs*, op. cit., p. 103.

16 Rodgers, Bill: *Fourth Among Equals*, Politico's, London, 2000, p. 47.

17 Morgan, Janet (ed): *The Backbench Diaries of Richard Crossman*, Book Club Associates, London, 1981, pp. 136–7 (entry for 14 August 1952).

18 Whiting, Richard: *The Labour Party and Taxation: Party Identity and Political Purpose in Twentieth-Century Britain*, Cambridge University Press, 2000, p. 137.

19 Fabian Society Papers, British Library of Political and Economic Science, London: C/65/1, Douglas Jay, 'Britain's Economic Survival', lecture given on 25 November 1952. For a summary of the main points of the lecture, see Jay, Douglas: 'The Price of Survival', *New Statesman and Nation*, 13 December 1952.

20 Morgan: *Backbench Diaries of Richard Crossman*, op. cit., pp. 185–6 (entries for 1, 2 and 3 December 1952).

21 Jay: *Change and Fortune*, op. cit., p. 226.

22 Jay, Douglas: *Socialism in the New Society*, St. Martin's Press, London, 1962, p. 27.

23 Jay: *Change and Fortune*, op. cit., p. 34. See also Jay, Douglas: in G.E.G. Catlin (ed): *New Trends in Socialism*, Lovat Dickson and Thompson Ltd., London, 1935, pp. 105–22.

24 See Toye: '"The Gentleman in Whitehall"', op. cit.

25 Hugh Gaitskell Papers, University College, London: C33, speech by Douglas Jay at a meeting in Stafford Borough Hall on 28 January 1950.

26 Ilaria Favretto: '"Wilsonism" Reconsidered: Labour Party revisionism 1952–64', *Contemporary British History*, vol. 14, no. 4 (2000), pp. 54–80, at p. 63.

27 See for example Jay, Douglas: 'Socialist Plan for British Trade Drive', *Forward* (London edn.), 17 January 1953; and Jay: *Socialism in the New Society*, op. cit., pp. 165–7.

28 Parliamentary Debates, House of Commons, 5th series, vol. 493, col. 344, 8 November 1951.

29 Jay, Douglas: 'The Price of Survival', *New Statesman and Nation*, 13 December 1952.

30 Streeten, Paul: in G.D.N. Worswick and P.H. Ady (eds): *The British Economy in the Nineteen-Fifties*, Clarendon Press, Oxford, 1962, p. 109.

31 Parliamentary Debates, House of Commons, 5th series, vol. 493, col. 348, 8 November 1951.

32 Ibid., vol. 657, col. 1355, 11 April 1962.

[33] See Cairncross, Alec: *Diaries of Sir Alec Cairncross: the Radcliffe Committee/Economic Adviser to HMG, 1961–64*, Institute of Contemporary British History, London, 1999, p. 37. For a succinct discussion of the impact of 'stop-go', see Howlett, Peter: in Paul Johnson (ed): *Twentieth-Century Britain: Economic, Social and Cultural Change*, Longman, London, 1994, pp. 335–7.

[34] Parliamentary Debates, House of Commons, 5th series, vol. 551, col. 1462, 23 April 1956.

[35] Tomlinson, Jim: 'Modernising Britain? The Economic Policies of the Wilson Government, 1964–70', Manchester University Press, Manchester, forthcoming, ch. 4.

[36] John Callaghan, 'The Left and the "Unfinished Revolution": Bevanites and Soviet Russia in the 1950s', *Contemporary British History,* vol. 15, no. 3 (2001), pp. 63–82.

[37] For Gaitskell's anxieties along these lines see Gaitskell, Hugh: *The Challenge of Co-existence*, Methuen, London, 1957, pp. 81–3.

[38] See Favretto: '"Wilsonism" Reconsidered', op. cit., pp. 61–2.

[39] See his comments in the preface to the 1962 Pelican edition of Galbraith, J.K.: *The Affluent Society*, Penguin, Harmondsworth, 1962, p. 10.

[40] Jay: *Socialism in the New Society*, op. cit., p. 144.

[41] Jay, Douglas: 'The Man who pleads for more taxes', *Forward*, 16 January 1959.

[42] Jay, Douglas: 'Beyond State Monopoly', in *Where?* Fabian Tract 320, 1959, pp. 20–25 at p. 24.

[43] Davenport: *Memoirs*, op. cit., p. 204. Jay, Douglas, 'Beyond State Monopoly', in *Where?* Fabian Tract 320, 1959, pp. 20–25 at p. 24.

[44] Labour Party archive (henceforward LPA), National Museum of Labour History, Manchester: Jay, Douglas: 'Equity Shares and the Small Saver', Labour Party Finance and Economic Policy Committee, Re: 480, January 1959.

[45] Davenport, *Memoirs*, op. cit., p. 204.

[46] Jay, Douglas: 'Tories keep the brake on action over monopolies', *Forward*, 1 March 1957.

[47] TNA: PRO PREM 8/1183 'Note of a Meeting held at the House of Commons on 17th May, 1950 at 7.30 P.M. to discuss the Memorandum on the State and Private Industry'; Jay, Douglas: 'Public Capital and Private Enterprise', *Fabian Journal*, July 1959, pp. 9–14.

[48] Favretto: '"Wilsonism" Reconsidered', op. cit., pp. 58–9.

[49] Jay: *Change and Fortune*, op. cit., pp. 271–5.

[50] Jay, Douglas: 'Are We Downhearted?', *Forward*, 16 October 1959.

[51] The article had not in fact mentioned Clause 4. Benn, Tony: *Years of Hope: Diaries Papers and Letters 1940–1962*, Hutchinson, London, 1994, p. 318 (entry for 21 October 1959).

[52] Jay: *Change and Fortune*, op. cit., pp. 272, 332–3.

[53] *Labour Party Annual Conference Report 1959*, Labour Party, London, 1959, p. 121. Institute of Contemporary British History, 'Witness Seminar: The Campaign for Democratic Socialism 1960–64' in *Contemporary Record*, vol. 7 no. 2 (1993), pp. 363–85 at p. 368.

[54] Jay: *Change and Fortune*, op. cit., pp. 276, 278–9.

[55] Fletcher, Raymond: 'Ends and Means', *Tribune*, 26 January 1962.

[56] Crossman, R.H.S. : 'The Taxolaters', *New Statesman*, 23 January 1962.

[57] 'More Than Equal', *The Times*, 22 January 1962.

[58] 'Eternally Deluded?', *The Economist*, 27 January 1962.

[59] 'The Last Puritan', *Times Literary Supplement*, 26 January 1962. For evidence of Hutton's authorship, see the *TLS* Centenary Archive database.

[60]   Clore took over J. Sears (True-Form Boot Company) in 1953 and subsequently masterminded a further string of aggressive takeovers in the footwear industry. Parliamentary Debates, House of Commons, 5th series, vol. 657, 11 April 1962, col. 1355; 'Clore: Where will this man strike next', *Forward*, 23 November 1956; Jay, Douglas: 'The Lessons of Clore and Chambers', *New Statesman*, 12 January 1962.

[61]   Jay: *Socialism in the New Society*, op. cit., pp. 349–50.

[62]   Douglas Jay, *Socialism in the New Society*, op. cit., pp. 350.

[63]   Ibid., pp. 350–1.

[64]   Ibid., pp. 351, 353.

[65]   Gaitskell Papers, University College, London: A139.1, Jay to Hugh Gaitskell, 15 May 1956.

[66]   Jay, Douglas: 'Don't Stop the Press', *Forward*, 17 May 1957.

[67]   Black, Lawrence: *The Political Culture of the Left in Affluent Britain, 1951–64, Old Labour, New Britain?*, Palgrave, Basingstoke, 2003, p. 84.

[68]   Parliamentary Debates, House of Commons, Fifth Series, vol. 596, 26 November 1958, cols. 449–50.

[69]   Jay: *Change and Fortune*, op. cit., p. 274.

[70]   Jay, Douglas: 'Too Smug!', *Forward*, 20 November 1959.

[71]   See Toye: 'The Gentleman in Whitehall', op. cit.; and also Jay: 'Britain's Economic Survival', op. cit., p. 8.

[72]   However, in regard to (d), see LPA: RD.112, Finance and Economic Policy Sub-Committee, Douglas Jay, 'The Labour Party and the Common Market', February 1961: 'We should urge that the U.K. ... should offer *to join the Common Market, if, but only if, the Common Market common external tariff were reduced to zero on all those foods and raw materials which are now imported Duty-free into the U.K. from the Commonwealth.* This is the only issue, economically, which seriously matters' (emphasis in original). This suggestion was probably a matter of political tactics only, as the Six were unlikely to agree to the condition; but it does imply that Jay took a slightly more ambiguous approach to the European issue at this time than he recalled in his memoirs. See Jay: *Change and Fortune*, op. cit., pp. 280–6.

[73]   Favretto: '"Wilsonism" reconsidered', p. 55.

[74]   Pimlott, Ben: *Harold Wilson*, HarperCollins, London, 1992, pp. 300–301.

CHAPTER 5

Total Abstinence and a Good Filing-System? Anthony Crosland and the Affluent Society

*Catherine Ellis**

If total abstinence and a good filing-system are to be the banners under which we march towards Socialism, well, a good many of us will fall by the way-side.[1]

When Anthony Crosland commented wryly in 1951 that human frailty was an obstacle to building the New Jerusalem, he struck at the heart of a matter that plagued the Labour Party throughout its years in opposition between 1951 and 1964. The popular characterization of Labour as a party of abstinence in a period of rising affluence has often been used to explain the party's successive electoral defeats in 1951, 1955 and 1959.[2] Much of this characterization derives from the Conservative Party's portrayal of Labour as the party of austerity, rationing and controls, a tactic that undoubtedly made a significant contribution to Conservative electoral success.[3] Whilst it is clear that the political left and right differed substantially in their responses to post-war conditions and expectations, the relationship between affluence and socialism, both ideologically and in policy-making, has been examined primarily from the perspectives of election results and public opinion. A clear connection has been made between the Labour Party's poor showing at the polls and the apparent inability of prominent Labour politicians to comprehend the 'affluent society'. 'Why,' as Nick Tiratsoo has asked, 'was Labour so incapable of understanding what was going on around it?'[4]

This chapter will argue that the problem was not Labour's understanding of contemporary Britain, but rather the difficulties that the party experienced in trying to choose an appropriate response to the 'age of affluence'. Labour was acutely aware that any such choice would entail both a rethinking of its conception of socialism and the reformulation of its policies to reflect the new circumstances of post-war Britain; however, the multiplicity of voices within the party hampered its ability to respond decisively to this dual challenge.[5] This chapter illustrates the diversity of Labour's reactions to affluence through the work of one of the party's most influential thinkers, Anthony Crosland.

The basis of Crosland's socialism was a detailed analysis of Britain's economy and society. The foundations of Crosland's ideas were laid during his undergraduate education at Oxford and, more importantly, his military service in the Second World War, when he began to develop a conception of socialism that reconciled self-interest with public interest. With Labour active in Churchill's coalition government, Crosland often considered the possibility of a Labour government after the war, but his army experience taught him much about the alleged 'psychological argument' for socialism. As early as 1942, he was concerned that the intellectuals of the left were 'out of touch with popular feeling.'[6] Through his wartime service, Crosland learned not to overestimate the appeal of politics to the average person:

> On the basis of intensive mass-observation, I am prepared to state categorically: that, generally speaking, it would make no difference to the morale of the population, or of their determination to win this war, what the Govt. was & what the social system was – let alone any particular measure of Socialism, which [would] pass literally unnoticed.[7]

Throughout his career, Crosland returned repeatedly to the psychological aspects of socialism and politics, stressing the importance of free choice in a socialist society and the need to seek out the underlying causes of social inequality and industrial disputes.

After the war, he turned his attention to Britain's perilous economic situation, but as austerity gave way to abundance, Crosland became convinced that in order to recover their electoral popularity and act effectively in government, socialists must engage with the effects of affluence on both the individual and the community. Throughout the 1950s, Crosland argued that socialists should build on their accomplishments in government and develop a programme that reflected modern society. He also believed that socialists should distinguish between ends and means: Long-standing socialist goals could be reached through a variety of means. Central to his vision were definitions of equality, fellowship and individual freedom that required, not rejected, material plenty. Crosland did not condemn affluence; he welcomed it. He demonstrated that affluence did not compromise socialists' economic and moral goals, but strengthened them. Crosland's significance to the study of the 'affluent society' was the marriage of affluence and socialism. Although Crosland's ideas were never completely accepted by the Labour Party, both the party's internal policy debates and its published programmes contained important elements of his arguments, particularly after Labour's electoral defeat in 1959. Crosland provides an important example of how British socialists engaged with, shaped, and were shaped by, post-war culture and society.

'Socialism is not bread alone'

Affluence presented British socialists with challenges to both ideological development and policy formation. These challenges were widely recognized, but opinions varied about the effects that sustained full employment, individual prosperity and a rising standard of living would have on the British people and how, by extension, socialists should respond. To begin with, the conditions that had fostered affluence also seemed to have reduced the economic necessity for socialism. As Labour's General Secretary, Morgan Phillips, observed in 1960, 'Brute poverty and unemployment can, happily, no longer be expected to act as the recruiting sergeants of the Labour Movement.'[8] Accordingly, the appeal of socialism had to be more than material. It had to inspire with moral force and the conviction that despite the improvements that had taken place since the war, a still more desirable model of social life and human relationships was possible. Jenkins recognized this challenge as early as 1950:

> Now we have to devise measures which are experiments, which are not overdue, and which will not be removing continually felt discomfort and grievance so much as offering to satisfy certain general aspirations which people are very unlikely to think about frequently. Most men will go to more trouble to get rid of a shoe that pinches than to save up for a trip to Naples. We have helped people to get rid of their pinching shoes, but it is at least possible that they will not allow us to conduct them to Naples.[9]

As the standard of living rose across all classes, but especially for the working class, it became essential to address the role that private consumption would play in a socialist society. Should socialists welcome affluence for its contribution to equality and personal freedom, or did the emphasis on individual gain that affluence implied pose a threat to the development of a socialist community? How would the balance between public and private responsibilities be articulated? And, critically, would the ultimate goal of a socialist society have any appeal to people who had 'never had it so good'?

Responses to these questions frequently drew upon older traditions within the ideology of the British left. One important element, which Crosland found particularly objectionable, was a strong strain of grim self-denial. It was exemplified perhaps most clearly in the person of Stafford Cripps urging restraint as Chancellor after the war, and also by what many saw as the coldly bureaucratic influence of the Fabians. Crosland, for example, accused Beatrice and Sidney Webb of casting socialism in a Spartan mould, complaining that 'their lack of temptation towards any of the emotional or physical pleasures of life ... *would*, if universally influential, make the Socialist State into the dull functional nightmare which many fear.'[10] Similarly, in a lecture delivered in 1952, R.H. Tawney recalled being treated to 'one of the famous exercises in asceticism described by Mrs. Webb as dinners.'[11] Austerity for the individual was inseparable from austerity for the nation. Although the redistribution of wealth and a rising standard of living for the majority of Britons were central to the socialist project, during the Second World War and the years that followed, Labour believed that its duty was to subordinate individual to collective needs, not only in the nation's interest, but also in pursuit of its own ethical commitments. The long-term project of national solvency had to take precedence over short-term material benefits.[12]

Returned to opposition in 1951, Labour continued to advocate austerity. As far as the party was concerned, the individual was not first and foremost a consumer, but rather a citizen within a community and – ultimately – a socialist society. This citizen was a person with 'obligations to fulfil as well as rights to enjoy.'[13] Citizens enjoyed 'equality of opportunity' and had 'equal rights to freedom and to satisfaction of their basic needs.' At the same time, they had a 'social duty' to 'contribute to the good of the community according to their abilities.'[14] The framework within which individuals and communities developed was set by the state, which provided economic planning and social services that furthered the principle of equality and ensured the effective distribution of scarce resources.[15] The creation of a healthy community thus depended upon the combined efforts of the individual and the state – neither was independently sufficient. Labour therefore emphasized that 'socialism is not bread alone.' Its vision of socialism extended beyond 'material security and sufficiency' to 'the evolution of a people more kindly, intelligent, co-operative, enterprising and rich in culture,' who would together build communities that reflected 'all the finer constructive impulses of man.'[16] Austerity was not popular with the electorate, but in the early 1950s the party held to it on both economic and moral grounds, insisting that man was more than 'an economic animal,' susceptible only to economic incentives. As Richard Crossman explained, the community should not be seen 'as a collection of individual consumers of material goods.' Socialists needed to persuade voters that although capitalism was an effective system under which to produce and distribute goods, 'Socialism is *more moral* than Capitalism,' and thus 'economic materialism' was insufficient.[17]

'Unnatural morality and priggish Puritanism'

While these ideas broadly reflected Crosland's own views in the 1940s and early 1950s, his vision of socialism already extended beyond economic stability and public services to include private prosperity. As Crosland demonstrated in his first book, *Britain's Economic Problem* (1953), he understood the need for austerity in order to construct a socialist society; however, he also argued that Attlee's governments had only just begun to scratch the surface of the enormous task that lay before socialists.[18] What the situation demanded was a reconciliation of socialism with the dramatic social and economic changes that had occurred in Britain during and since the war. As early as 1940, Crosland believed that he was witnessing 'the birth of a new social order.'[19] Power was shifting from the old propertied elites to those who held power in the new system, trade unionists, managers, professionals, and most of all the state itself. In his contribution to *New Fabian Essays* (1952), Crosland reinforced his conviction that major reforms had taken place since the war. On the whole, he found that 'Britain had, in all the essentials, ceased to be a capitalist country.' The new society was characterized principally by a shift in the balance of power from owners to managers, and from private industry to the state. Economically and socially, he described the new form as 'pluralist' – capitalist in its acceptance of private ownership and the market, managerial to the extent that the new class of managers had 'usurped the position of the old capitalist class,' and socialist because the market was centrally planned according to 'traditional socialist ends.'[20]

The Labour government's defeat in 1951 underlined the urgency of Crosland's calls for a restatement of socialism to suit post-war conditions. While economic growth and stability remained Crosland's priorities in the early 1950s, some of his work clearly foreshadowed his later and more influential views. Crosland was calling for a re-thinking of socialism well before 'affluence' had become prominent in the political landscape. In particular, Crosland was already convinced that socialists must take into account individual preferences, which would inevitably include more discretionary spending and higher consumption. In 1951, for example, he complained to a Fabian audience that 'the Webb tradition' was imperilling the possibility of building a 'happy Socialist society' along the lines he envisioned:

> Indeed, the truth is we must get rid of the Webb tradition in every sphere. It is hanging around our necks like a millstone at the moment. It is a tradition of total indifference to art and beauty and freedom and radical individualism, a tradition of unnatural morality and priggish Puritanism. If we have too much of this tradition, we may produce Socialism of a kind, but not of the kind that most of us want to see.[21]

Crosland was already advocating the liberalization of divorce, abortion and licensing laws, and he called for more support for cultural and artistic endeavours. Seeking nomination as Labour's candidate in South Gloucestershire in 1949, he defined socialism as 'a state of affairs in which every single citizen has the chance to live the same sort of graceful, cultured & comfortable life that only the lucky few can live to-day.'[22] Crosland was unmoved by critics who worried that Britons were losing interest in political and community engagement in favour of more private pastimes; indeed, he observed that 'some of the best of human activities are … rather personal than social.'[23] Affluence would become an essential component of this vision of socialist Britain.

Crosland did not address the concept of 'affluence' directly in the early 1950s, but he acknowledged that post-war wage increases raised important questions for socialists. In particular, he was concerned that a future Labour government might be tempted to respond to higher wages by raising taxes in the name of equality. Instead of returning money to taxpayers in the form of additional services 'determined by the fiat of the State,' Crosland encouraged Labour to balance the demands of equality and freedom by leaving more funds for people 'to spend as they like.' 'We must allow our citizens to spend future increases in their income as they want,' Crosland argued, 'even if we think they are likely to spend them unwisely.'[24] The challenge of reconciling what individuals *should* want with what they *did* want was a recurrent theme in Crosland's work, one that was closely related to his criticism of the Soviet Union, and also placed him in opposition to many in the Labour Party throughout this period.

The Future of Socialism

Preparing for the 1955 election, Labour's strategy included a message of 'Fair Shares in Prosperity' and a vigorous rebuttal of the Conservatives' accusation that a Labour government would reintroduce rationing.[25] However, these efforts seemed to have little influence on the electorate's perception of Labour as the party of austerity, controls and nationalization, and the Conservatives were returned with an increased majority. This election defeat marked the beginning of a significant change in Labour's approach to the expression of socialism both in policy-making and for public consumption. A new research programme was organized and Labour began to commission its own public opinion surveys and consider the motivation of the individual voter. 'Our task,' the party insisted, 'must be to convince the electorate that there is an important role for a democratic socialist Party working within a framework of a "successful" and expanding economy.'[26] As the likelihood of economic crisis grew more remote, the challenge of recruiting supporters for socialism became more acute. Crossman asked the question that was on many socialists' lips: 'If welfare capitalism can provide the majority with security, how can we ever persuade them to prefer Socialism?'[27]

Labour tried to answer that question by giving the individual consumer a larger role in Labour's programme, and from the mid-1950s Labour strengthened its claim to be the party of the consumer. The emphasis was not on expanded opportunities for the purchase of goods, however, but on the protection of consumers, especially 'the housewife', from shoddy goods and rising prices.[28] Yet protecting the shopper did not mean that Labour was unconcerned about rising personal consumption. The protection of consumers pointed socialists back to the difficulty of balancing an appeal to the electorate on moral as well as material grounds, but the moral case for socialism was still advanced as the best option in the second half of the 1950s.[29]

In many respects, the Labour Party's policy revisions in the late 1950s were not very successful.[30] Returning to Crossman's question about the moral appeal of socialism, Crosland provided some alternative answers. While he agreed that there were both moral and economic reasons for supporting socialism, he wanted socialists to be more open to the benefits of individual material gain. This was a message that built on many of Crosland's earlier ideas, but was outlined most fully in his second book, *The Future of Socialism* (1956).

Noel Annan has suggested that for Crosland, the goal of socialism was to give everyone equal access to 'the good things of life' and that in *The Future of Socialism*, Crosland had produced 'a theoretical justification for pleasure.'[31] Crosland would likely have agreed with this assessment. Although he had supported Attlee's austerity measures and was critical of the Conservatives' economic management in the early 1950s, Crosland had never shown any tolerance for those who wanted to make socialism cold and bureaucratic. In the second half of the 1950s, Crosland set out to remove all traces of Puritanism and to stress the benefits of socialism for the community as a whole. He insisted that socialism was not about drab uniformity and efficient bureaucracy, but must be based upon a clear acceptance of personal liberty and happiness in an atmosphere conducive to the realization of individual goals in private as well as public life. Not only were economic growth and a healthy balance of payments important to Crosland, but they also had to be accompanied by the encouragement of 'non-economic value-judgments' that laid emphasis on beauty and creativity after the provision of basic material necessities.[32]

Crosland saw an opportunity to use the resources of the affluent society to enrich Britons both culturally and materially. Rather than condemning the excesses of affluence and prophesying the decline of socialism into a vehicle for more efficient acquisitiveness and competition, Crosland argued that the Labour Party must approach the affluent society from a very practical point of view, analysing and resolving its shortcomings, but not condemning the higher standards of living and greater material equality that it produced. Britain in the 1950s was not Tawney's acquisitive society. In the new era of reformed capitalism, Crosland told socialists to pay more attention to wooing Beatrice Webb's 'average sensual man' and to accept 'rising consumption' as a 'socialist objective.' Increasing consumption would reduce the sense of inferiority often felt by the working classes and contribute to greater equality between classes. Therefore, 'higher personal consumption must form part of any statement of the socialist goal on fundamental egalitarian grounds.'[33]

High personal consumption did not pose a threat to socialism, provided that consumption was located in an atmosphere of continued commitment to greater equality, fellowship and freedom. Crosland believed that post-war Britain, while not socialist, was capable of maintaining the necessary rate of economic growth to support his economic, social and cultural objectives. Even the long-standing ideal of 'brotherly love' among socialists was not at odds with affluence. 'Why should not the brothers be affluent,' Crosland asked, 'and the love conducted under conditions of reasonable comfort?'[34] Crosland rejected any suggestion that rising personal consumption was 'unsocialist' or would 'lower the moral tone of society.' Consumption should not become 'an over-riding priority' for socialists, but 'one out of many desirable aims of social policy.'[35]

In *New Fabian Essays*, Crossman had claimed that it was 'not the pursuit of happiness but the enlargement of freedom which is socialism's highest aim.'[36] Crosland disagreed. For him, freedom and happiness were inseparable; they were fostered by affluence and together they formed the 'more important spheres' of socialism that make up the concluding chapter of *The Future of Socialism*. Crosland wanted to encourage more emphasis upon 'private life, on freedom and dissent, on culture, beauty, leisure, and even frivolity.' It was essential to stress these virtues as the state made ever larger inroads into everyday life and socialist governments had come to be associated with austerity. Many socialists, Crosland again lamented, still believed that the road to the New Jerusalem was marked out by 'total abstinence and a good filing-system.' He called for, among other things, divorce reform, extended licensing hours, an end to the censorship of books and plays, better designs for clothing and furniture, and equal rights for women, as examples of the way the state could set a positive example for 'a change in cultural attitudes.'[37]

The origins of Crosland's views on happiness and personal fulfilment are diverse, but ultimately they reinforce the notion that this aspect of his socialism, although readily applied to the affluent society of the 1950s, did not originate in it – it was built on much deeper foundations. Crosland attributed most of British socialism's reputation for austerity to the Fabian legacy and a tendency for the 'moral ascetics' of the left to be hostile toward consumption of all types, particularly working-class spending habits. Despite the significance of the Second World War and the Attlee governments for both Crosland and the Labour movement, the direct impact of the war on this aspect of Crosland's thought seems to have been minimal. He claimed that his proposals for cultural reform had the sanction of William Morris and his belief in expressing socialism in terms of beauty and artistic achievement in all aspects of life.[38] The idea that socialism was inseparable from both cultural and material enrichment also draws upon Evan Durbin's wish for 'the common happiness of mankind' in a creative society.[39] Susan Crosland has suggested that her husband's upbringing in a family of strict Exclusive Brethren was also influential on this side of his socialism. Crosland's faith lapsed into agnosticism as he grew older, but he still recalled the Brethren's image of life in the kingdom of God. In contrast to the Brethren, however, Crosland 'was occupied with what was happening in this world: he felt the grossness of inequality; he thought that some of the unfairness could be righted here and now.'[40] Crosland's secular message was infused with a desire to create the Brethren's community of fellowship and equality in this world, not the next.

Socialism in the affluent society

Labour's electoral defeat in 1959 provided Crosland with expanded opportunities to urge reform. He observed in the immediate aftermath of the election:

> The will to socialism has always been based on a lively sense of wrongs crying for redress; and before the war the wrongs were manifest indeed. But now, instead of glaring and conspicuous evils ... we have full employment, the Welfare State, and the prospect in ten years' time of a car to every working-class family. For a party of protest, there is a good deal less to protest about.[41]

In his contributions to the debate sparked by the 1959 election results, Crosland urged socialists not to become nostalgic for the deprivation of earlier times, but rather to welcome affluence for its beneficial effects on both the individual and the community. He continued to believe that changes in the nature of capitalism had rendered much of the traditional socialist programme obsolete, and the fact of continued affluence was central to the rethinking of socialism at this time.

Much of the debate was conducted in Fabian tracts and the pages of *Encounter* magazine, which published a series of articles addressing 'The Future of the Left'. Crosland fired the first salvo in March 1960. He observed that increased prosperity and fading class identity were the most common factors blamed for drawing voters away from socialism and the Labour Party. For Crosland, these explanations raised two critical questions. First, did the much-vaunted 'swing to the right' in European and North American politics really exist? And second, if voters were no longer responsive to socialist politics, was there any way to make left-wing parties electable again? In response to the first question, Crosland found little conclusive evidence of a rightward trend, and therefore rejected the argument that Labour's unpopularity was connected to a larger international swing of the political pendulum. To answer the second question, Crosland acknowledged that many social and economic factors were taking voters away from socialism, but he also noted that the more successful left-wing parties in Europe were those that had proven to be most adaptable to changing circumstances. 'Adaptability' was the key to success.[42]

Crosland's prescription was blunt. Labour was associated in the public mind with 'a sectional, traditional, class appeal' and was reinforcing this image by bickering over nationalization. The solution was 'revisionism,' which Crosland described as 'a long-term effort to enable the Labour Party to survive in mid-twentieth-century conditions.' Crosland argued that to adapt to contemporary circumstances and become once again electable, Labour must drop its commitment to nationalization. He demonstrated the extent to which nationalization had ceased to be central to Labour's programmes since the early 1950s, and he urged the party to stop equating nationalization with socialism, and to focus instead on maintaining the distinctiveness of the socialist programme in areas such as social welfare, the redistribution of wealth, and 'the proper dividing line between the public and private spheres of responsibility.'[43]

At the heart of Crosland's argument was an appeal to socialists to reconsider their fixation on economic questions such as nationalization and planning, and to try instead to gain a better social and cultural understanding of post-war Britain, particularly the significance of affluence. Crosland asked how, for example, socialists could justify the need for additional economic planning when 'the existing degree of planning appears adequate to ensure full employment and a steady rise in consumption-standards.'[44] Rather than attacking modern society as 'evil' and 'rotten' and castigating the British people for seeking a higher standard of living, Crosland appealed socialists to 'stop describing the present prosperity as 'phoney' and begin incorporating popular attitudes as part of a natural process of adaptation. While he acknowledged that some aspects of the transition might seem 'extremely unattractive' to socialists, to flout them betrayed 'an arrogant indifference ... to the lives and fears and hopes of ordinary people.' Crosland was disgusted by what he interpreted as a return to the 'coals in the bath' argument:

> Surprisingly enough, ordinary people like to be materially well off. And any normal socialist will wholeheartedly rejoice at the spread of material affluence – on grounds of personal freedom, since rising standards widen the area of choice and opportunity: on grounds of social justice, which surely requires that the masses should now also be admitted to the world of material ease which others have so long enjoyed: on general egalitarian grounds, since rising consumption increases both the fact and consciousness

of social equality: and on grounds of democratic anti-paternalism, since this
is clearly what the workers want.[45]

Crosland did not, however, accept the affluent society uncritically. Rather, he
observed that some socialists seemed unable to distinguish between 'the fact of
affluence, which is to be welcomed unreservedly since it widens the range of
choice and opportunity open to the average family,' and the less welcome aspects
of an affluent society, such as the uneven distribution of wealth, 'the neglect of
social spending' and 'the vulgar commercialization of culture.' In other words,
plenty of causes remained for socialists who were prepared to demote
nationalization, and Crosland was certain that embracing them would make Labour
electable again.[46]

Crosland's ideas found support within the Labour Party from figures such as
Hugh Gaitskell, Douglas Jay, Roy Jenkins, and Patrick Gordon Walker, but they
also provoked considerable controversy among left-wingers such as Aneurin
Bevan, Ian Mikardo and Crossman. To his critics, Crosland's apparent acceptance
of affluence was a betrayal of the core values of socialism and a dangerous
misreading of an 'ugly,' 'vulgar' and 'meretricious society.'[47] The most prominent
riposte came from Crossman. At the height of the debate, Crossman was convinced
that optimism about the ability of reformed capitalism to provide boundless
prosperity was misplaced. 'I believe that we must give warning of the crisis ahead,'
he wrote, 'and condemn the Affluent Society as incapable of coping with it.'
Crossman's proof lay in the example of the Soviet Union, which he believed was
quickly outstripping the decadent countries of the west in both industrial efficiency
and economic growth. Crossman insisted that complacency in the face of this
threat would lead to the erosion of Britain's economic strength and 'fatty
degeneration' among the British people, and he encouraged Labour to maintain its
commitment to nationalization and economic controls to compete with growing
Soviet power.[48]

Crosland replied forcefully, accusing his critics of a 'Pharisaical attitude'
toward the fruits of affluence. 'Of course there are innumerable things wrong with
the affluent society,' he wrote. 'But why, the moment that the workers acquire the
cars, holidays, and gadgets which the critics have been enjoying all their lives,
should they be condemned as "fatty" and "degenerate"?' He demonstrated that the
Soviet Union would not be able to overtake the levels of consumption reached in
the west, and he accused Crossman of a willingness to sacrifice democracy and
consumer choice at the altar of higher economic growth. Crosland also found
Crossman's commitment to nationalization flawed, because Crossman had failed to
demonstrate that nationalization would actually lead to the economic expansion
that Crosland considered essential. Crosland accepted a limited expansion of
controls and public ownership, but he still believed that the price-mechanism was
the best available expression of consumers' freedom. People, he argued, 'should
have what they want, and … they themselves are the best judges of what they
want.' To reject consumers' desires would be paternalistic and authoritarian, not
socialist. Again, this is not to suggest that Crosland advocated higher personal
consumption as an isolated goal, nor that he aimed to create a 'socialism of

shopping,' but as a means to greater equality, economic welfare and happiness, he believed that affluence should be accepted as a central part of socialist policy.[49]

In the late 1950s and early 1960s, Crosland accepted that the spread of affluence and the resultant reduction in social tension had made a greater degree of overlap between the Conservatives and Labour inevitable, but he insisted that the grounds for remaining a socialist were as clear as ever. Indeed, socialism and affluence had become inseparable. Crosland's socialist convictions were based on moral and humanitarian grounds that required active support for affluence. Although culture and personal liberty were not the unique preserve of socialists, Crosland argued that Labour's record in these areas, as well as its traditional economic and social priorities, still set Labour very clearly apart from the Conservatives. With Britain's urgent economic problems fast disappearing, Crosland hoped that the next Labour government would use the wealth of the affluent society to take the lead not only on economic, but also on cultural and libertarian issues. Crosland urged socialists to see the unique opportunity that post-war affluence offered not only to enrich Britons materially, but also to spare more resources in the pursuit of 'beauty and culture,' from architecture and town planning to the abolition of capital punishment and artistic censorship. As Crosland concluded in *The Future of Socialism*: 'We do not want to enter the age of abundance, only to find that we have lost the values which might teach us how to enjoy it.'[50]

Affluence, community and democracy

Crossman and other critics argued that the waste inherent in perpetuating affluence was inefficient, morally corrupt, and damaging to the socialist project, while Crosland insisted that affluence was central to a vision of a socialist society and was, moreover, no more than people were entitled to and clearly wanted. The area of fundamental agreement, which brought together a range of socialists, was the relationship between affluence, community and democratic society. In this respect, socialists were returning to the question that had plagued them since the late 1940s: How could voters be convinced to support the Labour Party in conditions of full employment and unprecedented prosperity?

Following the 1959 election, this question returned with even greater urgency, as it appeared that it was precisely contemporary economic conditions that were distancing voters from socialism.[51] Crosland argued that this need not be the case. In the early 1960s, the stamp of Crosland's thinking was clear in Labour's growing acceptance that affluence was not a threat to socialism, but a justification for its continued relevance. However, Crosland's ideas were not adopted wholesale. In particular, the party's public statements were very much influenced by John Kenneth Galbraith's analysis in *The Affluent Society* (1958),[52] but Crosland did not wholly accept Galbraith's preoccupation with production patterns and the stimulation of 'purely artificial wants' to explain America's maldistribution of public and private spending.[53] Labour's policy reviews also still found it difficult to resist blaming the 'get-rich-quick ethos of the affluent society' for a 'weakening of moral fibre,' although they nevertheless echoed Crosland's warning that any such weakening (real or imagined) could not be blamed on irresponsibility fostered by the welfare state, but on a wider culture of acquisitiveness.[54]

Crosland explained in 1962 that socialists were not hostile to affluence; rather, they believed that 'the present *balance* between public and private spending is wrong.'[55] In public statements leading up to the 1964 election, Labour followed this model in its discussion of affluence. Morgan Phillips' pamphlet, *Labour in the Sixties*, written for the party's 1960 conference, became the blueprint for the party's subsequent statements. When Labour was critical of affluence, it was not because of 'pessimistic assumptions about a recurrence of mass unemployment,' but because of 'the demands of the new world towards which we are moving.' Labour did not advocate depriving individuals of material gains, but sought to ensure that the balance between public and private provisions was inclusive and would strengthen rather than destroy the fabric of democratic society. The growth of private purchasing power was not an evil in itself, but without state controls and a clear plan for future development, the foundations of the affluent society would remain weak and the balance between 'community needs and individual self-interest,' already abused by successive Conservative governments, would be lost, to the detriment of society as a whole. Accordingly, Labour called on the British people to 'subordinate private interest to the needs of the community' so that essential resources would be available for 'social justice' and the revitalization of democracy.[56] In the 1964 election campaign, Labour avoided overt expressions of hostility towards affluence, but continued to lay emphasis on the needs of the community over the desires of the individual, condemning the Conservatives' 'economic free-for-all' that 'put the narrow needs of the market before the wider needs of the man.'[57] Although Labour never became as enthusiastic about affluence as Crosland had hoped, his influence was nevertheless strong and he remained a very significant force in Wilson's governments.

Conclusion

During the 1950s and early 1960s, there were real differences among British socialists over appropriate responses to the 'affluent society'. Crosland and Crossman represented the most public face of the debate, but it was Crosland whose vision proved to be the more influential. Post-war socialists, like their earlier counterparts, were concerned with the extension of democracy (economic and social as much as political democracy), and with the promotion of equality and the enlargement of individual freedom. Crosland demonstrated how affluence could – indeed *must* – play a part in reaching these goals. Consequently, by the early 1960s, debate within the Labour Party was less concerned with condemning affluence than with addressing the means through which socialists should respond to its impact on the relationship between the individual, the community and the state. Much of Crosland's diagnosis and prescription stemmed from his long-standing conviction that socialism could provide Britons with not only the material goods that they sought and deserved, but also with a moral vision that separated Labour from the Conservatives. He returned to this point in 1968:

> I do not think election victories can be guaranteed by concentrating solely on people's private standard of living. I therefore believe that we need to take some risks, to exert a positive leadership, to catch a glimpse of some kind of vision other than a rise in personal spending, and to create again a sense of valid idealism so that we can offer the electorate, when we come to face them, a positive and distinctive policy.[58]

Labour's electoral difficulties after 1951 highlighted the need for the party to rethink its relationship with contemporary society. Labour understood that post-war Britain had changed and indeed took credit for much of the transformation through the Attlee governments. The party had no doubt that affluence was part of that transformation; however, Labour's thinking about affluence produced diverse reactions. British socialists did not ignore, misunderstand, or uniformly reject affluence, but questions about affluence invariably led to questions about the character of socialism itself. As Crosland insisted, many of the challenges that Labour faced in the 'affluent society' did not originate outside the party, but within it. The party's main weakness was its adherence to a model of socialism that placed affluence in opposition to national solvency, expanding democracy and equality. Instead, Crosland offered socialists a formula that reconciled affluence with economic growth, social responsibility and individual freedom. In so doing, Crosland not only provided the Labour Party with a means of adapting to contemporary society, he also reaffirmed his long-standing belief that the New Jerusalem should be founded on affluence, not abstinence.

Notes

* Research for this article was supported by the Association of Commonwealth Universities in the United Kingdom and the University of Lethbridge Travel Fund. I would like to thank Susan Crosland and Raymond Plant for discussions about Anthony Crosland's work and access to his papers, and Matthew Ellis, Stephen Brooke, and José Harris for their helpful comments on earlier versions of the text.
1. British Library of Political and Economic Science, London School of Economics [henceforward BLPES], C.A.R. Crosland Papers [henceforward CARCP]: 13/38, 'Is This Socialism?' Anthony Crosland, 20 November 1951.
2. Abrams, Mark, Rose, Richard and Hinden, Rita: *Must Labour Lose?* Penguin, Harmondsworth, 1960. Bogdanor, Vernon: 'The Labour Party in Opposition, 1951–1964', in Bogdanor, Vernon and Skidelsky, Robert (eds): *The Age of Affluence 1951–1964*, Macmillan, London, 1970, pp. 81–114. Tiratsoo, Nick: *Reconstruction, Affluence and Labour Politics: Coventry 1945–60*, Routledge, London, 1990, especially pp. 88–120. Jefferys, Kevin: *Retreat From New Jerusalem: British Politics, 1951–64*, Macmillan, Basingstoke, 1997. Brooke, Stephen: 'Labour and the "nation" after 1945', in Lawrence, Jon and Taylor, Miles (eds): *Party, State and Society: Electoral Behaviour in Britain since 1820*, Scholar, Aldershot, 1997, pp. 153–175. Fielding, Steven:

'Activists against "Affluence": Labour Party Culture during the "Golden Age", circa 1950–1970', *Journal of British Studies*, vol. 40, no. 2 (2001), pp. 241–267.

3   Zweiniger-Bargielowska, Ina: 'Rationing, Austerity and the Conservative Party Recovery after 1945', *Historical Journal*, vol. 37, no. 1 (1994), pp. 173–197.

4   Tiratsoo, Nick: 'Popular Politics, Affluence and the Labour Party in the 1950s', in Gorst, Anthony et al. (eds): *Contemporary British History, 1931–1961: Politics and the Limits of Policy*, Pinter, London, 1991, p. 56.

5   Black, Lawrence: *The Political Culture of the Left in Affluent Britain, 1951–64*, Basingstoke, Palgrave Macmillan, 2003, especially pp. 124–54. Tanner, Duncan: 'Labour and its Membership', in Tanner, Duncan, et al. (eds): *Labour's First Century*, Cambridge University Press, Cambridge, 2000, pp. 248–80. Fielding, 'Activists against "Affluence"', op. cit. pp. 241–49.

6   BLPES: CARCP, 3/26/I, Crosland to Philip Williams, 25 January 1942.

7   Ibid., undated [1940–1942].

8   Phillips, Morgan: *Labour in the Sixties*, Labour Party, London, 1960, p. 15.

9   BLPES: Hugh Dalton Papers, 9/10/40, Jenkins to Dalton, 31 October 1950.

10 Cited in Crosland, Susan: *Tony Crosland*, Jonathan Cape, London, 1982, p. 47.

11 Tawney, R.H.: *The Webbs in Perspective*, Athlone Press, London, 1953, p. 4.

12 For example, Labour Party: *The Old World and the New Society*, 1942, pp. 9–10. Labour Party: *Challenge to Britain*, 1953, p. 20. All Labour Party documents were published by the Labour Party in London.

13 Labour Party: *Labour Believes in Britain*, 1949, pp. 3–4, 7.

14 Labour Party: *Labour and the New Society*, 1950, pp. 11–12, 16.

15 For example, Labour Party: *The Welfare State*, Discussion Pamphlet no. 4, 1952.

16 Shore, Peter: *The Real Nature of Conservatism*, Labour Party Educational Series no. 3, 1952, pp. 39–41. Labour Party: *Look Forward: The Labour Party*, 1961, p. 4.

17 Crossman, R.H.S.: *Socialist Values in a Changing Civilisation*, Fabian Tract no. 286, Fabian Society, London, 1951, pp. 4–5, 7.

18 Crosland, C.A.R.: *Britain's Economic Problem*, Jonathan Cape, London, 1953, pp. 212–22.

19 BLPES: CARCP, 3/26/i, Crosland to Williams, 5 July 1940 and 22 April 1941.

20 Crosland, C.A.R.: 'The Transition from Capitalism', in Crossman, R.H.S. (ed): *New Fabian Essays*, Turnstile Press, London, 1952, pp. 42–44. On Crosland and managerialism, see Reisman, David: 'Crosland's *Future*: The Missing Chapter on Burnham's *Managerial Revolution*', *Research in the History of Economic Thought and Methodology*, Archival Supplement no. 6 (1997), pp. 207–27.

21 BLPES: CARCP, 13/38, 'Is This Socialism?' Anthony Crosland, 20 November 1951.

22 Quoted in Reisman, David: *Crosland's Future: Opportunity and Outcome*, Macmillan, London, 1997, p. 201.

23 BLPES: CARCP, 4/1, '? Title', undated [1951–1955]. CARCP, 16/1, notebook entry, 3 April 1946.

24 BLPES: CARCP, 13/38, 'Is This Socialism?' Anthony Crosland, 20 November 1951.

25 Labour Party Archives, National Museum of Labour History, Manchester [henceforward LPA]: Research Department [henceforward RD], R.463, Informal Group on Party Propaganda, 'Propaganda Themes', January 1955. RD, R.479 (revised), 'Propaganda and the General Election: Interim Report', March 1955.

26 LPA: RD, R.522, Policy and Publicity Sub-Committee, 'A New Research Programme', July 1955. RD, Re.56 (revised), 'Memorandum on Proposed Pilot Scheme for a Public Opinion Survey', May 1956. RD, Re.68, 'Note on Available Public Opinion Material', May 1956.

[27] Crossman, R.H.S.: 'Planning for Freedom' (1956), in his *Planning for Freedom*, Hamish Hamilton, London, 1965, p. 61.

[28] Labour Party: *Your Guide to the Future Labour Offers You*, 1958. Labour Party: *Fair Deal for the Shopper*, 1961. Black, Amy and Brooke, Stephen: 'The Labour Party, Women and the Problem of Gender, 1951–1966', *Journal of British Studies*, vol. 36, no. 4 (1997), pp. 419–52.

[29] For example, Socialist Union: *Twentieth Century Socialism*, Penguin, Harmondsworth, 1956, pp. 40–43.

[30] For example, Ellis, Catherine: 'The Younger Generation: The Labour Party and the 1959 Youth Commission', *Journal of British Studies*, vol. 41, no. 2 (2002), pp. 199–231. Black, *Political Culture of the Left*, op. cit.

[31] Annan, Noel: *Our Age: Portrait of a Generation*, HarperCollins, London, 1990, p. 219.

[32] Crosland, C.A.R.: *The Future of Socialism*, revised edition, Schocken, New York, 1963, p. 172.

[33] Crosland, *Future of Socialism*, op. cit. pp. 212, 217–20.

[34] Crosland, C.A.R.: 'Production in the Age of Affluence' (1958), reprinted in his *The Conservative Enemy: A Programme of Radical Reform for the 1960s*, Jonathan Cape, London, 1962, pp. 97–103. Quote from Crosland, *Future of Socialism*, op. cit., p. 217. Crosland subsequently became much less optimistic about Britain's rate of economic growth. See Crosland, C.A.R.: *A Social Democratic Britain*, Fabian Tract no. 404, Fabian Society, London, 1971. Crosland, C.A.R.: 'Socialism Now', in Leonard, Dick (ed): *Socialism Now and Other Essays*, Jonathan Cape, London, 1974, pp. 15–58.

[35] Crosland, *Future of Socialism*, op. cit., pp. 222, 219.

[36] Crossman, R.H.S.: 'Towards a Philosophy of Socialism', in Crossman (ed), *New Fabian Essays*, op. cit., p. 29.

[37] Crosland, *Future of Socialism*, op. cit., pp. 355–57. BLPES: CARCP, 4/1, '? Title' (sic), undated [1951–1955], op. cit.

[38] Crosland, *Future of Socialism*, op. cit., pp. 219–22, 356. For the origins of British socialists' views on consumption, see Thompson, Noel: 'Social Opulence, Private Asceticism: Ideas of Consumption in Early Socialist Thought', in Daunton, Martin and Hilton, Matthew (eds): *The Politics of Consumption*, Berg, Oxford, 2001, pp. 51–68.

[39] Durbin, Evan: *The Politics of Democratic Socialism*, George Routledge and Sons, London, 1940, p. 334.

[40] Crosland, Susan, *Tony Crosland*, op. cit., p. 8.

[41] Crosland, C.A.R.: 'Orientation: Socialism Today and Tomorrow', in *Report of the Conference on the Situation in Western Europe, Part 2*, Socialist International, Amsterdam, 1959, p. 39.

[42] Crosland, C.A.R.: 'The Future of the Left', *Encounter*, vol.14 (March 1960), pp. 3–5.

[43] Crosland, 'Future of the Left', op. cit., pp. 5, 7–10. See also Jay, Douglas: *Socialism in the New Society*, Longmans, London, 1962, especially pp. 384–89.

[44] Crosland, 'Orientation', op. cit., p. 40.

[45] Crosland, C.A.R.: 'How Labour can kill the image that haunts its future', *News Chronicle*, 11/1/60. Crosland, 'Future of the Left', op. cit., p. 12. The last quote is very similar to a passage in *Future of Socialism*, p. 222.

[46] Crosland, C.A.R.: *Can Labour Win?* Fabian Tract no. 324, Fabian Society, London, 1960, pp. 14–16.

[47] Foot, Michael: *Aneurin Bevan: A Biography*, vol. 2, Davis-Poynter, London, 1973, pp. 641–50.

[48] Crossman, R.H.S.: 'The Spectre of Revisionism: A Reply to Crosland', *Encounter*, vol. 14 (April 1960), pp. 26–27. Crossman, R.H.S.: *Labour in the Affluent Society*, Fabian Tract no. 325, Fabian Society, London, 1960, pp. 9–12.

[49] Crosland, C.A.R.: 'On the Left Again: Some Last Words on the Labour Controversy', in his *The Future of the Left and Other Political Commentaries*, Encounter, London, 1961, pp. 12–18. Crosland, C.A.R.: 'Monopoly, Advertising and the Consumer', in *Conservative Enemy*, op. cit., p. 67. 'Socialism of shopping' is Reisman's term in *Crosland's Future*, op. cit., p. 152.

[50] Crosland, 'Future of the Left', op. cit., pp. 8–9. Crosland, C.A.R.: *The New Socialism*, Dissent Pamphlet No.1, Dissent Trust, Melbourne, 1963, pp. 9–13. Plant, Raymond: 'Democratic Socialism and Equality', in Fawcett, Helen and Lowe, Rodney (eds): *Welfare Policy in Britain: The Road from 1945*, Macmillan, Basingstoke, 1999, pp. 94–115. Crosland, *Future of Socialism*, op. cit., pp. 357–61.

[51] Abrams, Rose and Hinden, *Must Labour Lose?* op. cit.

[52] For example, Labour Party: *Signposts for the Sixties*, 1961, pp. 7–10.

[53] Crosland, 'Production in the Age of Affluence', op. cit., pp. 97–103.

[54] For example, Labour Party: *Crime – A Challenge to Us All*, 1964, p. 5.

[55] Crosland, 'Public and Private Spending', in *Conservative Enemy*, op. cit., p. 12.

[56] Phillips, *Labour in the Sixties*, op. cit., pp. 5–8. The same argument was presented in Labour Party: *First Things Last?* 1961, pp. 2–6, and Labour Party, *Look Forward*, op. cit., pp. 2–8.

[57] Northcott, Jim: *Why Labour?*, Penguin, Harmondsworth, 1964, pp. 153–7. Labour Party: *Let's Go with Labour for the New Britain*, 1964, p. 5.

[58] Crosland, C.A.R.: *Socialists in a Dangerous World*, Socialist Commentary Supplement, November 1968, p. 5.

CHAPTER 6

The Impression of Affluence: Political Culture in the 1950s and 1960s

Lawrence Black

Despite what can routinely be described as the 'biggest improvement in the material standard of living in Britain since the middle ages', it is the relative stability not extent of change that impresses in accounts of post-war British party politics.[1] Even electoral behaviour seemed more predictable than for decades before and after. The era was long dubbed 'consensus' by politicians and historians alike. This could indicate: that the change involved in affluence was limited; that politics was efficient at managing or immunized from them; or that affluence did not have any automatic political effects.

It might also mean historians have too readily inherited the terms of contemporaries. Late twentieth century British political history has irrefutably been less engaged by the newer turns (cultural, linguistic) and foci than writing on the eighteenth and nineteenth century. Studies of popular politics and Martin Francis' opening up of 'high politics' to issues of masculinity and emotional codes, have begun to address this. Expanding upon and beyond high/popular politics, this chapter uses diffuse political sites to scrutinize established narratives. It assesses the politics of affluence through party efforts to cultivate support, but also through affluence's representation by organizations in civil society. It looks beyond analyses of the state, policy and elections to the culture of politics itself, its instincts, conduct, style and remit of influence in the wider culture. This is detailed via the fortunes of organizations straddling the socio-political dimensions of affluence. Informed by the possibilities of a cultural history of politics, its concern (and discursive approach) is with the impression politics had of affluence as much as the impression affluence had on politics and with meanings besides causation and structure.[2]

Representations of affluence: the subtopia of Admass

Affluence registered variously on the landscape and imagination of post-war Britain. A useful example was the Retail Price Index's calculation which in 1956 reduced the weighting of food items, discarded candles and added dog food, washing machines, telephone rentals and second hand cars – as motor scooters, refrigerators and sherry were in 1963. Unlikely a location as it might seem, *The Times* reported in 1959 from West Germany on 'conditions of army life brought about by the increasing affluence of the private soldier': 'Naafi hire purchase helps the British soldier to indulge his taste for Italian shoes', 'Naafi shops bulge with refrigerators and washing machines' and 'sherry parties ... for newly married privates'. 'As usual the Americans are taking the lead, but ... the British Army will soon have to take notice' of measures like Europe's largest frozen food facility or a punishment barring use of private cars, which were owned by a third of US soldiers. Indeed army life in the form of national service (compulsory for men until 1960) was by some accounts, good training in the ethos of affluent Britain. In Sillitoe's *Saturday Night and Sunday Morning*, Arthur Seaton told: 'In the army it was: "F___ you Jack, I'm all right". Out of the army it was: "Every man for himself". It amounted to the same thing.' A 1960 Gallup Poll commissioned to show the popularity of sport in how Saturday afternoons were spent, was instead topped by 'went shopping' and 'did jobs about the house or garden'. 'Worked' was third followed by 'watched BBC TV *Grandstand*'.[3] 'BOOM', *Queen* magazine's September 1959 headline, referred not to the reigning nuclear threat, but the buoyancy of business, consumers and youth and toasted Britain as the world's leading champagne importer.[4]

Such developments were mostly represented critically by political and cultural elites; conceived in terms of moral and cultural loss besides material gain. 'Affluence' imputed their cultural poverty. For such critics, material progress did not necessarily mean a better quality of life – as dilemmas of choice, environmental consequences or heightened expectations attested. Articulated as negatively in other nations, 'affluence' in Britain supplemented and resonated with narratives of decline.[5]

Politicians of all shades regarded affluence as cloaking real economic achievement or as late-imperial ostentation.[6] Psychologists held 'affluence is synonymous with decadence' and character-weakening pleasures like pastel, soft toilet paper.[7] It was virtual and artificial – bought on hire-purchase for as little as one per cent down[8] and based on false needs contrived by advertising, as J.K. Galbraith's *The Affluent Society* argued. All told, it was argued, private affluence came at the expense of public squalor. The champagne cork cover of the Penguin edition of *The Affluent Society* symbolized less celebration than the superficial fizz of affluence, society's muddle-headedness under the influence of affluence. Working titles had been more explicit, *Why People are Poor* or *The Opulent Society*. 'Affluent' was settled upon as 'neither wholly neutral nor pejorative'. Galbraith concluded with the (aptly domestic) analogy that 'to furnish a barren room is one thing, to continue to crowd in furniture until the foundation buckles is another.'[9] Never having had so many goods, it was maintained, was not the same as never having had it so good.

Hoggart's *The Uses of Literacy* iterated the point, maintaining that social change whilst of quantitative benefit, involved a cultural impoverishment and the loss of much of value in working-class culture. The paperback wore a LS Lowry cover – both Hoggart and Lowry's pictures of the people nostalgically evoked vanishing landscapes.[10] Wilmott and Young's studies of Londoners' suburban dispersal, published by Penguin after 1961, highlighted similar themes – the loss of community and kinship. In another negative title, *The Affluent Sheep*, journalist Robert Millar reported British consumers unworthy of affluence; a largely apathetic flock under the sway of advertising and big business. Downbeat as contemporary usage of 'affluence' was, its hegemony was such that poverty was forgotten, as was the fact that for many Britons the symbolic goods of affluence were more an aspiration than achievement. [11] Even its critics contested affluence's qualities not existence. But real or imagined, the consequences of affluence were feared.

Far from anything desirable, affluence was a by-word for what seemed wrong in society. Attorney General Sir John Hobson told Hampstead Young Conservatives (YCs) early in 1964 that 'the affluent society was one of the main causes of Britain's rocketing post-war crime figures ... there is far greater temptation in an affluent society'. Bristol's Consumer Group reported that County Court actions for recovery of hire purchased goods more than doubled in the decade to 1962. By 1970, a perturbed Barbara Wooton paired affluence with permissiveness and acquisitiveness as *Contemporary Britain*'s value system. [12]

Material salvation and consumerism seemed to many Christians to be what Britons worshipped, if a nativity scene in a Workington store, showing the three kings offering up a washing machine, electric cooker and refrigerator, was any guide. In a 1966 Anglo-American study, sex, HP, loneliness, TV violence and laziness were amongst a litany of ills 'flourishing in the midst of affluence'. 'Affluence in the hands of fallen man', the Peterhouse-educated authors decided, was 'a double-edged sword.' [13]

Critics could point to deleterious by-products of affluence – its effluence for instance. Through the 1960s the volume of rubbish Britons threw out increased by 50 per cent. Reclamation was itself big business – contributing £90 million to Britain's (ailing) trade balance by 1970. Collection and disposal costs for local councils grew annually. It was not only rising consumption that increased this burden, but the expectation that private rubbish would be collected as a public service – a literal instance of private affluence and public squalor. John Green, deputy director of the Local Government Operational Research Unit, proposed consumers must be 're-educated' to dispose of more of their own rubbish or replace house-to-house collections with communal dumps. [14]

Civil society was littered with initiatives critical of yet contingent upon popular affluence – attempting to pick-up cultural, commercial, popular and professional standards. Keep Britain Tidy, which flourished from 1958, its voluntary fund-raising matched by the Housing and Local Government Ministry, campaigned with T-shirts, postal franks and novelty records. 'Our aim is to make litter-dropping socially "not on"', its Director explained. [15] Akin to Keep Britain Tidy was Mary Whitehouse's 'Clean-Up TV' campaign. A middle-class 'anti-permissive moral protest' for good taste, the 'nation's watchdog' of TV sex and violence, it suspected a new establishment were 'pro-dirt' and filthy plays. If affluence relaxed Victorian strictures, it simultaneously stirred traditional, Christian values. Secularization was striking in the 1960s because the churches had recruited strongly until then. Affluence emerged in an environment where prudish moral reflexes and resources remained. [16] The founding manifesto of Whitehouse's National Viewers and Listeners Association in 1964 attracted more than 300,000 signatures. [17] Also filling this spiritual void and posing a middle-class, 'romantic challenge to post-war affluence', Veldman argues, were fantasy literature (Tolkein,

C.S. Lewis), ecological thought from the Soil Association to anti-growth economics and the Campaign for Nuclear Disarmament (CND).[18]

The advertising-mass culture complex J.B. Priestley (a CND founder) developed, 'admass', admonished the consuming values of the day. The private, homely character of ordinary Britons Priestley celebrated as the essence of national identity, seemed threatened and un-resistant to the changes afoot in domestic life. 'If you didn't think too much, the consumers' England the Tories created seemed quite pleasant ... like living in America but under royal patronage', but, Priestley feared, 'in danger of turning into a *faceless* nation.' Marcuse's *One Dimensional Man* likewise remonstrated the conformism of mass culture and its consumers. Cliff hints Whitehouse and Marcuse's (dis)likes were similar, if not their remedies. Just like CND for Labour, Whitehouse pricked the moral instincts of Conservatism, responsible after all for loosening up TV regulation.[19]

In 1955's *Architectural Review*, Ian Nairn, coined 'subtopia' to express 'outrage' at the blighting of the landscape with homogenized 'suburban sprawl'. Advertisers were amongst the professions lashed, but it was concluded 'we are all offenders as well as victims.' Nairn's 1957 sequel pictured Los Angeles as the 'prophecy of doom' current 'progress' foretold. Subtopia became an 'indispensable ... contemporary verbal coinage' and spawned a play, *The Subtopians*, set in a Southern English town living room.[20] Clapson argues distaste for subtopia occurred 'within the context of a pervasive anti-suburban ethos in England', longstanding amongst literary and intellectual elites. 'Subtopia' rapidly became a derisive term for suburbia in general, rather than specific environmental transgressions.[21]

Other pressure groups – whose proliferation it is tempting to regard as taking up issues mainstream politics was not – propounded the idea that Britain was affluent, but used the term almost disparagingly, seeing and representing in it a loss of values or requiring improvement. Invariably, they bore a moral tone of middle class discrimination from *hoi polloi* tastes. The Consumers' Association (CA), post-war Britain's largest new voluntary body, and the quintessential organization of affluent Britain, was a product of consumer choice, but aimed to inform this. As presently constituted, affluence was no recipe for happiness. The *Good Food Guide* (a CA publication from 1963) intended to educate the (conservative) taste and etiquette of British diners. Editor Raymond Postgate sided the *Guide* (with E.P. Thompson against T.S. Ashton) in debates about the industrial revolution, contending it had driven food standards downwards.[22]

The Anti-Ugly Group from the Royal College of Art lead successful protests against Jack Cotton's proposed high-rise on Piccadilly Circus in 1959. Cotton, a Birmingham and New York property developer, had proposed the entire building front would be an advertising façade. So outraged was public opinion, that the Housing Minister 'called in' London County Council's planning permission.[23] This illustrates that affluence's critics were not always at odds with Britons and that Britons were not uncritical in their reception of affluence. Film historians Harper and Porter show the average 1950s cinema-goer was fairly discriminating – their enthusiasm for Hollywood was often to do with domestic producers not supplying preferred genres. Likewise, TV viewers rationed their viewing and tastes, liked the choice of ITV and its regionalism (compared to the BBC), but less so advert breaks. As Jackson's 1968 study (meekly) proposed, there were a range rather than one mass response to TV, sagely adding, 'any working-class has a fairly strong degree of scepticism about politicians or pop stars.'[24]

What is worth underscoring here is that not all criticisms of affluence were unfounded or transferred disgruntlement at imperial or comparative economic decline. 'Life is more than washing machines alone' could be an austere or idealistic belief. But pessimistic accounts – difficult not to relate to the declinist context in which affluence materialized – were imperious, marginalizing a more contested sense of affluence. Fears of the breakdown of traditional values or at what was replacing traditional working-class communality were based more on impression than evidence. Even in more judicious accounts, prison was used as an analogy for suburban lifers, escaping via pet ownership.[25] Rule's discussion of overtime contends critics overplayed the pace of change and degree to which it ruptured existing patterns of life. Clapson holds the 'textual hegemony' Young and Wilmott's studies enjoyed through the 1960s, sidelined research more positive about suburbanization, like Gans' studies of 'Levittowners' in the USA.[26]

More often, similarly critical accounts of US affluence provided cues for the pejorative sense of affluence sustained by British commentators. America was concomitant with affluence and British 'decline'. Its dynamism – where politicians 'ran' not 'stood', the JFK myth – contrasted with Britain's more dignified-*cum*-dilapidated state.[27] But America was also rich in critiques of affluence. In *Challenge to Affluence*, Gunnar Myrdal, argued an 'underclass' was excluded from work even during a boom by modern production's technical demands, thus capping the reach of affluence. David Riesman, analysed suburban lifestyle psychology, even 'suburban sadness', asking *Abundance for What?* Michael Harrington's *The Other America* revived poverty as an issue in the early 1960s, as it would shortly be rediscovered in Britain. Consumer campaigner Ralph Nader influenced British consumer activists after 1965 and Transport minister (1965–8) Barbara Castle, responsible for introducing seat belts and breathalyzers.[28]

Vance Packard's *The Hidden Persuaders*, *The Status Seekers* and *The Waste Makers* were also influential. Penguin editions were published between 1960 and 1963. For Winston Fletcher, an applicant for Labour's Director of Publicity in 1962 and later a leading advertising executive and President of the Institute of Practitioners in Advertising (IPA), *The Hidden Persuaders* was 'the most important book about advertising ever written'. *The Waste Makers* critiqued consumerism's 'throw-away spirit' and was dedicated (Galbraith-style) to those 'who have never confused the possession of goods with the good life.' Though as Horowitz notes, Packard's success was partly that his books aped the values they regretted: written in derivative journalism (Packard's trade) and with a knack for catchphrases that entered popular parlance. Even sympathetic reviewers, like Hoggart, wondered if they were reading a diagnosis or symptom of affluence's ills. Whilst not springs to political action like Harrington or Nader, *The Waste Makers* originated in an H.H. Wilson Princeton class. Wilson also taught Nader and documented the political manoeuvrings behind the advent of British commercial TV.[29]

Packard found a ready audience amongst advertising's critics. As with 'subtopia', longstanding elite suspicions helped make advertising a blame-magnet for contemporary culture. TV was key to advertising: its novelty meant advertising was qualitatively more apparent[30] and involved a higher proportion of professional agency productions than in the press. Expenditure was steady as a proportion of national income and consumer spending (never more than double 1948's post-war low, 1.4 per cent). Nor was it disproportionate internationally – in 1968 West Germany spent 2.9 per cent of GNP on advertising, the USA 2.1 per cent and the UK 1.2 per cent. As Labour's advertising commission pointed out, 'the USA has ... both a higher standard of living and a higher advertising ratio than Britain.'[31] A specific relationship between advertising expenditure and living standards might be elusive, but critics targeted its values more than cost.

Likewise, affluence was not to be measured in numbers alone, but by the perceived social priorities – acquisitiveness, individualism, domesticity – as much as the income with which it was acquired. Noteworthy then were the growth of the domestic pet food industry; Gallup's 1958 report on Britain's six million lawn mowers or the do-it-yourself 'cult', which seemed particularly metaphoric of broader changes.[32] An important process in making the politics of affluence was the ways in which such values and lifestyles were assumed to have or attributed with political qualities.

Cultivating affluence's politics

So, for example, Gaitskell sensed the standard of living having 'risen in ways that especially affect people's homes' meant 'people nowadays are more family and less community conscious ... wondering all the time whether they can do better for themselves alone'. He alleged such DIY values had 'created problems for the Labour Party.' The parochialism of suburban living or gardening were equated with similarly limited political ambitions. Potter's 1960 rant, *The Glittering Coffin* – another title alleging the pretence of affluent Britain – thought it 'not the most natural thing in the world to be a radical when surrounded by suburban hedgerows and new supermarkets.'[33]

The Galbraithian formula of the private detracting from the public was apparent in this investing of consumer goods and affluent living with political attributes. Hearth and home were regarded as a private, not public and political sphere – and affluent Britons seemed to be an ever more domestic, family-oriented species. The process of making the 'politics of things', by which goods took on social qualities, was closely linked to the 'sex of things'. As two pro-Labour economists argued the limits to consumer politics: 'in organisations dominated by women, the emphasis and direction of consumer activity is often focused on the household and away from deep involvement in the political and economic decision-making that shapes our society.'[34] Smith and Martin's case – a default instinct in Labour's unconscious – signals why it struggled to cultivate support amongst consumers and women. The left was more reluctant than Conservatism to accept that, 'the majority prefer to lead a full family life and cultivate their gardens' (as Crosland put it) or to regard these as anything other than empty, apolitical lives.[35] Yet it was precisely these domestic, private spheres – televiewing, shopping – that were key, everyday sensibilities in affluent Britain and as key as Westminster or Keynes to its politics.

Political and pressure groups, just as advertisers endeavoured to do, imbued lifestyles and goods with particular meanings. The CA was potent in associating consumer activity and commodities with qualities beyond the private sphere. Its tests on all manner of goods, from cars to zips, were used as ciphers for the condition of the nation's economy and skills of its consumers. Its focus on domestic goods raised their symbolic importance as epitomes of affluence higher than consumer spending on them. *The Economist* depicted Macmillan thanking a roomful of consumer durables after the 1959 election, as if they had turned out to vote. A correlation, between car ownership and voting Tory, was assumed to be a causal relationship. In *Room at the Top*, Joe Lampton's (Labour) father tells his son, 'If ah'd joined t'Con Club, ah'd be riding to work in my own car.' But any tenability this assumption might have had was precisely what affluence was eroding. Joe, then, could not share his 'father's pride, because the hypothetical car which he'd so highmindedly rejected was all too real to me.'[36]

That psephologists and politicians (and historians) commonly assumed social change was the motor of politics, was important to the ways affluence was conceived politically. Such assumptions (suburbia as a conservative environment, property ownership a conservative attribute) were vital components of mid-century political culture deciding how change was represented and voters addressed. As Jacobs argues, abundance has also been understood to exert 'a fundamentally depoliticizing and privatizing influence'. Consumerism was desiccating political passions – 'the sound of class war is drowned by the hum of the spin-dryer', Tory MP Charles Curran's obituary of Aneurin Bevan noted. Curran offered a variation on this theme in another soundbite, suggesting that as an 'escalator from *Coronation Street*', Britons were better off riding individual consumerism than re-distributive politics.[37] In *Must Labour Lose?*, pollster Mark Abrams argued social changes in the 1950s were undermining Labour's support.[38]

Richard Hamilton's 1967 study of French workers and affluence aimed 'to locate the social structural roots of political attitudes and voting behaviour.' But in 'account[ing] for the immunity of ... left voting to real changes in living standards', Hamilton came to 'question seriously the presumed effects of affluence' and reversed the connection, such that political behaviour was not contingent upon social factors, but 'depend[ed] rather on the ability of the left to ... mobilize ... workers.'[39] In Britain, sociological research (prompted by *Must Labour Lose?*, but emerging into 1968's debates about workers' revolutionary potential) concluded similarly that the 'affluent worker' was 'not so bourgeois after all'.[40] They might not have withstood much scrutiny, but assumptions about the social background to politics, unless affluence arrived pre-packaged with political meaning, were vital to how the political meaning of affluence was constructed – holding out the prospect of doubling living standards in 25 years as Butler and 1955's Conservative manifesto did or the left's proclivity to see embourgeoisement.[41]

More recently, historians have regarded electoral fortunes less as the upshot of social changes than of how effectively parties have approached voters and change. They have distinguished between Conservative and Labour articulation of post-war social change. Zweiniger-Bargielowska has argued the Conservative's ability to construct an alliance of support in opposition to rationing and controls was at the heart of their electoral recovery after 1945 and in securing an advantage amongst women voters. By contrast Labour struggled to acknowledge consumerism matters, articulate successfully to women voters or relate successfully to affluent voters in 1959.[42] But tempting as upending the idea of consensus is, evidence tempers too sharp a differentiation between the parties and such differences as can be identified should not be over-interpreted.

The left often took a dim view of affluence, rejecting material salvation. Capitalism was the devil that failed to live up to the left's expectations – producing not economic crisis, but the goods. The 1959 slogan 'Life's Better with the Conservatives' was illustrated with cars and TV, but for Labour 'better' (in 'Let's Have a Better Britain') did not mean more affluent. Delegates at Labour's 1964 Women's conference wondered 'what had become of the housewives of the past, who had known exactly what a shilling meant' and harangued 'gullible ... housewives buying a washing machine when they did not even have a plug to plug it in.' Frozen food 'was ... women's fault too' – however 'quick and easy to cook', its taste reminded one delegate of Charlie Chaplin stewing his boots in *The Gold Rush*. Later in the 1960s, this would be recognized not as an instance of an exploitable generation of consumers, lacking the disciplines of austerity, but as one of the pressures on time affluence meant for women in the labour force.[43]

Wrapping themselves in popular affluence, Conservatives might aver Britons had never had it so good, but they were less certain (than either Labour, contemporary and subsequent commentators) that it would profit them electorally or suited their vision for Britain. In the *Conservative Agents' Journal*, a month after the 1959 election, an agent wrote an article entitled 'Never had it so Good', telling how the slogan had been thrown back in their face by rail commuters disgruntled at fare increases. Middle class discontent with price rises and a fear that voters would attribute their new spending power to trade union strength also made them wary.[44] Besides this were anxieties about affluence's cultural and moral impact. Peter Goldman's 1961 *Principles of Conservatism* saw the present as 'an age darkened by materialism.' 'We have so much the dollar cannot buy,' one local councillor concluded of a US visit. It was stressed 'spiritual progress must keep pace with the material' and that it was Labour's appeal that was 'materialistic'.[45] Conservatives were no more at ease with cavalier materialism than Labour puritans, especially when in instances like the introduction of Premium Bonds, it seemed to be appealing to the wrong constituency and values. As one disgruntled Tory put it: 'it is not that ... section of the community which has always supported the Conservative Party that is now responsible for the increased millions spent on alcohol, tobacco and gambling ... that money is being provided by the poverty stricken followers of Mr. Frank Cousins.'[46]

Conservative ideology was evident here – sceptical less of change itself than that it represented progress. The 1959 Conservative manifesto celebrated TV and car ownership as 'fruits of our policies' and 'signs of the increasing enjoyment of leisure', but also asserted 'this represents a challenge to make the growth of leisure more purposeful and creative, especially for young people.'[47] This had been registered in Voluntary Service Overseas created in 1958. The Pilkington Committee, Consumer Council and economic planning after 1962 further evince Conservative unease at unregulated affluence.

Clear-cut differences are not easily found in the parties attitudes towards advertising. If, as Tunstall argued, 'the major political antagonism towards advertising comes from the Labour Party', nor did Tories entirely acquit it in publications like *Advertising on Trial*. A Banbury Young Conservative (YC) complained of 'Jonesmanship', 'pre-occupation with sex' and 'mass corruption by the sheer vulgarity of commercial advertisers.'[48] The main defence was mounted by the free-market Institute of Economic Affairs, marginal to mainstream Conservatism. Labour's enmity had limits too. George Darling (Board of Trade), told advertisers in 1964 that their voluntary regulation (the Advertising Standards Authority) was wanting, but that their help in boosting exports was very much wanted.[49]

Nor was it always apparent – as an alternative to the assumption that they were bound to benefit from growing consumerism – that Conservatives were better able to voice consumer issues. Goldman, director of the Conservative Political Centre, was shock loser in a 1962 by-election in the safe, Tory, Kent commuter suburb of Orpington – where their 1959 majority of almost 15,000 was overturned by the Liberals. According to Ian Gilmour, Goldman was 'cabinet material', but 'not good on the doorstep'. Liberal (the victors) and Conservative research also reported that the blame the local Tory establishment took for the 'lack of provision of shopping facilities to serve rapid population growth' was decisive.[50] Perversely, consumers did benefit from Conservatism's defeat, as Goldman left to become CA's new director in 1964.

Rather than local particularity, Orpington reveals a fragmented national pattern. Supportive or critical, a Conservative audience was more easily mobilized by consumer issues of this order. In Coventry, another booming city, the Labour Council's rebuilding of the shopping precinct did not bring Labour support. Coventrians apparently found, 'connections between the availability of consumer goods in bright new shops and the ideals of municipal socialism... difficult to make.' The Tories were not necessarily more in touch with consumers and could fall foul of consumer issues since its audience was more readily activated by them. A 1960 Gallup Poll for Michael Young's proposed consumers' party corroborated this. Of the 25 per cent in favour, more were Conservative than Labour voters from 1959 – suggesting they were most interested in consumer issues or dissatisfied with Conservative articulation of them.[51]

How social changes like popular consumerism registered politically was not predestined, but mediated by political choices. Both main parties' producer links – trade unions and business – complicated an unalloyed appeal to consumers. Debates on the 1949 Board of Trade report into Resale Price Maintenance (RPM, whereby manufacturers fixed retail prices) demonstrated this. The early 1960s saw what Mercer terms a 'cold war' between retailers and manufacturers. As the

Conservatives enjoyed close ties with both, this raised RPM's sensitivity. Abolition appealed to free marketers, to combat the Co-op's built-in (as producer and retailer) advantage and to the cohort of Tories who wished to broaden its appeal by detaching its close association with industry and appealing to consumers. The CA also favoured abolition and the prospect of lower prices, as did the majority of public opinion, although relatively divided and uninformed. Townswomen's Guilds and small shopkeepers, constituencies to which the Conservatives appealed, defended RPM.[52] The essential and close call was whether Britain was more a nation of shoppers than of certain manufacturers and shopkeepers? Findley argues that when abolition came in 1964 it cost the Tories the election, through the opposition of shopkeepers (amongst whom support for the Tories fell from 74.5 per cent in 1959 to 44.5 per cent a poll found), manufacturers and backbenchers.[53]

If affluence haunted the left, then Conservatism felt hostage to it – not an embarrassment of riches, but conscious its own fortunes were contingent upon popular affluence. Both could see something to suit their principles in affluence – advancing equality or individualism. But to the extent that parties imagined society in their own image, affluence left both uneasy. As the first *Guardian* editorial of the sixties remarked: 'Macmillan ... Gaitskell ... Butler ... Bevan – none of them seems to fit happily into the Britain of coffee bars ... commercial television ... and "Room at the Top"'[54]

Just as politics was irreducible to social determinants, so parties' relations with voters were scarcely intimate enough to allow more than a highly contingent relationship between electoral fortunes and political language to be deduced. Party utterances were rarely known to many voters in such detail as historians can excavate. Political historians would do well not to assume their interest in politics was widely shared – if the past was another country, so often was politics. If, as many contended, 'advertising has ... become one of the chief creators and communicators of social values', not to mention the power of TV, then politics faced stiff competition. 'Political apathy', a Leicester Tory admitted in 1956, was hardly a 'new phenomenon like Rock n' Roll or Premium Bonds'.[55] Given this, party articulation of affluence should be interpreted as evidence of the production of political discourse (of party culture, perceptions of the electorate) rather than of its reception (or electoral performance). Political language was most obviously used in forging discursive positions portraying each other. In 1955 the Conservatives cited Douglas Jay to depict Labour as bureaucratic. Labour retorted in 1956 that Premium Bonds, were 'a squalid raffle.' In 1964 the Tories posed as defenders of 'the "affluence" at which socialists sneer'; Labour that 'Britain could and should have had it a whole lot better' and that 'no nation ... was ever inspired to become great (or greater) with the venal philosophy of '"I'm all right, Jack".'[56]

Politics' boundaries, politics' new look

Affluence afforded concerns beyond the immediate standard of living and issues of the quality of life were conceived of increasing political pertinence. Labour revisionists were as animated by culture and leisure as wage and work. Roy

Jenkins' 1959 Penguin election special concluded with a chapter asked, 'Is Britain civilized?' Jenkins's Home Office tenure (1965–8) saw permissive personal and cultural legislation introduced. But the quality of life issues being raised by politics did not particularly reflect the popular mood. Since politics was immunized from social change, so its ability to influence it, even wielding governing power, was constrained. *New Society* found many Britons ambivalent (to issues like immigration or homosexuality, for example), such that it wondered if it was more apt to 'talk of the cautious sixties rather than the swinging sixties?'[57] Like affluence, permissiveness, divided more within than between both main parties and between political elite and popular 'interests' – whether the politician was 'bound to limp along behind the society he represents' as the *Guardian* reflected on the fifties or attempting to nurture attitudes, as the sixties might be viewed.[58]

As revisionists wished to shed Labour's cloth cap associations, Conservatives were concerned 'not to tie the Party's public image too closely to industry.' To this end, extensions of share ownership were mooted and a Recreation, Arts and Sport committee established.[59] Bow Tories considered leisure 'within the purview of the politician' as the 'post-industrial society' increased 'true leisure, as distinct from mere recuperation from work.' The state should 'safeguard' the 'high' arts (on which mass culture was 'parasitic') and be 'stimulatory ... not coercive'. This 'voluntary' aspect recognized affluence detached wishes and needs and that if the 'cultural pyramid was not likely to be pushed from the bottom ... it must be pulled from the top.' The aim was that 'the leisure society' as 'successor to the industrial society' should be 'a Tory development'. Bow Group preferences signal this meant 'highbrow' – 'serious music', ballet, the Hallé Orchestra and Kenneth Clark's ITV series, *What is Good Taste?* [60]

Concern with the quality of life was apparent in newer political formations induced by affluence. Not that ideas of British decline were confounded. Revisionists like Crosland debated 'What's Wrong with Britain?', chiding the 'middle-aged conservatism, parochial and complacent ... settled over the country'. Like revisionism, the New Left espoused cultural and moral interests and took decline as read. Dworkin argues 'discourses of decline' underpinned much of its output – from Anderson, Nairn, Hall and Gilroy. CND, also avowing moral over material issues, saw in unilateralism the potential for British world leadership, something the post-imperial Cold War world had divested it of.[61]

The CA also understood Britain as in decline. Young, its founder, twinned affluence and decline, arguing in 1967 that whilst 'the consumer movement has been expanding, the country of which it is part has been declining.' 'The prospect of Europe' Young explained in 1962, would lift the 'myth-laden fog' shrouding Britain. Likewise, the consumer politics of 1960's *The Chipped White Cups of Dover*, would arrest decline – discerning consumers would improve production quality and competitiveness and a consumer 'interest' would counter those of business and the unions and the inflationary wage-price spiral.[62]

CA's monthly, *Which?*, gave a gloomy audit of the quality, reliability and use-value of the array of new consumer goods, the underhand methods of credit deals, salespeople and advertising and the skills of consumers themselves – the perils of prosperity not of scarcity. With more than half a million members by the later

1960s, CA was powerful and critical in representing Britain and Britons as affluent. But it struggled to reach beyond a middle-class, conservative audience – tribute to affluence's distribution and to how a definitive consumer 'interest' was as elusive as other political identities. Members more often treated it instrumentally, as a value-for-money guide, than a social movement. This reined in the broader aspirations of activists and leaders – mainly liberal-left figures, disgruntled by Labour's attitude (Young, Crosland) or disgruntled with party (Goldman). But CA still realized Young's prediction that 'politics will become less … the politics of production and more … the politics of consumption'. If unable to trump the main parties, CA raised consumerism's political salience for them, making consumerism and goods the stuff of politics – not least in legislation it lobbied for, like the 1968 Trades Descriptions Act, that had brought 38,000 cases by 1970, mainly against second-hand car dealers [63]

The Co-Op also experienced affluence in terms of consumerism and politics, but unlike the flourishing CA, was dying of consumption – its new patterns and tastes. One quarter of Britons were Co-op members and almost half a million employees in 1962. This formidable presence could not disguise trading problems: between 1957 and 1961 Co-op retail trade increased by 6 per cent, that of the multiples (like Marks and Spencer) by 37 per cent; its almost 12 per cent market share in 1957 had fallen to under 8 per cent by 1970.[64] It had been an early innovator in self-service supermarkets – 90 per cent of self-service stores in Britain in 1950 were Co-ops, but by 1960 less than half and by 1968 one quarter. Politics was a poor recruiter for the Co-op – only one of 204 respondents to a 1958 survey of new Manchester members had joined for political reasons – a third joined for the 'divi'. Traditions of cash-only trading meant a smaller proportion of Co-op trade than that of the multiples was undertaken on H-P. Affluence seemed at odds with self-help Co-Op style. As a Coventry Co-Operator put it to Richard Crossman in 1955: 'What are we to do when our members draw the "divi" to spend at M&S round the corner?'[65]

Yet as a three-year commission reported in 1958, many of the Co-Op's difficulties were self-inflicted rather than the result of social change. Crosland, its secretary, rehearsed arguments he later applied to Labour and Britain. 'Conservatism and complacency' were impeding modernization and profess-ionalization. In Liverpool-Cheshire, the commission reported, 'the buildings, the atmosphere, and … managers … dreary and uninspiring.' Societies resisted amalg-amation. There were 37 societies within a seven-mile radius of Huddersfield – many sustaining stores of 'Edwardian majesty'. 'What the Co-ops need', CA's director ventured, 'is a Dr Beeching.'[66] Other evidence, of the difficulties the Council of Industrial Design experienced in trying to bring good, modern furniture design and marketing to the Co-Op shopfloor, suggested a strong institutional resistance.[67] Local management was 'largely inbred', boards of directors elected from (and by) 'a restricted circle' of employees, guildswomen and socialists, much less the average shopper-member. Less than half a per cent of members attended society meetings, 1.41 per cent voted in board elections in 1960 – by all comparisons, the 'lowest extremity of membership apathy.'[68]

Most damning was the sense that the Co-Op was at odds with the modern consumer. Its retail outlets were ill-sited for the demographic changes of post-war Britain and were often of too poor a quality for 'the consumer, working class as well as middle class', who was 'more exacting than her predecessor of even two decades ago' and would 'no longer endure blowzy buildings and dowdy display.' Its clothing lines had 'a certain dowdiness' and were 'not always "smart" enough to appeal to the younger generation'. The commission was bluntly told: 'women in Southampton don't buy their clothes [at the Co-op] because they are made of cheap, shoddy material and not modern in style and at a dear price.'[69] The picture was not uniformly bleak. The Co-Op in Britain's second new town, Crawley, impressed the Commission. *Which?* tests were mostly positive about Co-Op products. But the '"image" of a Co-operative shop in the public mind' as 'built in the early 1900s, still operating counter-service ... window display old-fashioned ... exterior ... badly in need of paint ... interior frowsy' was hard to budge and not entirely unfounded.[70]

Within Co-Op circles the sense was that the Commission proposals 'modif[ied] the traditional conception of Co-operative democratic control in the pursuit of business efficiency.' Critics (like the Co-op executive) and proponents agreed it amounted to 'bouquets for capitalism'.[71] But the Co-op contrived change in such unforgiving terms regarding bright lights, modern goods and efficient managers as ills – as to struggle to make progress with it. This discloses much about the left's difficulties with affluence, but also, according to Halsey and Ostergaard's survey, about a 'secular drift towards apathy'. They found the Rochdale Pioneers meant nothing to 89 per cent of members, whose time was spent not in rival voluntary organizations, but gardening or watching TV. Most saw the Co-op instrumentally, as a shop not social movement, upholding their conclusion that 'active public participation is characteristic only of a small minority.'[72]

Also at the confluence of social and political life were the Young Conservatives. Formed after the war, it branded itself, Cold War style, the 'largest voluntary political youth movement in the free world', though 'the end of ideology' might have been as apposite. With 2,500 branches in 1954 and even as membership halved to 80,000 in 1963 and further as the 1960s progressed, it easily out-performed Labour.[73] This comparative advantage was located in its social acumen, as even opponents attested. Raphael Samuel recalled, the Conservatives 'enjoyed a near exclusive command of social glamour' as 'the party of people with big houses ... who had cars ... carried themselves with poise' and were 'a magnet to the socially aspiring.' By contrast Labour was judged to 'lack the necessary social skills for the successful organisation of whist drives, dances.'[74]

The YC's social presence exhibited longstanding Conservative talent for building social organizations (Primrose and Housewives' League, Ratepayers' Associations), blending (deliberately apolitically on occasions) into local society. In locations like Banbury, close ties to the Chamber of Commerce and such innocuous pastures as the Sweet Pea Society, made Conservatism an unofficial part of everyday, private life, whereas Labour seemed interferingly political. Mind, its seven YC branches were a vital canvassing resource.[75]

Its social reputation was central to the YC's appeal. Organized with great budgets and skill, YC life seemed one long round of endless balls. Diaries brimmed with dances, car rallies and treasure hunts, factory visits or Miss YC contests (judged by Keith Joseph amongst others in 1964, on criteria like 'poise and deportment', 'dress-sense' and quizzed on The Beatles). Critics mocked it as a 'middle class marriage bureau', but the agenda evidently engaged members – women particularly, a 1964 *Times* profile noted.[76]

YCs did not have a monopoly on social allure. As the Bow Group's *Crossbow* featured a semi-clad woman in a 1967 discussion of the YC's public image (Chesham YC's chair had infamously strip-teased in 1965), so a recruiting section of the Young Communist's *Challenge* did early in 1968. Social besides pacific reasons attracted some CND joiners. By the mid-1950s, in a sure sign of affluence, miners held the car rallies long popular with YCs.[77] Even as membership shrank, YCs denounced Labour's attacks on 'pirate' radio ('free' radio, broadcasting what the BBC would not, not living by plunder) and Tony Benn, the minister responsible, as 'the Mrs Grundy of our time.' Juliet Gardiner snappily analysed women's magazines and fashion and *Impact* resisted the sorts of moral censure of drugs, permissiveness and campus protests that elder Conservatives often revelled in.[78]

Falling membership lead YCs to ask whether 'in an affluent age people can find enough social entertainment without joining the Young Conservatives'. Iain Macleod's 1965 Report attempted to revive its social prominence. University expansion also depleted it, but most reasoned the YCs 'simply cannot compete on their terms with the professional pastime makers.' It was concluded 'customary … thinking that the pill should be thickly sugared' now meant 'the political work of the Young Conservatives [was] being hidden from the view of potential members'. A 1965 joiner, interested in drama and banning arms sales to South Africa, was told: 'we talk about everything here except politics'. He thought the YCs had 'stepped into dad's clothes' and YC women 'too frivolous … constantly talking about … getting married and watching the telly'. Rather than a 'social club catering only for political lightweights', it now aimed to 'concentrate more on involvement in the local community', such as marching for Oxfam or tidying local gardens. YCs became more political than social party animals then, in the belief 'political organisations will only ever interest a small per centage of the community'.[79]

Politics – formal, associational political outlooks – seemed to be struggling to maintain a presence, due to the difficulties in convening a party of interests from the fragmentation of interests and in competition with the plethora of pressure groups affluence gave rise to. More than apathy this would account for both the relative success but limits to CA, the condition of the Co-Op and YCs and declining party membership from the early 1950s.[80]

One of the more obvious impressions affluence had on politics was that in striving to be accessible and relevant, party politics was itself increasingly domestically-minded and conducted as marketing or 'pop'. Referencing The Beatles was *de rigueur* in the 1964 election.[81] Political scientists saw Heath depicted 'as if advertising a new cigarette'; journalists regarded Macleod as 'the best TV anchorman in the business ... he can smile on cue.' Wilson associated with *Coronation Street*, *Z-Cars* and comedian Jimmy Tarbuck during the 1966 campaign. 'The phrase "the trivialization" of politics began to be heard ... mostly from the politicians', Levin reported; and the £2½ million bet on the 1966 election evinced politics was a pastime like the horses.[82]

The YC's glossy *Impact*, replacing *Rightway* in 1964, pitched itself: '*Impact* provides a unique opportunity of reaching thousands of today's most important spenders – the affluent 16–24 age group.' The *Daily Herald* closed in 1964, because (hinting at limits to affluence's distribution) of the advertising profile of its chiefly working-class audience. Even Labour, whose ads increasingly targeted floating not confirmed voters, was minded to 'cut down on the amount of money we spend in the *Herald*.'[83] If advertising rescued newspapers from undue political interest, it now subjected them to commercial forces. *Reynolds News* survived, briefly, by morphing into the 'more "magaziney"' *Sunday Citizen* in 1962. Though the Co-op lamented the 'concessions to public taste' required for a day when 'people tend to put slippers on their minds as well as on their feet'.[84]

Politics had rarely been propagated in such explicitly commercial language. 'The Product – Politics' was regarded as a consumer durable. Abrams' Research Services Ltd. told in 1956 how, 'Labour faces problems similar to those of a commercial organisation', needing to know 'the reactions of consumers to our product.' By 1963, a more discriminating approach recognized, 'Labour ... is not a mass-consumer product bought over the counter once or twice a week' like 'tinned salmon or biscuits'. A 'reminder advertising schedule', low-key but regular, was thus less appropriate than 'a short, sharp, concentrated' campaign using 'larger spaces' which 'targets stand a better-than-average chance of seeing.' This also acknowledged that 'however cynical, apathetic, naïve or stupid people are', voting was an act 'they attach great importance to.'[85]

Politicians with formal connections to advertising/PR firms doubled between 1959 and 1963. They were more evident amongst Tories, like MPs Ian MacArthur, an Associate Director of US advertisers J Walter Thompson or Geoffrey Johnson Smith, who sat on the IPA's parliamentary committee.[86] Despite such networks, the emotional culture of Conservatism was uneasy with the 'culture of sensation' such media seemed to fuel within and beyond politics and of which they would fall foul in the Profumo scandal. Differentiating between the parties' attitudes to new techniques is blurred. Taylor argues Conservative dealings with pollsters proved both their 'scepticism of the consequences of social change to be well founded as well as exposing the limits of opinion research.' Labour's instinctive misgivings – 'Labour had no need to resort to Hidden Persuaders of their own', as one MP put it – did not prevent a professional publicity director being appointed in 1962. This was not quite the novelty diehards or modernizers believed. Francis Williams, as Attlee's PR advisor in the 1940s was known, not as a hidden persuader, but as Labour's '*éminence grise*'.[87]

A Conservative PR consultant argued, 'in a world of OMO ... and hard-selling TV ads, the meagre resources of a local association may seem ... swamped', but the local and even domestic remained important despite (indeed because of) the professional, national trends in politics.[88] One 'political *sequelae*' of the 'consumption society', was commonly understood to be that 'the comfortable, box-equipped living room keeps the average voter away from the hustings', ensuring they saw 'only th[e] mass consumer political products.'[89] CND's street politics was one reaction to this. But TV also brought voters and politicians together in the living room. Conservatives advised broadcasters, besides avoiding shiftiness and sharply-coloured clothes, to: 'remember you are not addressing a meeting', but the voter 'in his own living room ... speak and behave as if you were also in that living room ... because that's virtually where you are.'[90]

In other ways, little changed. Trenaman and McQuail found TV politics had increased public knowledge, but not voting behaviour. TV did not prevent politicians being satirized (a booming TV genre) or heckled, since audiences could not be ticketed. In *The Loneliness of the Long Distance Runner* Colin Smith turned the TV volume down and became a ventriloquist for the pictures: 'we did it to some Tory telling us about how good his government was going to be if we kept on voting for them ... hands lifting to twitch moustaches and touching their buttonholes ... so that you could see they didn't mean a word.' In Tony Richardson's 1962 film version, the Tory broadcaster is heard, to derision from his settee audience, telling how Britons had the 'self-discipline' demanded by 'the challenge of prosperity', but lacking in 'our American cousins in affluence'. More often, political TV meant the channel was switched or TV turned off.[91]

That affluence privileged the private/domestic over the public/imperial was variously apparent politically. Macmillan remarked upon securing Polaris missiles from Kennedy in 1962, that Britain was, 'keeping up with the Joneses'.[92] Dress sense, Elizabeth Wilson remembers, was an effective means of distinguishing YCs – in 'cavalry twills and paisley cravats' – from other activists. For 1962's 'Brighter Premises' competition, Labour constituencies were advised by leading designer Misha Black. A pamphlet offered tips on gardening, interior and exterior decoration and if not corporate branding, then at least a Co-Op Gloss and Emulsion colour paint chart. Conservatives were also conscious, 'people today expect ... efficient presentation and modern packaging.' Enoch Powell asked 'how can a party with its paint peeling off' and 'often ... antiquated, dilapidated, ill-furnished' premises, 'persuade people that it is selling them a prosperous future?'[93]

Conclusion

It is tempting to conclude that in looking for a prosperous future, Britons were looking less to party politics and that the politics of decline has obscured the decline of politics. But, the purpose of this chapter has been to suggest, albeit speculatively, the potential of a more cultural history of post-war politics. This approach generates new themes (notably, the domestic/private and political coalescing – a theme extended through the 1960s), but does not reject existing themes. Above all, it delimits politics as discrete in important ways from the impact of affluence. This explains both a sense of relative stability and of the limits to its popular relevance and influence. If formal political authority was waning, civic networks and 'social capital' were not. Affluence excited this elite-popular tension, if at the same time blurring, reconfiguring politics' boundaries. The socio-political sensibilities of affluent Britain are more richly described and obtained by this approach and in this way affluence makes a case for re-interpreting post-war British politics.

Notes

[1] Obelkevich, James: 'Consumption' in Catterall, Peter and Obelkevich, James (eds): *Understanding Post-War British Society*, Routledge, London, 1994, p. 141.

[2] Francis, Martin: 'Tears, Tantrums and Bared Teeth: The Emotional Economy of Three Conservative Prime Ministers, 1951–1963', *Journal of British Studies,* vol. 41 no. 3 (2002), pp. 354–87.

[3] Hopkins, Harry: *The New Look: A Social History of the Forties and Fifties in Britain*, Secker and Warburg, London, 1963, p. 310; Millar, Robert: *The Affluent Sheep*, Longman, London, 1963, pp. 19, 193; *The Times*, 30 April 1959; Sillitoe, Alan: *Saturday Night and Sunday Morning*, Pan, London, 1960, p. 114.

[4] *Queen*, 15 September 1959; Samuel, Raphael: 'The Quality of Life' in *Where?*, Fabian Tract 320, Fabian Society, London, 1959, p. 35.

[5] See later discussion of the USA; also McCormack, Gavan: *The Emptiness of Japanese Affluence*, M.E. Sharpe, Armonk NY, 2001.

[6] See (amongst many), Darling, George: *Advertising and the Labour Government*, Institute of Practitioners in Advertising, London, 1964, p. 9.

[7] Phillips, Robert: 'After Affluence?', *Twentieth Century,* nos. 1039, 1040 (double issue, 1968–9), p. 42.

[8] Montgomery, John: *The Fifties*, Allen and Unwin, London, 1966, p. 275.

[9] Galbraith, John Kenneth: *The Affluent Society*, Penguin, Harmondsworth, (1958) 1971, p. 284; and *A Life in Our Times*, Houghton Mifflin, Boston, 1981, p. 339.

[10] Hoggart, Richard: *The Uses of Literacy*, Penguin, Harmondsworth, 1958; 'Pictures of the People', *The Observer*, 15 November 1959. Waters, Chris: 'Representations of Everyday Life: LS Lowry and the Landscape of Memory in Post–war Britain', *Representations* no. 65 (Winter 1999).

[11] Wilmott, Peter and Young, Michael: *Family and Kinship in East London*, Penguin, Harmondsworth, 1962; Millar, *Affluent Sheep* op. cit.; Silburn, Richard and Coates, Ken: *Poverty: The Forgotten Englishmen*, Penguin, Harmondsworth, 1970. Such as Kerr, Madeline: *The People of Ship Street*, Routledge and Kegan Paul, London, 1958.

[12] *The Times*, 5 February 1964; *Bristol Evening Post*, 5 November 1962; Wootton, Barbara: *Contemporary Britain*, Allen and Unwin, London, 1971.

[13] Montgomery, *Fifties*, op. cit., p. 276; Fuller, Reginald H, and Rice, Brian K.: *Christianity and the Affluent Society*, Hodder and Stoughton, London, 1966, ch. 7, pp. 95, 170.

[14] Southworth, June: 'The Wastemakers', *Focus* (UK Consumer Council, April 1970), pp. 2–7; 'Rubbish', *Consumer News* (Research Institute of Consumer Affairs, RICA), 24 May 1965.

[15] Southworth, 'Wastemakers', op. cit., p. 4.

[16] Brown, Callum: *The Death of Christian Britain: Understanding Secularisation 1800–2000*, Routledge, New York, 2001, ch. 8; Fryer, Peter: *Mrs Grundy: Studies in English Prudery*, Corgi, London, 1965.

[17] Not to be confused with the educational broadcasting group of the same name fronted by Peter Laslett or the left-wing Screen Viewers Council that protested the syrupy, violent content of TV. Cliff, Dallas: 'Religion, Morality and the Middle Class' in King, Roger and Nugent, Neill (eds): *Respectable Rebels: Middle Class Campaigns in Britain in the 1970s*, Hodder and Stoughton, London, 1979, pp. 128, 149.

[18] Veldman, Meredith: *Fantasy, the Bomb and Greening of Britain, 1945–80*, Cambridge University Press, Cambridge, 1994.

[19] Priestley J.B.: 'What Is Wrong With Britain?', in Montgomery, *Fifties*, op. cit., pp. 286, 364; Cliff, 'Religion', op. cit., pp. 138–9; Marcuse, Herbert: *One Dimensional Man*, Routledge, London, 1964.

[20] Nairn, Ian: *Outrage* and *Counter-Attack Against Subtopia*, Architectural Press, London 1955 and 1957; Hopkins, *New Look*, op. cit., p. 477; Frisby, Terence: *The Subtopians*, Samuel French, London, 1964.

[21] Clapson, Mark: *Invincible Green Suburbs, Brave New Towns: Social Change and Urban Dispersal in Post–war England*, Manchester University Press, Manchester 1998, pp. 5–7.

[22] *Good Food Guide* (1965–6), pp. 10–11.

[23] RICA: *Town Planning – The Consumer's Environment*, London, 1965, p. 25; Lewis, Peter: *The 50s*, Book Club, London, 1978, pp. 36, 200.

[24] Harper, Sue and Porter, Vincent: 'Throbbing Hearts and Smart Repartee: The Reception of American Films in 1950s Britain' *Media History* vol. 4 no. 2 (1998). O'Sullivan, Tim: 'TV Memories and Cultures of Viewing, 1950–65' in Corner, John (ed): *Popular Television in Britain: Studies in Cultural History*, BFI, London, 1991, pp. 169–74; Jackson, Brian: *Working Class Community*, Routledge and Kegan Paul, London, 1968, p. 165.

[25] Hopkins, *New Look*, op. cit., p. 332 – after a section on how suburban life was breaking down sexual segregation in working-class culture and before noting the million dogs enrolled in the Tailwagger's Club.

[26] Rule, John: 'Time, Affluence and Private Leisure: The British Working Class in the 1950s and 1960s', *Labour History Review*, vol. 66 no. 2 (2001), pp. 223–42; Clapson, *Invincible Green Suburbs*, op. cit., pp. 66–7, 198. Also Procter, Ian: 'The Privatisation of Working-Class Life: A Dissenting View', *British Journal of Sociology*, vol. 41 no. 2 (1990), pp. 157–80.

[27] Snowman, Daniel: *Britain and America: An Interpretation of Their Culture, 1945–75*, Harper and Row, New York, 1977, p. 266.

[28] Myrdal, Gunnar: *Challenge to Affluence*, Gollancz, London, 1963; Riesman, David *Abundance For What?*, Doubleday, New York, 1964, pp. 226–308; Harrington, Michael *The Other America*, Penguin, Harmondsworth, 1963. Castle on Nader, *Focus* (September 1966), p. 18. For a recent critique see Goff, Brian and Fleischer, Arthur A III: *Spoiled Rotten: Affluence, Anxiety and Social Decay in America*, Westview Press, Boulder CO, 1999; Putnam, Robert D.: *Bowling Alone: The Collapse and Revival of American Community*, Simon and Schuster, New York, 2000 is central to the debate.

[29] Horowitz, Daniel: *Vance Packard and American Social Criticism*, University of North Carolina Press, Chapel Hill, 1994, pp. 152 (Fletcher), 86, 123, 178, 202; Packard, Vance: *The Waste-Makers*, Longman, London, 1960, p. 5; Wilson, H.H.: *Pressure Group*, Rutgers University Press, New Brunswick, 1961.

[30] See Laski, Marghanita: 'Sacred and Profane', *Twentieth Century* (February 1959); Tunstall, Jeremy: *The Advertising Man in London Advertising Agencies*, Chapman and Hall, London, 1964, pp. 232–9.

31 Labour Party: *Advertising – Green Paper* (March 1972), pp. 18, 21; Labour Party: *Report of a Commission of Enquiry into Advertising*, 1966, p. 26; Offer, Avner: 'The Mask of Intimacy: Advertising and the Quality of Life' in Offer, Avner (ed): *In Pursuit of the Quality of Life*, Oxford University Press, Oxford, 1996, pp. 211–55.

32 Hopkins, *New Look*, op. cit., pp. 332–3. See Browne, Jen: 'Decisions in DIY: Women, Home Improvements and Advertising in Post-war Britain' in Andrews, Maggie and Talbot Mary M.: *All the World and Her Husband: Women in Twentieth-Century Consumer Culture*, Cassell, London, 2000, pp. 131–45.

33 Potter, Dennis: *The Glittering Coffin*, Gollancz, London, 1960, p. v; Hugh Gaitskell in Sampson, Anthony: *Anatomy of Britain*, Hodder and Stoughton, London, 1962, pp. 108–9.

34 Martin, John and Smith, George: *The Consumer Interest*, Pall Mall Press, London, 1968, p. 255.

35 Crosland, C.A.R.: *Socialism Now*, Jonathan Cape, London, 1973, p. 89. For an example see Hobsbawm, Eric: *Interesting Times*, Allen Lane, London, 2002, pp. 221–2.

36 Braine, John: *Room at the Top*, Eyre and Spottiswoode, London, (1957) 1971, p. 102.

37 Jacobs, Meg: 'The Politics of Plenty in the 20th Century United States' in Daunton, Martin and Hilton, Matthew (eds): *The Politics of Consumption*, Berg, Oxford, 2001, p. 223.

38 Curran, *London Evening News*, 7 July 1960; *Crossbow* (October–December 1967), p. 32; Abrams, Mark and Rose, Richard: *Must Labour Lose?*, Penguin, London, 1960.

39 Hamilton, Richard F.: *Affluence and the French Worker in the Fourth Republic*, Princeton University Press, Princeton NJ, 1967, pp. 3, 156–79, 275 296.

40 Goldthorpe, John, and Lockwood, David, 'Not So Bourgeois After All', *New Society*, 18 October 1962, pp. 18–19; and with Bechofer, Frank, Platt, Jennifer: *The Affluent Worker*, 3 vols., Cambridge University Press, Cambridge, 1968–9, vol. 3, pp. 22–9.

41 Craig, F.W.S. (ed): *British General Election Manifestos, 1918–74*, Macmillan, London, 1975, p. 189.

42 Zweiniger-Bargielowska, Ina: 'Rationing, Austerity and the Conservative Party Recovery After 1945', *Historical Journal*, vol. 37, no. 1 (1994), pp. 173–97; Hinton, James: 'Militant Housewives: The British Housewives' League and the Attlee Government', *History Workshop Journal*, no. 38 (1994), pp. 129–56; Black, Amy and Brooke, Stephen, 'The Labour Party, Women and the Problem of Gender, 1951–66', *Journal of British Studies*, vol. 36 no. 4 (1997), pp. 419–52; Laing, Stuart: *Representations of Working-Class Life, 1957–64*, Macmillan, Basingstoke, 1986, p. 13. Clapson, Mark: 'Suburbia and Party Politics', *History Today* (September 2001), pp. 16–18.

43 Labour Party: *Labour Women's Conference*, (1964), p. 47; Scott, Rosemary: *The Female Consumer*, Halsted Press, London, 1976, pp. 102–3.

44 'Never Had it so Good', *Conservative Agents' Journal*, no. 457 (December 1959), p. 210; Turner, John: 'A Land Fit For Tories to Live In: The Political Ecology of the British Conservative Party, 1944–94', *Contemporary European History*, vol. 4, no. 2 (1995), pp. 198–203.

45 Goldman, Peter: *Some Principles of Conservatism*, Conservative Political Centre (CPC), London, 1961, p. 2; Cooke, Margaret: 'Impressions of America', *Swinton College Journal;* vol. 3, no. 2 (1954), p. 32; Butler, R.A.B.: 'Conservatism today and tomorrow', *Swinton College Journal*, vol. 1, no. 1 (1951), pp. 4, 8.

46 Letter, *Conservative Agents' Journal*, no. 425 (November 1956), p. 314.

47 Ramsden, John: *The Making of Conservative Party Policy: The Conservative Party Research Department Since 1929*, Longman, London, 1980, p. 205.

[48]   Tunstall, *Advertising Man*, op. cit., p. 235; Haynes, M: *Advertising on Trial: The Case for the Consumer*, Bow Group, London, 1961; Wilkins, Nancy: 'Anything Goes', *Impact* (February 1965), pp. 26–7.

[49]   Amongst Ralph Harris and Arthur Seldon's titles see, *Advertising in a Free Society*, IEA, London, 1959. Darling, *Advertising*, op. cit., pp. 6–7, 9–11.

[50]   Young, Ken: 'Orpington and the "Liberal Revival"' in Cook, Chris and Ramsden, John (eds): *By-elections in British Politics*, UCL Press, London, 1997, p. 171; Gilmour, Ian and Garnett, Mark: *Whatever Happened to the Tories?*, Fourth Estate, London 1997, p. 170.

[51]   Lancaster, Bill and Mason, Anthony: 'Society and Politics in 20th Century Coventry' in Lancaster, Bill and Mason, Anthony (eds): *Life and Labour in a Twentieth Century City: The Experience of Coventry*, Cryfield Press, Coventry, 1986, p. 358. Young, Michael: *The Chipped White Cups of Dover: A Discussion of the Possibility of a New Progressive Party*, Unit 2, London, 1960, p. 20.

[52]   *Economist*, 24 June 1950, p. 1375; Mercer, Helen: *Constructing a Competitive Order: The Hidden History of British Antitrust Policies*, Cambridge University Press, Cambridge, 1995, ch. 8, pp. 164–69; Millar, *Affluent Sheep*, op. cit., pp. 117–8.

[53]   Findley, Richard: 'The Conservative Party and Defeat: The Significance of Resale Price Maintenance for the General Election of 1964', *Twentieth Century British History*, vol. 12, no. 3 (2001), pp. 327–53. *Daily Telegraph* 16 March 1964.

[54]   *Guardian*, 1 January 1960.

[55]   Williams, Lord Francis: *The American Invasion*, Anthony Blond, London, 1962, p. 21; *Conservative Agents' Journal*, no. 425 (November 1956), p. 313.

[56]   Craig, *Manifestos*, op. cit., pp. 192, 257; Conservative Party: *Prosperity with a Purpose*, London, 1964, p. 26; Wilson in Levin, Bernard: *The Pendulum Years: Britain in the Sixties*, Cape, London, 1970, p. 15.

[57]   Jenkins, Roy: *The Labour Case*, Penguin, Harmondsworth, 1959; Barker, Paul and Hanvey, John: 'Facing Two Ways: Between the 60s and 70s', *New Society*, 27 November 1969, pp. 847–50.

[58]   Thompson, Peter: '"Labour's Gannex Conscience?": Politics and Popular Attitudes in the Permissive Society', in Coopey, Richard, Fielding, Steve and Tiratsoo, Nick (eds): *The Wilson Governments, 1964–70*, Pinter, London, 1993, pp. 136–50; *Guardian*, 1 January 1960. On the liberal elite-illiberal public see also, Hansen, Randall: *Immigration and Citizenship in Post-War Britain*, Oxford University Press, Oxford, 2000.

[59]   Ramsden, *Conservative Party Policy* op. cit., pp. 200–1; Conservative Party Archive (CPA), Bodleian Library: CRD 2/52/13, Policy Committee on Recreation, the Arts and Sport.

[60]   Fairbairn, David: 'An Approach to Leisure: Conservatism in a Post-Industrial Society' in Bow Group: *Principles in Practice*, CPC, London 1961, pp. 87, 94, 98; Carless, R. and Brewster, Pat: *Patronage and the Arts*, Bow Group, CPC Series 205, London, 1959, pp. 68–73.

[61]   Crosland, C.A.R.: 'What is Wrong with Britain?', *The Listener*, 5 July 1962; Crosland, C.A.R.: 'On the Left Again' *Encounter* (October 1960). Dworkin, Dennis: 'Cultural Marxism Revisited: The New Left and British Decline', paper to the North American Conference on British Studies, Baltimore, 2002.

[62]   'Proceedings of Consumer Assembly', London, 3 November 1967, p. 38; CA Archive, A67; *Daily Mail*, 23 November 1962; Young, *Chipped Cups*, op. cit., pp. 19–20.

[63]   Young, *Chipped Cups*, op. cit., p. 19; Labour Party: *Labour Women's Conference*, 1970, p. 27; Black, Lawrence: '*Which?*craft in Post-war Britain: The Consumers' Association and the Politics of Affluence', *Albion*, vol. 36, no. 1 (2004).

64 RICA: *British Co-Operatives*, London, 1964, pp. 5, 14, 26; Crosland, C.A.R.: *A Critical Commentary on Co-operative Progress*, Co-op Party, Manchester, 1971, p. 1.

65 Bonner, Arnold: *British Co-operation*, Co-Op Union, Manchester, 1970, pp. 247–48. CWS Market Research Department: *Survey Among New Members of the Manchester and Salford Society* (February 1958), pp. 3, 7 in Hugh Gaitskell Papers, University College London, C309, 6. Hodgkinson, George: *Sent to Coventry*, Pergamon, Oxford, 1970, p. xxvii.

66 C.A.R. Crosland Papers, British Library of Political and Economic Science: Vis/Carc/12,3 in 14/1. Casper Brook in RICA, *British Co-operatives*, op. cit., p. 31.

67 With it should be added the traditional tastes of shoppers, Woodham, Jonathan: 'An episode in post-utility design management: the Council of Industrial Design and the Co-operative Wholesale Society' in Attfield Judy (ed): *Utility Reassessed*, Manchester University Press, Manchester, 1999, pp. 39–57.

68 RICA, *British Co-operatives*, op. cit., p. 27. Halsey, A.H. and Ostergaard, G.N.: *Power in Co-operatives: The Internal Politics of British Retail Societies*, Blackwell, Oxford, 1965, pp. 74, 76, ch. 3.

69 *Co-Operative Independent Commission Report*: Co-op Union, Manchester, 1958, pp. 44–50. Gaitskell Papers: C309, 3E, Wilson to Gaitskell (Commission Chair), 31 January 1956.

70 Crosland Papers: Vis/Carc/19. RICA: *British Co-Operatives*, op. cit., p. 34. *Independent Commission Report*, op. cit., p. 45.

71 Perkins, Alfred: 'First Impressions of the Commission's Report', *The Bulletin* (Co-Op Educational Secretaries Association), July 1958, p. 11. 'Bouquets for Capitalism', *Sunday Times*, 13 July 1958.

72 Halsey and Ostergaard: *Power in Co-operatives*, op. cit., pp. 70, 78, 94–5.

73 'Young Conservatives History' (c. 1954); CPA, CCO506/17/2: 'Notes for Compilation of Pocket Politics' (c. 1955).

74 Ellis, Catherine: 'The Younger Generation: The Labour Party and the 1959 Youth Commission', *Journal of British Studies*, vol. 41, no. 2 (2002), pp. 199–231; Samuel, Raphael: 'The Lost World of British Communism', *New Left Review*, no. 154 (1985), p. 10; Holroyd-Doveton, John: *Young Conservatives*, Pentland, Bishop Auckland, 1996, pp. 52, 153; Birch, Alan: *Small Town Politics*, Oxford University Press, Oxford, 1959, pp. 76–7.

75 Stacey, Margaret: *Tradition and Change: A Study of Banbury*, Oxford University Press, Oxford, 1960, pp. 50, 54. Berrington, Hugh: 'Banbury', in Butler, David: *The British General Election of 1955*, Frank Cass, London, 1969, p. 132.

76 CPA, CCO506/17/1: 'Miss YC 1964'. *The Times*, 18 September 1964.

77 *Crossbow* (October–December 1967). She resigned but was re-elected – see Fryer, *Mrs Grundy*, op. cit., p. 283. *Challenge* (February 1968), p. 11. CND member in *New Statesman*, quoted in *IRIS News* (January 1962), p. 7. Crosland C.A.R: *The Future of Socialism*, Jonathan Cape, London, 1956, p. 285.

78 Morgan, Henry: 'Pop Pirates', *Impact* (Spring 1966), pp. 14–15; (Winter 1967), p. 14. Gardiner, Juliet: 'I Took My Flower to a YC Ball But Nobody Asked Me to Frug', *Impact* (Winter 1968), p. 13.

79 CPA, CCO 506/23: Macleod Report. '65 Generation YC', *Impact* (February 1965), p. 25; 'Community Service', *Impact* (Summer 1967), p. 17. On 'politicization' see Evans, Timothy: *Conservative Radicalism: A Sociology of Conservative Party Youth Structures and Libertarianism, 1970–92*, Berghahn, Oxford, 1996.

80 For political science literature on this see Curtice John: 'Political Sociology, 1945–92' in Catterall, Obelkevich, *Post-War British Society* op. cit., pp. 31–2.

[81] Newton, Francis: 'Pop Goes the Artist', *New Statesman*, 6 July 1962, p. 25. Butler, David and King, Anthony: *The British General Election of 1964*, Macmillan, London, 1965, p. 39.

[82] Rose, Richard: 'One Man's Election', *Twentieth Century*, no. 1043 (1970), p. 10; Booker, Christopher: *The Neophiliacs: A Study of the Revolution in English Life in the Fifties and Sixties*, Collins, London, 1969, pp. 279–80; Levin, *The Pendulum Years*, op. cit., p. 339.

[83] *Impact* (Spring 1964), p. 2. Mark Abrams Papers, Churchill College, Cambridge: Box 67, 'The Past, Present and Future of Labour Party Advertising', 9 December 1963.

[84] Co-Op: *Press Power for the People*, Co-Op Union, Manchester, 1962, p. 16–17. See also Hirsch, Fred and Gordon, David: *Newspaper Money: Fleet Street and the Search for the Affluent Reader*, Hutchinson, London, 1975.

[85] Dowson, Graham (Marketing Director, Rank Organisation): 'The Product – Politics', *Impact* (Summer 1967). Labour Party Research Department, Re. 47, 'Memo on Proposed Pilot Scheme for a Public Opinion Survey' (April 1956). 'The Past, Present and Future of Labour Party Advertising' op. cit.

[86] Waller, Ian: 'Pressure Groups: MPs and P.R.O.', *Encounter* (August 1962), pp. 7–11. MacArthur, Ian: 'The Adman's Reply', *Impact* (Autumn 1965). 'Tory Funds', *Guardian*, 29 January 1964.

[87] Taylor, Andrew: 'Speaking to Democracy: The Conservative Party and Mass Opinion From the 1920s to 1950s' in Ball, S. and Holliday, I. (eds): *Mass Conservatism*, Frank Cass, London, 2002, pp. 90–5. Pearson, John and Turner, Graham: *The Persuasion Industry,* Eyre and Spottiswood, London, 1965, p. 258. Williams, Lord Francis: *Nothing so Strange*, Cassell, London, 1970, p. 217. See Francis, 'Tears', op. cit.

[88] Watts, Reginald: 'Bringing the Party Up To Date', *Crossbow* (October–December 1967), p. 34.

[89] Abrams, Mark: 'Why the Parties Advertise', *New Society*, 6 June 1963; David Tribe, 'Galloping Consumption', *Twentieth Century*, nos. 1039, 1040 (1968–9), p. 7.

[90] Abrams Papers: Box 58, Conservative Party central office, *Talking on TV and Radio* (1963), pp. 6–10, 24.

[91] Trenaman, Joseph and McQuail, Denis: *Television and the Political Image*, Methuen, London, 1961; Sillitoe, Alan: *Loneliness of the Long-distance Runner*, Longman, London, 1966, p. 170 (Sillitoe was the film's screenwriter); Black, Peter, *The Mirror in the Corner*, Hutchinson, London 1972, pp. 53–4.

[92] *Foreign Relations of the United States*, vol. XIII, 20 December 1962, p. 1109.

[93] Wilson, Elizabeth: 'All the Rage', *New Socialist* (November/December 1983), p. 26; Labour Party: *Brighter Party Premises*, London, 1962; Powell, Enoch: 'The Party with the Paint Peeling Off!', *Conservative Agents' Journal*, no. 513 (February 1965), pp. 12–13.

CHAPTER 7

Affluence, Relative Decline and the Treasury

*Hugh Pemberton**

In economic terms, the 1950s and early 1960s present us with a paradox. On the one hand one has the concept of 'affluent Britain' – almost unprecedented rates of economic growth, full employment, rising real incomes, and rising consumption of goods and services (such as regular holidays) that had hitherto been the province of an affluent minority. On the other hand we find mounting concern regarding Britain's poor economic performance – in fact the very concept of Britain's long-term relative economic decline was virtually invented during these years – with fear of decline prompted by a range of new international statistics demonstrating Britain's relatively poor (and deteriorating) economic performance. This paradox has led to a particular fascination with the period amongst both economic historians and political economists.

As the years 1948 to 1973 have receded they have come increasingly to be seen as a 'golden age' of economic development. With this shift has come an increasing emphasis on the experience of 'affluence' rather than on Britain's economic 'decline': in other words the focus is increasingly on absolute growth rather than on relative decline.[1] As this shift has taken place there has been a redefinition of the meaning of 'decline', with fears of economic decline in the 1950s and 1960s increasingly ascribed to a 'declinist' mindset. In this view, 'declinism' is seen as an ideology and thus as a political construct.[2] The debate becomes centred not on an apparently objective truth, but on subjective ideas, and on the ways in which these ideas have motivated both policy makers and public opinion.[3] In this way, the concept of 'declinism' can be a powerful one; for it can highlight a potential gap between the assumptions of contemporary economic commentators and policy makers and the reality of Britain's actual economic performance. There is a danger here, of course, of taking an overly Panglossian view of British economic performance – of seeing it as all for the best in the best of all possible worlds – and of underestimating the potential of relative decline to have real economic effects and to generate justified fears for the future in the minds of contemporary policy-makers. This concern is the starting point for this chapter.

The chapter has three purposes. The first, is to describe some of the economic changes experienced by Britain in the 1950s. The second is to consider the extent to which fears of decline were justified. The third is to assess the impact of such fears, whether real or imagined, on economic policy and, in doing so, to reassess the traditional view of the Treasury in this period. The chapter will argue that too little importance has been attached to the rapid increase in British living standards at this time and that 'declinism' in the 1950s overstated the problem of Britain's relative economic decline since the war. Nevertheless, the chapter suggests that relative decline should not be airbrushed out of the picture, that the superior performance of many of Britain's continental competitors was not simply a product of post-war reconstruction and that it had the potential to become more than simple 'catch-up and convergence', that real shortcomings in the prevailing Keynesian policy making framework were already apparent by the beginning of the 1960s, and that the Treasury made a serious attempt to address these problems.

A 'golden age'

In 1962, Worswick and Ady noted that 'Measured by almost any of the available indicators, the fifties was a decade of economic progress for the British economy.'[4] By 1950, a vigorous post-war recovery had restored consumption to pre-war levels and the ensuing decade saw continuing growth. Gross domestic product, for example, virtually doubled; up from £13,162m in 1950 to £25,681m in 1960.[5] Even when adjusted for inflation, the growth in GDP was marked (see Figure 7.1), with an average annual rate of growth across the decade of 2.73 per cent per annum. Feeding this growth was a marked increase in investment, as Figure 7.1 clearly shows, and in productivity.[6] This against a background of low unemployment which, although pockets of regional unemployment persisted,

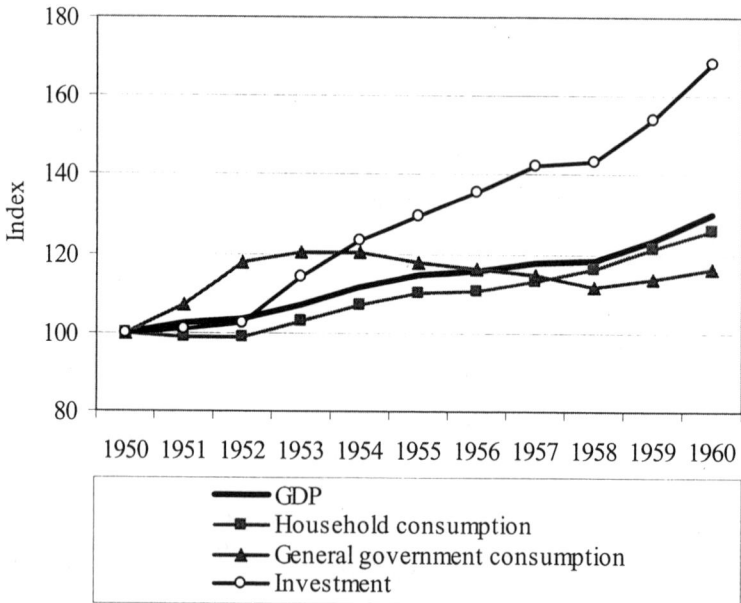

Figure 7.1 UK growth indices, 1950–60 (at 1995 market prices, 1950=100)
Source: Own calculations using data from ONS Statbase, November 2002.

averaged around 1.6 per cent of the workforce during the 1950s and in some years fell as low as 1.1 per cent.[7] Impressively, despite such low levels of unemployment, inflation too was relatively low. Although there were steep rises in prices in 1951 and 1952 as a consequence of the Korean war, between 1953 and 1960, the average annual rate of inflation was just under 4 per cent. Viewed from the perspective of the quarter century following the OPEC I oil price rise in 1973 (during which time the average rate of inflation was virtually 10 per cent), the price inflation of the 1950s looks pretty benign. One should not underestimate, however, the worries that were generated in the minds of those who had lived through the deflationary inter-war period, and the (soon to be justified) fear that the use of demand management to exploit a Phillips-type trade-off between employment and inflation in a fully (perhaps over-fully) employed economy had the potential to generate a relentless increase in the level of inflation over time.

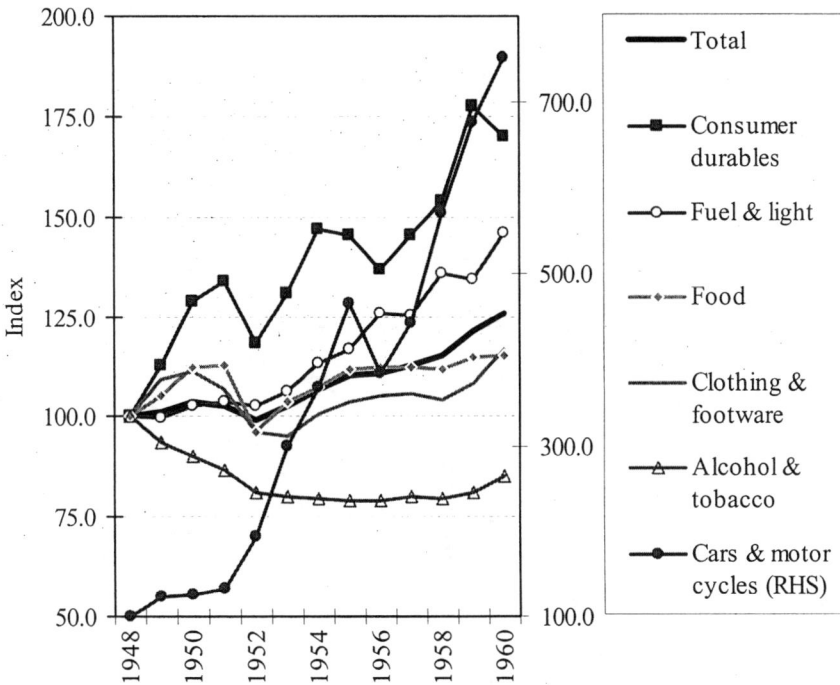

Figure 7.2 Real consumer spending (selected items), 1948–60 (1948=100)
Source: *Economic Trends* (London: Central Statistical Office), various years.

This growth in national output, and the fact that the average growth in wages exceeded that in prices, translated into an increase in consumers' disposable income (up by over a quarter in real terms) across the decade (see Figure 7.1). This fed into rising consumer expenditure and rising living standards and, as the 1950s progressed, Britons were increasingly able to purchase goods that had hitherto been beyond their reach. The most spectacular growth in consumption can be found in sales of consumer durables such as washing machines, refrigerators, televisions (up by 70 per cent in real terms between 1948 and 1960). Sales of cars and motor bikes were even more impressive, up by a staggering 750 per cent over the same period (see Figure 7.2). With this growth in consumers' real incomes and purchasing power came a recognition of consumers' interests and the period saw the formation of consumers' associations and legislation against restrictive trade practices.[8]

Relative decline and 'declinism'

Paradoxically, however, despite Britain's absolute (and unprecedented) increase in the size of its economy and in the wealth and purchasing power of its citizens, as the decade wore on it became increasingly apparent that the British economy was performing poorly in comparison with its competitors. By the end of the decade, new comparative statistics were available from post-war institutions such as the United Nations, GATT, the IMF and the OEEC.[9] These revealed that, whilst the performance of the post-war British economy was historically very good, and particularly good in relation to the extremely lacklustre inter-war period, it was markedly less good than her European competitors. For example, new comparative national income statistics from both the UN and the OEEC showed Britain slipping down the league table. Similar data showed a relative decline in UK industrial production (see Figure 7.3) – seen at the time as fundamental to the health of any

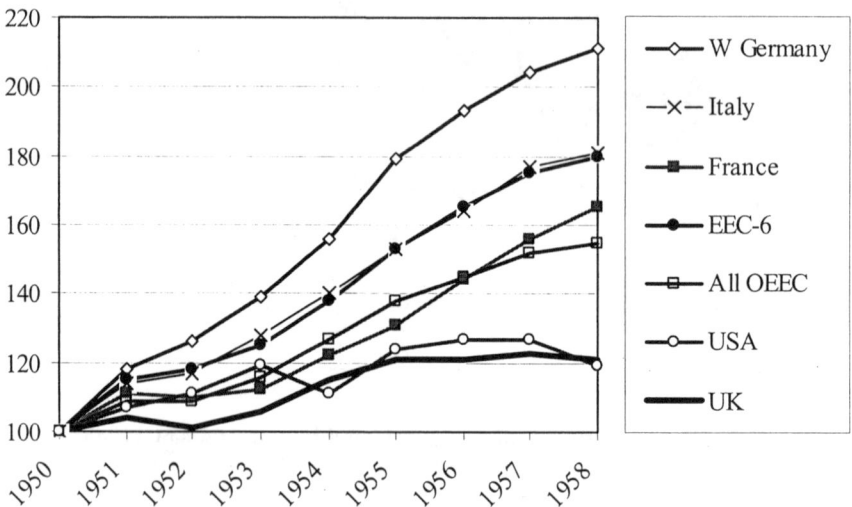

Figure 7.3 Indices of industrial production, selected countries, 1950–8
Source: OEEC, *General Statistics, 1959*
(Paris: Organisation for European Economic Co-operation).

economy. This relatively poor growth of industrial production was reflected in comparative figures for industrial productivity growth (see Table 7.1).

Table 7.1 Productivity growth (GNP per employee year), 1950–9

	1950–59	1954–59
UK	1.7	1.6
France	3.6	3.3
W. Germany	4.5	3.6
Italy	4.7	3.8
Netherlands	3.4	2.9
Sweden	2.8	3.0
Japan	6.1	7.6
Canada	2.0	1.8
USA	2.2	2.2

Source: National Institute Economic Review, no. 16 (July 1961), p. 24.

These relatively poor levels of growth in industrial production and relatively poor industrial productivity compared to other OECD countries made themselves felt in two ways. Firstly, they translated in a decline in the relative superiority of

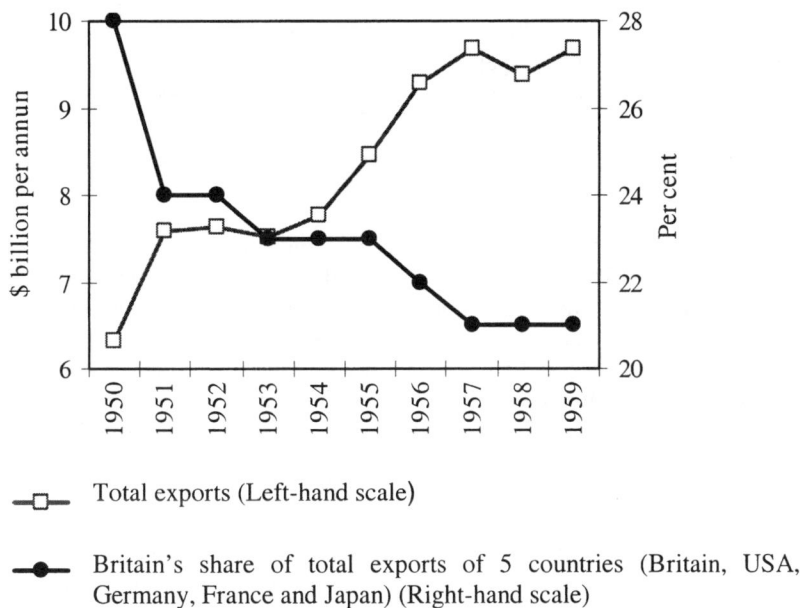

—□— Total exports (Left-hand scale)

—●— Britain's share of total exports of 5 countries (Britain, USA, Germany, France and Japan) (Right-hand scale)

Figure 7.4 Britain's export performance in the 1950s
Source: Worswick, G.D.N. and Ady, P.H., *The British Economy in the Nineteen-fifties*, Oxford, Oxford University Press, 1962, p. 117.

British living standards. Secondly, they had implications for international competitiveness. Indeed, Britain's export performance epitomized the paradox of absolute growth in conjunction with relative decline. British exports grew strongly in the 1950s, a reflection of the rapid expansion of world trade. Britain's share of world trade, however, declined quite markedly according to the best data available at the time (see Figure 7.4).

The question was did this relative decline in both living standards and share of world trade matter in the context of absolute growth on both measures? As Tomlinson has pointed out, it would have been grossly unrealistic for Britain to sustain the share of world trade that it enjoyed at the end of the Second World War, artificially bolstered as it was by the virtual economic destruction of significant competitors such as Germany.[10] 'Decline' in this context was inevitable. It was not, however, without repercussions.

Table 7.2 Top seven countries by GDP, selected years

	1938	% of UK	1950	% of UK	1960	% of UK	1973	% of UK
1	USA	309	USA	461	USA	478	USA	528
2	UK	100	UK	100	UK	100	Japan	177
3	Germany	75	France	61	Germany	95	Germany	111
4	France	63	Germany	59	Japan	81	UK	100
5	Japan	60	Italy	47	France	72	France	95
6	Italy	49	Japan	46	Italy	63	Italy	83
7	Canada	18	Canada	30	Canada	35	Canada	46

Source: Derived from Maddison, A., *Dynamic Forces in Capitalist Development*, 1991, pp.198–9.

As can be seen in Table 7.2, when compared simply in terms of total GDP – i.e. in terms of the size of the economy rather than in terms of relative living standards – the UK's economy was slipping further behind the USA during the 1950s. A number of other countries were rapidly closing the gap between the size of their economies and that of Britain. With higher rates of growth in these competitor economies, this situation could be expected to continue to worsen – and indeed by the beginning of the 1970s the Britain economy had become smaller than those of both Japan and Germany, and was soon to be overtaken by France. As Alec Cairncross noted: 'The fundamental change was a loss of economic power: commercial power, bargaining power, financial power.'[11] In short, Britain was becoming a much less significant actor in the world economy, with much less influence on its behaviour. If nothing else, this was a psychological shock. It was more than this, however, for Britain continued to see itself as a world power with world-wide strategic commitments. Increasingly, the UK found that it was having to 'punch above its weight'. This had both economic and political implications. Economically, it became increasingly difficult to sustain Britain's military, intelligence, and diplomatic expenditure commitments.[12] Politically, it required a painful series of strategic adjustments as Britain was forced gradually to accept the consequences of its reduced power.[13]

Moreover, the question arises whether Britain's relative decline was simply due to the catching-up process as the continentals reconstructed their economies after the war, or whether there were other factors at work. This is (and was) a difficult judgement to make. Tomlinson notes that the superior rates of economic growth of many of Britain's continental competitors was largely based on the much greater scope for continental Europe to shift labour out of agriculture into more productive occupations.[14] Nevertheless, the most salient facts are that by the end of the 1950s it was clear that Britain would, in terms of the size of its economy, shortly be overtaken by Germany and Japan and thus cede its number two league table position, and that by 1961 both France and Germany had overtaken Britain in income per head for the first time since the industrial revolution.[15] In other words, Britain was not just being caught up by its competitors in the 1950s and 1960s, by the 1960s it was being overtaken. This had obvious psychological consequences in terms of 'declinism', and led to widespread finger-pointing but, as we shall see, it could also be seen as an objective economic problem rather than just a subjective issue of perceptions.

Relative decline and the Treasury

A persistent theme advanced in the late-1950s and early-1960s by critics of the government's economic policy was the disjuncture between the actual nature of Britain's state and the state it seemed to require if it was to meet the challenge of relative decline. In a civil service still dominated by the Northcote-Trevelyan reforms of 1854, it was asserted, the British state was conceived in purely negative terms, to be restricted as far as was possible to 'night-watchman' functions, whereas it was widely accepted that relative decline could only be reversed by an active state. Probably the most coruscating such attack was that of Thomas Balogh in his accusation that the civil service, and particularly the Treasury, was 'The Apotheosis of the Dilettante' – dominated by classically educated Oxbridge 'generalists' rather than trained economists, obsessed with a 'candle-ends' approach to public expenditure, totally inadequate to the task of managing and developing a modern economy, and thus a major obstruction to faster growth.[16] The Treasury, argued Balogh, was institutionally predisposed to favour the status quo rather than embracing change, and suffered from a chronic 'lack of imagination, initiative and capacity for planning ahead'.[17] In Balogh's view, the 'lack of competent and well-trained economists would have serious implications on our prospects at a juncture when British relative strength is ebbing away and needs utmost efforts for its reinforcements'.[18] Balogh's attack was fairly extreme, but the general thrust of his argument was a relatively common one at the time and it was to shape Labour's decision in 1964 to remove responsibility for long-term planning from the Treasury and hand it over to the new Department of Economic Affairs.

Such attacks on the Treasury were supplemented by criticisms that its management of demand during the 1950s had helped to retard Britain's rate of economic growth – with the Treasury's response to up- and down-swings in demand tending to be both too late and too great, the result being that 'stabilization' policy was anything but.[19] Such problems were exacerbated by operational difficulties with economic forecasting (see Roger Middleton's chapter below) and by political pressures to increase demand in advance of elections – this latter problem being a particular issue in 1959, as the Treasury later privately acknowledged.[20] The result, it was argued, was a pattern of 'stop and go' that was exacerbating the business cycle – excessive upswings leading to wage inflation, increased imports and thus inevitably, in a situation of fixed exchange rates, to a sterling crisis, which would then precipitate a panicky deflationary response and consequently an excessive downswing during which production, and productive capacity, would be unnecessarily and permanently lost.[21]

Criticisms of the Treasury in terms the malign effect on growth of both a 'generalist' mandarinate and its poor management of demand in the 1950s were trenchant at the time and continued to shape perceptions for many years thereafter.[22] Recently, however, we have started to revise our views of the Treasury at this time. Booth, for example, whilst also criticizing the malign role of Treasury generalists during the 1950s, has emphasized the contribution to economic policy of Keynesian economists in the Treasury's Economic Section.[23] Peden's recent history of the Treasury has dispelled many myths, emphasizing the Treasury's pragmatism and ability to adapt to changing circumstances, though acknowledging the fact that it has always operated within canons of economic belief that emphasize the need for expenditure control and the advantages of a free-market.[24] In respect of the late-1950s and early-1960s, Ringe and Rollings argue it is a mistake to see the Treasury as part of the problem rather than the solution and argue that by 1961 the Treasury was not just interested in promoting higher economic growth but had become desperate to achieve it.[25] We seem, therefore, to be moving towards a more nuanced account of the Treasury's approach to economic policy during this period.

The acknowledgement by the Treasury of deficiencies in its stabilization policy during the 1950s, and the perception that urgent changes in policy were needed if growth was to be increased, did not mean that its officials necessarily agreed that growth would be improved by further raising the level of demand. Both Frank Lee (its Permanent Secretary), Thomas Padmore (head of its Home Finance section) and some economists in its Economic Section, for example, were initially impressed by the proposals advanced by the academic economist Frank Paish on macro-economic management. They were attracted by the idea of operating the economy at a lower pressure of demand and allowing unemployment to rise above 2 per cent, the level then regarded as the trigger for reflation.[26] Having a margin of excess capacity, it was argued, would reduce inflationary pressures and force industry to export. It would also shake out inefficiently used labour, improve industrial efficiency and increase international competitiveness. By doing so, it was hoped, the rate of economic growth would not be reduced by the lower level of demand but increased.

Others in the Treasury thought differently. An alternative analysis was that advanced by the government's chief economic adviser and head of the Treasury's Economic Section, Robert Hall. This was to maintain fairly high demand to avoid the wasteful effects of unproductive capacity and unemployment but to address stop-go by improving the government's stabilization policy via new instruments of economic control.[27] Improving the government's ability to manage the level of demand in the economy, Hall argued, would raise the trend rate of growth by avoiding the debilitating effects of excessive 'stops' in the 'stop-go' cycle. This, however, raised the problem of inflation since the already relatively high level of demand would be further increased in this scenario. To cope with this, Hall proposed that an incomes policy be adopted to ensure that wage rises were not allowed to outstrip the growth of productivity.[28]

Such contrasting views produced a vigorous debate within the Treasury during 1960–61 regarding the relationship between stabilization policy and growth, about how growth might be raised, and about how to deal with the potential inflation that this might cause. Such a debate is indicative of the Treasury's growing concern that Britain's rate of economic growth was unacceptably low. By 1960, growth was 'getting in to the air' in the Treasury, as Hall put it.[29] This was not just the product of internal debate but the result of the wider change in the intellectual climate. This had been wrought by a growing interest amongst academic economists in the means by which faster growth might be attained; by the advocacy of financial journalists and other 'ersatz economists' (as Roger Middleton terms them in his chapter below); by the efforts of pressure groups such as Political and Economic Planning to promote new policies on growth; by a perception in industry that output could be higher (epitomized by discussions at the Federation of British Industry (FBI) annual conference in November 1960); by discussions in tripartite institutions such as the Economic Planning Board (EPB) and National Joint Advisory Council (NJAC); and by the input of think tanks such as the National Institute for Economic and Social Research.[30] Lee, for example, attended the FBI's November 1960 conference and had returned with his views on the potential of British industry to improve both output and productivity radically altered, and fired with an enthusiasm to harness industry's apparent concern with efficiency to the ends of higher growth.[31]

In January 1960 Lee, with the support of the Economic Section, began a reappraisal of the Treasury's policy on growth. To drive this process, Lee set up a secret inter-departmental committee of Permanent Secretaries to look at how growth might be raised.[32] Clearly, if the Treasury had been guilty of neglecting the question of growth during the 1950s this was now no longer the case.[33] The impact of Lee's initiative was soon evident. Almost immediately, a Treasury memorandum for the Economic Planning Board acknowledged Britain's poor relative growth and recognized the adverse impact on industrial confidence of the government's management of demand.[34] That growth was now becoming the subject of debate in existing (if somewhat moribund) tripartite institutions and the discussions in the EPB, NJAC and National Producction Advisory Council for Industry suggested to Otto Clarke (whose dominant personality meant he was a powerful influence on Treasury thinking) and to his deputy Peter Vinter that there was fertile ground upon which to sow Treasury seed.[35] Clarke suggested that a submission on growth be prepared for the Chancellor. As a consequence of this, Lee created a working party of officials from the Treasury, the Ministry of Labour and the Board of Trade to report to his *ad hoc* committee of permanent secretaries. Its terms of reference were to prepare a submission to ministers on economic growth and on the possibility of tripartite action to increase it.[36]

The result was a report by officials to the Chancellor and cabinet in July 1961 entitled 'Economic Growth and National Efficiency'. This clearly set out the Treasury's position on growth and the economic policies that it thought might improve it.[37] The report began by acknowledging that it was the product of mounting public concern that Britain's rate of growth was inadequate in comparison with rates of growth being achieved by its continental competitors. In this sense, the report can be seen as a product of late-1950s declinism. In other respects, however, the Treasury's analysis differed significantly from the analyses and economic policy panaceas emanating from other quarters. Firstly, it emphasized what it saw as the achievements of post-war economic policy – the elimination of unemployment and an historically impressive economic growth record – and the reasonably flexible way in which the economy seemed to be adapting to changing patterns of demand and to changing production possibilities. Secondly, whilst acknowledging that Britain's rate of growth of national income per head was lower than that of many countries, the report queried whether the country's relative position had deteriorated during the 1950s to the extent often claimed. Most significantly, it located the 'growth problem' not in fears about Britain's economic performance in the recent past, but in the future. In this sense, the Treasury was acknowledging that Britain's relative economic decline during the past decade had been an almost inevitable product of continental reconstruction, whilst expressing its concern at the effects, particularly the political effects and the repercussions for sterling, that would result if this relative decline continued. This was not 'declinism', but it did indicate concern that the British economy needed to perform better in the future.

The report's title was significant. In one sense the Treasury's analysis was firmly located in a contemporary zeitgeist in which higher growth was seen as a necessity. In another sense, however, the report's evocation of the Edwardian concept of 'national efficiency' suggested that the Treasury's policy prescription amounted to 'shiny new bottles for the good old cough mixtures', as Otto Clarke put it.[38] This, however, was a trifle harsh and an example of Clarke at his most cynical. Whilst there were certainly familiar elements in its policy proposals, the report proposed a radical break with past Treasury policy – for it concluded that higher growth would not be achieved without a much greater degree of government intervention in the economy to correct a range of market failures.

The report was highly sceptical that a breakthrough into higher growth could be achieved simply by raising the level of demand in the economy as suggested, for example, by Sir Roy Harrod in his voluminous correspondence with the prime minister.[39] In the view of the Treasury, raising demand alone would simply run into bottlenecks on the supply-side, increase costs and prices, suck in imports and lead to an inevitable balance of payments crisis.[40] The report therefore suggested a war on two fronts. Firstly, it proposed that the rate of growth of home demand should in the short-term be set at a level rather below that currently prevailing – the theory being that this would encourage manufacturers to seek overseas markets and thus eliminate the chronic balance of payments problems that had dogged the country since the war. Secondly, it proposed a longer-term programme of concerted government action on the supply-side to promote 'national efficiency'.[41] In effect, therefore, it was proposing short-term restrictions in the growth of consumption whilst simultaneously embarking on a radical and wide-ranging overhaul of the supply-side of the economy – the theory being that in the medium- to longer-term supply side reform would allow demand to rise again, and to rise more swiftly. In the longer-term, therefore, the Treasury hoped that its twin track approach would deliver higher economic growth.

To this end, the report suggested a thorough review of supply-side policy. It argued, for example, that the economy needed to be re-balanced via more and better micro-economic policies to encourage higher and better directed investment, whilst ensuring allocational efficiency by leaving investment decisions as far as possible to the operation of the free market. Tariff protections should be removed the better to expose British industry and commerce to international competitive forces. A more active labour market policy was required and to this end the Treasury proposed a series of major policy reviews in the field of taxation, pensions, and conditions of work that would aim to encourage more people, particularly women to enter the labour force. It also suggested that regional policy and housing policy should be used to encourage the mobility of labour. In addition, it proposed that the government should use education and training policy to raise the volume of trained and technically qualified workers, and that action should also be taken to increase the quality of training provided both by the government and by employers. The government should implement an incomes policy that would ensure that the growth of wages did not outstrip that of productivity – thus ensuring that higher growth did not trigger inflation and reduce Britain's international competitiveness. The government should also, suggested the Treasury, bring an end to restrictive practices on *both* sides of industry: via action on business in respect of monopolies, the abolition of resale price maintenance, and the removal of anachronistic restrictions on shop opening hours; and by endeavouring to find a means to remove restrictive labour practices in industry and the professions and other action to create a more flexible work force. The tax system should be reviewed and if necessary reformed to ensure that it did nothing overly to restrict, and preferably promoted, both growth and productive efficiency. Public expenditure decisions should henceforth be made in the context of improvements in growth and national efficiency. Most importantly, it suggested that the government should seek to emulate French and German 'success in instilling an attitude of mind in business which has confidence in future growth and the development of the economy'.[42] The report concluded by emphasizing the need to develop a coherent policy 'mounted on a wide front', one which ministers should recognize would require the adoption of a more interventionist approach that would 'call for "difficult" battles with vested interests'.[43]

In short, the policy proposals in 'Economic Growth and National Efficiency' envisaged a radical change in the direction of economic policy; a change that would revise the very objectives of economic policy, with growth promoted to a key aim rather than being seen as a policy by-product, and radically alter the policy instruments used to attain these objectives.[44]

Viewed from the perspective of 2003, although tripartite co-operation between government, industry and the trade unions to raise industrial efficiency and the idea of a voluntary incomes policy to limit the growth of wages now seem positively 'historic', in other respects a number of the proposals in 'Economic Growth and National Efficiency' seem remarkably familiar. The emphasis on competition, on flexible labour markets, on the role that an active labour market policy can play in improving economic performance, and on the importance of improvements in the supply-side of the economy, for example, would not be out of place today. Ringe and Rollings find the Treasury diagnosis of the causes of relative decline and the 'growth problem' similar to that advanced by Broadberry and Crafts.[45] Indeed, in a sense one sees in the Treasury's proposals a harbinger of later ideas emanating from post-neoclassical endogenous growth theory – particularly regarding the scope for government action to help raise the long-run growth rate, and in the importance accorded to developing human capital.[46]

The policy failure

Submission of the Treasury's report to the Cabinet in July 1961 was followed almost immediately by a marked shift in the government's economic policies – ushered in by the Chancellor's address to Parliament on 25 July in a debate on emergency measures to deal with yet another in the succession of post-war sterling crises. In announcing the introduction of 'indicative' planning to achieve higher levels of both industrial investment and productivity the Chancellor set out the first element of what was to be a radical new policy package.[47] This led directly to the creation of the National Economic Development Council (NEDC) in 1962 – an institution chaired by the Chancellor and including representatives from industrial employers, the nationalized industries and the Trades Union Congress (TUC). 'Indicative' planning involved the agreement by the interested parties of targets for indices such as the rate of growth and of investment – the most important such target being the 4 per cent target for the growth of GDP that was agreed by the NEDC in 1962 and immediately endorsed by the government as a primary objective of its economic policy. The targets were not binding but simply indicated what was likely to happen if the tripartite participants acted as they had said they intended.[48] By such a 'psychological conjuring trick', it was hoped, the participants would gain the confidence voluntarily to play their part in the attainment of these ambitious goals.[49]

The second plank of the new policy package, also announced by the Chancellor on 25 July, saw the implementation of a compulsory 'pay pause' for public sector workers – which Macmillan hoped would be 'the first – no doubt amateurish – attempt to move towards what has afterwards become known as an "incomes policy"'.[50] It certainly looked amateurish, since the unilateral imposition of compulsory wage restraint on the government's own workers was a strange way to go about tempting the wider trade union movement into support for a voluntary policy on wage restraint. This was in a sense a product of the hurried implementation of the new policies on growth, and of the way in which Macmillan and Treasury officials had used the sterling crisis to bounce the Chancellor into accepting them. The poisoned atmosphere it gave rise to, however, was to stymie substantive progress until the election of a Labour government in October 1964.[51]

Thirdly, the government sought to overhaul its fiscal policy. On taxation, the Chancellor announced two new 'economic regulators' that would improve its ability to manage the economy.[52] Behind the scenes, a wide-scale review of taxation policy was begun – with the intention of ensuring that both the existing tax structure and future amendments to it were consistent with the government intention to raise growth.[53] Parallel developments in public expenditure control were also set in train and these were to result in the creation of a new Public Expenditure Survey Committee responsible for planning public expenditure over a five-year horizon and for ensuring that spending decisions were taken within the context of the new 4 per cent growth target.[54]

This was more than an ad hoc alteration of policy by the government of the day. It was a wide-ranging overhaul of both the goals and instruments of government economic policy, and one implemented in short-order. It effectively implemented a new economic policy framework that was implicitly accepted by Labour when it was elected to office in October 1964 (for all their apparent novelty and excitement, Labour's economic policies on entering power in 1964 being in the main merely logical developments of the Conservatives' approach after 1961).[55]

Whilst the scale of the change of direction in 1961–2 was impressive, the achievements of the policies proved to be less so, with little discernible impact on the rate of growth. In July 1966, indicative planning, the attempt to build a voluntary incomes policy, and the idea of a specific growth target all expired as the economy was deflated in an attempt to save sterling from devaluation. Nor can the array of radical new policies be said to have achieved much during their five-year life. As Leruez pointed out, and as Roger Middleton reiterates in his chapter below, neither the growth target set by the NEDC in 1962 nor that of the 1965 National Plan were attained.[56] There was a small improvement in the average annual rate of growth in the 1960s (up around 0.2 per cent compared with the 1950s) but this was scarcely significant.

One reason for the failure of the new policies may be that, whilst the Treasury's analysis was acute, there was clearly a contradiction between, on the one hand, a co-operative approach to raising industrial efficiency and securing wage restraint and, on the other hand, the promotion of free markets and greater competition. To a certain extent, this reflected the lack of theoretical grounding for the Treasury's proposals highlighted by Middleton in his chapter. The contradiction also reflected the constraint posed for restructuring the economy by the continuing commitment to full employment.[57] It was also indicative, however, of a serious shortcoming in the Treasury's proposed reform programme – its dependence on others to implement and ensure the success of the programme.

As Ringe and Rollings have pointed out, whilst the apparent failure of the market to make the most of growth opportunities in the high demand post-war environment seemed to put the onus on government to address the problem of relative decline, it was easier for the Treasury to analyse the problem than to solve it. Whilst 'Economic Growth and National Efficiency' was incisive, 'The Treasury could not simply impose its solution on Whitehall and the rest of the economy, however much it wished to and however persistently it tried'.[58] Ringe and Rollings were talking specifically about the proposal to explore tripartite solutions via the new NEDC – arguing that the decision to adopt this course sprang out of the Treasury's awareness of potential opposition from other ministries within Whitehall, on which it would depend to implement many of its proposed reforms, and from both sides of industry. Nevertheless, what was true of indicative planning was true of the wider 'growth project' on which the government had now embarked.

In terms of Whitehall, the fact was that the Treasury's analysis of the 'growth problem' and of the ways in which it must be addressed was far ahead of other government departments. This was a serious problem, as the Treasury conceded.[59] Since it would be dependent on these departments to implement its proposed policy changes it recognized the need for 'missionary work' within Whitehall.[60] Lee's creation of the inter-departmental committee of permanent secretaries, and of the inter-departmental working party on growth, was part of this campaign.

Despite this attempt to bring other departments round to the Treasury's view, it was to find itself balked on several fronts. In incomes policy, for example, the Ministry of Labour, which must necessarily be responsible for overseeing such a major intervention in the labour market, feared that to do so would prejudice its traditional role as a conciliator between employers and unions.[61] It therefore resisted the idea – only succumbing when Macmillan took personal control of economic policy in the summer of 1962. Even so, it was not until the advent of a Labour government, and the transfer of responsibility for administering the incomes policy from the Ministry of Labour to the new Department of Economic Affairs, that real progress began to be made on obtaining the support of the unions and on building effective institutions to support the policy. Similarly, the Board of Trade proved extremely reluctant, both at first and as the policy developed, to countenance action to restrain increases in prices or dividends.[62] This made it hard to make progress on a policy which was bound to involve intervention in both fields if incomes policy was not to operate to the disadvantage of wage-earners.

Even in fiscal policy, in a field normally seen as its fiefdom, the Treasury found itself having to trim its sails in the face of departmental opposition. This was particularly so in its attempt to overhaul Britain's tax structure and make it more conducive to higher growth. Both the Inland Revenue and the Customs and Excise, on which the Treasury depended for the administration of taxation, proved doughty opponents of the idea that changes to taxation should now be assessed primarily on a measure of their contribution to economic policy rather than the traditional criteria of equity and of ease and efficiency of collection.[63] Together they were able to ensure that the inter-departmental review of taxation policy ran into the sands, and to see off proposals for (inter alia) an overhaul of indirect taxation, a payroll tax (the aim of which was to encourage the more efficient use of labour), and a variant of the Swedish 'investment reserve' scheme in which companies would pay profits, free of tax, into a fund on which they would be allowed to draw in times of recession. They also resisted, and through this resistance helped to reduce the efficiency of, the introduction of the national insurance 'regulator' in 1961, the introduction of the 'payroll regulator' in the same year (so effectively neutered that it was never possible to use it) the taxation of capital gains (finally introduced in 1965), and proposed changes to company taxation culminating in the 1965 corporation tax.[64]

Outside Whitehall, as Ringe and Rollings point out, the Treasury faced the problem of how to encourage the active participation of the FBI and the TUC, and of how to demonstrate its willingness to pursue new policies on growth 'while at the same time not moving in to "take charge of" the subject' and antagonizing either, or both, sides of industry.[65] It therefore sought to shape opinion on both sides of industry via the NEDC.[66] The decision to seek a co-operative solution through the NEDC, and its failure either to achieve its aims or to form the basis for the creation of a 'developmental state' in Britain, were therefore a product of the weakness of central government and of the profound fragmentation and the marked interdependence of its economic policy institutions.[67]

What was true of the NEDC was also true in other areas of supply-side policy in which the Treasury attempted to overhaul Britain's economic institutions. In industrial training, for example, identified then (as now) as a key supply-side problem and as an area in which British standards were below those of most of her competitors both in terms of quality and quantity, and in which radical improvements must be made if growth was to be raised, the government's attempt to intervene via the 1964 Industrial Training Act has come to be seen largely as a failure.[68] Whilst the employers organizations and the TUC were persuaded that reform was required, many of their members feared the consequences of radical change – particularly small firms, who would be required to pay a training levy and the craft unions, which saw reform of apprenticeships as likely to end the wage premium attached to 'craft' jobs. Their opposition to reform caused their respective peak organizations to resist the proposal to create a strong central authority able to impose change across the new structure of industrial training boards in the face of low level opposition from employers and unions.[69] The Ministry of Labour proved extremely reluctant to take powers to enforce change, or even to use its funding as a lever – mainly because it feared that to do so would spoil its relations with industry and prejudice its traditional role as an industrial conciliator.[70] In addition, although logically one might have expected the overhaul of training to have been undertaken within the context of the NEDC, and the new structure of industrial training boards subsumed within the industrial level EDCs. This did not happen. The failure arose because the Treasury, recognizing the problems it faced in bringing both sides in the NEDC to a common agreement on the means to faster growth, was reluctant to muddy the waters by widening the scope of its considerations.

This weakness of the Treasury in the face of fragmented labour market institutions can also be found in incomes policy. Again, logically one would have expected any voluntary incomes policy to have been built via negotiations in the new NEDC. Yet this did not happen because the Treasury, only too aware of its difficulties in tempting the TUC into negotiations on growth, recognized that to introduce incomes policy into the equation, given the unions' attachment to free collective bargaining, would be to invite disaster.[71] Thus the new incomes policy institutions (first the National Incomes Commission and then the National Board for Prices and Incomes) were built in parallel to the institutions of planning rather than integrated with them. This was a serious weakness.[72] In addition, although progress began to be made on incomes policy after the election of a Labour government in 1964, national agreements proved largely illusory since neither the employers organizations nor the TUC had the power to compel their members to comply. The result was that an array of plant- and company-level bargains were struck which broke with agreed norms. This led to 'wage drift' and thus undermined incomes policy from within. Once again, therefore, Treasury policy makers thereby again found themselves balked by the fragmented nature of Britain's industrial and economic institutions in their attempt to overhaul economic policy and intervene in the economy to raise growth.

Conclusion

We find, therefore, that in absolute terms the economic performance and rising living standards of the 1950s were impressive. The Treasury recognized this. It also recognized that 'declinist' fears regarding the rate of Britain's relative decline in the 1950s were overstated. Our analysis indicates that in 1960–61 the Treasury accepted that Britain's economic 'decline' in the 1950s was largely the product of a catch-up and convergence process resulting from the reconstruction and restructuring of war-ravaged economies on the continent and in Japan.

Nevertheless, at the beginning of the 1960s the Treasury was extremely concerned about the political and economic implications of relative decline if projected into the future (i.e. if catch-up and convergence was succeeded by overtaking), and about the emergence of problems with the prevailing Keynesian framework of demand management to stabilize the economy, control inflation and maintain full employment.

In an attempt to deal with both these problems the Treasury, with the support of Macmillan, embarked on a 'great reappraisal' of economic policy which resulted in the adoption of the 4 per cent growth target and the adoption of an array of new policy instruments, and adjustments to existing policy instruments, to achieve it.[73]

We conclude, however, that this attempt to avoid a continuation of relative decline and to correct perceived deficiencies in the Keynesian policy framework failed, and that it failed largely as a result of the Treasury's inability to impose its analysis and its proposed policy solution on either other government departments or on extra-governmental actors on whom it depended to implement the new policy framework and to make it work effectively.

Notes

* This chapter builds on research funded by the ESRC (awards R00429734705 and T026271086) and the Institute for Historical Research, London University. It was written during an ESRC postdoctoral fellowship at the University of Bristol and a British Academy postdoctoral fellowship at the London School of Economics. Thanks are due to all these institutions for their support.

1 Hobsbawn, Eric: *Age of Extremes*, Michael Joseph, London, 1994, ch. 9; Middleton, Roger: *Government Versus the Market*, Edward Elgar, Cheltenham, 1996; Tomlinson, Jim: *The Politics of Decline*, Longman, Harlow, 2000.

2 Supple, Barry: 'Fear of Failing: Economic History and the Decline of Britain', in Clarke, P., Trebilock, C. and Supple, B.: *Understanding Decline: Perceptions and Realities of British Economic Performance*, Cambridge University Press, Cambridge, 1997, p. 9. Gamble, Andrew: 'Theories and Explanations of British Decline', in English, R. and Kenny, M. (eds), *Rethinking British Decline*, Macmillan, London, 2000, p. 5; Tomlinson: *The Politics of Decline,* op. cit.

3 Tomlinson: *The Politics of Decline*, op. cit., p. 2.

4 Worswick, G.D.N. and Ady, P.H.: *The British Economy in the Nineteen-fifties*, Oxford University Press, Oxford, 1962, p. 68.

5 All figures are from Statbase, Office of National Statistics [www.statistics.gov.uk], November 2002.

6 Maddison, Angus: *Economic Growth in the West*, Allen and Unwin, London, 1964, pp. 231–2 and 240.

7 Worswick and Ady: op. cit., p. 536.

8 See chapters by Hilton and Black in this volume. See also Hall, Margaret: 'The Consumer Sector' in Worswick and Ady, op. cit., pp. 429–59; and Zweiniger-Bargielowska, Ina: 'Living Standards and Consumption' in Addison, Paul and Jones, Harriet: *A Companion to Contemporary Britain, 1939–2000*, Blackwell, Oxford, forthcoming 2003.

9 Tomlinson: *The Politics of Decline*, op. cit., pp. 12–21.

10 Tomlinson, Jim: 'Economic Policy' in Floud, Roderick and Johnson, Paul: *The Cambridge Economic History of Modern Britain. Volume 3: Structural Change 1939–2000*, Cambridge University Press, Cambridge (forthcoming, 2003).

11 Cairncross, Alec: *The British Economy Since 1945* (2nd edn), Blackwell, Oxford, 1995, p. 297.

12 A consequence of such high levels of overseas spending for both the balance of payments and levels of domestic investment being highlighted by Shonfield, Andrew: *British Economic Policy Since the War*, Penguin, Harmondsworth, 1958.

13 Examples being the 1956 Suez debacle; the decision in 1960 to request the USA to supply Skybolt missiles and thus the acceptance that Britain could no longer sustain a fully independent nuclear deterrent; the attempt to join the EEC in 1961; the even more humiliating rejection by De Gaulle of this application; and the 1968 withdrawal from east of Suez.

14 Tomlinson: 'Economic Policy' in Floud and Johnson: op. cit. See also Feinstein, Charles: 'Structural Change in Developed Countries During the Twentieth Century', *Oxford Review of Economic Policy*, vol. 15, no. 4 (1999), pp. 35–55.

15 Cairncross, Alec: *Managing the British Economy in the 1960s*, Macmillan, London, 1996, p. 6.

16 Balogh, Thomas: 'The Apotheosis of the Dilettante' in Thomas, Hugh: *The Establishment*, Ace Books, London, 1962 (first published by Anthony Blond in 1959).

124 AN AFFLUENT SOCIETY?

[17] Ibid., p. 95.

[18] Ibid., p. 92.

[19] The criticism was most effectively outlined by Dow, J.C.R.: *The Management of the British Economy, 1945–1960*, Cambridge University Press, Cambridge, 1964.

[20] Public Record Office, Kew (henceforth 'PRO'): T 267/20, Treasury Historical Manuscript, 1971, 'The Control of Demand: 1958–1964'.

[21] Worswick and Ady: op. cit., pp. 273–4); Brittan, Samuel: *The Treasury Under the Tories, 1951–1964*, Penguin, Harmondsworth, 1964, pp. 135–6; Dow: op. cit., p. 365.

[22] Leruez, Jacques: *Economic Planning and Politics* in Britain, Martin Robertson, London, 1975, p. 104; Ham, A: *Treasury Rules: Recurrent Themes in British Economic Policy*, Quartet, London, 1981; Pollard, Stephen: *The Wasting of the British Economy: British Economic Policy 1945 to the Present*, Croom Helm, London, 1984.

[23] Booth, Alan: 'Britain in the 1950s: A "Keynesian" Managed Economy?', *History of Political Economy*, vol. 33, no. 2 (2001), pp. 287–8; and Booth, Alan: 'New Revisionists and the Keynesian Era in British Economic Policy', *Economic History Review*, vol. LIV, no. 2 (2001), pp. 346–66.

[24] Peden, George: *The Treasury and British Public Policy, 1906–1959*, Oxford University Press, Oxford, 2000.

[25] Ringe, Astrid and Rollings, Neil: 'Responding to Relative Decline: The Creation of the National Economic Development Council', *Economic History Review*, vol. LIII, no. 2 (May 2000), pp. 331–53.

[26] TNA: PRO T 230, 26 July 1960, F. Lee, 'Personal note for the [new] Chancellor'. Paish's ideas are summarized in Paish, Frank: *Studies in an Inflationary Economy: the United Kingdom 1948–1961*, Macmillan, London, 1962 – a volume of collected essays. In effect, Paish was a proto-monetarist, arguing that higher growth would be best achieved by lowering the rate of growth of monetary demand (Glynn, S. and Booth, A: *Modern Britain: An Economic and Social History*, Routledge, London, 1996, p. 310). A useful summary of his position appeared in an article written by him for the *Financial Times*, 14 September 1960 and this was read with interest in the Treasury.

[27] TNA: PRO T 230/493, 25 August 1960, 'Answers to the Chancellor's questionnaire'.

[28] British Oral Archive of Political and Administrative History, Library of the London School of Economics and Political Science: Transcripts of two interviews with Lord Roberthall (on 23 April 1980 and 13 May 1980) conducted by Anthony Seldon.

[29] Hall, Robert: *The Robert Hall Diaries, 1954–1961* (edited by A. Cairncross), Unwin Hyman, London, 1991, p. 257.

[30] Pemberton, Hugh: 'Policy Networks and Policy Learning: UK Economic Policy in the 1960s and 1970s', *Public Administration*, vol. 78, no. 4 (2000), pp. 771–92; and Pemberton, Hugh: *Policy Learning and British Governance in the 1960s*, Palgrave Macmillan, London, 2004.

[31] TNA: PRO T 171/524, 28 November 1961, 'Note by the Permanent Secretary'.

[32] TNA: PRO T 230/523–6, passim; T 298/334–5, passim; TNA: PRO T 230/579, 30 January 1961, Vinter to Hopkin; Lowe, Rodney and Rollings, Neil: 'Modernising Britain, 1957–1964; A Classic Case of Centralisation and Fragmentation?' in Rhodes, R.A.W.: *Transforming British Government*, vol. 1, Macmillan, London, 2000, p. 112. The committee comprised permanent secretaries from the Board of Trade and ministries of Labour, Transport, Aviation and Power, as well as senior officials from the Treasury and its Economic Section.

[33] Ringe, A. and Rollings, N. op. cit., p. 346. Sir Douglas Wass could not remember the words 'economic growth' being mentioned in any official document before 1960 according to Keegan, William and Pennant-Rea: *Who Runs the Economy?*, Maurice

Temple Smith, London, 1997, p. 91. The chairman of the inter-departmental working party on growth ascribed its creation to increased public discussion of growth and, in particular, to the discussions on growth in the EPB and NPACI (TNA: PRO T 230/579, 30 May 1961, Vinter to Cairncross).

34 TNA: PRO CAB 134/1816, 3 January 1961, EPB(60)35, 'Economic Growth: Note by the Treasury'.

35 TNA: PRO T 325/72, 23 February 1961, Clarke to Lee; TNA: PRO T 230/579, 27 February 1961, Vinter to Clarke, 'Elements of a Policy for Economic Growth'; TNA: PRO T 230/579, 13/03/1961, Clarke to Hall, Padmore, and Lee, 'Economic Growth'. The impact can be seen in TNA: PRO T 325/72, 14/03/1961, Hall to Sir Frank Lee and Sir Thomas Padmore, 'Economic Growth', in which Hall called for an 'urgent examination' of economic policies in respect of the balance of payments and growth.

36 TNA: PRO T 230/525, 23 March 1961, WPEG(61)1), 'Scope of the enquiry'. The submission was to consist of an appreciation of post-war UK growth and a comparison with other countries; details of the attitudes of industry, labour and other relevant non-governmental institutions to the problem and details of any discussions that have taken place with them to date; an examination of the relationships between economic growth, competitive power and the balance of payments; and, finally, the identification of possible tripartite action to stimulate economic growth and competitiveness.

37 TNA: PRO CAB 129/105, July 1961, C(61)94, 'Economic Growth and National Efficiency'.

38 TNA: PRO T 325/72, 23 February 1961, Clarke to Lee.

39 TNA: PRO PREM 11/2973, 'Correspondence between Prime Minister and Sir Roy Harrod on economic policy and growth', 1957–1960, passim; and TNA: PRO PREM 11/3287, 'Correspondence with Sir Roy Harrod on economic problems and policy', 1960–61, passim.

40 TNA: PRO CAB 129/105, C(61)94, op. cit., p. 9.

41 Ibid., pp. 40–109.

42 Ibid., para. 39d.

43 Ibid., para. 39e.

44 Pemberton, Hugh: 'Learning, Governance and Economic Policy', *British Journal of Politics and International Relations*, vol. 5, no. 3 (in press, 2003); and Pemberton: *Policy Learning and British Governance in the 1960s*, op. cit.

45 Ringe and Rollings: op. cit., p. 348; Broadberry, S.N. and Crafts, N.F.R.: 'British Economic Policy and Industrial Performance in the Early Post-war Period', *Business History*, vol. 39, no. 4 (1996), pp. 65–91; and Broadberry, S.N. and Crafts, N.F.R.: 'The Post-war Settlement: Not Such a Good Bargain After All', *Business History*, vol. 40, no. 2 (1998), pp. 73–9.

46 Crafts, N.F.R. : '"Post-neoclassical Endogenous Growth Theory": What are its Policy Implications?', *Oxford Review of Economic Policy*, vol. 12, no. 2 (1996), pp. 30–47.

47 House of Commons, Parl. Debs., 25 July 1961, col. 220.

48 See Shanks, Michael: *Planning and Politics: the British Experience, 1960–1976*, George Allen and Unwin (for Political and Economic Planning), London, 1977, p. 105.

49 Dow: op. cit., p. 398.

50 Macmillan, Harold: *At the End of the Day, 1961–1963*, Macmillan, London, 1973, p. 36.

51 Dorfman, Gerald A.: *Wage Politics in Britain, 1945–1967*, Charles Knight, London, 1974, pp. 97–115; Fishbein, Warren H.: *Wage Restraint by Consensus: Britain's Search for an Incomes Policy Agreement, 1965–79*, Routledge and Kegan Paul, London, 1984, pp. 31–3.

[52]   Pemberton, Hugh: 'A Taxing Task: Combating Britain's Relative Decline in the 1960s', *Twentieth Century British History*, vol. 12, no. 3 (2001), pp. 354–75.

[53]   TNA: PRO T 233/2330–1, 'Review of Taxation Policy, 1960–1961', passim.

[54]   Lowe, Rodney: 'The Core Executive, Modernization and the Creation of PESC, 1960–64', *Public Administration*, vol. 75, no. 4 (1997), pp. 601–15.

[55]   Brittan, Samuel: *Steering the Economy: the Role of the Treasury*, Secker and Warburg, London, 1969, p. 190; Pemberton: *Policy Learning and British Governance in the 1960s*, op. cit.

[56]   Leruez, Jacques: *Economic Planning and Politics in Britain*, op. cit., figure 11.1.

[57]   Norman Macrae, a senior journalist on *The Economist*, was one of those who attempted to provide the missing theoretical justification (see Macrae, Norman: *Sunshades in October*, Allen and Unwin, London, 1963).

[58]   Ringe and Rollings: op. cit., p. 349.

[59]   TNA: PRO T 325/72, 13 March 1961, 'Economic Growth', Clarke to Hall, Padmore and Lee.

[60]   Ringe and Rollings: op. cit., p. 346.

[61]   This fear was evident from the first (see TNA: PRO CAB 134/1690, 28 April 1961, EA(61)30, 'Wages Policy').

[62]   In October 1964, its permanent secretary told the Treasury Group on Incomes Policy that it 'would be better to abandon all attempts to seek an agreed incomes policy than to embark on a course which might lead to controls of this kind' (TNA: PRO T 311/188, 8 October 1964, TGIP(64) 7th meeting).

[63]   The Inland Revenue, for example, argued that the aims of economic regulation and equity were incompatible (TNA: PRO T 233/2331, 18 October 1961, RTP(61)2, 'Inland Revenue Taxation: note by the Inland Revenue').

[64]   Pemberton: 'A Taxing Task', op. cit.

[65]   TNA: PRO T 325/72, 23 February 1961, Clarke to Lee; TNA: PRO T 230/523, 7 July 1961, Vinter to Clarke.

[66]   A slightly revised version of 'Economic Growth and National Efficiency', was submitted by the Treasury to the NEDC as a starting point for its consideration of obstacles to growth, and potential ways of addressing them. Initially dismissed as 'Treasury trash' by some NEDC representatives (Brittan: *The Treasury Under the Tories*, op. cit., p. 240) the Treasury's analysis nonetheless clearly formed the foundation of the NEDC's first report (the 'Orange Book') which appeared a year later (NEDC: *Conditions Favourable to Faster Growth*, HMSO, London, 1963).

[67]   Ringe and Rollings: op. cit.

[68]   King, Desmond: *Actively Seeking Work? The Politics of Unemployment and Welfare Policy in the United States and Great Britain*, University of Chicago Press, Chicago, 1995, p. 130; Finegold, David and Soskice, David W.: 'The Failure of Training in Britain: Analysis and Prescription', *Oxford Review of Economic Policy*, vol. 4, no. 3 (1988), pp. 21–53; Shonfield, Andrew: *Modern Capitalism*, Oxford University Press, Oxford, 1965, p. 119. Sheldrake, Sarah and Vickerstaff, John: *The History of Industrial Training in Britain*, Gower Publishing, Aldershot, 1987, pp. 37–8 detected some improvement in engineering, but overall their assessment was also negative.

[69]   For the BEC's opposition to a strong central authority, see Records of the British Employers' Confederation, Modern Records Centre, University of Warwick: MSS.200/C/3/EDU/24/5, 14 Feb. 1963, 'Central body under the Training Act'. For the TUC's retreat from the General Council's initial desire for such a body, see TNA: PRO LAB 18/835, 6 March 1963, 'Note of a Meeting with Representatives of the TUC'.

[70] Brittan: *Treasury Under the Tories*, op. cit., pp. 328–29. For the Ministry of Labour's awareness of the possible consequences of radical government intervention, see TNA: PRO LAB 9/382, 5 March 63, Nash to Stewart and 7 March 1963, Maston to Rossetti; and TNA: PRO LAB 9/378, 10 May 1963, file note.

[71] Pemberton: *Policy Learning and British Governance in the 1960s*, op. cit., ch. 5.

[72] Tomlinson: 'British economic policy', op. cit., pp. 272–73; Wilensky, Harold L. and Turner, Lowell: *Democratic Corporatism and Policy Linkages: The Interdependence of Industrial, Labor-market, Incomes and Social Policies in Eight Countries*, Institute of International Studies, University of California, Berkeley, CA, 1987.

[73] Significantly, what Brittan: *Treasury Under the Tories*, op. cit., ch. 7 called the 'great reappraisal' had by 1969 been downgraded by him to merely an 'appraisal' in Brittan: *Steering the Economy*, op. cit., ch. 6.

Plate 1   Lawrence Harvey as Joe Lampton in the film version of John Braine's *Room at the Top*, produced by John and James Woolf and directed by Jack Claton. Here Joe visits the scene of his childhood in the northern industrial town of 'Dufton'

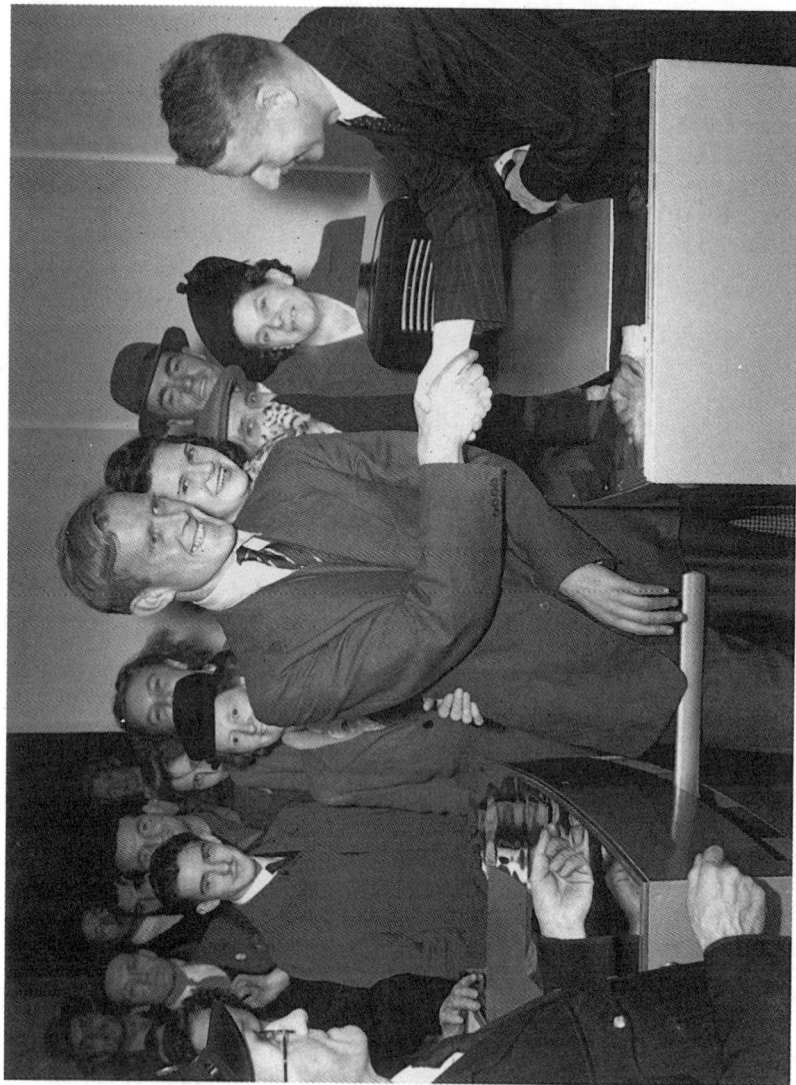

Plate 2 The (anonymous) 500,000th visitor to the Britain Can Make It exhibition receives a radio set from the Deputy Director of the Council of Industrial Design, N.E. Kearley, 1946

Plate 3   The Industrial Designer; detail of the exhibit 'What Industrial Design Means' at Britain Can Make It, 1946

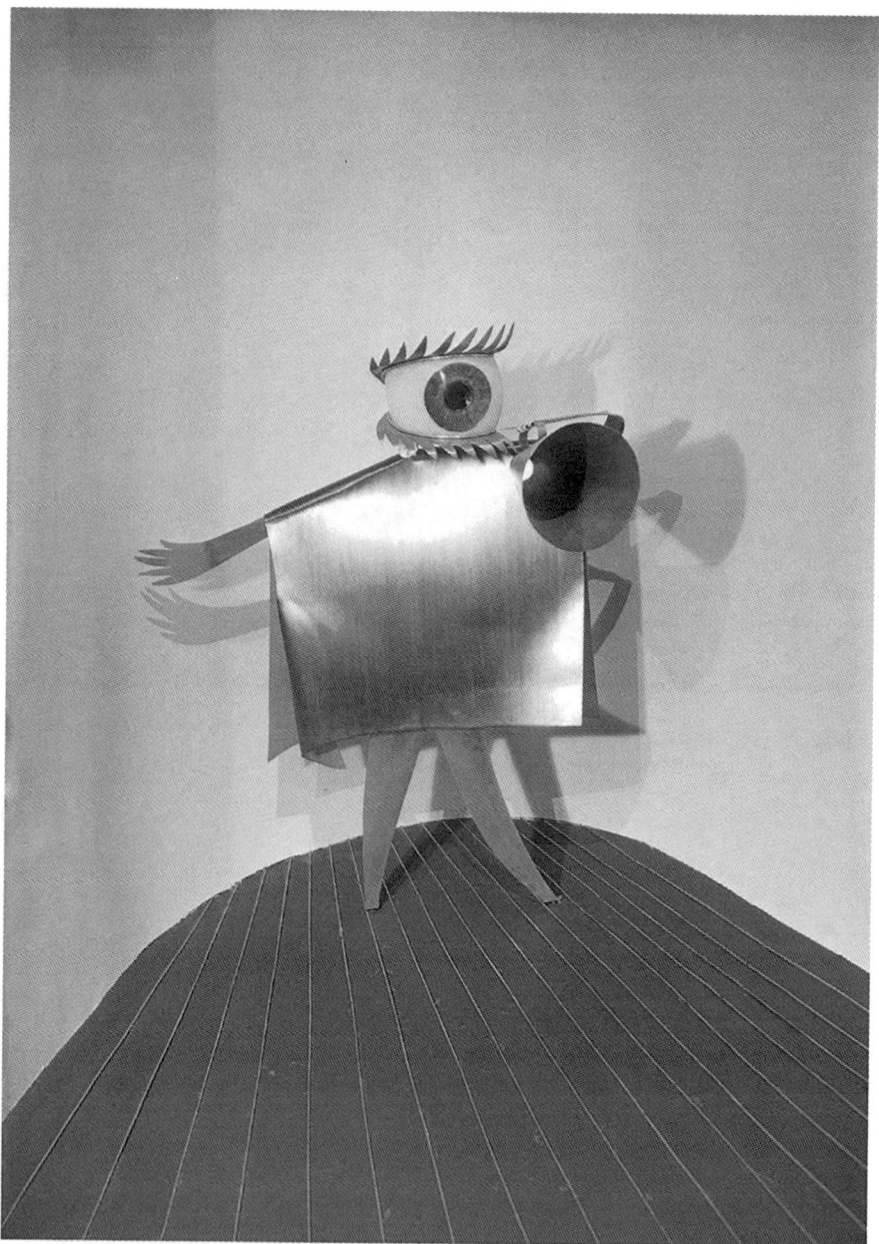

Plate 4   The Figure of 'Mr Designer' directed visitors at the Britain Can
Make It exhibition and brilliantly embodied the Council of
Industrial Design's core message to consumers

CHAPTER 8

Economists and Economic Growth in Britain, c.1955–65

Roger Middleton[*]

The role of economists[1] in the rise to prominence of economic growth promotion as an explicit policy objective has recently been given a fillip by two emerging literatures which have deepened our understanding of what Hutchison called the developing 'growth consciousness' of this era.[2] The first of these, which has been inspired *inter alia* by the literature on social learning and policy networks, concerns the so-called 'Keynesian plus' policies, namely the augmentation in the early 1960s of 'classic' short-term Keynesian demand management techniques and objectives for stabilization purposes with a range of supply-side initiatives directed at promoting higher growth.[3] The second is much broader in scope, that is recent work – mostly part of, or inspired by, the ESRC's Whitehall programme – into the underlying administrative and political failures of the various modernization programmes – of which Keynesian plus was a part – initiated in the post-Suez era of national re-evaluation and policy reorientation.[4]

Both literatures have much broader ambitions than merely explaining the rise to prominence of the growth objective, but in both it is a constant preoccupation because of what we might call the big 'what if' question which is implicit (occasionally explicit) in the dominant 'declinist' historiography of post-war Britain:[5] what was that counterfactual set of policies which, *if* introduced, and *if* resulting in higher growth (all other policy objectives also being simultaneously and satisfactorily attained), would have moderated relative economic decline, saved Keynesian social democracy from the traumas of the 1970s and thus made unnecessary the Thatcherite reaction against the so-called post-war consensus. In the following I take no position on most of those debates.[6] My concern is only incidentally with specifying and defining this big 'what if'; rather, it is more to do with 'who', the 'why' and the 'how': that is with the actors who generated the new growth consciousness and the mechanisms whereby it was diffused into the policy-making community, but above all with the effectiveness of those actors claiming economic expertise, the extent to which (in an operational and epistemological sense) their knowledge was useful and what culpability they might have for the eventual fate of that growth strategy which culminated with the Labour government's National Plan, the life cycle of which was so aptly described by Opie, one of the academic economists who served briefly as an 'irregular' in the new Department of Economic Affairs (DEA), as 'conceived October 1964, born September 1965, died (possibly murdered) July 1966'.[7]

Died, possibly murdered, for let us not be under any illusions that, relative to its ambitions, the growth strategy failed. The first question to address, therefore, is what the implications of that failure were in terms of the now dominant declinist perception of Britain's golden age economic performance, in other words how much the 'what if' might have mattered. We can then consider three interrelated questions: what role did economics and economists play in the advocacy coalition that fermented the developing growth strategy of this era; what limited their effectiveness; and what were the consequences for the economics profession and for economic policy of the eventual failure of the strategy? Our sights are thus set on the market for economic advice, the internal workings of the policy process and the sociology of economics. On these issues we will be somewhat sceptical of existing accounts; we hope also to rescue from the condescension of posterity those economists who, displaying both useful economic knowledge and realistic aspirations of what might be possible, were deeply sceptical of the developing growth consciousness and anxious about its implications for the standing of professional economics.

Relative economic decline and the 1960s growth strategy

As can be seen from Figure 8.1, which uses the latest Maddison dataset to generate an updated version of the much reproduced chart by Leruez,[8] the actual path of real GDP by the end of the golden age was well below the original growth plan of the 1963 National Economic Development Council (NEDC) and the 1965 National

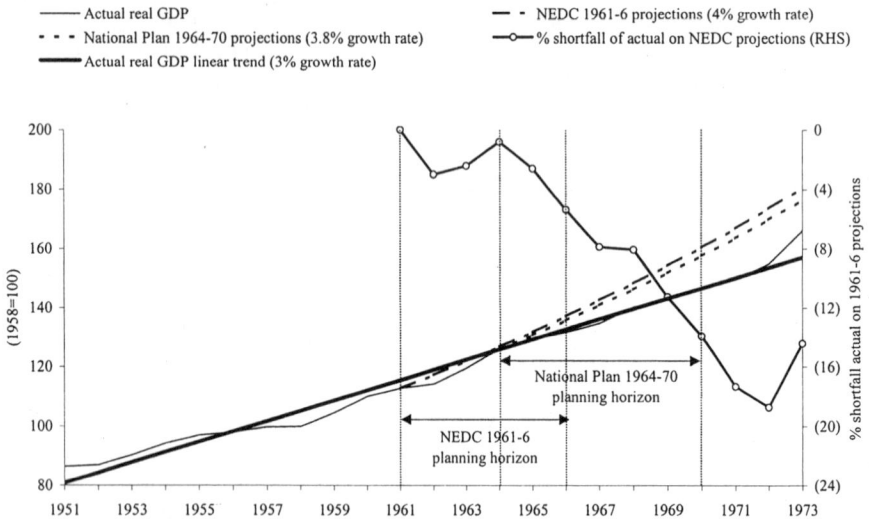

Figure 8.1 Real GDP at 1995 market prices (1958=100): actual and trend, NEDC 1961–6 projections and National Plan 1964–70 projections
Source: National Statistics databank.

Plan which had annual growth targets of 4.0 per cent and 3.8 per cent respectively.[9] By 1973, and in relation to the 1963 plan, the per centage shortfall was 14.4 per cent, and it was only this low because of the temporary and unsustainable boost afforded by the Barber boom.[10] Put differently, because growth is cumulative, and thus so is underperformance, the decadal shortfall by 1973 was (in 1995 prices) just over £300bn or 64 per cent of actual 1973 GDP. £300bn is an enormous sum, and, of course, hugely hypothetical but it does give a measure of the enormity of the stakes as economics but above all as politics.[11] Accordingly, had the growth strategy been successful then Britain would by 1973 have attained a standard of living so much closer to the leading OECD economies that the narrative of relative economic decline which now pervades the literature could not have developed. Affluence thus resonates here more as under-achievement and as failure than as progress and celebration, as of course befits its hallowed status in the declinist historiography. However, had the growth strategy succeeded, there could have been a very different narrative, not of unprecedented relative decline, but one of exceptional historic catch-up on the productivity leaders provoked by a modernizing British state.

To complete the process of situating Britain's actual growth record in relation to contemporary aspirations for yet greater affluence, we note the longer-term implications of successive and sustained one per centage point increases in the compound growth rate. The use of integers is deliberate, for it became the currency of political competition: if 3 per cent then *surely* 4 per cent?; *only* 4 per cent!; *come on* why not 5 per cent!? I term this 'intoxication by integers', and explore later how it came about. For the present, we note the power of compound arithmetic in terms of how successive step integers work to transform the standard of living. Thus a 3 per cent growth rate translates into a doubling of GDP every 23.5 years (broadly the doubling of the standard of living in a generation of Butler's 1954 pledge); a 4 per cent growth rate every 17.7 years; and a 5 per cent growth rate every 14.2 years. These are beguiling figures when other countries were then growing at double the rate of Britain's economy, but they must be set alongside the long-term growth rate for the British economy (1856–1973) which was 2.0 per cent; that, and notwithstanding all the talk of relative decline, it was half as high again as this long-term rate during the golden age (that is a 3 per cent growth rate); and that the target aspiration was for a growth rate double the long-term trend (that is 4 per cent).

What do economists know?

Abramovitz, the originator of the now ubiquitous catch-up and convergence framework for understanding why growth rates differ, observed in an essay reviewing the field in the early 1950s that 'the problem of economic growth lacks any organized and generally known body of doctrine'.[12] There was a considerable corpus of individual work but nothing systematic that explained why growth rates differed. Subsequently, as Mueller puts it, 'the growth rate of the "growth literature" far exceeded that of the phenomenon it tried to explain',[13] but during our period formal economic theory had little practical immediate contribution to make and was rarely the inspiration for those economists advocating new policies on growth or for those who, achieving insider status, were charged with making it operational. Thus, in Britain as in the US, the relationship between theory and policy was the obverse of what might be expected: it was policy that drove theory and even then rather indirectly.[14] Rostow's stage theory is about as close as we get to an inspirational work at this time.[15]

'Mind the gap'

Before considering what economists knew that was useful about how to promote faster economic growth there is a prior issue to consider, that of limited contemporary empirical knowledge and how this contributed to the presumption that relative economic decline was specifically a consequence of British economic underperformance as against temporary above-trend performance elsewhere. The origins of the ideology of declinism can be traced to the early post-war statistical revolution,[16] which generated a league table approach to national economic performance such that from the late 1950s onwards the growth statistics were studied 'eagerly, not to say, morbidly' by successive governments.[17] To begin with, higher growth by the defeated continental European powers had been explained by their recovery from wartime damage, but there came a point – given substance by the statistical revolution – that Britain's relatively low growth rate must eventually reflect British underperformance.[18] Great credence is now placed on the catch-up process in explaining slow growth in Britain during the golden age, to the extent that very recent accounts of British economic performance have an overly Panglossian quality. But all that is ahead of us and here we note that concerns about competitiveness were hardly new; they date at least to the 1890s; and that if economists did not distinguish clearly between absolutes (the level of labour productivity actually attained) and relativities (the growth rate of labour productivity as a country converges or does not on the productivity leader) then it would be difficult to expect any other group of policy actors to do so.

There were serious informational problems during the 1950s and into the 1960s for economists – there being little or no published data on the absolutes of the productivity gap which would allow verdicts to be made about whether growth rates were an adequate measure of comparative performance or not, i.e. at what point did faster growth elsewhere really begin to matter. There was some quality research available on the Anglo-American productivity gap, but given that in so many ways the American example has proved an unhelpful comparator it is particularly unfortunate that in assessing the gap little was known about comparative productivity performance with Europe.[19] The fixation on growth rates was accordingly understandable and permeated through all of the strands of the literature.[20]

The 'old' new growth theory

Modern growth theory has developed through three phases since the Second World War.[21] The first, originating in pioneering papers by Harrod and Domar, sought to make the Keynesian system dynamic and was concerned as much with issues of stabilizing demand as with increasing productive capacity to accommodate rising demand. Although they provided key building blocks for later theorizing, their approaches were actually rather different and it is important that Harrod's theorizing drove him towards a pessimism about the possibility of attaining steady and high growth. The policy implications of this early theorizing were not altogether obvious, but in essence the Harrod-Domar approach modelled economic growth as a function of three explanatory variables: the savings rate, the labour force growth rate and the capital-output ratio. However, as Solow noted, his 'Discomfort [with Harrod-Domar] arose because they worked this out on the assumption that all three of the key ingredients ... were given constants, facts of nature. The savings rate was a fact about preferences; the growth rate of labour supply was a demographic-sociological fact; the capital-output ratio was a technological fact.'[22]

The second phase, which began in the mid-1950s with Swan and Solow and which continued to the 1980s, is that of mainstream neo-classical theory which, during our formative period, comprised a series of highly abstract models which rested on a number of more or less strenuous assumptions about the characteristics of modern capitalism. From these pioneering efforts the literature on the neo-classical growth model mushroomed in the 1960s with efforts to relax somewhat the 'heroic abstractions' made in Solow's initial formulation. More realistic models were developed, the differing vintages of capital (and thus latent productivity potential) were introduced, and investment was then augmented with human capital. But in almost all of this emerging literature the long-run equilibrium growth rate was taken as exogenous, determined by the growth rates of population and productivity. Population growth was not immediately tractable in public policy terms, while the rate of technological progress was assumed exogenous (the so-called Solow residual). Equally significant was that such theorizing about the causes of growth, grounded as it was on the assumption of the operational superiority of the market as an allocational device, was antipathetic to the planning movement of the 1960s.[23]

It was thus not immediately clear how the developing growth literature offered a practical guide to growth-hungry policy-makers. What was clear was that investment in physical capital mattered and that there was some potential in human capital, but as Robert Shone – the first Director General of the NEDC – complained from experience it was extraordinarily difficult in practice to determine the magnitude of their coefficients in any aggregate production function.[24] Neo-classical theory did, however, spur the development of major empirical enquiries – growth accounting exercises – into why growth rates differed,[25] from which it emerged that in Britain, as with other leading economies, high post-war growth derived less from applying additional factors of production (capital and labour, in sum total factor inputs) than from significantly increased productivity of those inputs, so-called total factor productivity. Of course, this was the Solow residual and thus such exercises left unexplained the ultimate and fundamental sources of growth.

The absence of a menu of obvious policy choices or signposts of what British policy-makers ought to be doing was compounded by politicians' ignorance about the growth process. Thus, in Alec Cairncross's judgement, neither of the first two Chancellors he served (Selwyn Lloyd, 1961–2; Maudling, 1962–4) 'had any real insight into the mainsprings of economic growth ... they simply assumed that if expansion was sufficiently prolonged, industrial productivity would move upwards to a new, steeper curve.'[26] He further noted that:[27]

> Britain had set about planning without really understanding how growth took place – growth in productivity, rather than growth in output. There was little theory about what determined the rate of growth that was worth a hoot – though what there was was in the Orange Book. Indeed, that was the only attempt to set down what could usefully be done to affect the rate of growth.

Indeed, there is something of an irony that the 'old' new growth theory, which actually accorded little theoretical role to government, was dominant during the golden age when many western governments actively intervened to promote growth, whereas the 'new' new (endogenous) growth theory, which sanctions a stronger role for governments, emerged in the 1980s whilst governments were trumpeting the virtues of the market and minimal government. Before proceeding to that third phase of post-war growth theory we need to introduce one now little cited conclusion of Denison's early work, and some important notes of dissent about theoretical developments during this second phase of theorizing.

Denison concluded his first growth accounting exercise, that solely on the US economy, by stressing that:[28]

> large and costly changes would be required if deliberate policy was to raise the high-employment growth rate appreciably above what it would be otherwise. 'The tale of a kingdom lost for want of a nail appears in poetry, not economic history.' This finding contrasted with a common view that it would be easy to add whole per centage points to the growth rate.

We have stressed the neo-classical provenance of this second phase, and indeed it was an important component of the emerging neo-classical synthesis of this period.[29] However, there were Keynesian dissidents, and especially Cambridge UK dissidents in the form of Joan Robinson, Pasinetti and Kaldor. They questioned Solow's strong assumptions of smoothly substitutable factors of production, competitive markets and equilibrium state method, and instead offered alternative theories of growth and distribution which *inter alia* might be conceived as of more appropriate to the British case. Unfortunately, the most visible manifestation of this dissent was the infamous Cambridge capital controversy, which for economics' growing number of critics marked the apotheosis of the discipline's descent into sterile theorizing.[30]

The 'new' new (endogenous) growth theory

Recent endogenous growth theory takes us well beyond our temporal borders but has a twofold relevance: first, as a means of looking back to golden age growth; and second as a means of looking forward to assess how practical policy dissatisfaction with neo-classical theory yielded ·further insightful theorizing and the possibility of progress in economics. Thus, the first point to observe is that in this third phase, which begins in the 1980s, growth theory emerged to occupy a much more prominent position in the mainstream research agenda and also cast off some, although not all, of its previous intellectual detachment from the puzzling question of why some countries are persistently poor and others persistently rich. With technology now endogenous, scale economies admitted and growth accounting exercises maturing to model and measure the influence of politics, policy and institutional arrangements on the behaviour of key economic actors, at last something resembling the ultimate and fundamental causes of why growth rates differ lay in the grasp of economists and policy-makers. Or so the most optimistic readings of the potential of endogenous growth theory would have it.[31]

The 1960s growth strategy has not yet been interpreted through an endogenous growth lens, but the growing body of theoretical and empirical work suggests the importance of the supply-side (with obvious implications for Keynesian plus); of broad rather than just physical capital (Robbins report and other vocational and educational initiatives); of raising the rate of technological change (R&D and competition policy); and of enhancing the appropriability of returns to investment in innovation and physical capital.[32] Moreover, as Crafts, a somewhat sceptical but still positive analyst of the endogenous approach, has stressed:[33]

> better supply-side policies tend to have their pay-off in the far distant future, while frequently jeopardising the votes of powerful interest groups initially. Absent effective ways of achieving pre-commitment, the short-termism of politicians is always likely to be an obstacle to faster long-run growth.

Accordingly, whilst it remains a potentially fruitful avenue to undertake such a retrospective, Crafts usefully brings us back to political and institutional capabilities and constraints. As for the economics, the growth process has recently and usefully been likened to a mosaic whereby there is no single vantage point that can encompass the full range of influences.[34] However, whilst economists continue to disagree about important short-term issues there is much fuller agreement about the necessary conditions – pro-education, pro-investment and pro-technology – if market economies are to deliver sustained long-term growth. All are recognizable themes in the emerging growth strategy of the late 1950s and early 1960s. The central question thus becomes whether the instruments for remedying the productivity shortfall were firmly based in appropriate penalty and incentive structures; in short back to politics and policy design.

What sort of economics proved decisive?

Hitherto, we have worked with an implicit, rationalist and modernist assumption: that policy could be improved by 'better' academic economics. If we now factor in the long-standing tension facing all economists, that between doing well (in a professional sense), by foregoing preaching and remaining wholly scholastic,[35] and doing good (in a welfare enhancing sense), by seeking to improve the quality of decision-making,[36] we can begin to confront what sort of economic thinking proved decisive and why in the 1950s and 1960s and what its longer-term implications were for economic policy and the reputation of economics.

The market for economic advice

The policy-making process has been described by Cairncross,[37] a key actor-observer, as a noisy conversation conducted through multiple networks which draw upon many types of economic expertise involving multiple producers of economic ideas.[38] It is, however, arguable that all post-war British economists who sought to forge a career as a senior policy adviser, consciously or unconsciously, had the example of Keynes in mind of how to do well and to do good. Accordingly, to be heard in this noisy, highly contestable market required strong and varied attributes which were as much to do with social endowments – understanding the networks of Whitehall and (for some) the possibilities afforded by Fleet Street and the media – as with one's standing as an elite professional economist with something interesting and relevant to say. Moreover, having gained access to the networks and then moved on to become a policy insider, the next issue to confront is how to make effective your comparative advantage. As Cairncross warned: 'Those who have never served in a large Government department are inclined to take too exalted a view of the rationality of the process of decision-making'.[39] The representation of 'economists as supermen able to transform the economy by technical wizardry and rendering administrators and ministers alike redundant', might now seem laughable but was a not altogether unfair caricature at the height of the Keynesian hegemony.[40]

　　Cairncross's observations accord with our understanding of how professional economists first made significant inroads into Whitehall during the Second World War, that is in the construction of the planned war economy. The challenge in the 1950s and early 1960s, however, was substantially different: not to override markets, but to support their more effective operation. Unfortunately, the political rhetoric, occasionally the economists' pronouncements also, suggested something more antipathetic to the market. None the less, when actually in Whitehall the economist policy insiders typically found themselves occupied as economist-administrators. For example, both Cairncross at the Treasury,[41] and Donald MacDougall at NEDO and then the DEA,[42] recount that a very great part of their time was allocated to drafting and redrafting documents. This was less to get the economics perfect – the technical nature of which rarely rose above the basic analytical tools imparted in any good undergraduate economics degree – than to find suitable wording which would offend the least number of interested parties in the corporatist melting pot that NEDC/NEDO and the DEA came to represent, and all under the careful and ever vigilant watch of a Treasury committed to ensuring that any 'creative tension' – Labour's phrase for the new Treasury/DEA-demand/supply-side policy axis – would not rebound to its disadvantage.

We have abundant evidence that far from these insiders being responsible for talking up the target growth rate, the intoxication by integers, it was the very opposite. Again, diaries and memoirs attest to the insider's efforts to contain politicians' ambitions for challenging targets and their frustration that neither the underlying qualitative issues or the hard allocational choices were being addressed. Cairncross, as Robert Hall before him, combined inherent Treasury pessimism with scepticism about the possibilities of making significant changes in short-term economic behaviour. MacDougall, who would replace Cairncross at the Treasury, was perhaps a little more optimistic about the prospects for growth promotion (as was Robert Neild), and probably also the most informed (and optimistic) of all of the advisers about the reality of the UK-US productivity gap and British competitiveness.[43] Even Kaldor, who with Balogh would become the bogeymen of Labour's dirigiste ambitions for certain City-business constituencies, would prove his worth with the Treasury he served, although his most public innovation, the Selective Employment Tax, remained an embarrassment.

Financial journalists and the advocacy coalition

An important component of Pemberton's advocacy coalition are the economic journalists whose writings 'lagged behind that of the academics [but] Nevertheless, they were much more able to communicate to the public the new ideas about the "growth problem" and its solution.'[44] Our dissent here concerns the respective significance of the participants and the content of their messages. First, if theory did lag policy, then actually the second group did not so much lag the academics as operate in parallel, and with economics but one element in their rhetorical armoury. This becomes clear not just from an assessment of the low technical content of their writings – pretty minimal beyond basic principles of economics, with few direct references to current theoretical work – but in relation to these journalists being as much cultural as economic critics. Accordingly, Shonfield, Shanks and Sampson, rightly identified as the key propagators of the growing mood for modernization, of which faster growth was becoming the rallying cry,[45] represented first and foremost a developing style of political discourse which was anti-Establishment in a cultural sense. Thus, to a certain extent, economics was the means to achieve the desired cultural and political reform (growth as change). This is not to deny the advocacy goal, that of a rejuvenated British economy, but it is to ground it in a wider context. Academic economists were not much involved in this critique, although Balogh's excoriating attack on the civil service rightly attracted attention, and some economists who achieved policy insider status in the 1960s (for example, Neild) would try to influence the Fulton Commission – which was the Establishment's response to these attacks.[46]

We draw this distinction, between the cultural content of these anti-Establishment attacks (Britain as a 'stagnant society') and the technical economic nature of the message about what reform was necessary in economic policy and behaviour, because the voices of the economic and financial journalists were the ones most heard and the ones to which politicians necessarily had to listen as perceptions of economic management competency became the subject of party political competition.[47] That this part of the advocacy coalition was able to dominate is a testimony to the competitiveness of the British market for economic advice; and to the fact that professional economics and economists had not managed to eclipse the power of non-professional economics, i.e. potentially ersatz economics.[48]

What mattered here is that relative to the academic economists, the journalists propagated a much more straightforward diagnoses of slow growth as caused by a combination of 'Stop-Go' and deep-seated administrative-policy failures, and a version of its remedy (in administrative reform and above all 'planning') which finessed the difficulties associated with implementing the new growth strategy. In short, in their advocacy of planning and of economic policy reform as part and parcel of broader modernizing reform, it was this group which fuelled policy-makers' growing preoccupation with securing greater macroeconomic stability and investment-led accelerated growth. The latter, of course, presumed, first, that growth was currently being constrained by 'low' investment; and, secondly, that business investment itself could be promoted by public policy. For some contemporary critics, the former was highly debatable,[49] while the latter posed all sorts of dangers for allocational inefficiencies and rent-seeking behaviour.[50]

In political economy terms we might conceive of the developing growth strategy as designed to widen the policy space by pasteurizing much of the conflicts that bedevilled contemporary politics. That growth was a palliative which would finesse long-standing distributional conflicts is a commonplace of this period. For contemporary critics, new growth promoting agencies such as NEDC and the growth targets that would emerge from them were an attempt to avoid the hard choices and the politically difficult changes that would be necessary to attain higher growth.[51] One is reminded here of the critique applied by Hayek and others against Keynes between the wars, namely that denying the obvious (if hard) solution for unemployment – allowing the labour market to clear through real wage flexibility – required extraordinary ingenuity, brilliance and administrative flexibility to be applied to construct a second-best solution, otherwise known as the Keynesian revolution. For the developing anti-planning lobby of the early 1960s, the complaint was naturally that planned growth was an oxymoron: what was required was freer markets and much more intense competition. Of course, for the Conservatives, there existed no straightforward dichotomy between government and market; they sought both greater planning and more intense competition, at least in product markets. That this was not how it appeared in political discourse was intrinsic to the bogus dilemmas that were increasingly characteristic of post-war British politics.[52]

A plague of economists?

It is now a commonplace that the growth targets were unrealistic, but where should we allocate culpability for these and other assumed errors which comprise what Harry Johnson's called the 'rich store of stupid decisions' which are the hallmark of post-war British economic policy?[53] The case against the economist insiders was first put effectively by Postan in a famous tirade which asked rhetorically whether 'with their models, measurements and forecasts' they had 'helped the economic recovery, or ... on the contrary, aggravated Britain's predicament by misdirecting the attention of the government and the public?' Reporting entirely in the negative, and suggesting that it was the economists' 'greater sophistication of ... theoretical constructions, ... much refined statistical and economic methods, [which] have put it out of touch with real economic situations',[54] these charges were not easily dismissed. Unlike much else of the reaction against growthmanship and growthmania they could not be derided as the mere rantings of second-rate economists who could only find a publishing home in the Institute of Economic Affairs (IEA).

Nonetheless, with the official records now available to supplement the potentially self-serving diaries and memoirs of the participants, and with the benefits of time, we can largely absolve the economists of technical errors, explaining the 4.0 and 3.8 per cent 1963/1965 growth targets in terms of a complex of factors, some of a largely economic character and others relating more to political factors. Of the former we highlight:

1. The problem of overinterpretation, in particular of the 1955–8 recession in which zero growth of industrial output combined with growing concerns about 'Stop-Go' were interpreted as something systemically wrong with the British economy, rather than as a set of contingent events which had produced policy overshoots in the 'Stop' (too much and for too long) and subsequent 'Go' phases (determined by the impending 1959 election).[55]
2. The growing pro-growth bias in public debate made it increasingly difficult to restrain above-trend growth, resulting in a policy cycle which was more 'Go-Stop' than 'Stop-Go'.
3. The problem of starting point, in which recovery from the 1955–8 recession was necessarily above trend and this generated the expectation by those less numerate and less informed about trend and cycle that if 4 per cent could be attained 1958–63 than it could easily be sustained thereafter. This necessarily established a 4 per cent floor to the target range.[56]
4. The problem of informational weaknesses, especially in 1964 when for a time the industrial production index appeared stuck despite contrary evidence about the developing boom. On the one hand there were apparently justifiable concerns about unemployment, while on the other, as the election campaign drew towards polling day, a classic balance of payments crisis was gathering pace. 'A crisis atmosphere was created just as the election was about to take place',[57] and in the refusal of the incoming government to immediately devalue

we have the orthodoxy that Labour's version of the growth strategy was fatally compromised from the outset.

The principal political factors include:

1. The naiveté of politicians in that, as Croham put it: 'Whatever the achieved growth rate, they wanted a target significantly bigger and that was liable to mean bigger by 1 per cent[age point]',[58] with Selwyn Lloyd particularly identified in this respect as being difficult to persuade – by Cairncross – that 5 per cent was unrealizable and that even 4 per cent was substantially higher than that achieved in the 1950s.
2. The intensity of political competition and the politicization of economic policy, of which the apogee must be the 1964 general election. This was the first and only election in which claims and counter-claims about the achievability of a growth target held centre stage,[59] resulting in a mood in which Macmillan's 'You've never had it so good' became 'You could have it better'.[60]
3. The confusion between growth targets and the policies necessary for their attainment, which in this context relates to the presumption by many (especially MacDougall) that the problem was not the target but Maudling's 'dash for growth' (1963–4) and Labour's subsequent error in not devaluing upon taking office.
4. The conflation of growth with planning, in which ideological opposition to the latter prejudiced opinion about desirability of promoting the former, and the tendency to backward project from the flaws associated with the National Plan to the NEDC initiative.

The dominance of political motives in Labour's exchange rate non-decision of October 1964 is, of course, the foundation of the economists' defence against much of the charge sheet levelled against their public and policy activities.[61] But is this an adequate defence given the broader charge of hubris? As Friedman put it:[62]

> we economists in recent years have done vast harm – to society at large and to our profession in particular – by claiming more than we can deliver. We have thereby encouraged politicians to make extravagant promises, inculcate unrealistic expectations in the public at large, and promote discontent with reasonably satisfactory results because they fall short of the economists' promised land.

Friedman's complaint was mirrored by many other economists at the time and subsequently who did not necessarily share his pro-market sympathies.[63] None the less, a necessary degree of confidence and ambition are a requirement for successful policy entrepreneurship (of which Friedman was hardly innocent), and as we have already demonstrated the insider economists were for the most part trying to deflate expectations about what was possible.

The political naivety of the economists

If the professional economists can largely be absolved of the more serious charges levelled against the economics of their advice, what about the second order charges that they were extraordinarily politically naïve? This charge embodies two elements: the first, the sense of hubris that if they got involved in politics they would not be compromised by it; and the second, their naivete about planning and particularly the National Plan. A further charge has also been made which goes to the heart of a common perception of economists' professional responsibilities: that politicians are weak and credulous and must be saved from themselves by high-minded economists.[64] In relation to all of these elements, and whether it be the spectre of Leviathan conjured up by Friedman's version of political economy, or Buchanan and Tulloch's developing public choice analysis, we need to be realistic that before at least the mid-1960s government failure in Britain was presumed to be less in practice than was market failure. O'Brien goes too far when he says that assumptions of 'omniscient and impartial government' swept aside all reservations about governmental capability,[65] but what was the alternative? Hardly an IEA version of the world, not at least in the 1960s.

The idea that there was a potential for perverse relationships between politics and economics, and between politicians and economists, was hardly novel.[66] What was new was that the results of the growth consciousness reconfigured power and authority within the state and as between the state, capital and labour. New constituencies, of which the economists were but one, acquired a vested interest in the growth strategy as they had previously in the full employment policy. Admittedly, the numbers involved were now larger, which was part of the IEA inspired reaction to the growth strategy, but as we have seen, economist insiders did try to discipline the politicians by deflating their expectations. At the NEDO and then at the DEA, MacDougall referred constantly to indicative planning as a 'confidence trick' (albeit with some – largely *ex* post – foundations in the theory of asymmetrical information) and sought to deepen government's understanding of how the economy functioned.[67]

Unfortunately, in the minds of the public and business economics was increasingly associated with forecasting, and as we have seen all of the planning experiments came to nought in this respect. The failures of forecasting became a special focus for adverse comment, with the expansionary bias of the economics establishment forensically examined on a number of occasions to its discredit.[68] This developing critique of the economists activities, of course, was in any case superimposed upon longer- and deeper-running lay perceptions that economists' predisposition to disputation limited their capacity to offer agreed solutions to practical problems. That the degree of professional economists' unanimity on economic questions was very much greater than that of the politicians they tried to serve, as Brittan's attitude survey of 1971 made clear,[69] came as a surprise to Britain's chattering classes, evidence of the deeply based and erroneous cultural assumptions about economists and economics and of how errors in forecasting rebounded to their political disadvantage.

Conclusions

In his seminal 1946 paper, Domar concluded that *'the rate of growth* [was] a concept which has been little used in economic theory'.[70] Less than 20 years later, the growth rate was to dominate not just economic theory but economic policy and, above all, British political discourse. Intoxicated by the possibilities afforded by compound arithmetic, via step-up integer growth rates, the Chancellors Selwyn Lloyd and Maudling, although not Callaghan (George Brown at the DEA, however, more than made up for any intoxication shortfall), were both grossly over-optimistic about the growth strategy and guilty of gross manipulation of economic policy for short-term political ends. But why should we expect otherwise of the politicians? And does it matter? The conventional wisdom has it that Labour's economic failure to guarantee the affluent society through its growth strategy not only robbed it of victory at the 1970 general election but, in that disappointment, was responsible for the leftwards shift thereafter in the Parliamentary Labour Party which made the Wilson–Callaghan years so traumatic and ensured that the following 18 years were ones spent in opposition.

To these big claims were appended the accusation that the economists' hubris was dangerously irresponsible in terms of economic policy and the profession's public reputation. It is now accepted that it was the faltering of the growth strategy, rather than the slightly later perception of the breakdown of the Phillips curve, that initiated the reaction against the Keynesian conventional wisdom. In no small part, disillusionment with economics resulted from the public having accepted the image that economists sought to present of their discipline as a positive science advancing theories with high predictive power and open to empirical testing and falsification. No one doubts that the 1960s were years of bitter disappointments, but as Sinclair concluded 'The real failure of governments lay not so much in their economic policies as in their extravagant claims of omnicompetence.'[71] If so, what else could have been done given that most of the policy insiders tried to contain the politicians' ambitions?

What would a more realistic growth strategy have looked like? For many, the answer almost begins and ends with devaluation to another fixed but adjustable parity (or moving to a floating exchange rate) and doing something radical about the sterling balances and Britain's geo-political overload which was placing untenable pressures on the balance of payments.[72] Beyond this we then have a class of arguments about which great care is needed, for much of the anti-planning school carries covert embryonic New Right baggage. Much does not, however, and it needs to be emphasized that under both the Conservatives and then Labour the advice given and the policies pursued were all mindful of market incentives/penalties and did not generally mark further deviations away from the balance between government and market that became the cornerstone of the post-war settlement. Whatever the rhetoric, there were in practice few *new* assaults upon the canons of professional economics – in particular upon value theory, on which the edifice of demand-supply, competition, optimal resource allocation, etc. resided – and therefore succour for the producers and consumers of ersatz economics. But with tax levels rising, with Labour forced into all sorts of devices to avoid the unavoidable, namely devaluation, and with the language of planning the dominant discourse, the growth strategy could be spun in such a way by its opponents.

It is not difficult to see that cooler language on the part of the politicians (and a few economists), greater restraint in target setting, greater transparency about the distribution of the costs/benefits of change, etc., could all have made an important contribution, but it must be remembered that a number of the politicians believed that they also had some credentials as economists. Be it Macmillan's interwar planning ideas, or Harold Wilson's apprenticeship in the wartime command economy, reservations about the market economy were much more marked amongst some of the political leaders than the majority of the economists, or at least the latter group *sans* Balogh. Of the politicians, Macmillan is more straightforward: an expansionist to his finger tips. Wilson, however, is more difficult to locate, and here of course we have two associated political liabilities: the great unmentionable (the exchange rate) and the great ungovernable (George Brown). Both Wilson and Brown spent the early part of the new government blustering about managing the economy in entirely new ways and railing against the gnomes of Zurich, no doubt to the delight of the left of the PLP. They also allowed the tactical electoral value of using the developing balance of payments crisis in the late summer of 1964 to derail totally their strategic economic vision.

The economic ideas that came to dominate between c.1955–65 had good academic provenance and Britain's economics establishment tried hard to contribute positively to policy needs. We have identified certain problems to do with the culture of economics and with the organization of research which limited the immediate utility of economics for policy, but the stronger charges against the professional economics establishment do not hold water. One characteristic of this time was that many were bruised by their experience of being a policy 'irregular'.[73] It was certainly more difficult to entice university economists into the Government Economic Service thereafter,[74] and this provided opportunities for an anti-Keynesian economics 'disestablishment'[75] to develop which that would take hold by the mid-1970s. In this sense the failure of the growth strategy established the groundwork for the monetarist-neo-liberal experiment to which Britain would be subjected under Thatcher and successive governments.

Notes

[*] This chapter is an output of the ESRC-financed project (R000237856) which produced Ringe, Astrid; Rollings, Neil; and Middleton, Roger: *Economic Policy under the Conservatives, 1951–64: A Guide to Documents in the National Archives of the UK*, IHR, London, 2004.

[1] Hereafter, if the noun 'economist' is unqualified by an adjective, such as 'professional' or 'policy insider', it refers to any person/group either self-identified as possessing economic expertise or viewed as such by potential consumers of such expertise.

[2] Hutchison, Terrence: *Economics and Economic Policy in Britain, 1946–1966*, George Allen and Unwin, London, 1968, p. 125; see also Arndt, Heinz: *The Rise and Fall of Economic Growth*, University of Chicago Press, Chicago, 1978.

[3] Pemberton, Hugh: 'The Keynesian-plus Experiment: A Study of Social Learning in the UK Core Executive, 1960–1966', Ph.D. dissertation, University of Bristol, 2001; to be published as *Policy learning and British governance in the 1960s*, Palgrave, London.

[4] Ringe, Astrid and Rollings, Neil: 'Responding to Relative Decline: The Creation of the National Economic Development Council', *Economic History Review*, vol. 53, no. 2 (2000), pp. 331–53; and Lowe, Rodney and Rollings, Neil: 'Modernising Britain, 1957–64: A Classic Case of Centralisation and Fragmentation?', in R. Rhodes (ed): *Transforming British Government*, Macmillan, London, 2000, vol. I, pp. 99–118.

[5] Tomlinson, Jim: *The Politics of Decline: Understanding Post-war Britain*, Longman, London, 2000.

[6] See, however, Middleton, Roger: *The British Economy since 1945*, Macmillan, London, 2000.

[7] Opie, Roger: 'Economic Planning and Growth', in W. Beckerman (ed): *The Labour Government's Economic Record, 1964–1970*, Duckworth, London, 1972, p. 170.

[8] Leruez, Jacques: *Economic Planning and Politics in Britain*, Martin Robertson, London, 1975, figure 11.1.

[9] Respectively, NEDC: *Growth of the United Kingdom Economy to 1966*, HMSO, London, 1963; and Cmnd. 2764, Department of Economic Affairs, *The National Plan*, HMSO, London, 1965.

[10] Maddison, Angus: *The World Economy*, OECD, Paris, 2001, table A1–c. We calculate that UK real GDP per capita in 1973 was some 93 per cent of the OECD-17 average, a gap significantly less than the hypothetical shortfall of actual GDP relative to the NEDC 1963 projection of Figure 1. Had the hypothetical 14.4 per cent shortfall been made good then Britain's OECD ranking by this measure would have risen from eleventh to fifth, two places above its 1950 ranking.

[11] That this is not entirely an anachronistic exercise can be defended on the grounds that, concurrent with the developing growth strategy, the National Institute of Economic and Social Research was undertaking a major forecasting exercise on what the British economy might look like in 1975 were the NEDC target growth rate attained.

[12] Abramovitz, Moses: 'Economics of Growth', in B.F. Haley (ed): *A Survey of Contemporary Economics*, R.D. Irwin, Homewood, IL, 1952, vol. II, p. 132.

[13] Mueller, Denis C. (ed): *The Political Economy of Growth*, Yale University Press, New Haven, 1983, p. 1.

[14] See Tobin, James: 'Economic Growth as an Objective of Government Policy', *American Economic Review*, vol. 54, no. 3 (1964), pp. 1–20.

[15] Rostow, Walt: *The Stages of Economic Growth: A Non-Communist Manifesto*, Cambridge University Press, Cambridge, 1960.

[16] Tomlinson, *Politics of Decline*, op. cit.

[17] Arndt, *Economic Growth*, op. cit., p. 51.

[18] Middleton, *British Economy*, op. cit., pp. 6–9 ff.

[19] Comparative and historical studies of national product per capita made a substantial advance with Gilbert, Milton and Kravis, Irving B: *An International Comparison of National Products and the Purchasing Power of Currencies*, OEEC, Paris, 1954, but investigations of this form into comparative absolute labour productivity lagged a good half decade or so. Hence, policy-makers had to wait until Maddison, Angus: *Economic Growth in the West: Comparative Experience in Europe and North America*, George Allen and Unwin, London, 1964, before they had solid and useful estimates with which to assess absolute values of the gap.

[20] E.g. Denison, Edward: *Why Growth Rates Differ?*, Brookings Institute, Washington, DC, 1967; Matthews, Robin; Feinstein, Charles; and Odling-Smee, John: *British Economic Growth, 1856–1973*, Clarendon Press, Oxford, 1982.

[21] Solow, Robert: 'Perspectives on Growth Theory', *Journal of Economic Perspectives*, vol. 8, no. 1 (1994), p. 45. Any competent general history of economic thought should provide an account of post-war growth theory's development which makes clear some of the implications for policy, for example, Backhouse, Roger: *A History of Modern Economic Analysis*, Basil Blackwell, Oxford, 1985, ch. 25; see also Coates, David: *Models of Capitalism*, Polity, Cambridge, 2000, appendix.

[22] Solow, Robert: 'Growth Theory and After', *American Economic Review*, vol. 78, no. 3 (1988), p. 308.

[23] Coates: *Models*, op. cit., pp. 265–6.

[24] Shone, Robert: 'Problems of Planning for Economic Growth in a Mixed Economy', *Economic Journal*, vol. 75, no. 1 (1965), pp. 8–9.

[25] Denison: *Why Growth Rates Differ?*, op. cit.; and, eventually, Matthews, *et al.*: *British Economic Growth*, op. cit.

[26] Cairncross, Alec: *Managing the British Economy in the 1960s*, Macmillan, London, 1996, p. 65.

[27] Cairncross in discussion on Croham, Lord: 'Were the Instruments of Control for Domestic Economic Policy Adequate?', in F. Cairncross and A. Cairncross (eds): *The Legacy of the Golden Age*, Routledge, London, 1992, p. 105. The Orange Book was NEDC: *Conditions Favourable to Faster Growth*, HMSO, London, 1963.

[28] Cited in Denison, Edward: 'Growth Accounting', in J. Eatwell *et al.* (eds): *The New Palgrave Dictionary of Economics*, Macmillan, London, vol. II, p. 572.

[29] Middleton, Roger: *Charlatans or Saviours?: Economists and the British Economy from Marshall to Meade*, Edward Elgar, Cheltenham, 1998, pp. 206–11.

[30] Ibid., pp. 227–8.

[31] Barro, Robert: *Determinants of Economic Growth*, MIT Press, Cambridge, MA, 1997.

[32] Crafts, Nick: '"Post-neoclassical Endogenous Growth Theory": What are its Policy Implications?', *Oxford Review of Economic Policy*, vol. 12, no. 2 (1996), p. 42.

[33] Ibid., p. 44.

[34] See Landau, Ralph *et al.* (eds): *The Mosaic of Economic Growth*, Stanford University Press, Stanford, CA, 1996, pp. 1, 12, 15.

[35] Stigler, George: *The Economist as Preacher*, University of Chicago Press, Chicago, 1982.

[36] Klein, Daniel: *What Do Economists Contribute?*, Macmillan, London, 1999.

[37] Cairncross, Alec: 'Academics and policy makers', in F. Cairncross (ed): *Changing Perceptions of Economic Policy*, Methuen, London, 1981, p. 5.

[38] Middleton, *Charlatans or Saviours?*, op. cit., pp. 50–51.

[39] Cairncross, Alec: 'Writing the History of Recent Economic Policy', unpublished paper, 1970, p. 5.

[40] Cairncross, Alec: *Essays in Economic Management*, George Allen and Unwin, London, 1971, p. 203.

[41] Cairncross, Alec: *The Wilson Years: A Treasury Diary, 1964–1969*, Historian's Press, London, 1997.

[42] MacDougall, Donald: *Don and Mandarin: Memoirs of an Economist*, John Murray, London, 1987, pp. 140–41.

[43] See MacDougall, Donald: 'Does Productivity Rise Faster in the United States?', *Review of Economics and Statistics*, vol. 38, no. 2 (1956), pp. 155–76.

[44] Pemberton: 'Keynesian Plus', op. cit, p. 62.

[45]   Shonfield, Andrew: *British Economic Policy Since the War*, Penguin, Harmondsworth, 1958; Shanks, Michael: *The Stagnant Society: A Warning*, Penguin, London, 1961; and Sampson, Anthony: *Anatomy of Britain*, Hodder and Stoughton, London, 1962.

[46]   Balogh, Thomas: 'The Apotheosis of the Dilettante: The Establishment of Mandarins', in H. Thomas (ed): *The Establishment*, Anthony Blond, London, 1959, pp. 83–126; and Hennessy, Peter *et al.*: 'Symposium: Fulton, 20 years on', *Contemporary Record*, vol. 2, no. 2 (1988), pp. 44–51.

[47]   Parsons, D. Wayne: *The Power of the Financial Press*, Edward Elgar, Aldershot, 1989, p. 109.

[48]   Parsons, *Financial Press*, op. cit., p. 110. Ersatz economics, born of lay participants in economic discourse, embodies the concepts of substitute (of vulgar for professional economics) and inherent danger (of resulting incorrect economic behaviours founded on erroneous conclusions). In the US it has been a particular target of McCloskey and Krugman; and in the UK in the do-it-yourself-economics targeted by Henderson, P. David: *Innocence and Design: The Influence of Economic Ideas on Policy*, Basil Blackwell, Oxford, 1986.

[49]   Clark, Colin: *Growthmanship: A Study in the Mythology of Investment*, IEA, London, 1961.

[50]   Ringe *et al.*: *Economic Policy*, op. cit., ch. 7.

[51]   Ringe and Rollings: 'Responding', p. 333.

[52]   Rollings, Neil and Middleton, Roger: 'British Economic Policy in the 1950s and 1960', paper delivered to Economic History Society Annual Conference, University of Birmingham, 6 April 2002.

[53]   Johnson, Harry: 'The Man who turned Economics into Commonsense', *The Times*, 9 March 1976.

[54]   Postan, Michael: 'A Plague of Economists?: On Some Current Myths, Errors and Fallacies', *Encounter*, vol. 30, no. 1 (1968), p. 42.

[55]   This appears a key period in generating the impression of British macroeconomic instability during the golden age because the business cycle phase with the highest amplitude (1955–60) was also that with the slowest average growth. It was also coincident with, first, the beginnings of that policy inquest into relative decline and, second, following the proximity of an (unwarranted) expansionary budget and the 1955 general election, the accusations that 'Stop-Go' had assumed the character of political business cycles.

[56]   MacDougall, discussion on Croham: 'Instruments of Control', op. cit., pp. 102–3.

[57]   Cairncross: *Managing the British Economy*, op. cit., p. 87.

[58]   Croham: 'Instruments of Control', op. cit., pp. 91–2.

[59]   Butler, David and King, Anthony: *The British General Election of 1964*, Macmillan, London, 1965, pp. 132–4.

[60]   Proudfoot, Mary: *British Politics and Government, 1951–1970: A Study of an Affluent Society*, Faber and Faber, London, 1972, p. 160.

[61]   Middleton, *Charlatans or Saviours?*, op. cit., pp. 253–68.

[62]   Friedman, Milton: 'Have Monetary Policies Failed?', *American Economic Review*, vol. 62, no. 2 (1972), pp. 12, 17–18.

[63]   Not least from some of the actors in the British growth experiment, and particularly Cairncross who, in a number of publications after he left the civil service and returned to academe, made the implicit charge of hubris and more explicit critique of political naivete on the part of the economics profession.

[64]   Jewkes, John: 'The Perils of Planning', *Three Banks Review*, no. 66 (June 1965), pp. 3–14.

[65] O'Brien, Denis: 'The Emphasis on Market Economics', in A. Seldon (ed): *The Emerging Consensus?: Essays on the Interplay Between Ideas, Interests and Circumstances in the First 25 Years of the IEA*, IEA, London, 1981, p. 64.

[66] There has always been a literature critical of economics and economists, but from the 1960s onwards some of it became pretty strident in its critique of the dismal science and the supposed political and policy pretensions of its practitioners because of the growing association of economists with forecasting; see, for example, Rubner, Alex: *Three Sacred Cows of Economics*, MacGibbon and Kee, London, 1970; and Pringle, Robin: *The Growth Merchants: Economic Consequences of Wishful Thinking*, CPS, London, 1977. Such literature has been unduly neglected by historians of economic thought, as indeed has that of financial journalists.

[67] MacDougall, *Don and Mandarin*, op. cit., p. 139.

[68] Hutchison: *Economic Policy*, op. cit. and Pringle: *Growth Merchants*, op. cit.

[69] Brittan, Samuel: *Is There an Economic Consensus?: An Attitude Survey*, Macmillan, London, 1973.

[70] Domar, Evsey: 'Capital Expansion, Rate of Growth and Employment', *Econometrica*, vol. 14, no. 2 (1946), p. 147.

[71] Sinclair, Peter: 'The Economy: A Study in Failure', in D. McKie and C. Cooks (eds): *The Decade of Disillusion: British Politics in the Sixties*, Macmillan, London, 1972, p. 94.

[72] Middleton, Roger: 'Struggling with the Impossible: Sterling, the Balance of Payments and British Economic Policy, 1949–72', in A. Arnon and W.L. Young (eds): *The Open Economy Macromodel: Past, Present and Future*, Kluwer Academic Press, Boston, MA, 2002, pp. 103–54.

[73] Brittan, who spent an unhappy fourteen months in the DEA, has made clear that the origins of his 'second thoughts' on the Keynesian conventional wisdom lie in that period, while Beckerman, who did not reject Keynesianism, also had a personally and professionally unrewarding experience in the DEA which coloured his preparedness thereafter to become too enmeshed in public policy; see their contributions to Backhouse, Roger and Middleton, Roger (eds): *Exemplary Economists*, Edward Elgar, Cheltenham, 2000, vol. II, pp. 165–8, 280–82. Another irregular was Michael Stewart (Economic Section, then Cabinet Office) who once free of the civil service used his experience to publish a sharp and accurate critique, *The Jekyll and Hyde Years: Politics and Economic Policy Since 1964*, J.M. Dent, London, 1977. Finally, of course, Cairncross expressed on a number of occasions his delight at returning to academic life in 1969, although alas his published writings on Whitehall were far less indiscreet.

[74] An interesting comparison can also be made between the positive press reception to Cairncross's appointment as chief economic adviser in 1961 and the chilliness afforded to his successor, MacDougall, in 1968; see Middleton, *Charlatans or Saviours?*, op. cit., p. 268.

[75] Singer, Otto: 'Knowledge and Politics in Economic Policy-making: Official Economic Advisers in the USA, Britain and Germany', in B.G. Peters and A. Barker (eds): *Advising West European Governments: Inquiries, Expertise and Public Policy*, Edinburgh University Press, Edinburgh, 1993, pp. 76–79.

CHAPTER 9

The Polyester-Flannelled Philanthropists: The Birmingham Consumers' Group and Affluent Britain

Matthew Hilton

In its famous fictional portrayal, Birmingham, or Rummidge, was 'a large, graceless industrial city sprawled over the English Midlands at the intersection of three motorways, twenty-six railway lines and half-a-dozen stagnant canals.'[1] David Lodge was a little unfair in his dour description, creating as it does an image that looks backwards to a city founded on manufacture, production and trade. It does not capture the spirit of affluence, the optimism of post-war regeneration or the forward-looking design of much social and urban planning. It does not embrace the liberating potential of egalitarian consumption so famously evoked in J.B. Priestley's *English Journey* and commonly celebrated in the speeches of post-war politicians and social commentators. No longer dressed in ragged trousers, the British working class, together with an expanding middle class, housed in Birmingham across the leafy suburbs to the south of the city, were turning instead to the nylons and polyesters of a more scientific age. If not exactly offering the solutions to consumer society provided by Alec Guinness' *The Man in the White Suit* (Alexander Mackendrick, 1951), new technological and electrical gadgets seemed to provide everybody with the chance to share in the good life and the leisured society. In the ten years after 1945, national expenditure on these items – refrigerators, stereos, cookers, electrical appliances and motor cars – shot up from £189 million to £1,268 million per annum.[2]

Yet this apparent shift to affluence was met with tensions and anxieties as households negotiated the new array of goods. If affluence represented a brave new world it was one which offered various pitfalls and dangers for consumers. Higher wages may well have reduced any alienation felt in the workplace, but consumers sensed a growing alienation in the store and on the high street. The problem felt by many was that the traditional skills and resources associated with the shopper – being able to touch and test the product, rely on the verbal guarantee supplied by a trusted retailer or trust in the ethic of commerce practised by the Co-operative movement – were no longer useful in a market dominated by anonymous manufacturers and highly technical products where only a qualified scientist or engineer could assess the quality or fitness for purpose. Instead, consumers were becoming what one commentator called the philanthropists of consumer society,[3] wilfully handing over cash to companies engaged in a great value-for-money trick: hire purchase agreements did not make clear the true cost of a good; resale price maintenance hid a number of unpopular collusive trading agreements which exploited the consumer; poor labelling tended more to misinformation than useful advice; advertising praised the shoddy and over-inflated the value of the cheap; contract law failed to set out precisely the duty of care owed by manufacturers; guarantees were often worthless; prices gave no indication of exorbitant maintenance and repair costs; many products simply broke down or were found to be faulty within days; unskilled sales staff cared more for their commissions than they did to helping consumers find the product most suitable to their needs; and, worst of all, poor design, negligent manufacture and a dismissive regard to the mass public ensured that many products were even dangerous and potentially lethal for their users. This was the 'consumer jungle' to which many journalists and critics referred as individuals were left to fend for themselves amidst a hostile and alien environment.[4]

The Birmingham Consumers' Group

In Birmingham, a group of affluent professionals determined to help the city's public put a stop to its unwitting benevolence. In January 1963, the Birmingham Consumers' Group was established and held its first annual general meeting. Led by Gordon Burley, a lecturer in product design and development at the Birmingham College of Advanced Technology, who became the first chairman and secretary, it quickly obtained over 100 members largely from the relatively prosperous south side of the city. Its initial Executive Committee reflected the geographical and social base of its membership: Burley was from the more opulent end of Edgbaston, as was the first editor, Dr J.C. Gunn; the Treasurer, Miss J. Edlin, was from Hall Green; the projects officer, Michael Steward, from Kings Heath; the programme secretary, Clive Waterman, and the information officer, Ray Burgess, from Moseley; while later figures appeared from other established prosperous districts such as Harborne, Kings Norton and Solihull.[5] They committed themselves to the creation of an 'independent, autonomous, non-profit-making, non-sectarian and non-party-political organisation' which aimed 'to increase the awareness of consumers, to identify and promote the proper interests of consumers and the means of their protection and to provide a channel for consumer opinion and representation.'[6] In practice, this meant conducting local surveys of shops and public services, publishing the results in the *Birmingham Consumer*, the Group's quarterly magazine, and acting as the spokesbody for the consumer on local issues.[7] Members paid an annual subscription of 10s, though recognizing that much of its membership would be made up of married couples, a family subscription rate was introduced at 12s 6d. Within a year, there were 207 subscriptions to the *Birmingham Consumer*, of which 106 were from single members (who, against the Executive's expectations, were predominantly male), 102 were from double members (that is, married couples) and a further nine from various public institutions and private organizations (who paid an annual rate of £1).[8]

This was a reasonably successful beginning and the very fact that a group of relatively anonymous middle-class suburbanites could come together in such an organization suggests much about affluent lifestyles in post-war Britain. It demonstrates at least that consumers not only participated in the purchasing of a growing number of consumables, but that affluence itself created a new social environment which promoted renewed voluntary activity across suburbia. Admittedly, this voluntarism could be based as much on self-interest as on a regard for the lives of one's fellow consumers and citizens, but it represented a move into the socio-political sphere outside of the commercial bodies and trade unions usually associated with post-Second World War political debate. Furthermore, the Birmingham Consumers' Group was to assume a wider prominence as many of its leading figures would help place the 'consumer interest' at the heart of any national discussions over politics, society and the economy. Members of the Birmingham Group went on to take up prominent positions in the Consumers Association (CA), the Office of Fair Trading and the National Consumer Council and their agendas, arising from their experience of affluence in the 1950s and 1960s, shaped much consumer protection legislation and state intervention from the 1970s onwards.

In the early 1960s, the Group got off to a reasonably successful start. It received favourable coverage in the press, with the *Birmingham Post* and *Birmingham Evening Mail* both picking up on the willingness of men to become 'alert customers' and the desire of the Group not to be portrayed as anti-business or the enemy of retailers.[9] But the Group was to achieve even greater prominence the closer its links became to the University of Birmingham, itself situated in Edgbaston and with a staff largely scattered through the residential areas already associated with the new breed of consumer 'activist'. By the end of the Group's first year, Colin Harbury had returned from the United States to take up a post as a senior lecturer in the Economics department at the University. He helped make the Group a more positive and wide-ranging movement, rather than one concerned with narrow personal interests as typified by Burley's well-publicized request in 1959 to have the cost of his cinema ticket refunded when the film failed to live up to the expectations of that promised in the publicity posters.[10] By the summer of 1964 Harbury stressed the need for greater information to ensure consumers knew their legal rights and to help them obtain value for money, but he also emphasized 'the aesthetic development of standards of taste in things personal and civic; and for the politico-economic discussions of institutions,' especially the role of consumer groups in relation to private bodies and local and central government bureaucracies concerned with consumer affairs.[11] Earlier in 1958, Harbury had published a Fabian pamphlet entitled *Efficiency and the Consumer,* arguing that affluence had created a society which reduced the individual to 'embarrassing ignorance', 'inability', 'short-sightedness' and 'wasteful, irrational' expenditure. He advocated instead a form of empowered consumerism whereby consumers cast aside fashion, religion, national identity and custom to reach the 'enlightenment' of 'rational' 'efficiency'.[12] In this politics of consumption rather than production, the consumer, through information, representation and discrimination, could overcome the advantages given to the manufacturer in a technical age.

Harbury's consumer vision was in line with the technologically and rationally minded professionalism of his University colleagues. Along with him came

Leonard Tivey, a lecturer in politics with a background in Political and Economic Planning and before that, as with Harbury, a training at the London School of Economics. Tivey went on to represent the consumer in the gas industry and, in line with his academic interests which led to a chair in political science, wrote several pieces on the position of consumer protection and the consumer movement in the modern state.[13] Gordon Borrie, who had already written a book with Aubrey Diamond on *The Consumer, Society and the Law* before he took up a senior lectureship in the Law department in 1965, was 'seized upon immediately' by the Consumers' Group and became another prominent member with useful contacts.[14] Later, he became Dean of his faculty before having to resign in 1976 to take up the post of Director General of Fair Trading. These men were often joined by their wives and other women who had received a university education, had started families and were, as Tivey put it, 'looking for something to do'.[15] Cynthia Walton was a professional journalist living in Moseley who became an early editor of the *Birmingham Consumer*. Tivey's wife, Marjorie, became the secretary and, with him, another editor and central member of the Group in the 1970s and beyond and is still a member today. So too is Ruth Klemperer, the editor immediately after Walton. She had obtained a DPhil from Oxford and had settled into being a housewife in Selly Oak, literally on the University's doorstep, but by the mid-1960s had time on her hands to employ her talents beyond the home. Similarly, Rachel Waterhouse, wife of another lecturer, had completed a PhD in the University's History department in 1950 but had then focused on raising four children. However, as a member of the CA from the very beginning, Harbury obtained her name from the subscription list and encouraged her to become the Group's secretary in 1964. She would hold several positions throughout the 1960s and 1970s and remains a vice-president, but she was also convinced by Harbury, Tivey and Borrie, in a meeting at the University, to stand for the CA Council as the 'Birmingham housewife'. She went on to become a member of the National Consumer Council in 1975 and chair of the CA from 1979.[16] Finally, Janet Upward, who had been secretary of the Wolverhampton Consumers' Group, founded by Gordon Burley in 1968 after he had moved from Birmingham, followed her husband to Kings Heath in 1970. She immediately joined the Birmingham Group and, from 1972, acted as secretary to the National Federation of Consumer Groups.[17]

With such close connections, the Group was often referred to as the 'Birmingham University Consumers' Group' and it saw as its rivals the Oxford Consumers' Group which drew on a similar social base. But its membership reached beyond the campus and in the mid-1960s it continued to grow. In early 1965, just two years after the Group's formation, subscriptions had reached a figure of 369, representing a total membership of 540.[18] Membership dipped slightly towards the end of the decade, but following successful recruitment drives in the spring of 1968 and the soliciting of 253 new members of staff at the University in 1969, membership figures persisted around the 500 mark.[19] Nevertheless, the active membership was substantially less than this, with around 25 committed consumers – who were often housewives – being relied upon for project work. The main focus of the Group was the *Birmingham Consumer*, but it began with the intention of being the centre for general discussions of consumer issues. Discussion Groups were set up in 1963, held in members' houses, so that topics such as public services, electrical repairs and household maintenance could be explored. District Section Meetings were also begun in order to reach out beyond the south Birmingham area, though the absence of committed consumers elsewhere prevented this becoming a permanent activity. Members worked to collate information that may have been of use for the informed consumer in the Birmingham region with Burgess, the Information Officer, immediately collecting the names of 500 organizations which were of some use to the Group. The intention was then to communicate constantly with these other bodies so that the Group became 'the local centre of consumer interest', a grass roots independent body which participated on an equal footing with the more established institutions of provincial civil society.[20]

But the life of the Group always revolved around the quarterly publication of its magazine. Members submitted proposals for subjects they wished to be researched, else complaints – often in the form of letters to the magazine – were analysed by the Executive to determine priorities, upon which project teams were then assigned to head the investigation. The first study undertaken by the group – and here its choice reflected the social and economic background of the membership – was of garage services. Members questioned nearly 40 garages around the city and compiled a list as to whether there existed an automatic car wash, a wheel balancing machine, a crypton engine tester, a headlamp beam setter, the hours of opening, the rates charged for labour and, most crucially, whether the owner had signed up to the Fidelity Scheme of the Motor Agents' Association. The results were published in the first issue of the *Birmingham Consumer* and this limited form of comparative testing formed the model for many future projects.[21] In the 1960s the Group analysed a range of private goods and services from Christmas crackers, delivery delays, dry cleaning, taxis and restaurants: even the University students were enrolled on one survey of the resale of electricity by landlords in rented accommodation.[22] Such a local group with limited funds and expertise could never hope to engage in the value-for-money testing of branded goods and there was a natural drift to the testing of municipal services. Here a certain narrow-mindedness could creep in as the group consolidated established middle-class concerns over the state of council refuse collection and the length of waiting times in general medical practice.[23] Yet the civic commitment of the Group must also be noted. Indeed, one can only imagine and admire the sight of several university-educated women, led by Anji La Touche-Cliff and including some who would soon go on to lead prominent public lives, visiting every public lavatory across the city centre, giving each a rating and concluding that 'all the old Birmingham Council lavatories seem to be the very worst to use, and we would advise readers to keep a list for emergency use only.'[24] Unfortunately for these housewives, their husbands, though also members of the Group, had not volunteered in sufficient numbers for this weekday project and a solitary John Martin was left to visit the male toilets, though he presumably gave up since gentlemen's facilities were not included in the tabulated survey results.

Other examples could be cited as the Group increasingly turned its attention to public services – from bus stations to playgrounds, facilities for the young and the elderly, public health, street numbering and libraries. Attempts were made to make the Group a crucial support to any national consumer organization. Price surveys were conducted for the Prices and Incomes Board, the Group publicized the outlets where the CA's *Which?* magazine 'best buys' could be purchased and closer contacts were established by Upward with the Office of Fair Trading in the 1970s. As it gained a greater knowledge of consumer issues within Birmingham the Group did begin to take on the role of a more general consumer advocate. In addition to the journal, the Group published special supplements, one on *Leisure Activities for Young People* in 1964 and another on *Birmingham After 7pm* in 1967. Later, though for members only, and invoking the concerns of several late-nineteenth century international Consumers' Leagues and trade union campaigns, they issued a *White List* of services in the home, so that reliable decorators, builders, plumbers, carpenters and so on could be called upon.[25] Initially it had planned to establish an advisory service to complement the activities of the local Citizens' Advice Bureau in this field, though it never had the resources to do this effectively.[26] Instead, it took to forms of direct intervention on specific issues. It issued press statements on topics as diverse as rising prices, resale price maintenance and lead-free paint, and it policed national regulations such as the Home Office prohibition of flammable children's nightdresses: when members of the Group discovered these being sold in the 1964 summer sales of some of Birmingham's largest stores a public campaign led to their removal from the shelves.[27] Later, they pressurized the Midlands Electricity Board into publishing more information about its maximum prices and they stirred up local interest in garage tyre gauges.[28] Such campaigns encouraged Council authorities to encourage the representational work of the Group. Members were frequently approached by the local media to provide the consumer view and meetings were often held with representatives of retailers, Chambers of Trade and advertising agencies. In 1966 the Group was asked to nominate one of its members to the Birmingham Post Office Advisory Committee and this was soon followed by requests for nominations to Community Health Councils, the municipal Transport Advisory Committee and the Citizens' Advice Bureau Committee.[29] Increasingly, the Group interested itself in urban planning and one of its most prominent roles was in its call for the pedestrianization of Birmingham city centre. Although the final scheme was not to the Group's taste, it was an important initiator and a constant contributor to public consultation meetings.[30]

Reform of the affluent society was to come not only through the market place but through the individual shopper. Consumer education was seen as crucial to rectifying many of the imbalances involved in the exchange of goods and the Group made this its principal activity beyond its assessment of local services. Beginning with its own members, articles were published in the *Birmingham Consumer* on 'the art of complaining' and specific guidelines were written in its 'advice to shoppers'.[31] Experts were invited to contribute articles on their own work, be it in the local weights and measures inspectorate, the Citizens' Advice Bureau, the City Council's Information Department or the municipal Analytical

Laboratories. The Group was able to draw on the many contacts of its several prominent public figures to arrange lectures by national consumer figures. For instance, in the autumn of 1964, a series of talks were given in Birmingham Library featuring Mary Adams, deputy chair of the CA, Noel White, deputy chair of the Council for Industrial Design, Aubrey Diamond, chair of the National Federation of Consumer Groups, Roger Diplock, director of the Retail Trading Standards Association, Brian Groombridge, research director of the Research Institute for Consumer Affairs, and Elizabeth Ackroyd, director of the Consumer Council.[32] Members of the Group went on to give talks around the city, to schools, colleges, residents' associations, church groups, women's groups and professional institutions. From 1971, the Group was even provided with its own slot on Radio Birmingham, a fortnightly programme which discussed topics such as 'what is a consumer?', food concerns, consumer safety, local services and legislation such as the Trade Descriptions Act of 1968.[33] 'Buyer Beware' was broadcast on alternative Thursdays at 5.50pm and by 1978, the Group had taken greater control of its content, the invited experts, the script and even the signature tune.[34]

Consumerism's great oration

Consumer education was also to be provided in more formal settings. Following the low attendance at many of its own meetings on general consumer issues, the Group decided to embark on specific educational courses, beginning with 'The Consumer and Society' organized in collaboration with the Extra-Mural Department of Birmingham University.[35] This was followed by a 13-week evening course – 'Shopping for Value' – run by members of the Group at the Bournville Institute for Further Education in 1967.[36] The message of the courses formed the great oration of Birmingham consumerism and could sometimes be taken to the heart of irrational consumption's spending beano such as when the Group set up a stall in the Pallasades shopping centre during the 1981 'Consumer Week'.[37] Members of the Group placed great faith in the potential of organized, activist consumerism and empowered individualism. Informed and knowing consumers would not blindly hand over their money to exploitative tradesmen but would carefully select, choose and discriminate in their purchasing decisions such that the market worked for them and not the interests of business. There was a great sense of optimism as to what local organizations could achieve. Janet Upward has suggested that at the time they thought they were 'the new force in the land': by 'collectivising our resources we could get information for consumers which would enable them to be better shoppers and get a better deal. And then as we got more sophisticated we would say, "Well, if you've got better educated or informed consumers they will help drive up the quality of goods and services because they will be more discriminating".'[38] Popular with such consumers were the works of Vance Packard whose The Hidden Persuaders pointed to the ability of advertisers to control the consuming desires of the mass public.[39] In order to overcome such a situation it was up to this generation of 1960s consumers who entered adulthood in a time of affluence to ensure they were not manipulated and, to this end, a proliferation of self-help manuals for consumers appeared throughout the 1960s and 1970s.[40]

Robert Millar's *The Affluent Sheep* was widely read by the leading activists within the Birmingham Consumer Group. The *Daily Express* journalist argued that consumers were being herded into consuming decisions through the manufacturer's grip on subconscious desire: 'They are like sheep being joggled by sheepdogs. They run hither and thither, not knowing why and totally unaware of where they are going.'[41] He asked 'Who will be the shepherds?' and saw in consumerism the opportunity to create a new world. He imagined 'two nations' of consumer emerging: on the one hand the 'efficient', 'rational', 'scientific', 'objective', 'informed' and 'discriminating', motivated purely by a desire to obtain value-for-money; on the other, the 'fickle', 'ignorant', 'deluded' and 'illogical'.[42] Later, the Birmingham consumers would follow Robin Wight's advice and 'refuse to be driven to market' building a revolution based on 'no marches, no manifesto, no real leaders and few formal followers.'[43] Out of the move to empowered individualism would emerge a 'new consumer' establishing a 'new coincidence of self-interest between business and the consumer.'[44]

Birmingham consumers also set their own agenda and worked out for themselves the role of the consumer in modern society. Borrie, through his work at the Office of Fair Trading, saw the consumer as a handmaiden to industry. Consumerism, at least through its representation in his role as Director General was not so much a 'watchdog' but 'a *regulator* of business, a *monitor* of markets and laws, a *proposer* of policies, and *educator* of the public and a *promoter* of high trading standards.[45] Rachel Waterhouse shared this non-aggressive stance and would later set out the purpose of the consumer movement as a means to assist 'an individual or person in one part of their life: that is, as purchaser or user of goods or services, whether privately or publicly supplied.'[46] This implied a 'preoccupation with the immediate' and a focus on practical concerns but the local consumer activist was to form just one part of a wider model of consumer protection. Writing in the *Birmingham Consumer* at the close of the government's Consumer Council in 1970, she argued that all consumer organizations had to co-ordinate their activities more effectively such that 'the organised consumer may have a voice commensurate with his importance in the production/selling/buying cycle.'[47] Finally, Leonard Tivey, several years after publishing his more academic pieces on the role of consumer protection in the modern state, set out his views on consumerism as a form of 'constitutional opposition, responsible yet critical, always vigilant for its clientele and asking for improvement.'[48] From 1978 Tivey began a series of 'Consumer speculations' in the *Birmingham Consumer* which ran on throughout the 1980s and into the 1990s in which he shied away from making consumerism a 'third force' in the political sphere but emphasized its practical capabilities in solving a whole range of problems 'concerned with truthful information and honest dealing': from defining its boundaries, the role of free trade, the extent of free choice, the relationship between consumers and workers, the nationalized industries and competition policy.[49]

Consumerism abridged or complete?

Tivey also spoke of a perceived backlash against consumerism in 1979 as the Confederation of British Industry sought to place limits on the consumer's role and the new Conservative government criticized 'rampant consumerism' and advocated instead the panacea of 'choice'.[50] It is in such actions that the double meaning of consumerism has been forgotten. Increasingly over the last two or three decades it has lost its original associations with voluntarism, organized campaigning and even Ralph Nader-esque political activism and, instead, has come to be associated only with individual acquisitiveness and all the other pejorative terminology regularly invoked by critics of modern capitalist society.[51] An abridged version of the history of the Birmingham Group might therefore end at this point and one could perhaps endorse the conclusion of a businessman in the 1960s who dismissed local consumer activists as 'uninitiated amateurs who are insufficiently informed to assess the standards of experienced traders and that they are run by a few carping cranks.'[52] Membership figures for Birmingham had been in decline for some time and as early as 1966 the Sutton Coldfield Consumer Group had been forced to amalgamate with Birmingham due to a lack of interest.[53] The Birmingham Group had long recognized the difficulties of getting its members involved in projects and meetings even in the 1960s but this was exacerbated in the 1970s as total membership fell. In 1972, it still stood at a comparatively respectable 426, but declined gradually to 341 by 1976 (of which 116 were family subscriptions: that is, two members per one subscription) and just 237 by 1987 (87 single members, 63 double members and 24 organizations).[54] These dwindling numbers always operated on an extremely limited annual budget at an amount only ever in double figures in the 1960s and only a few hundred pounds in the late 1970s. One gets the impression that the majority of these shared few of the wider concerns of Harbury, Waterhouse, Tivey and Borrie. Indeed, when the Information Officer, Raymond Fletcher, attended a meeting with other local consumer groups he returned infuriated at having spent a day discussing such trivial issues as the great deception perpetrated by fish fryers selling chips by weight after, rather than before, cooking.[55] By the 1980s, then, Tivey's more abstract interventions on the nature of consumerism were read by very few consumers and the Group's continuation owed much to his joint editorship of the *Birmingham Consumer* with his wife, Marjorie, who continued to take an active role in the Group's organization. Lacking in support and with little direct impact on Birmingham civic society, local consumerism might simply be regarded as the product of a well-meaning body of affluent professionals whose purpose and functions were only ever relevant to a transitional stage of post-war consumer society.

But consumerism as an organized movement was always about much more than the state of Birmingham's lavatories. The role of figures such as Harbury should not be analysed solely in terms of often futile goals to transform the shopping mentality of the Birmingham public. The Consumers' Group was but one manifestation of a wider phenomenon which transformed post-war British society and politics. In the fuller history of consumerism, the Group looked far from being an isolated voluntary body of amateurs and at one point seemed part of a more popular outgrowth of grass-roots activism. In October 1961 over 500 'ordinary' consumers met in Aylesbury with a view to developing local consumer organizations. Within ten days, the first local consumer group had been set up in Oxford which, 12 weeks later, was publishing the *Oxford Consumer*, a magazine, like Birmingham's, dedicated to local consumer issues and surveys of local prices, goods and services.[56] Other groups soon appeared, giving 'expression to a genuine grassroots consumer feeling' made up of 'lively young people' of the type found across the south Birmingham suburbs.[57] For instance, in 1963, the chairs of the various new groups included 'a housewife, a BOAC pilot, a serving soldier, two University dons, a GP, a medical consultant, an industrial designer, an architect and a quality control engineer.'[58] By March 1963 there were 50 consumer groups in existence (Birmingham had been the 21st), with a total of 5,000 members. They had all come together under the National Federation of Consumer Groups (NFCG), the purpose of which was 'to give the groups a national voice, to maintain ethical standards in group activities, to encourage and assist the formation of new groups and to act as a central agency to maintain communication between groups and to arrange so far as possible facilities and services to individual member groups.'[59] By 1967 there were 100 groups with a total membership of 18,000 consumers.[60] Most published their own magazines and engaged in practices almost identical to those in Birmingham. For instance, the Basildon group published the *Buyer's Broadsheet*, the Sutton Group the *Vigilant*, North West Surrey the *Spotlight*, Tunbridge Wells *Shop!*, Durham *Pick and Choose*, Derby and District *Choice*, the Islington *Fair Deal*, the Bromley *Watchdog*, South Humberside *Cash*, and York's *The Yorkshire Consumer*.[61] As this short selection suggests, just as in Birmingham the consumer groups were located in the more affluent areas of the country, though there were nevertheless flourishing organizations across the north of England and in and around Glasgow.

What all these groups represented were the local manifestations of a wider movement spearheaded by the creation of the Consumers' Association in 1956 and the publication of its comparative testing magazine, *Which?*, from 1957. The CA was established by the sociologist and former Labour Party researcher, Michael Young, together with a number of other like-minded professionals from across the political spectrum but with a bias firmly towards the centre-left or the revisionist wing of the Labour Party. By the end of its first year, the CA had captured the imagination of the press and the public. It received free publicity in over 300 publications and had 47,000 members paying an annual subscription of 10s. By the end of March 1961, there were already a quarter of a million members, and over half a million by the beginning of the 1970s. By 1987, membership figures would peak at just over one million.[62] The socio-economic profile of these readers matched that of the Birmingham Group. Members of the CA tended to be readers of *The Times, Guardian, Observer, Telegraph, Spectator*, and *Economist*; by contrast, reports on the activities of CA in the pages of the *Daily Mirror* brought few, if any, new members.[63] According to a 1960 survey, 49 per cent of members were 'professional' (with annual incomes over £1,000), 40 per cent were 'lower professional' or junior managerial, leaving just 7 per cent from the skilled or semi-skilled working class.[64] Furthermore, just about every member of a local consumer group was also a subscriber to *Which?* and it was to maintain closer links with its membership that the CA had organized the initial meeting to promote consumer groups in Aylesbury in 1961. Indeed, the CA went on to provide the secretariat and much of the funding for the NFCG, though this was also a means of keeping a tight reign on a set of organizations which it felt were open to the infiltration of business which the fiercely-independent CA was keen to prevent.

Precisely because of these concerns, the CA began to give much less support to the local groups from the late-1960s, though it was also felt that they could offer much less practical help to the national body which increasingly saw its success in a concentration on its own publishing activities. Yet the view of consumerism as propagated by the CA remained one to which the local groups largely adhered. *Which?* was to be the means by which individual shoppers could inform themselves of the real information about a product, leading to better value-for-money and more rational expenditure. The consumer movement as a whole recognized that the problems of the market place could not be resolved through individual action alone and, just as the Birmingham Group sought to increase its activity in municipal politics, so too did national consumer organizations demand a wider range of consumer protection measures. The 'consumer's decade', as Rachel Waterhouse and others termed the 1960s, began with the report of the Molony Committee on Consumer Protection in 1962. This led directly to the creation of the government-funded Consumer Council in 1963 and the Trade Descriptions Act of 1968 which, in turn, was followed by a flurry of legislation in the 1970s that included the 1973 Fair Trading Act, the 1974 Consumer Credit Act, the 1977 Restrictive Trade Practices Act and the 1978 Consumer Safety Act.[65]

Although the Consumer Council was generally criticized for lacking teeth, existing as it did on a limited budget, having no powers of compulsion and being restricted to the general promotion of consumer welfare rather than the pursuit of specific grievances, it did act as a point of focus for the expanding consumer movement in the 1960s. Furthermore, it became the institution through which more reformist agendas were developed and articulated, to be taken up by MPs and other pressure groups. Its magazine, *Focus*, became the outlet for the Council's campaigning voice, calling for an overhaul of the legal system and, in particular, the creation of small claims courts that would enable consumers to seek redress over minor problems without incurring the considerable expenses usually associated with the recourse to law.[66] When the Council was abolished by Ted Heath in 1970, it provoked an outcry among consumer groups and the press, forcing politicians to realize the seriousness which the public attached to consumer issues by this time. The Conservatives immediately backtracked and appointed Geoffrey Howe as Minister for Consumer Affairs (within the Department of Trade and Industry) in 1972 and established the Office of Fair Trading in 1973. The Labour Party too joined the consumerist bandwagon and, after coming to power, it upgraded consumer representation in government by establishing a Secretary of State for Prices and Consumer Protection in March 1974, the very act of which seemed to confirm that consumers had an important role to play in inflation policy, a position deliberately denied by the Conservatives.[67] Labour's most significant contribution to the redevelopment of consumerism was, however, the establishment of the National Consumer Council in 1975 which has devoted itself to representing all consumers, but especially the poor and disadvantaged, recognizing the social limits of the consumerism embodied within the Birmingham Group.

The consumers of Edgbaston, Harborne and Moseley were therefore far from alone in Britain nor, given the economic circumstances which formed the backdrop to their emergence, the rest of the world either. Grass-roots local consumer activism was perhaps more pronounced in Britain than anywhere else, but the development of the rational, comparative-testing-type consumerism to which the Birmingham Group adhered spread around the world in the 1950s. Modern affluent consumerism began in the United States in the late 1920s and was given momentum with the creation of the Consumers' Union in 1936 which published its test results in *Consumer Reports*. In Britain several attempts were made to develop similar organizations in the 1940s and 1950s before Young directly modelled his CA on the US model. However, across Europe, similar organizations also appeared such that by 1959 the CA was joined by the *Consumentenbond* in the Netherlands, the *Union Belge des Consummateurs* in Belgium and the *Union Fédérale de la Consommation* in France and, one year later, the Australasian Consumers' Association in Sydney. In 1960, these independent bodies came together to found the International Organisation of Consumers Unions designed to 'act as a clearing house for information on test programmes, methods and results; to regulate the use of ratings and reprints of materials of member organizations; and to organize international meetings to promote consumer testing.'[68] Immediately, however, it spread out of this model, first taking on board the agendas of the state-assisted consumer councils of the Scandinavian countries and, from the 1970s, the interests of developing world consumers, concerned less with value for money and more with the right to enjoy a basic standard of living. Nevertheless, this institutional product of affluence grew out of the pockets of individuals exactly like those of the Birmingham consumers and today it consists of over 250 affiliated institutions from well over 100 states.[69]

The impact of local consumer groups may well have been limited within their own cities, but as part of this wider movement to consider the consumer in economic and social life, the consequences have been far more profound. 'Affluent Britain' is therefore not only a debate about standards of living, of macroeconomic policy or political machinations in Whitehall and Parliament, but how the world of goods has shaped the socio-political outlook of different cohorts of the population. Organized consumerism may have been deliberately non-party political but it has clearly influenced policy decisions by both the two main political parties. The emphasis placed on value-for-money, choice and competition has clearly fed into a Conservative faith in the free market, but consumerism's fight to have the interests of end-users given greater regard in both the private and the public sector has built on more established social democratic traditions.[70] For idealists such as Michael Young, consumerism was a means to free British politics from the perceived stranglehold of the trade unions and the employers and an opportunity for the interests of the individual not to be forgotten in the large-scale bureaucratic structures of the modern state and market place. Complaints from Birmingham consumers about the contents of a portion of chips may well have reduced consumerism to a petty-minded and even selfish individualism, but their work to achieve greater representation on civic issues such as pedestrianization represents a broader commitment to participative democracy and many of the goals associated with third-way political formulations. And, as a politics of pragmatism, so often espoused by the likes of Waterhouse, consumerism has been able to achieve notable victories on a range of single issues. Indeed, by 1980, *The Times* was able to claim that the CA had 'filled more pages of the statute book than any other pressure group this century.'[71]

The consumer as professional

To explain this impact requires an understanding of the social characteristics of the consumer activists of affluent Britain. The Birmingham Group was a product of its affluent time, so much so that although it continues to meet in 2003, much of its membership is retired and includes many of the same individuals who had initiated activities in the 1960s. Even by the 1980s, the Birmingham Group was visibly in decline, though its fortunes must be recognized as part of a broader national trend. By 1982, there were only 31 operational groups remaining within the National Federation of Consumer Groups, and half this number again ten years later.[72] Yet, when they had initially come together in the 1960s, inspecting lavatories, playgrounds and refuse collection across the city, there was much to confirm Upward's belief that they were 'the new force in the land.' Indeed, strength came from the homogeneity of their social world and they seem far distant from the neighbouring suburb of Smethwick where issues of racism, poverty and housing featured so notoriously in the 1964 election. It is indicative that the *Birmingham Consumer* had to remind its readers on several occasions that the Groups' 'primary function' was not that of a 'social organisation'.[73] Yet it is quite evident that the most successful meetings held by the Group at one another's homes were those which doubled up as social events, most typically that bastion of 1970s bourgeois Britishness, the 'cheese and wine' party.[74] From 1976, Rachel Waterhouse held the first of her annual garden parties which was to become a fixed date on the calendar of Birmingham consumerists well into the 1990s.[75] A survey of members in 1973 noted their concentration within the south Birmingham area and a further indicator of the Group's socio-cultural uniformity was given by the acknowledgement 'that one of our secret vices is listening to the Archers.'[76] On a surface level, these were the educated middle classes, sharing an economic and social universe which had given rise to the existence of 4,250 voluntary bodies in Birmingham alone in the 1960s.[77]

But it is simply too easy to identify all these consumers as middle class and in this case class is insufficient as an analytical category. Politically, their interests were not class specific and their allegiances did not neatly coalesce with the divisions within formal party politics. Economically, they may have been within the higher income bracket, but they were lawyers and lecturers rather than factory owners and company directors. Socially, they appear relatively uniform but this was the product of no specific interest and they were indeed concerned to extend their organization beyond the southern suburbs of the city. And, culturally, their tastes may have appeared middle class, but their outlook reflected a particular type of middle class. It is better, then, to refer to the activists as the professionals of post-war planning, the experts of Harold Perkins' 'professional society' who played a quantitatively more significant role in post-war reconstruction than they had in any other period.[78] They were the sons and daughters who had often been the first within their family to receive a university education and they were now the recipients of a secure and relatively sizeable salary. They were exactly those 'younger sons of the bourgeoisie' whom Orwell had predicted would bring about a mild-mannered English revolution: 'Most of its directing brains will come from the new indeterminate class of skilled workers, technical experts, airmen, scientists, architects and journalists, the people who feel at home in the radio and ferro-concrete age.'[79] In the early 1960s, they were still young, optimistic and wanted to share in all aspects of affluence, from controlling its growth to sharing its lifestyle. These experts were central to not only 'economic management and social policy, but also to areas of cultural taste, the urban and rural environments, consumer behaviour and the psychological well-being of communities.'[80]

In this focus on professionalism, Birmingham consumerists were not a class but a 'habitus' as Bourdieu would put it, a distinct social group with a set of shared dispositions structured by their social and economic capital but with the ability to participate in the developments of their own tastes, beliefs and preferences.[81] Class and habitus are nevertheless closely related but to refer to a professional habitus perhaps better encapsulates the world view and actions of this one section of the middle class. Organized consumer activists were admittedly unlike the majority of subscribers to *Which?* who were united only within an income bracket and not through a set of social, cultural and political dispositions. Activist consumers were defined by an ethos of professionalism and technocratic expertise and a commitment to socio-economic planning and reconstruction. They were committed to the virtues of independent information which, provided it was given to consumers through objective criteria, could solve many of the problems and inequities of the marketplace and lead the nation to an egalitarian participation in the affluent society. They aimed not to oppose the market society and mixed economy within which they found themselves, but to redirect its developments to suit the concerns of consumers as much as the profits of directors or the wages of workers. Most of all, these amateur yet professionally-oriented consumers placed their faith in rational discrimination, such that shopping and cultural life were to follow the same efficient and logical principles of the expertise they applied in engineering, economics, politics and social policy. They shared a faith in the ability of polyesters, rayons and nylons to build a new technical age, but outside their workplace, shopping too had to succumb to the same imperatives. When the affluent consumers of Moseley, Harborne and Edgbaston first met in 1963, then, their aims, and that of most of the national and international organizations to which they were ultimately attached, were to direct consumption according to their own criteria and not to make it a mere outlet for what they saw as ignorant, irrational philanthropy.

Notes

1. Lodge, D.: *Changing Places*, Penguin, Harmondsworth, 1978, p. 13.
2. Mitchell, B.R. and Deane. P.: *Abstract of British Historical Statistics*, Cambridge University Press, Cambridge, 1962, p. 371.
3. Millar, R.: *The Affluent Sheep: A Profile of the British Consumer*, Longman, London, 1963, p. 4.
4. Giordan, M.: *The Consumer Jungle*, Fontana/Collins, London, 1974.
5. *Birmingham Consumer*, no. 1, 1963, p. 1.
6. Birmingham Consumers' Group (BCG), *Constitution* (1964), private papers of author. I am grateful to Len and Marjorie Tivey for this and many other materials of the BCG.
7. *Birmingham Consumer*, no. 2 (1963), p. 3.
8. *Birmingham Consumer*, no. 4 (1964), p. 3.
9. *Birmingham Consumer*, no. 2 (1963), front cover.
10. Ibid.
11. *Birmingham Consumer*, no. 5 (1964), p. 3.
12. Harbury, C.D.: *Efficiency and the Consumer*, Fabian Society, London, 1958, pp. 2–5.
13. Tivey, L.: 'Quasi-government for consumers', in Barker A. (ed): *Quangos in Britain: Government and the Networks of Public Policy Making*, Macmillan, Basingstoke, 1982, pp. 137–51; Tivey, L.: 'The politics of the consumer', in Kimber R. and Richardson, J. J.: *Pressure Groups in Britain: A Reader*, Dent, London, 1974, pp. 195–209.
14. Borrie G. and Diamond, A.L.: *The Consumer, Society and the Law*, Penguin, Harmondsworth, 1973; Interview with Rachel Waterhouse, 8 March 2002.
15. Interview with Len Tivey, 7 March 2002.
16. Interview with Rachel Waterhouse, 8 March 2002.
17. Interview with Janet Upward, 3 April 2002.
18. BCG, *Annual Report, 1964–1965*, p. 1.
19. BCG, *Annual Report, 1967–1968*, p. 3; *Annual Report, 1968–1969*, p. 4; *Annual Report, 1969–1970*, pp. 2–3.
20. *Birmingham Consumer*, no. 1 (1963), p. 2.
21. Ibid., pp. 6–9.
22. BCG, *Annual Report, 1968–1969*, pp. 4–5.
23. *Birmingham Consumer*, no. 10 (1966), pp. 3, 21–31.
24. *Birmingham Consumer*, no. 13 (1966), p. 7.
25. BCG, *White List: A List of Services in the Home* (Birmingham, n.d.), author's private papers.
26. BCG, *Annual Report, 1963–1964*, p. 3.
27. BCG, *Annual Report, 1964–1965*, p. 1.
28. BCG, *Annual Report, 1968–1969*, p. 1; various press cutting from *Birmingham Evening Mail*, author's private papers.
29. *Birmingham Consumer*, no. 13 (1966), p. 2; BCG, *Annual Report, 1974–1975*, p. 1.
30. BCG, *Annual Report, 1971–1972*, p. 1.
31. *Birmingham Consumer*, no. 1 (1963), pp. 9–10; no. 2 (1963), p. 12; no. 10 (1966), pp. 14–15.
32. *Birmingham Consumer*, no. 5 (1964), p. 3.
33. *Birmingham Consumer*, no. 28 (1971), p. 1; BCG, *Annual Report, 1971–1972*, p. 3.
34. BCG, *Annual Report, 1974–1975*, p. 3; BCG, *Annual Report, 1977–1978*, p. 4.
35. BCG, *Annual Report, 1964–1965*, p. 2.
36. *Birmingham Consumer*, no. 16 (1967), p. 2; BCG, *Annual Report, 1967–1968*, p. 5.
37. *NFCG Newsletter*, no. 40 (1981), paragraph 650.

38 Interview with Janet Upward, 3 April 2002.

39 Packard, V.: *The Hidden Persuaders*, Penguin, Harmondsworth, 1960 (first published 1957). See also idem: *The Waste Makers*, David Mackay, New York, 1960.

40 See especially the works of Elizabeth Gundrey which were often reviewed in the *Birmingham Consumer*: *Your Money's Worth: A Handbook for Consumers*, Penguin, Harmondsworth, 1962; *At Your Service: A Consumer's Guide to the Service Trades and Professions*, Penguin, Harmondsworth, 1964; *A Foot in the Door: An Exposé of High Pressure Sales Methods*, Frederick Muller, London, 1965. *Help!*, Zenith Books, London, 1967.

41 Millar, *Affluent Sheep*, p. 3.

42 Ibid., p. 196.

43 Wight, R.: *The Day the Pigs Refused to be Driven to Market: Advertising and the Consumer Revolution*, Hart-Davis, MacGibbon, London, 1972, p. xii.

44 Ibid., pp. xiii, 73.

45 Director-General of the OFT: *Annual Report, 1986*, Office of Fair Trading, London, 1987, p. 10.

46 Waterhouse, R.: 'New frontiers for consumerism', *RSA Journal*, vol. 136, no. 5383 (June 1988), p. 466; Interview with Rachel Waterhouse, 8 March 2002; Waterhouse, R.: 'Memorandum on the objects of the Group' (1969), author's private papers.

47 *Birmingham Consumer*, no. 28 (1971), p. 4.

48 *Birmingham Consumer*, no. 19 (1968), p. 17.

49 *Birmingham Consumer*, no. 57 (1979), p. 2, plus various issues, 1979–1990; Interview with Len Tivey, 7 March 2002.

50 *Birmingham Consumer*, no. 57 (1979), p. 1; Confederation of British Industry: *Principles of Consumer Policy*, Confederation of British Industry, London, 1979; Conservative Party: *Manifesto 1979*, Conservative Central Office, London, 1979.

51 On the definition of consumerism see *Oxford English Dictionary* plus Swagler, R.: 'Evolution and applications of the term consumerism: themes and variations', *Journal of Consumer Affairs*, vol. 28, no. 2 (1994), p. 350.

52 *Focus*, vol. 1, no. 1 (1966), p. 6.

53 *Birmingham Evening Mail*, 30 July 1966, press cuttings in author's private papers.

54 BCG, *Annual Report, 1971–1972*, p. 1; BCG, *Annual Report, 1975–1976*, p. 2; BCG, *Annual Report, 1986–1987*, p. 2.

55 *Birmingham Consumer*, no. 33 (1972), p. 2.

56 Archive of the Consumers' Association [hereafter CAA] Box 27: Gorse, D.H.: 'The growth of consumer groups', *New Outlook: A Liberal magazine*, no. 21 (July 1963), p. 20.

57 Curtis, H. and Sanderson, M.: *A Review of the National Federation of Consumer Groups*, Consumers' Association, London, 1992, p. 4.

58 Consumers' Association (CA), *Annual Report, 1962–1963*, p. 11.

59 Ibid.

60 Smith, G.: *The Consumer Interest*, Gollancz, London, 1982, p. 291.

61 *Focus*, vol. 1, no. 1 (1966), p. 6; vol. 1, no. 2 (1966), p. 6; vol. 1, no. 4 (1966), p. 6; vol. 1, no. 5 (1966), p. 6; vol. 1, no. 6 (1966), p. 6; vol. 1, no. 8 (1966), p. 6; vol. 2, no. 4 (1967), p. 10; vol. 3, no. 2 (1968), p. 8; vol. 3, no. 4 (1968), p. 6; vol. 5, no. 1 (1970), p. 19.

62 CA, *Annual Report, 1957–1958*, p. 2; CA, *Annual Report, 1960–1961*, p. 5; CA, *Thirty Years of 'Which?' 1957–1987*, CA, London, 1987.

63 CAA Box 27: E. Roberts, 'Consumer protection in foodstuffs', speech delivered in the Food and Nutrition Section at the Health Congress, 1 May 1959.

64 The remaining 4 per cent were categorized as 'other'. See CAA Box 27: 'Who reads "Which?"', article for *New Society*, final copy, 26 October 1962.

65 Borrie, G.: *The Development of Consumer Law and Policy,* Stevens and Sons, London, 1984.

66 *Focus*, vol. 2, no. 2 (1968), pp. 2–5; vol. 4, no. 10 (1969), p. 1; vol. 5, no. 4 (1970), pp. 19–22; vol. 5, no. 8 (1970), pp. 2–5.

67 Wraith, R.: *The Consumer Cause: A Short Account of its Organisation, Power and Importance,* Royal Institute of Public Administration, London, 1976, p. 16.

68 Sim, F.G.: *IOCU on Record: A Documentary History of the International Organisation of Consumers Unions, 1960–1990*, Consumers Union, New York, 1991, p. 27.

69 For further details on national and international consumer organisations see Hilton, M.: *Consumerism in Twentieth-Century Britain: The Search for a Historical Movement*, Cambridge University Press, Cambridge, 2003.

70 Hilton, M.: 'The fable of the sheep, or, private virtues, public vices: the consumer revolution of the twentieth century', *Past and Present*, vol. 176 (2002), pp. 222–56.

71 Cited in CA, *Annual Report, 1979–1980*, p. 13.

72 Curtis, H. and Sanderson, M.: *A Review of the National Federation of Consumer Groups*, CA, 1992, p. 6.

73 *Birmingham Consumer*, no. 10 (1966), p. 10.

74 *Birmingham Consumer*, no. 27 (1970), p. 3.

75 *Birmingham Consumer*, no. 47 (1976), p. 2.

76 *Birmingham Consumer*, no. 31 (1971), p. 1; no. 36 (1973), pp. 11–13.

77 *Birmingham Consumer*, no. 66 (1983), p. 1.

78 Perkin, H.: *The Rise of Professional Society: England Since 1880*, Routledge, London, 1990.

79 Orwell, G.: *The Lion and the Unicorn*, Penguin, Harmondsworth, 1982 (first published 1941), p. 113.

80 Conekin, B., Mort, F. and Waters, C.: 'Introduction', in Conekin, B., Mort, F. and Waters, C. (eds): *Moments of Modernity: Reconstructing Britain, 1945–1964*, Rivers Oram, London, 1999, p. 15.

81 Bourdieu, P.: *The Logic of Practice*, Polity Press, Cambridge, 1990; Bourdieu, P.: *Distinction: A Social Critique of the Judgement of Taste*, Routledge and Kegan Paul, London, 1986.

CHAPTER 10

Anticipating Affluence: Skill, Judgement and the Problems of Aesthetic Tutelage

Lesley Whitworth

This chapter is composed of two elements and two time-frames straddling the Second World War. The first prefatory comments utilize insights derived from research into the processes and practices of shopping in a buoyant Midlands city in the 1930s to notice the presence of certain characteristics associated with 'affluence', and hence to problematize its periodization. The second and larger element critically examines work carried out after 1944 by the newly established Council of Industrial Design with the British buying public. My aim in bringing these two elements together is to suggest that as well as encapsulating a sense of material well-being, the term 'affluence' could be said to refer with equal pertinence to a growth in sophistication of the discriminatory abilities of the ordinary buying public. The idea of 'wealth' can then be expanded to encompass a 'wealth of options' as well as a 'wealth of knowledge', allowing for the making of reasoned choices. Individually affluent workers can then be shown to have pre-dated the post-war period with which affluence is most commonly associated, and, most importantly for this chapter, exhibited particular aptitudes that the new body failed to acknowledge or respond to. In common with the political parties discussed elsewhere in this volume, it can therefore be said to have failed a significant proportion of its newly affluent constituency despite the hopes invested in it by government, and the state sponsorship that underpinned its task.

Skill and judgement

The first part of this chapter reprises an argument made elsewhere that a self-confident, technically sophisticated male workforce in a British Midlands town in the 1930s transferred many of its skills and capabilities into the domestic sphere and in particular to the processes and practices of shopping.[1] Coventry's time-served engineers and others among its prospering working classes showed an increased willingness to make money matters more transparent between husbands and wives, to mediate consumer choice between marriage partners, and to draw strongly on insights and identities deriving from the arena of work to inform and often determine the outcome of purchasing decisions.

Coventry has conventionally been identified by historians as one of those locations redolent of interwar industrial reconfiguration and economic regeneration. During the 1920s and 1930s it exhibited many features that were later to be associated with the affluence of the 1950s and 1960s. The city's dynamic manufacturing sector attracted a rapidly expanding workforce involved in the production of new synthetic fibres and iconic consumer durables such as radios, telephones, cars, and motorbikes. It was the country's fastest growing industrial centre.[2] Between 1921 and 1937 its population rose at a rate seven times that of the country as a whole.[3] Yet between 1933 and 1938 the per centage of unemployment in the city was generally half the national average.[4] It had the fastest rate of growth in house-building and the highest rates of working class owner occupation for a town of its size.[5] And by 1938 car ownership rates stood at double the national average.[6] In Coventry too, the lack of appeal of union membership and the concomitant emphasis on personal negotiation and self-presentation also parallels those aspects of the affluence thesis associated with 'instrumentalism'.

Within the factories, J.B. Priestley was told that workers could talk about nothing but 'gears and magnetos' even in their spare time, and himself struggled manfully with the urge to leap into one of the sleek new Daimler buses and take it for a spin.[7] Paul Thompson has written compellingly of the enduring quality of Coventry workers' conception of themselves as 'skilled'.[8] During the 1930s this identification had real if diminishing validity. Individual judgement, facility with materials and techniques, and familiarity with technical terminology garnered during lengthy apprenticeships furnished the time-served engineer with a strong sense of self, which proved to have interesting reverberations in the domestic sphere. In works' papers the 'For Sale and Wanted' columns provided a mechanism through which goods were traded and changed hands. Through them disposal and upgrading practices can be traced, and a particular engagement with technical language, product knowledge, and a delight in specifications – all intimately connected with the authors' working selves. In one of a series of remarkably prescient articles on photographic equipment in the works' paper of the country's most important machine tool manufacturer, the 'gadget fiend' was an identifiable type to whom some manufacturers of camera accessories were said to pander.[9]

Whilst men reported a certain inarticulacy around matters of aesthetic judgement, and the view was expressed that 'a woman spends more time in the house than a man does normally … and they should have the choice'; a distinction between the task of 'equipping', here gendered male, and the broader and conventionally feminine terrain of home-making is of paramount importance.[10] It was always men who bought the radios, for instance.[11] And cars as well as radios and holidays were readily justified by reference to the family-, as opposed to individual-, benefits that would accrue. Fathers encouraged children's hobbies and indulged playfulness with new kinds of toys; they built and made things that were understood as family resources. Although many historical accounts depict the shopper as female, at the close of my research I concluded that these men's shopping habits had modified more dramatically than women's during this period of relative prosperity, indeed that as breadwinners and technical arbiters men exerted a *pervasive* influence over a wide range of purchasing decisions.[12]

The skill attributed to women was managing money, not buying things, as Charlotte Luetkens recognized in a chapter on education in her 1946 book *Women and a New Society* in which she addresses the question of women's emerging role in an 'age of plenty':

> To take one instance of what the education of women of the future will have to deal with. Through the centuries, women have been taught the virtue of hoarding and saving – now they have to learn the art of spending. ... This ... should also educate women in the 'art of selfishness', the art of spending for ... herself.[13]

What I wish to underline here, is that men's transference of workplace skills and proficiencies into the realm of more domestically-configured consumption, filled both an operational and an aspirational vacuum that had opened up as increasingly technically sophisticated products came onto the market. In this environment, the enterprising retailers who placed an advertisement in *The Alfred Herbert News* which included the following appeal may have met with greater success than more cynical twenty-first century commentators will allow: 'Coventry engineers are known the world over for the quality of their workmanship. The same applies to our furniture, like your machines, it is made for service'.[14]

The problems of aesthetic tutelage

The British Council of Industrial Design (CoID, the Council) was founded in 1944 under the aegis of the Board of Trade, as a result of war-time concerns about the enormity of the task facing British industrialists in the post-war period. It was estimated that over a thousand million pounds worth of goods needed to be exported every year to pay for our pre-war volume of imports alone, and in the meantime other countries, most notably America, had massively improved their manufacturing efficiency, and, in the view of the government, the standard of design evident in their output.[15] The Council was therefore intended as a catalyst to animate British manufacturers' attitudes towards design and their awareness of the commercial imperative of adopting higher design standards. Its stated purpose was 'to promote by all practical means the improvement of design in the products of British industry', but alongside this was articulated a strong social impulse to improve lives.[16] Hugh Dalton's speech to the inaugural meeting of the Council contained the following statement:

> If you succeed in your task, in a few years' time every side of our daily life will be the better for your work. Every kitchen will be an easier place to work in; every home a pleasanter place to live in. Men and women in millions will be in your debt, though they may not know it ...[17]

At an early reception given by the Council in March 1945, its first Director S.C. Leslie went further, asking 'What is political and public work about, if it is not the achieving of a richer quality of life and enjoyment, in quite simple daily ways, for a man and his wife and their children?'.[18] Leslie savoured the élan of having 'money and Government money at that', which he posited as a token of the seriousness with which their sponsors regarded the task at hand, but also felt that 'lifting the quality of objects of common use in the hands and the homes of British people is a great objective in itself'.[19]

Magnanimous and benevolent impulses aside, it was clear from the outset to both government paymasters and Council activists that manufacturers and manufacturing policy – whilst indisputably at the heart of the problem – could not be dealt with in isolation. Part of the associated and needful work of the Council was therefore the bringing into sympathetic alignment of design education, retailing standards and the consuming appetites of the British buying public. The Council embarked on a programme of activities intended to draw each of its distinct and potentially competing constituencies (industry, education, retail, public) into a shared process necessary to achieve the sought-after transformation of design consciousness. In particular, the essential symbiosis being striven for by the Council between market and supplier was starkly apparent in the Chief Information Officer's description of the Council's aims and organization. He referred to the operation's precise symmetry:

> The Council treats the problem of raising design standards broadly as one of Supply and Demand. The staff is therefore divided into two main divisions, the Industrial Division to encourage the supply of well designed manufactures and the Information Division to stimulate a demand among the public for well designed goods.[20]

If this could be achieved an immense prize was attainable, as Hugh Dalton remarked, in a speech coloured by Council phraseology:

> Our export trade, and our volume of business at home, will both be the greater if our goods are planned and made, with skill and imagination, to meet the user's real need, and to give pleasure in the using.[21]

A very great deal, then, depended on the Council's tenets achieving the broadest possible acceptance. In his statement Dalton proffered one definition of 'design' among the many available to his contemporaries, and it was this view of design – logical, practical and inherently aesthetically satisfying – that the Council subscribed to.[22] The term 'design' was itself a relatively unfamiliar one as yet, and the deployment of scarce resources would need to be carefully managed during the early years to effect an educational engagement with each of the key sectors.[23] In this scenario the issue of 'real needs' was an abiding concern: a veiled reference to the vagaries of fashion and the unwanted admonitions of marketing (wo)men. Could all of the parties involved in this audacious economic reconfiguration be trusted to comply? If the public were to be useful allies, their susceptibility to such distractions needed to be reduced.[24]

S.C. Leslie's avowal of faith in the business element of the equation may have been mere window-dressing at a public event: 'Wouldn't you agree with me', he asked, 'that the business world is more animated than ever before by some sense of public obligation and public purpose?'.[25] For its answer we need look no further than its overwhelming rejection of the Council's model of regionally-located industry-specific design centres, a scheme which was abandoned a few short years later despite its centrality to their original agenda. Whilst it is not proposed to deal with the CoID's substantive relationship with industry in this chapter, the tensions apparent in the Council's relationship with the public lie at the heart of the discussion that follows.[26] Two quotations representing contrasting viewpoints serve here to signpost aspects of the argument developed hereafter. Leslie expressed the opinion 'that the public – whether because of war-time cynicism, or of war-time hardships, or both – is likely to expect better standards of quality, of convenience and of beauty in the things it buys, and to respond to any lead that it gets in those directions'. If sincere, this outlook could not be assumed to be shared by colleagues and collaborators. For instance, Mrs Lovat Fraser, a designer sitting on a 'Brains Trust' at a Council event in 1949, was pointed in her accusation that 'the public needs to be roused from the habit, caused by shortages, of taking what is put before it'.[27] However fallible, CoID literature constantly reminded the public of their heavy burden of responsibility, and endlessly exhorted them to demand well-designed goods and to let the manufacturer know through the intermediary of the retailer when goods were unacceptable.

From seeing to looking to searching

The Council's *First Annual Report, 1945–1946* shows that in response to Dalton's request that the Council 'arouse the interest of ordinary men and women', a three-pronged attack was outlined under the heading 'Reaching the Public'. After first making an assessment of the aforementioned 'real circumstances and needs', and secondly explaining the principles of good design whilst eschewing 'particular dogmas',[28] the third route was defined as 'affording plenty of opportunity for [the public] to see all kinds of good things, and get the idea for itself'. Seeing, then, occupied a privileged position in the Council's rubric, but the act of looking would become even more so.

The design promotional events that took place in the later 1940s arguably set the pattern for the whole of the subsequent period associated with the affluent worker, reinforced initially by the popular success and high profile of Britain Can Make It in 1946 and the Festival of Britain in 1951.[29] These and other smaller CoID events laboured to set a range of well-designed products before the public so that they could 'get the idea for themselves' in the face of continuing materials shortages and manufacturers' tentative return to full-scale peace-time production. Austerity added to the difficulty of locating good examples of product design at the same time as it increased the public's appetite to view them. The stated aim of 'rousing the public to a state of alert sensibility and giving it a lead' could not be achieved through passive spectating alone, however.

Whilst still denuded of its peacetime trophies, the Victoria & Albert Museum in London hosted Britain Can Make It between September and December during which time 1,432,369 people saw it (see Plate 2). The exhibition devoted a significant proportion of its overall effort to teaching visitors just what it was that a designer did (see Plate 3). So *new* was the conception, that professional recognition was still in its infancy, and people removed from the world of manufacturing as well as many within it were equally mystified by the role. The central organizing motif of the Council-authored exhibition was the iconic character 'Mr Designer', an animated eyeball which directed visitors, identified exhibits and, on occasions, spoke disturbingly through hidden speakers (see Plate 4). 'Mr Designer' brilliantly embodied the Council's core message. In parallel with this, a more actively conceptualized form of looking was encouraged through sales of a quiz pamphlet and the distribution of voting tokens to be placed in quiz banks located along the exhibition route. The Design Quiz was an exemplar of heavy-handed didacticism, offering firm guidance on the criteria against which products should be evaluated and concluding with the decisions of 'the judges' against which individuals' results could be compared. Nearly 500 copies of the quiz publication were sold per day, priced at 9d.

The exhibition-going public had in fact already had a foretaste of such exercises and the format appeared to be a popular one. At the *Daily Herald* Post-War Homes Exhibition held between June and August 1945, 37,000 CoID quiz entries were received, these represented 'an unusually high proportion of those who attended the exhibition'.[30] And at the *Daily Herald* Modern Homes Exhibition the following year it was reported that 'The Quiz stand at Dorland Hall is meeting with a very favourable reception and is certainly a huge popular success. We are having 1,000 entries sometimes. There is in fact considerable congestion around the posting box. ...'.[31] The tick sheet bore the legend 'Whether "Quizzing" or Shopping, Choose Carefully and Look for Design Points'.

The quiz was clearly understood to be part of the CoID propagandizing agenda. With reference to it Robin Darwin, then CoID Training Officer and later Principal of the Royal College of Art, wrote to Peter Moro, the Council's stand designer, that it was no bad thing to repeat a successful display formula 'from the point of view of propaganda'.[32] Letters from the Council's Mrs Murdoch request more lighting over the 'slogans' for 'full propaganda effect' from Moro, and explain to Mary Grieve, Editor of *Woman*, that quizzes are 'a favourite form of propaganda with us'.[33] The term was also used twice in headings in the *First Annual Report*. The use of such loaded terminology sits uneasily alongside contemporaneous claims by the Council that design was simply a matter of 'cleanliness and common sense'.[34]

In 1956 when the CoID finally succeeded in opening one centrally located all-embracing Design Centre in the Haymarket, London, one of its functions was to house a reference tool developed from a listing of well-designed products created for the Festival of Britain. It was hoped that by meticulously updating and adding to 'Design Index' an invaluable search mechanism could be made available to educators, buyers, industrialists and the buying public for whom the onerous task of looking and thinking would have been somewhat expedited. A poster advertising the Centre reads 'look before you shop'. Only two years later members of the public were excluded from accessing the Index before 12.30 between Monday and Friday. At these times it was reserved for the use of trade buyers. Shoppers were now encouraged to 'Look for the label' instead – a reference to a new scheme which allowed manufacturers whose products featured in the Index to append a Design Centre label to them, rendering them more readily identifiable in provincial shopping centres. One of the problems it was hoped that this scheme would rectify was the failure of the public to 'realise that in some towns one has to be a very persistent shopper if one is seeking well-designed things. ... Shoppers will soon learn the value of searching'.[35]

The indeterminate shopper

'Design Weeks', with a 'Design Fair' at their core, were the vehicle through which the Council chose to disseminate its message in the provinces. Travelling to the 'main centres of population', the Design Week was said to break 'new ground for the Council on a broad front' and to engage 'retail discussion groups, meetings of voluntary organisations, of teachers, of students and of housewives in open forum'.[36] A letter to Mr Poole of the Workers Educational Association in 1948 told that 'The intention of the Week is to stimulate interest in good design amongst *all sections of the community*' (my emphasis).[37]

The Fair made sure to claim its relevance for members of Britain's industrial workforce. It made a bold appeal for design's transformative power in all areas of working life; visitors were reminded that it might 'be possible to raise the whole standard of living in this country through good design, by removing petty irritations in the home, by reducing drudgery, by improving working conditions...'. A Design Fair press release from late 1948 invokes images of inter-activity of a kind likely to appeal to male visitors and redolent of one Council member's view that a 'gentleman's fun fair' would have been a desirable addition at Britain Can Make It.[38] 'There are handles to turn, buttons to press, switches to turn on and off, and a quiz answered by recorded voices'.[39] Furthermore an entry in the London County Council Educational Bulletin recorded that the Design Fair visitor 'is asked to compare, contrast, criticize and query; but *his* efforts are guided, so that *he* may find out how to make up *his* mind about the design of the things *he* sees' (my emphasis).[40] Yet groups of men are not foregrounded as beneficiaries of Design Fair in the quotation above, and the ambiguity of this routinely masculinized language is thrown into stark relief by the accompanying Design Fair guide which makes the assumed identity of the shopper very clear indeed; 'The way they make things in the factory is often like the way you make other things at home. Moulding a plastic radio cabinet is like cooking a waffle.'[41] Discussions and displays revolved around textiles and soft furnishings, and the failures of teapots to pour well rather than the harder edge of industrial design. Similarly, a display on the Festival of Britain ship *Campania* which toured British ports throughout 1951 conveyed the message that 'It is always the more DECORATIVE THINGS which turn a house into a home', a message guaranteed to alienate the many men who felt ill-equipped to make aesthetic judgements of this kind, and who typically deferred in such matters to the assumed authority of their wives. It also fails totally to recognize the many other things which might be said to turn houses into homes, particularly those pieces of equipment that men might be inclined to articulate a need for, predicated on the grounds of family resource: radios, cars, cameras and cine-cameras, toys, tools.[42] It was left to the newly formed Midland Industrial

Designers Association – an offshoot of the Birmingham 'Design Week' – to make the imaginatively conceived proposal to tour 'a photographic exhibition of members' work that had been selected for the 1951 [Festival of Britain], Stock List, ... round the more important Midland factories prior to the Festival'.[43]

A list survives of those considered for inclusion in the original make-up of the Council, but who were ultimately not invited to serve.[44] It provides little in the way of comfort however, in terms of the representation of the ordinary, or even the affluent worker. Perhaps the most significant omission in this regard was Councillor H. Slack of Sheffield, Treasurer and Secretary of the National Cutlery Union, who is named as a possible suitable Trade Union member of the Central Design Council. Also interesting in this context was Sir Miles Thomas in his capacity as Chairman of the Nuffield Foundation, which had as its aim the advancement of 'social well being' and, having been established by William Morris, Lord Nuffield, founder of Morris Motors in 1943, could at least boast appropriately industrial antecedents. Captain Black of Standard Cars is equally noteworthy. The General Manager of Standard's Canley works at Coventry responsible for the introduction of the 'Flying Standard', Black had a reputation for generosity in the car industry and paid higher wages with better fringe benefits than his competitors. We might also bemoan the absence of W.E. Williams from the list of candidates. Present at the reception for members of voluntary organizations held by the Council soon after its inception, Williams there represented the Institute of Adult Education. As the man behind the wartime Army Bureau of Current Affairs and the originator of the post-war scheme to develop art centres attuned to the leisure and cultural needs of local populations with funding from the Arts Council's forerunner, CEMA, Williams might have had much to offer debates about the popularization of messages about good design.[45] John Gloag, design commentator and author, wrote to the Council in early 1949 about precisely this glaring omission in the Council's approach to its work. Having seen their 'beautiful little pamphlet "Four Ways of Living",' he asked scornfully, 'Why do you always pick on the middle of the professional classes as your objectives? The big retail houses and trading organizations, who know what they are about, have realized that the new mass market lies in the proletariat; they must be your objectives too.'[46]

In January that year the Council had launched its own monthly periodical, *Design*. It had as its masthead 'A monthly journal for industry'. By issue three this had become 'A monthly journal for manufacturers and designers', and by 1951 '*The* monthly journal for manufacturers, designers and retailers' (my emphasis). At no stage however was it ever conceptualized as a magazine for the interested non-specialist reader. As the Council's Information Officer explained to conference delegates, its intended audience was emphatically 'not the general public'.[47]

Of the organization's other published outputs from this period, the magazine format *New Home* used fashion cameos to illuminate a message more centrally concerned with furniture, decoration and household goods, and books such as *Furnishing to Fit the Family* (1947) and *Ideas for Your Home* (1950) concerned themselves with the shape of furniture and its disposition within rooms; practical storage advice; the use of colour; and floor, wall and curtain treatments rather than defining desirable characteristics in household equipment.[48] It is tempting to lay the blame for this concentration on the softer aspects of design at the door of its second Director, Gordon Russell, himself a notable designer and manufacturer of furniture. Whether true or not, it is transparently the case that the medium was chosen and designed with a female readership in mind. Whilst *New Home* was clearly predicated on the Council's view (expressed elsewhere) that 'many young women appear to exercise far more skill and natural taste in dressing themselves than in furnishing their houses',[49] it nevertheless opened with the beguiling claim that 'Women know a great deal about shape ... because they get their eye in over clothes and hats'.[50] Even, then, when the Council believed it had the true shopper squarely in its sights, it operated with guile. A similar duplicity is evident in a statement made by a retailing Council member who spoke at a CoID Conference in 1949:

> Now the people who influence demand are, of course, ultimately the public who buy what they like. But the retailer is the link, and can influence what is placed before the public. This is a matter of great delicacy and not a thing that can be done all at once: but we must lead the public as well as serve them.

Later on he said that the public could be induced to 'go along certain lines'.[51]

The indeterminate quality of design

In the same year that Gloag wrote his letter about 'the proletariat' to the Council, two conferences were held for retailers and retail staff trainers. Occupying a 'key [strategic] position' as intermediaries in the Council's campaign to bring design awareness to the broadest possible audience, retailers might also be assumed to have some degree of pre-existing aesthetic-, or at least product-awareness.[52] Their response to the content of the course is therefore of some interest.

The conference report notes that an extra session was added to the last day because several people had expressed a wish for 'a practical talk' on what made an object well or ill designed. This was despite a full, two-day programme comprising lectures, workshops, discussion, a quiz, and films which were all design content driven and included a talk delivered by Gordon Russell, the Director himself, entitled 'What we mean by Good Design'. The feedback at the close of the conference makes it quite clear that the most useful session had been the one that was not even on the original itinerary: 'Mr Russell's critical examination of objects brought the conference *down to earth*' (my emphasis). His direct handling of a number of objects such as garden implements, pottery, china, clocks, etc, elicited a view from the participants that 'design can be best explained by practical analysis and demonstration rather than by talks and lectures'. A question had also been raised during discussion about the availability of a staff lecturer who could 'go out to the stores and speak with authority'. The Council's Information Officer indicated that they had insufficient resources but the Training Manager of Lewis's in Birmingham re-affirmed his view that it was most important that the lecturer 'should come from the Council as people are more ready to listen to the "expert".' The worrying implication of all of this is that far from being accessible as the CoID intended it should be, information about design had taken on the status of arcane knowledge and insights were seen to be in the gift of high level initiates.[53]

At the second conference later the same year a question arose about the need for a British quality research association similar to the American Consumers Union, which investigated goods and published bulletins.[54] Russell acknowledged the need for this kind of work but distanced the Council from such a sphere of activity, suggesting that whilst specifications might be helpful in raising the design standard of consumer goods, the British Standards Association (sic) was 'doing a lot of good work in this direction'. Pushed further, he gave as a reason the difficulty of dissociating the quality of a design from the quality of the workmanship and materials invested in it. This was an abdication of responsibility however. In response to its increased involvement in the preparation of standards for consumer goods after the war, the British Standards Institution had in fact been casting around for a 'consumer organisation' capable of articulating users' needs on its technical committees.[55] It was later to attract a great deal of criticism for its alleged mishandling of the consumer goods industries, leading ultimately to an official investigation.[56] The Council's establishment of its own design label in 1958, and of a liaison committee with the BSI in 1969 therefore represent rather belated attempts to respond to the real needs of consumers in relation to product evaluation criteria.

In the 20 years that passed between the 1949 retail conference at which great interest was expressed in the explanatory value of signs and labels, and the commencement of a reciprocal exchange between the CoID and the BSI, there was continuous activity, but little that availed the ordinary buying public anything. The Council instigated a programme of annual awards as a publicity vehicle for the new Design Centre. Both the Centre and its awards were founded 'primarily to stimulate improvement in the design of the kind of durable consumer goods that are normally bought through the retail trade'.[57] However, criticism of the value of the awards was swift to follow, focusing on ambiguities in the meaning of 'good design'. At the same time the journal *Design* wrestled with parallel debates about consumer protection. An article published in November 1957 noted that 'Interest in consumer needs is mounting' and had to include a 'stop press' item to reflect on the publication of *Which?* by the recently formed Association for Consumer Research, re-named the Consumers' Association shortly afterwards. The author of the article, Elizabeth Gundrey, was herself the recently appointed Information Officer of the new Consumer Council, and Editor of their publication *Shopper's Guide*. Both periodicals were available by subscription, this funding the operation of the Association for Consumer Research, whilst the Consumer Council had its own government grant and operated as a satellite of the BSI. Gundrey set out the case for independently verifiable test results and unbiased information. She said of the 'intelligent shopper', 'He is a minority, but an articulate and influential one'.[58] That a significant demand existed for such information can be demonstrated by early subscription figures; 10,000 took the first issue of *Which?* and this had reached 23,000 by January 1958.[59] Five thousand people and 'several hundred groups' were taking *Shoppers Guide* within six months.[60] By way of comparison, the potential reach of the CoID may be demonstrated by sales of its label, just under 50 million of which had been sold by the year ended 31 March 1965.[61]

An article appearing in *Design* just a few issues after Gundrey's provides a clue as to why the CoID may positioned itself rather differently to the other bodies.[62] The article represented a culmination of both the series on 'Consumer Needs' and a contribution to the 'Design Analysis' series being published concurrently. Its aim was synthetic; to 'set out the type of research into human and technical requirements that is becoming increasingly necessary as the *starting point* in the design of a new product' (emphasis in original). Although it validated the argument for product testing in the round, through analysis of basic design principles, followed by practical tests then laboratory examination, its chief wish was to find a successful formula for the refinement of designs ahead of production, *before* the mistakes had been both made and marketed. This is an entirely logical trajectory for a body charged with transforming industrial practice as well as educating consumers.[63] Nevertheless the closing comment, that 'The CoID welcomes co-operation with both these organisations' has a rather hollow feel to it, commensurate with the general quietness to be found in the organization's filing under these headings.

Whilst the issue of impending metrication, implemented nationally in 1971, provided a focus for the rapprochement with the BSI, the need to put the Council's product testing on a more rigorous and transparent footing also constituted a significant spur. But the larger project of ensuring absolute consistency between CoID and BSI product documentation, and manufacturers' compliance with both organizations' promotional schemes, proved less susceptible to resolution and an enduring trial to those members of staff charged with its delivery. By the time the Council had tentatively expanded the range of goods being tested at BSI's Hemel Hempstead test centre to include car accessories as well as garden tools and hand tools, other changes with more far-reaching consequences were taking place. A change of name from Council of Industrial Design to Design Council was said to be 'something which had been pending for several years' and 'in line with a broadening of its brief to include engineering design'. Furthermore the change was 'to be seen as an expansion of the Council's work and did not mean that the successful effort in consumer goods would be reduced'.[64] Notwithstanding this statement, a debate about future policy for the Design Centre Awards begun in 1965 had already thrown up a number of tensions. A memo from the middle of that year recognized the increasing attention which would be paid in future years to the capital goods section of the awards and the concomitant risk of appearing to downgrade the consumer goods awards, but thought that this 'evident participation in the capital goods industries' would give the Council 'greater authority among the consumer goods industries rather than less'.[65] A memo from a year later welcoming the slight reduction in the number of consumer goods to facilitate the introduction of the new capital goods section of the awards could be said to mark the Council's inexorable shift in emphasis. During the same debate it was noted in relation to the Council's supreme award, 'The Duke of Edinburgh's Prize for

Elegant Design', that 'although His Royal Highness and the Elegance Panels have in their selections been very careful to give serious and in some cases almost mathematical interpretations to the word Elegance, it might be difficult to extend the prize into wider fields without changing its name'.[66] A claim made by the Council in its very first *Annual Report* that 'design is a less esoteric field than science' appears untenable from this perspective.

Conclusion: the 'missing technician'

In an introduction to the work of the CoID given at the first liaison meeting with the BSI in January 1969, it was stressed that the Council's main purpose was to work for higher standards of design in British industry.[67] The speaker explained that 'the justification for this was that better design as a whole was bound to react to the advantage of the country as a trading nation and must add to the general well-being of the population'. This reads much less like a clarion call for the betterment of living standards for all Britons and much more as a generalized assertion of a putative outcome.

In 1946 the Council's first Director noted in a letter to the Ministry of Health that 'From the point of view of the public, housing on the one hand and domestic equipment and furnishing on the other are very close together'.[68] The CoID's determination therefore to produce, for example, '*a booklet for women,* of magazine format, on furniture, decoration and household equipment' (emphasis in original) seems mistaken for all of the following reasons.[69] The research commissioned from Mass-Observation into the 1946 Britain Can Make It Exhibition showed the Council that 'two men for every woman ... mentioned furniture as their special interest in the Exhibition'; also that 'men wanted to see mechanical items and electrical goods'; and lastly that the 'most widely represented class was very definitely artisan working class'.[70] Furthermore, as the authors of *'England Arise!'* have documented, working-class men had access to significantly larger amounts of disposable income than their wives, and substantially more time in which to spend it.[71] At a later point in the period we might also note, Ferdynand Zweig recorded the striking view that the affluent worker's home 'becomes his baby which he nurses'.[72] Lastly, a survey of adults' awareness of quality assurance symbols conducted by the British Market Research Bureau Ltd for the Quality Assurance Council in 1972 found that 'Consumer [labels] are something about which men are more knowledgeable than women'.[73]

In the same year that the Council was founded, 1944, the Council's scourge John Gloag published a book called *The Missing Technician* in which he bemoaned the absence of the vital figure of the industrial designer in the production process.[74] Copies of the book were held in the CoID Library. The Council would have done well to notice the equally damaging absence of 'technicians' from amongst the ranks of those with whom it wished to engage in the task of establishing new processes of consumption, the very kinds of men who emerge from the Coventry research profiled here as precursors of the affluent worker. Whilst people interested in 'educational' pursuits undoubtedly represented a minority of the British population, skilled workers, it should be noted, fell precisely into that group – as the ongoing exchange of textbooks, encyclopaedias and hobby-related items in Coventry works' papers of the pre-war period shows. In the campaign described here, there is no place for a strongly constituted model of active male consumption. Aesthetic tutelage, the guardianship and promulgation of a national design standard by state functionaries, disenfranchised many from a wider debate about design. The skilled male factory worker identified earlier, is relegated to the role of cypher, carrying out the plan of the industrial designer, even should that designer be the 'long-haired dreamer' who figured in Council nightmares.

In this brief chapter, a full explication of the Council's multifarious responses to the challenges set it by government cannot be attempted, nor can the success or failure of the strategies they adopted be adequately mapped against broader socio-political and economic factors. Nevertheless, by bringing to the published record an account of largely undocumented state-sponsored activities, it is hoped that readers' appreciation of the significance of this body and of its archive will be enhanced. Some of what has preceded in this chapter has been of a speculative nature. The close scrutiny of a much broader range of archival documents and contextual material will shortly take place, enabling the fuller development of an explanatory framework for the vacuum that appears to exist at the heart of the Council of Industrial Design's policy towards its largest potential audience.[75]

Notes

[1] This case has been most fully made in Whitworth, Lesley: 'Men, Women and "Little, Shiny Homes": The Consuming of Coventry, 1930–1939', unpublished PhD thesis, Centre for Social History, University of Warwick, 1997; but see also, Whitworth, Lesley: 'Shop and Shopfloor: Men's Sense of Belonging in 1930s Coventry' in Putnam T., Facey R. and Swales V. (eds): *Making and Unmaking: Creative and Critical Practice in a Designed World. Selected proceedings of the Design History Society Annual Conference, 2000*, Design History Society, Portsmouth, 2000; and Whitworth, Lesley: 'Fear and Loathing in West Germany? Contested Claims for Consumer Identities on either Side of the Second World War', in Playdon, P. (ed): *Proceedings of the Living in a Material World Conference*, Coventry University, Coventry, 1999.

[2] Thoms. D.W. and Donnelly, T.: 'Coventry's Industrial Economy, 1880–1980', in Lancaster, B. and Mason, T.: *Life and Labour in a Twentieth Century City: The Experience of Coventry*, Cryfield Press, Coventry ND [1986], p. 11.

[3] Richardson, Kenneth: *Twentieth-Century Coventry*, City of Coventry, Coventry, 1972, p. 277.

[4] University of London, Institute of Historical Research: *Victoria History of the Counties of England, Volume VIII*, Oxford University Press, Oxford, 1969, p. 236.

[5] Thoms and Donnelly, 'Coventry's Industrial Economy, 1880–1980', op. cit., p. 35; and Lancaster, B. and Mason, T.: 'Society and Politics in Twentieth Century Coventry' in Lancaster, B. and Mason, T.: *Life and Labour in a Twentieth Century City*, op. cit., p. 345.

[6] Prosser, R.: 'Coventry: A Study in Urban Continuity', unpublished MA dissertation, University of Birmingham, 1955, p. 94.

[7] Priestley, J.B.: *An English Journey*, Heinemann-Gollancz, London, 1934 (1968), p. 74.

[8] Thompson, Paul: 'Playing at Being Skilled Men: Factory Culture and Pride in Work Skills among Coventry Car Workers', *Social History*, vol. 13, no. 1 (1988), pp. 45–69.

[9] *The Alfred Herbert News*, March/April 1933, p. 45.

[10] Extract from transcript of author's interview with 'Mr G'.

[11] Evidence was gathered from pre-existing oral testimony, interviews, and published and unpublished autobiographies.

[12] Thankfully this situation is now changing. A strong example is Breward, Christopher: *The Hidden Consumer: Masculinities, Fashion and City Life 1860–1914*, Manchester University Press, Manchester, 1999. See also Hilton, Matthew: 'The Female Consumer and the Politics of Consumption in Twentieth-Century Britain', *Historical Journal*, vol. 45, no. 1 (2002), pp. 103–28, which discusses the un-gendering of the official image of the consumer by the later 1950s.

[13] Luetkens, Charlotte: *Women and a New Society*, Nicholson and Watson, London, 1946, p. 75.

[14] Jays advertisement, *Alfred Herbert News*, March 1930.

[15] Figure given by the CoID's first Director, S.C. Leslie, in Design Council Archive (hereafter DCA): ID125, speech given to representatives of voluntary bodies on 1 March 1945. Views on competitor nations taken from Hugh Dalton's speech to the inaugural meeting of the Council, reproduced in The Council of Industrial Design: *First Annual Report: 1945–1946*, HMSO, London, 1946, p. 6.

[16] Letter from Hugh Dalton to Sir Thomas Barlow, the CoID's first Chairman, dated 19 December 1944, reproduced in CoID: *First Annual Report,* op. cit., pp. 5–6.

[17] Extract from Dalton's speech reproduced in CoID: *First Annual Report,* op. cit., p. 6.

[18] DCA: ID125, speech by S.C. Leslie to representatives of voluntary bodies, 1 March 1945.

[19] Ibid.

[20] DCA: Printed and Published Material: 1949, Paul Reilly, 'The Aims and Organisation of the Council of Industrial Design' in 'Report on Design Conference for Retailers, 21st–24th February, 1949 at Westham House, Barford, Warwick' (Paul Reilly was Chief Information Officer of the Council). Similar formulations of words re-appear elsewhere.

[21] Extract from Dalton's speech to the inaugural meeting of the Council, reproduced in the COID: *First Annual Report,* op. cit., p. 6.

[22] A homespun version of European high modernism, the British conception of good design grew out of nineteenth century campaigns by John Ruskin and William Morris, and was concerned with 'truth to materials' and 'fitness for purpose'.

[23] Whilst industrial design consultancies such as that of the fearless self-promoter Raymond Loewy were a familiar feature of American commercial life by the 1930s, the same was not true for Britain. For international comparisons, see Woodham, Jonathan M.: *The Industrial Designer and the Public*, Pembridge, London, 1983; or Glancey, Jonathan: *Douglas Scott*, Design Council, London, 1988, for a rare British exception.

[24] The tradition of blaming the customer for the standard of goods on the market is longstanding, extending back through the nineteenth century. In the immediate pre-war period, the eminent design commentator Nikolaus Pevsner carried out an *Enquiry into Industrial Art in England*, Cambridge University Press, Cambridge, 1937, which produced damning accounts from manufacturers of the effect of popular taste on the quality of their output. Later on, the Consumers' Association would take up the same theme: see Black, Lawrence: '*Which?*craft in post-war Britain: The Consumers' Association and the politics of affluence', *Albion*, vol. 36, no. 1 (2004).

25   DCA: ID125, speech by S.C. Leslie to representatives of voluntary bodies, 1 March
     1945.
26   For more on the industrial aspect of their work see Maguire, Paddy: 'Designs on
     Reconstruction: British Business, Market Structures and the Role of Design in Post-War
     Recovery', *Journal of Design History*, vol. 4, no.1 (1991), pp. 15–30; and Maguire,
     Paddy: 'Craft Capitalism and the Projection of British Industry in the 1950s and 1960s',
     Journal of Design History, vol. 6, no. 2 (1993), pp. 97–112.
27   DCA: Printed and Published Material: 1949, 'Report on Design Conference for Retail
     Staff Trainers, 9–12 May 1949, at Stoke House, Bletchley, Bucks'. Notwithstanding the
     Council's brief to channel information back towards industry, its Information Officer
     was on record as saying that 'consumer research is dangerous'. He and Mrs Lovat Fraser
     then competed with one another in recounting the most horrific examples in their
     experience of public taste being pandered to.
28   A reference to European high modernism.
29   The Council of Industrial Design was solely responsible for the organization of Britain
     Can Make It, and selected the exhibits for many of the pavilions at the Festival of
     Britain.
30   From CoID: *First Annual Report*, op. cit., p. 20.
31   DCA: ID383 Pt 1, Mrs Murdoch (CoID) to Peter Moro (CoID's display designer), 29
     March 1946.
32   DCA: ID383 Pt 1, Robin Darwin to Peter Moro, 25 January 1946.
33   DCA: ID383 Pt 1, Murdoch to Moro, 29 March 1946, and Murdoch to Grieve, 25 March
     1946.
34   See 'DESIGN FAIR: Introductory Notes for schools' (by S. Morse-Brown) in DCA: ID
     1052 'Design Weeks Education Policy'.
35   *Design,* Issue 115, July 1958, 'Announcement', p. 6 and 'Comment', p. 21.
36   DCA: Printed and Published Material: 1949, Reilly in 'Report on Design Conference for
     Retailers', op. cit.
37   DCA: ID 930C, '"Design Weeks" – Reports'.
38   The Council member in question was Jack Beddington. See Woodham, Jonathan M.,
     and Maguire, Patrick J.: *Design and Cultural Politics in Post-War Britain: The Britain
     Can Make It Exhibition of 1946*, Leicester University Press, London, 1997, p. 128.
39   Papers contained in DCA: ID 930C, '"Design Weeks" – Reports'.
40   Ibid.
41   DCA: Printed and Published Ephemera, Council of Industrial Design: 'Design Fair: A
     Travelling Exhibition. Guide', ND.
42   See note 1 above.
43   DCA: ID 930C, '"Design Weeks" – Reports'.
44   List contained in DCA: ID 125.
45   For more on Williams see Weight, Richard: '"Building a New British Culture": The
     Arts Centre Movement, 1943–53' in Weight, Richard, and Beach, Abigail (eds): *The
     Right to Belong: Citizenship and National Identity in Britain, 1930–1960*, IB Taurus,
     London, 1998; and Fielding, Steven, Thompson, Peter and Tiratsoo, Nick: *"England
     Arise!": The Labour Party and Popular Politics in 1940s Britain*, Manchester
     University Press, Manchester, 1995, especially chapters 2 and 6.
46   DCA: ID 137, Gloag to Gordon Russell, 7 March 1949.
47   DCA: Printed and Published Material: 1949, Reilly in 'Report on Design Conference for
     Retailers', op. cit.
48   These were Council-authored and HMSO-published texts.
49   CoID: *First Annual Report,* op. cit., p. 20.

50 Council of Industrial Design: *New Home*, HMSO, London, 1946, p. 8.

51 DCA: Printed and Published Material: 1949, 'Report on Design Conference for Retailers', op. cit., G.R. Whalley, Director of Lewis's Ltd, spoke on 'Good Design is Good Business'.

52 This and subsequent quotations taken from DCA: Printed and Published Material: 1949, 'Report on Design Conference for Retailers'. op. cit.

53 At the closing forum of this event the provision of lecturers who 'could speak on specialised subjects' was again suggested as a way in which the Council could help.

54 DCA: Printed and Published Material: 1949, 'Report on Design Conference for Retail Staff Trainers', op. cit. For more on the American Consumers Union see McKellar, Susie: '"The beauty of stark utility": Rational Consumption in America – "Consumer Reports" 1936–54', in Attfield, Judy (ed): *Utility Reassessed: The Role of Ethics in the Practice of Design*, Manchester University Press, Manchester, 1999.

55 Explanatory notes contained in DCA: ID 80/18/1 Pt. I, minutes of BSI/CoID Liaison Meeting No. 3, held 15 September 1969.

56 See Tiratsoo, Nick: 'The American Quality Gospel in Britain and Japan, 1950–1970', in Sahlin-Andersson, K. and Engwall L. (eds): *The Expansion of Management Knowledge. Carriers, Flows and Sources*, Stanford University Press, Stanford, CA, 2002, pp. 175–92.

57 DCA: ID 1646/53, 'Proposed Future Policy for the Design Centre Awards', Paul Reilly, 12 July 1965.

58 Gundrey, Elizabeth: 'Guidance for Shoppers: Consumer Needs 8', *Design,* 107 (Nov 1957), pp. 62–64.

59 See http://www.which.net/corporate/history.html (5 March 2003). For recent scholarship on the Consumers' Association in addition to that already mentioned see Hilton, Matthew: *Consumerism in Twentieth-Century Britain: The Search for a Historical Movement,* Cambridge University Press, Cambridge, 2003.

60 Gundrey, 'Guidance for Shoppers' in *Design*, no. 107, pp. 62–64.

61 *Council of Industrial Design Twentieth Annual Report, 1964/65*, HMSO, London, 1965, p. 10.

62 'Consumer Needs 10', *Design,* no. 111 (March 1958), p. 32.

63 Although industry's receptiveness to even proven, cost-effective mechanisms for product improvement such as quality standards could not be relied upon. See Tiratsoo: 'The American Quality Gospel in Britain and Japan, 1950–1970'. op. cit.

64 DCA: ID 80/18/01, 'Minutes of BSI/CoID Liaison Meeting No. 6, held 14 June 1972'.

65 DCA: ID 1646/53, White to Reilly 1 July 1965.

66 DCA: ID 1646/53, 'Proposed Future Policy for the Design Centre Awards', Reilly, 12 July 1965.

67 DCA: ID 80/18/1 Pt. I, minutes of BSI/CoID Liaison Meeting No. 1, held 20 January 1969.

68 DCA: ID 383 Pt. 1, Leslie to T. Fife Clarke (Ministry of Health), 12 March 1946.

69 CoID: *First Annual Report*, op. cit., p. 21.

70 Typescript summary enclosed in. DCA: ID 903.

71 Fielding, Thompson and Tiratsoo: *England Arise!*. op. cit., pp. 141–43.

72 Zweig, Ferdynand: *The Worker in an Affluent Society: Family Life And Industry*, Heinemann, London,1961, p. 128.

73 DCA: ID 80/20 Pt. I, 'Quality Assurance Symbols: report on a Survey of Adults' prepared for the Quality Assurance Council by the British Market Research Bureau Ltd., p. 3.

74 Its full title was Gloag, John: *The Missing Technician in Industrial Production*, George Allen and Unwin, London, 1944.
75 A period of sustained research has been facilitated by an award from the Economic and Social Research Council with the Arts and Humanities Research Board as part of their 'Cultures of Consumption' programme. The two-year project 'Towards a Participatory Consumer Democracy: Britain, 1937–1987' began in 2003.

CHAPTER 11

'Selling Youth in the Age of Affluence': Marketing to Youth in Britain since 1959

Christian Bugge

Affluence in the post-war period has had a distinct impact on young people in Britain. Increased spending potential power has been one of the main contributing factors in providing post-war youth with the means to create a multitude of youth cultures and lifestyles which, as they grew in popularity, provoked varying degrees of outrage, excitement and commercial success. Traditionally youth cultures have been seen as one of the sites of counter-culture in society. The rebellious nature of youth cultures in the 1950s, when young people's new-found affluence brought them to the country's attention, and the social revolution pioneered in the 1960s led academics to focus upon youth as a site of societal rebellion. The spectacular and often what they have perceived to be the deviant nature of these cultural expressions have intrigued academics. Predominantly from the fields of sociology and cultural studies, numerous theories and observations have emerged which have sought to understand and rationalize this aspect of young people's lives.

'The New Left' history that emerged in the 1950s and 1960s moved away from a study of history that focused exclusively on elites to a new social history that focused on ordinary people. Drawing from the Marxist theory of the annales school and, personified by such historians as E.P. Thompson, this new academic approach focused on the autonomy and impact of ordinary people in the past. Similarly, within the discourses of sociology and cultural studies the assertion that 'Culture is ordinary', pioneered by Raymond Williams, led to studies which have applied an essentially Marxist interpretation to popular culture and, consequently, to youth culture. Led initially by the Birmingham Centre for Contemporary Cultural Studies (CCCS) in the 1970s, 'spectacular' youth cultures typified by the Mods, Skinheads and Punks were conceptualized as 'subcultures' a class-based collective resistance to capitalist structures.[1] Although the initial theories of the CCCS have been challenged and subsequently refined by cultural studies, the basic premise remains that youth cultures represent evidence of young people's resistance to the hidden hand of the market.

This approach, however, fails to consider some of the factors which are important to a fuller understanding of youth cultures, namely the way in which commerce has an effect on the lives of young people and how individual youth cultures have been constructed. By focusing upon youth cultures as an expression of young people's resistance, previous studies of youth culture have failed to consider the role of the capitalist superstructure, and more specifically commerce, in the way in which youth cultures are formed and become popular. This chapter, therefore, aims to explore an alternative explanation for the emergence of youth subcultures by taking a more detailed look at the commercial factors involved in the existence of youth subcultures. By analysing the response of marketing (broadly defined) to youth affluence, it explores the hypothesis that subcultures have come about partly due to the needs of commerce to segment markets into meaningful groups to which they can sell their products more effectively.

In order to address this hypothesis, it is important to understand what we mean by youth culture and more specifically by subcultures. Youth culture may seem ostensibly a straightforward concept, but in the light of the wealth of research on young people, it becomes complex and contestable. Young people are not easily split into individual cultural categories; they negotiate their identity for themselves and, especially in more recent times, may decide that they belong to a number of different subcultures. At its most simple, culture can be explained as the distinct patterns of life, and the ways in which social groups give expression to their social and material life experience.[2] Youth culture, therefore, refers to the distinct ways in which young people live their lives and can be distinguished by similarities and shared experiences based on age.

Once we look at youth culture in more detail, we discern the existence of a number of different and distinct ways of life within youth culture itself. There is a plurality of cultural groups that can be described as 'youth cultures'. This chapter is concerned with these specifically recognizable and defined cultures that exist within the encompassing concept of youth culture. 'Youth cultures', however is still a loose term. The most detailed attempt at explaining and defining these different youth cultures in the realm of academia has come from the CCCS. They have called these cultures 'subcultures' and defined them as collective class-based groups formed to express resistance to the cultural hegemony. However, subculture theory has many critics.[3] Firstly the theory focuses on an elite group within youth culture and fails to consider what happens to the subculture once it becomes popular. Moreover, by overemphasizing the role of class and resistance the theory ignores the role of the market in a subculture's development. The question remains then, whether youth subcultures, as the CCCS have claimed, rise spontaneously and lose their relevance once they become plundered and popularized by the media and commerce, or whether commerce plays a role in how subcultures emerge and become popular.

In more recent times, our understanding of youth subculture has changed significantly. Youth culture became more closely associated with commerce as the free market economy initiated by Thatcherism in the 1980s came to the fore. In the 1990s, the meaning of subculture as resistance began to lose its relevance. Advertising companies created departments that specialized in advertising to youth and increasingly used subculture's stylish appeal as a way of promoting 'brands' to consumers.[4] Similarly, more market research agencies focusing on youth alone were established to help brands comprehend subculture and to exploit its appeal in their marketing strategies. Youth subcultures became markets and no longer commanded any obvious resistance. The market, it appeared, had usurped the power of subculture. Steve Miles writing in 2000 argued, 'If they indeed exist at all, subcultures legitimize a world in which opposition is dead and consumer lifestyles are alive and well.'[5] Similarly, David Wheldon, Chief Executive Officer of a major advertising firm CIA, who throughout the 1990s was responsible for marketing brands such as Coca-Cola to young people, asserted, 'What people will tell you now, and they wouldn't be entirely wrong, is that everything is marketing.'[6]

Marketing to young people gained momentum in the 'age of affluence' and has grown in influence throughout the post-war period, but how did subcultures become the focus of marketing to young people? To what extent has youth culture become market driven? These are important questions for our understanding of the youth cultures of the past and for our appreciation of the lives of young people today. It seems of vital importance to discover as much as we can about the role of commerce and marketing in the history of youth culture. By moving away from a Marxist reading of youth culture to understand the role of commerce and marketing in the construction of youth cultures, we can begin to build a more robust appreciation of the role youth culture has played in contemporary Britain. This chapter explores how youth marketing in the age of affluence initiated a strategy of focusing on youth subculture as a way of targeting young people's consumption and as a way of appealing to the ever expanding youth market. It shows that this strategy has continued to the present day with increasing success. This allows us to gain a new appreciation of the meaning of youth culture and to begin to explore some of the consequences this may have had on young people. — + its culture

'Teenagers and hipsters': laying the foundations of youth marketing in the 1950s and 1960s

In the immediate post-war era the perception and nature of youth underwent a number of key changes. Firstly, young people's expectation of life improved. The Education Act of 1944 had provided more educational opportunities, particularly for working class youth, enabling some to pursue further education after the age of 15. Furthermore, 'day release' gave young wage earners the chance to pursue educational or training activities on a part-time basis.[7] Higher education also expanded. Before World War Two, the number of students in higher education in Britain, never rose above 70,000. By 1945–55 there were 122,000, by 1962–63 there were 216,000 and by 1965, 300,000.[8] In addition, youth represented a much more prominent demographic than before the war. This was due in part to the 'baby boom', but also by extending the amount of time in education, increasing numbers of people were postponing the responsibilities of adult life and choosing to remain young for a longer time. Moreover, when they did leave full-time education, most young people found life relatively easy. Military service ended in 1960 and unemployment remained at a minimal level. Earnings had risen faster than prices between 1951–63 and wage rates rose nominally by around 72 per cent.[9] By July 1957 Macmillan could famously state, 'Indeed, let's be frank about it; most of our people have never had it so good.'[10]

Another and possibly more significant part of the explanation of the emergence of subcultures in the post-war period was the increased amount of leisure time that youth experienced. Whereas youth cultures in the inter-war period were defined by their patterns of work and the industries to which they belonged, youth cultures in the 1950s and 1960s were now largely associated with leisure. Although poverty and inequality remained, and affluence did not spread to all regions of the country, on the whole youth had more disposable income. Added to this there were more places for young people to meet and exchange ideas. The expansion of the education system provided more chance for different classes to interact, particularly at art colleges, but also there were meeting places at 'skiffle parlours, jazz joints and rock and roll basements.'[12] Developments in mass communication coupled with increased urbanization also meant that the changing trends and development of youth subcultures reached many more parts of the country and at a faster rate. This new sense of youth and the attendant disposable income provided more opportunity for young people to experiment with different lifestyles in their consuming activities. Simultaneously these new developments in youth culture provided commerce with increasing reason to pursue youth as a market.

For the early parts of the 1950s, however, youth in Britain appeared to have initiated only deviant and troublesome subcultures. Newsworthy youth themes concentrated on the gang violence of the Teddy Boys and increases in incidences of youth crime.[13] At this point, except for the enlightened entrepreneur, young people were widely perceived by commerce as a problem and far from an accessible market. However, by the late 1950s this situation slowly began to change. The press began to switch direction and to depict young people as 'teenagers', a new strand to youth culture that had first appeared in America. This new conception of British youth portrayed young people in an altogether more favourable light. Presented as more docile, conformist and fun-loving, 'teenagers' with their passion for records, dancing and dressing-up, began to appear as the kind of youth culture that could constitute a market.[14]

The first serious attempt to exploit this emerging market on a broad scale in Britain was a market research report published by Mark Abrams in 1959 titled *The Teenage Consumer*. Mainly because Abrams was keen on showing the spending potential of young people, his study focused on those young people who had left full-time education and had not yet married. These 15–25–year-olds represented those young people with the greatest disposable income. Using the Ministry of Labour's Census of Wages for April and October of 1958 and the Blue Book on National Income and Expenditure, Abrams arrived at the conclusion that Britain's wage-earning youngsters were drawing about £1,480 millions annually, which equated to 8.5 per cent of all personal income in Britain. Furthermore, 'after his fiscal obligations to the state and to his parents the average young man is left with about £5 a week to spend as he chooses.'[15] Altogether, Abrams estimated that the nation's 4,200,000 working 'teenagers' had at their disposal £17 million a week, or £850 million a year, to spend as they liked. With pocket money added, this amounted to an estimated £900 million.

Most importantly, Abrams concluded that 'the quite large amount of money at the disposal of Britain's average teenager is spent mainly on dressing-up in order to impress other teenagers and on goods which form the nexus of teenage gregariousness outside the home.'[16] This acknowledged one of the most fundamental actions of belonging to a youth culture, 'dressing-up in order to impress other teenagers'. More significantly it established the fact that this was the very thing that teenagers spent most of their money on. Therefore, from the youth market's earliest beginnings, it was assumed that young people's spending was directed primarily at the activities associated with being part of youth subculture. Abrams's focus on 'Teenagers' exploited this popular conception of young Britons. Teenagers were not just an age category of 13–19 year-olds,[17] but a distinct and recognizable culture with popular appeal. In the popular press and in the popular imagination teenagers were the latest youth subculture. As a consequence of employing this tangible interpretation of youth culture, innocently or not, Abrams appealed to business wishing to tap the significant spending potential of the young and established a pattern in youth marketing which would continue to the present day.

Advertising's fascination with youth culture was also observed in the findings of the committee of *The Albemarle Report,* published in 1960.[18] The committee was appointed by the Minister of Education in November 1958, and charged with reviewing 'the contribution that the Youth Service of England and Wales can make in assisting young people to play in the Life of the Community.'[19] The report naturally focused upon young people's spending potential and concluded that marketing had already latched on to the potential of the new teenage subculture:

> A new market means new persuasions. Today as never before much advertising is addressed to teenagers, and to teenagers as 'teenagers' …
> They acquire therefore a sense of their own economic importance and independence.[20]

Even though the youth market was in its infancy, the committee's findings show that 'marketing' saw young people as part of a distinct subculture and most importantly that marketing used the media portrayal of the subculture to sell products to them. However, this was not the only way in which marketers used subculture. Marketers had long been aware that 'youth' had a very specific cultural and psychological appeal to consumers.[21] So at the same time the new youth subcultures were employed by marketers to sell to older consumers who wanted to feel young. This new departure meant that marketers reached out beyond the realms of the conformist and fun-loving teenager to draw from the more alternative youth cultures and to appeal to the youthful rebel in all consumers. As a result the size of the youth market increased significantly.

The rebellious youth cultures that satisfied these emerging consumer sensibilities most effectively, and the youth cultures that advertising and manufacturers strove to reflect in the 1960s, were those associated with the broad youth cultural phenomenon known as the 'counterculture'. The key characteristic of the counterculture was its desire to establish a creative revolution to break free from what it considered to be the staid, stolid, false and unimaginative culture of the 1950s. Above all the counterculture established the importance of creativity, innovation and 'coolness' in the way in which people consumed, and marketing geared its message accordingly. The desire of those in the counterculture to keep one step ahead in fashion trends and to challenge the orthodoxy had an obvious appeal to business. Clothing manufacturers, particularly, realized that if there were a more rapid pace of change in consumer fashion trends, the turnover and demand for their goods would increase. As consumers sought to keep up with changing fashions they were compelled to spend money on consumer products in order to keep up with the changing patterns of fashion.[22]

Advertising, in particular, strove to appeal directly to this youthful sense of rebellion, to this new creative revolution, and to the spirit of youth in consumers more generally. Business's obsession with rebellion was driven by the realization of what Warren Sussman calls the two 'moral orders'. Daniel Bell refers to these as a terrible 'contradiction'; a contradiction whereby on the one hand we have to work to earn a living and abide by the rules of economic production, but in our private lives, as consumers, we are taught to rebel.[23] This contradiction is resolved by the individual's ability to rebel in their consuming lives, to be an individual and free to be one's self. This recognition of the consumer's desire to 'be oneself' was evident in British marketing practice throughout the 1960s. Jeremy Bulger, who worked for the advertising agency Collet Dickinson, highlighted this recognition in his discussion of British car advertising in 1968.[24] Whilst appraising the latest selection of car adverts for that year, Bulger expressed the belief that cars were no longer being sold merely by their good mechanics or price, as they had in the past, but rather, 'on association of ideas, on image, on myth in the public mind. They sell them as a personality prop, not as a piece of private transport.' The intention was to escape the sense of mass production and to appeal to the consumer's desire to feel like an individual. The need to convey a sense of creativity and style was so important to marketing that Doyle Dane Bernbach, who were responsible for advertising Volkswagen, believed the car business had become more like the fashion business. In fact, as Bulger observed, the question of consumer taste had become almost as 'fine as couture'.[25]

Throughout the 1960s, marketers, who were based mainly in London, were absorbed by the various youth counter-cultures that sprang up around them. Andrea Adam, who helped produce the *Time* cover for its 'Swinging London' issue said, 'we were all totally riveted by London. London was special, it had a kind of mystique.'[26] The creative revolution eddying out of the capital had the young at its epicentre. As Mary Quant, one of London's leading pioneers of youth fashion at the time commented:

> London led the way in the changing focus of fashion from the establishment to the young. As a country we were aware of the great potential of this change long before the Americans or the French. We were one step ahead from the start ...[27]

In an article in the *Advertising Quarterly*, Richard Negus, a graphic consultant and a designer of advertising posters, revealed the growing fascination and premium attached to youth. 'Carnaby Street', he said, 'now has its very significant place alongside Bond Street; and a lot of the new excitement and new thought – vital, energetic and *young* – is springing from this source.'[28] Maxine Molyneux, writing in the *Advertising Quarterly* commented on how advertising had stolen ideas from the underground press, posters and record sleeves and that 'the youth explosion swept through Britain; advertising with a keen eye, followed by gearing its message to a new and different area of affluence.' Moreover, Molyneux believed that advertising's fascination with 'hip' affected the spread of these styles to a wider consumer audience. 'The feedback from the avant-garde into popular culture' was conveyed in advertising and provided the public with 'a kind of disposable art.'[29] The fascination with youth cultures amongst British marketers was therefore twofold. Firstly, youth was an attractive market, one with a distinct spending potential, but secondly, youth had an increasingly important symbolic role to play in appealing to the cultural and psychological needs of consumers in the 1960s. Increasingly people in Britain were choosing to act and remain young for longer, and marketers and manufacturers were there to provide them with the consumer products and, via marketing communications, the lifestyle instructions to explore these possibilities.

But to what extent were marketers successful in aiding the development of subcultures? Firstly, 'marketers' is a broad term. In the realm of advertising it is clear that Abrams' sentiments had filtered through to advertisers. Abrams' agenda with *The Teenage Consumer* was to alert advertisers to the potential spending power of the youth market. Douglas Kelly writing in the *Advertising Quarterly* in 1966 stated that:

> You are certainly aware of this challenge of the youth market and of the population explosion in which the balance is shifting from day to day in favour of youth. Their influence is also developing at the same astonishing rate.[30]

Advertising had responded to the new notion of youth and had begun to see youth as a market segment. Individual campaigns had a certain success. The popular 'twist' dance style was initially pushed hard in extensive publicity campaigns by the Paramount and Colombia film companies and latterly by the Mecca and Arthur Rank dance-hall chains. Moreover, if under the term 'marketers' we are to include the marketing activities of smaller scale commercial activities like fashion boutiques for example, we can say that the initiatives of designers such as Mary Quant had a great deal of impact on the subcultures of the 1960s. Similarly, Brian Epstein, the manager of The Beatles, in partnership with the record company EMI, was successful in developing and marketing a number of commercially successful groups under the title of the 'Mersey sound'.[31] Certainly from this perspective marketers were having an influence on the growth and development of subcultures.

Although it would be too ambitious then to state that advertising alone was directly responsible for the subcultures of the 1960s, important precedents had been set. Significantly, advertisers had now established and segmented the youth market and were aware of the subcultures within it. Simultaneously, young entrepreneurs had shown that subcultures could provide profitable markets. Although advertising may not have found it easy to communicate with subcultures it is clear that they were attempting to do so. What advertising was aware of, but found difficult to grasp, was subculture's stylish appeal, fashionableness, and its ever-changing sense of cool. Phillip Nathan, a copywriter in the 1960s, exemplified this in the *Advertising Quarterly*. Despite having completed three campaigns for youth, he claimed in frustration, 'today's vogue is tomorrow's anathema, while yesterday's bête noir may well be an overwhelming rage for several months ahead.'[32] The important precedent established, then, was that the marketers were aware of the commercial potential of youth subculture and in places had helped it to develop. Marketers had understood one of the most fundamental ways in which subcultures functioned; to define their members as 'hip', 'cool', and 'exclusive' and different from 'mainstream' culture. Whereas cultural studies would get lost in theorizing this aspect of subcultures as class-based resistance, marketing would continue to explore this important part of youth culture to develop and exploit its marketable appeal. Improvements in market research in the 1970s and in advertising practices in the 1980s would help marketers to understand subculture more effectively and firmly establish the template for selling to youth that was established in the 1960s.

From research to style: youth marketing in the 1970s and 1980s

Youth marketing in the 1970s faced a new set of challenges. The British economy struggled in comparison to the boom years of the 1950s and 1960s. The oil crisis of 1973 highlighted the extent of Britain's economic shortcomings, and indeed worsened the situation. The balance of payments, which had dogged the Labour governments of the 1960s, reached crisis point in the early 1970s and inflation and unemployment were rising at an alarming rate. Naturally marketing expenditure decreased. In 1971, *The European Journal of Marketing* (EJM) believed that, with the exception of only the top four or five agencies, agency revenues had fallen by as much as 10 per cent.[33] In the 1960s, the unprecedented levels of affluence and consumption played a significant role in the birth of the youth market. In the more depressed 1970s the youth market appeared to be less conspicuous and the youth marketing industry had to work harder to adapt to this change. In the marketing imagination, young people no longer constituted one large market segment with obvious spending potential. Now there was a need to delve deeper into the different nuances of how young people used consumption to form their identity and different cultural groupings. The focus therefore shifted to more detailed market research to understand the different youth markets.

One of the most important changes in youth marketing during the 1970s was the realization that youth consumption was as equally sophisticated as adult consumption. In the previous decade, when the focus of the youth market was directed primarily at free-spending teenagers, young people were viewed as distinct from the wider consumer market, with simpler consumer needs. Marketers now came to see young people more accurately as a complex consumer group and in some ways as more problematic than their older counterparts. As Adam Knowles claimed in the *Advertising Quarterly* in 1971, 'The isolation of the teenage market and its importance, notably by Dr Mark Abrams in the late-50s, directed perhaps too much attention to the "generation gap" idea. In fact, of course, the gap is non-existent.'[34] Christine Restall, international research co-ordinator for Europe at McCann-Erickson Advertising Ltd, also believed that the term 'teenager' was an irrelevant concept, and one that suggested that young people were 'a race apart.' In fact, teenagers did not use the term to describe themselves, either amongst their peers or to their parents. Restall believed that the focus on teenagers had blurred marketing's understanding of the youth market. McCann-Erickson's study revealed that despite their low-level of income, younger age groups still consumed as much in terms of records, clothes, toiletries etc., as older age groups. Moreover, it was naïve to consider youngsters as inexperienced consumers just because they had lower levels of income. The key to success was to appeal to young people's desire to express a connection with a certain way of life and to a particular cultural grouping. Restall believed that advertising worked in part because of the effectiveness of 'symbols which are used to project stereotypes, which in turn tell people about the product and its use, and imply the type of person who might use it.' Therefore, marketing began to consider 'the values that young people hold and the life styles to which they aspire.'[35]

Writing in *Advertising* in 1978, Paul Shay provides one such example of how market research was responding to this changed perception of the youth market. Shay, the executive director of Commercial Development and International Services, at SRI International, wrote that during the 1970s, the younger generation was experiencing a fundamental change. Having avoided the economic deprivation and uncertainty of previous generations, a change in values took place that promoted a search for more self-expression and self-fulfilment, as opposed to more basic materialist desires. The consumer cohort that directly reflected this cultural change was identified as the 'inwardly-directed.' SRI split the 'inwardly directed' into four subsections: those of the 'I-Am-Me' consumer; the 'experiential' consumer; the 'socially conscious' consumer; and the 'integrated' consumer. 'I-Am-Me' consumers were considered to be the most eclectic of all consumers and the type of consumer most likely to belong to a subculture. This group was young, either still at school or starting off in a career. They were considered as a 'far-out fringe market' that consisted of 'anything imaginable.' Interestingly, they were seen to be the 'trend-setters', worthy of scrutiny as the 'spawning ground for goods and services which subsequently spread to other more stable inner-directed groups.'[36] The commercial potential of subculture as the spawning ground of new consumer trends and as the precursors of wider consumer markets had been initiated.

If in the 1970s market research had recognized the heterogeneity and sophistication of youth culture and had increased its awareness of the effectiveness of subculture, in the 1980s, changing advertising practices would come to have a significant effect on the way in which 'youth' was used in advertising. From the early 1980s, led primarily by the advertising agency Saatchi and Saatchi, a new generation of advertising companies came to the fore of the marketing industry that increased the size and scope of the advertising business. Between 1976 and 1986 advertising expenditure grew by 66 per cent in real terms, and its expansion between 1985 and 1986 alone was 10 per cent. Above all, these new advertisers replaced the traditional maxim of the 'unique selling point' (USP) for the new 'emotional selling point' or 'ESP'.[37] As John Hegarty, partner in the new advertising agency, BBH, claimed, 'We don't sell, we make people want to buy.'[38] The aim of this new direction in advertising was to offer consumers an image of what they aspired to. Above all the new direction in advertising aimed to achieve this emotional appeal through the use of more creative adverts that placed a higher priority on style. This new creative impulse would draw from youth culture and employ images of youth style.

At the same time two important departments came to the fore in British advertising agencies: account planning and media buying. Account planning made use of the developments in qualitative market research in the 1970s that began to help segment markets more effectively and to appeal directly to the individual aspirations of different consumer segments. Research also helped media buyers to position their adverts more effectively. But most significantly, these two new areas took advantage of the growing media pluralization and the resulting fragmentation of the mass audience and readerships.[39] Stuart Ball, a planning and business director at KHBB revealed the account planners' approach to consumers. 'To be different, the consumer purchases a product on or around … signals that make a statement about him or herself – about what *kind* of person they are in society, or would like to be.'[40] This advertising practice grew alongside a significant social change. Whereas previously consumers had affirmed their identity by emulating the status standards of the people around them, the new breed of consumers purposefully affirmed their status by differentiating themselves from the group.[41] Rather than 'keeping up with the Joneses', consumers now wanted to get away from the Joneses. This meant that consumers embraced a 'style of life' rather than a place in the social hierarchy. John Seabrook sees this trend, in its more advanced 1990s state, as representing what he calls 'nobrow':

> Where the old hierarchy was vertical, the new hierarchy – Nobrow – seemed to exist in three or more dimensions. Subculture served in the role that high culture used to serve, as the trend giver to the culture at large. In Nobrow, subculture was the new high culture, and high culture had just become another subculture. But above both subculture and mainstream culture was identity – the only shared standard, the Kantian 'subjective reality'.[42]

This consumer sensibility, as we have seen previously, had its beginnings in the 1960s. Now, as advertising itself became more creative, the range of complex lifestyles could be better represented in a visual culture. Moreover, the variety of lifestyles depicted in these new visual representations drew heavily on the styles of youth culture. Young people were increasingly expressing their affiliation to these different lifestyles by consuming the products attached to these various media representations. As Miles has claimed, by the 1980s 'it was almost as if consumerism had emerged as a way of life for young people.'[43]

Brands as subculture: Youth subculture and youth marketing in the 1990s

In 1993 *Marketing Week* stated that, 'Getting on the same wave-length as young people is vitally important for companies' and that each brand had their own approach. 'Coca-Cola divides youngsters into different types and markets to each one; Nike tries to construct images that are beyond fashion; Sega taps into rebellion; and Tango gets them laughing.' By the 1990s, for bigger brands with endless budgets the way to appeal to consumers was to own a subculture themselves. Steve Jones, marketing director of Coca-Cola GB and Ireland provided an example of how far brands were associating themselves with different youth cultures. 'By dividing youngster into different groups – such as mainstreamers, Rappers, Rockers and Surfers – and tailoring ads to each, Coke hopes to "have credibility and be relevant to their lives".' Due in part to economic recession, and partly as a reaction to Thatcherism, the first half of the 1990s was dominated by a return to 'realism', which was reflected in marketing practice. The 1980s aspirational lifestyles had been replaced by a more 'realistic' view of young people. The early 1990s then, gave rise to what marketers referred to as 'Generation X.' Young people were seen as 'Anti-materialistic, media-literate and with the attention span of a gold fish.'[44] It was perhaps this belief that youth culture was more media savvy, immune to marketing and less materialistic that encouraged marketers to explore the more anti-materialistic and more attitude driven environs of youth subculture. It was no longer the belief that marketing could offer merely a superficial image of youth style that young people would aspire to, now it was important to understand the attitude and the essence of youth culture.

The important ingredient that marketers aimed to extract from youth culture in the 1990s was the 'lifestyle' of the various innovative new subcultures. Mike Perry, account director at Simons Palmer Denton Clemmow and Johnson, the agency working for the sportswear brand Nike, explained that attitude was more important than style. 'You are better off finding an attitude that gels rather than keeping up with the latest fashion – and we feel attitude is more important than age.' Each of the large brands aimed to associate itself with a youth cultural attitude. Rather than merely trying to keep up with developing style trends, brands aimed to be seen as having a particular attitude or lifestyle, and in effect to own for themselves a part of a subculture. It became important therefore to own a lifestyle and marketers busily hunted out developing subcultures with which they could associate before the trend became more popular. As Perry added: 'It is important to talk to the style-makers and those behind the playground chat. We interview fashion magazine editors and stylists, as well as influential young people.'[45]

It is certainly clear that in the 1990s marketers began to focus more directly than they had done in the past on individual youth subcultures. By the 1990s, the double-action appeal of youth merged together. Now subcultures were not just used to appeal to consumers, they actually became individual markets. The focus on subculture became so important, and the ability to reach segments became so much more effective, that subcultures were actively sought and developed as youth markets. As Seabrook argues:

Prior to Nirvana there had been overnight pop sensations, of course, but
never before had a cult band – a band that defined itself against the
mainstream culture – become part of the mainstream so quickly. After
Nirvana, it became common for hip-hop acts who were on the street six
months ago to sell millions of records, or for a band like Radish, who had no
folk following other than the band's parents and friends – a band that had
never even performed live before – to have millions of 'fans' with one song
and a hit record.[46]

Qualitative research now began to explore deeper into the subcultural realm and
companies that specialized in understanding the mentality of the young could
discover and define 'cool' and sell it to the eagerly awaiting advertising companies
and brands. The 1990s saw a whole host of descriptions and explanations of both
the lifestyles and spending habits of Britain's young. Mark Ratcliff was one
researcher who benefited from this development. He was employed by HK
McCann, Coca-Cola's British agency and spoke of a 'post-rave culture' as 'the
single most important development in youth culture since the invention of the
teenager in the 1950s.' Ratcliff had been employed by HK McCann to attend raves
in order to glean an understanding of this powerful youth subculture. Ratcliff saw
rave culture as the most dominant influence in the six years prior to 1994. 'Not
every young person is an active participant in rave culture,' Ratcliff argued, 'but all
are influenced in some way by its values.' The challenge to advertisers in the mid-
1990s according to Ratcliff was to appeal to the values within rave culture rather
than the obvious iconography. Ratcliff believed the most successful television
adverts were those which were 'wilfully silly, irreverent and energetic' such as the
adverts for Tango orange drink which had borrowed from the fly-posters of illegal
raves.[47]

Understanding the implications of the rise of youth marketing

The growth of the youth market cannot be explained alone by the fact that young
people became more affluent in the post-war period. Although young people's
affluence has attracted the attention of youth marketing, the increase in the
amounts of money and time invested in the youth market has also been affected by
older consumers who aspire to, and emulate, the lifestyles of the young. 'New
youth' consumers have sought the large amounts of cultural capital that is available
in young subcultures by purchasing products and brands that allude to aspects of
young people's style and lifestyles. One of the most common ways in which
consumers are able to realize the cultural capital of the young is through the
consumption of media representations or commercial reinterpretations of
subculture. As we have seen in this chapter this is a commercial template that was
established from the very beginning of the youth market in the 1960s.
So how did youth subcultures that were first identified by marketers in the
1960s become so entwined with commerce? Part of the explanation is the
emergence of new social groupings and their stereotypes, new social values and

ideologies in the 1980s. During the 1980s stereotypical social groupings such as the 'yuppie', the 'new man', the 'career woman' and the 'lager lout' were created and developed by different aspects of the media.[48] At the same time consumption took on a higher priority in the 1980s, partly due to the collapse of communism, and the triumph of capitalism as *the* world system of economic organization and the lionization of free market politics over more orthodox politics of state intervention and the welfare consensus.[49] In this environment image took on a hitherto unprecedented importance as style, form and aesthetic came to dominate the commercial world. Increasingly, consumers used commodities to help construct a wide range of identities.

Aided and abetted by marketing, products and brands were increasingly used to confirm membership of particular cultural communities and to signify invidious and often antagonistic social and cultural differences between different groups.[50] 'Lifestyles' came to the fore. The style-obsessed media developed a number of social stereotypes to reflect and enhance this popular preoccupation. Marketing, in this increasingly consumerist environment, embraced these lifestyles as a way to increase brand identities and as a way of segmenting, developing and creating new markets. Subcultures could fuel these new desires for new markets and new segments. At the core of segmentation was style, the allusive quality which youth subcultures had in abundance. With increased media these new markets drew on increasingly focused advertising to nurture these markets.

Increasingly brands have been used to answer fundamental questions about our social selves. For example, to quote Jane Pavitt, author of *Brand.New*, 'wearing Diesel jeans rather than Levi's emphasises my youth.'[51] Furthermore, marketing is responsible for developing and encouraging the connection between commodities and lifestyle. For Giddens, working out who we are is partly a process of acquiring desired commodities and the pursuit of the 'artificially framed styles of life.'[52] Marketing aims to associate its brands with certain styles of life, so that the lifestyles can be assumed when purchasing its products. Growing numbers of consumers in their middle age seek these artificially framed styles of life. They satisfy these desires by consuming signals that make a statement about what kind of person they want to be. With the ever-increasing insatiability for new market segments and consumable lifestyles, consumers and marketers have eagerly pursued youth culture for its constantly replenished stock of subcultures. As a result consumer focus is increasingly switched to young people, their culture and style.

More importantly, consumers of varying ages have become more interested in consuming the 'cool' qualities of products, brands and lifestyles. Increasingly this has become a means of measuring social status. As Bob Tyrell of the Henley centre for forecasting states, 'Lifestyle is all about knowing the style code, and the fewer the people that know, the slicker the lifestyle.' Tyrell calls the process the lifestyle pyramid: 'The more you know the style, the fewer are the people that can de-code your own lifestyle, and the higher your place in the pyramid. This is the cornerstone of modern marketing.'[53] Increasingly 'cool' has become more important as a gauge of cultural capital and differentiation in society, and therefore subcultures are incorporated into marketing as they represent the quintessence of cool. The youth market has engulfed a larger number of older consumers who are interested in consuming products that are symbols and signals of young people's lifestyles.

So, if marketers have sought out the latest subcultures and attempted to use aspects of their styles, music and attitudes in advertising, what affect has this had on youth subcultures? The commercialization of subculture and the development of an ageing 'youth market', willing to consume the latest youth culture, would appear to have denied young people an important cultural outlet. With greater numbers of older people aiming to express an affiliation with youth cultures, it is harder for young people to use youth subculture as an expression of their difference and as a way of constructing a unique identity. Therefore we might assume that young people have lost possession of youth subcultures and that this cultural mechanism has become obsolete. However, young people still participate in youth subcultures, but that participation is likely to manifest itself through consumption. Critically, this is still limited to those who have the necessary financial resources. Those without the necessary resources are increasingly excluded.[54] Young people are still creative in how they consume and it can be argued that their interaction with the market is a two-way process. However, the question still remains – who holds the more powerful hand in that interaction?[55]

Conclusion

In an age where affluence has had an overwhelming effect on society, there has been a great deal of concern about youth consumption and the ability of the market to influence the lives of impressionable youngsters. The existence of subcultures has previously been championed as evidence of young people resisting the hidden hand of the market. However, this theory is beginning to fall apart. As youth subcultures have increasingly been absorbed in the commercial world to fulfil the hunger of lifestyle marketing there is now less evidence that subcultures represent resistance. Marketing and other forms of media readily portray emerging youth subcultures such that young people often experience subculture from these media portrayals before they experience it for themselves. Young people are no longer actively pursuing subcultures as a way of life, if indeed they ever were; they are merely consumers of the styles of subcultures. There is now an abundance of subcultures in the youth cultural environment, and young people choose elements of each of these in their consuming lives. It means that youth subcultures are rapidly reused and retrospectively reborn. In an environment where the media constantly portrays new youth cultural innovation, there is a decreasing opportunity for young people to be subcultural, to be alternative and different. Moreover, older and more affluent consumers can have a more active participation in subcultures as they have the financial resources to consume sub-cultural accoutrements. Marketing plunders the subcultures of the young so those older consumers can incorporate them into their lifestyles. As Wallace and Kovatcheva have argued, it is increasingly hard for young people to shock, to create new subcultures and to find a voice of their own.

> It seems that the proliferation of youth subcultures and their absorption into commercial mass media, rock and fashion industries has on the one hand resulted in the increasing importance and acceptance of them but, at the same time, youth as a cultural force is dissolved.[56]

Evaluating the role of marketing in the culture of young people's lives is inextricably bound to social theory debates over *structure* and *agency*. The age of affluence that dawned from the later 1950s increased the potential both for popular agency and for the control of everyday lives by the structures of consumer capitalism. By focusing on the various aspects of the marketing industry, we can see that the young people's agency has been overemphasized. It is essential then, that we develop these initial findings of marketing's engagement with youth subculture to develop a greater understanding of the role of commerce in everyday culture. Cultural studies has been preoccupied with attempting to discover multiple ways in which young people display agency and avoid the grasp of the producers of popular culture by turning any number of commodities into objects of rebellion.[57]

In certain cultural studies' discourses it is assumed that consumerism is a democratic process whereby young people pick and choose between the commodities they require, that there is a dialogue between producer and consumer, so that consumers get more of what they like and less of what they dislike.[58] But is it this simple? What degree of agency do young people really have within the structure of the market? Can we really continue to see these commercial youth cultures as resistant and indicative of young people's freedom from commerce? Cultural studies has developed in opposition to Frankfurt's 'mass culture' theory and debates over the value of low versus high culture. It has aimed to stress both that popular culture is worthy of study and more importantly that popular culture is expressive of people's creativity, freedom and even resistance to the capitalist structure. This academic trend has an important place, but we need to keep a balance. Admittedly, not all studies of culture express the enfranchising aspects of consumerism. Bauman argues that freedoms associated with consumption are determined by levels of income and are therefore socially divisive.[59] What we need is a more critical evaluation of the culture industry. We need to recognize the hand of commerce in producing modern day culture. This is not to suggest that we should embrace the Frankfurt school's notion that popular culture is plebeian and amenable to social control, or that people do not exercise choice, taste judgements and discretion about popular culture. But we should question the extent to which these opinions are formed in isolation from commercial marketing com- munications. In the pressure to find young people's creativity in the face of potential manipulation, the power of marketing has been under explored. We need to consider how marketing plays a part in how culture is produced so that we may more fully comprehend the way in which people construct their individual and group identities in an affluent and consumer-driven society.

Notes

[1] Hebdige, Dick: *Subculture: The Meaning of Style*, Methuen, London, 1979. Brake, Mike: *The Sociology of Youth Culture and Youth Subcultures: Sex and Drugs and Rock'n' Roll?* Routledge and Keegan Paul, London, 1980. Hall, Stuart and Jefferson, Tony (eds): *Resistance Through Rituals, Youth Subcultures in Post-war Britain*, Hutchinson, London, 1976.

[2] Wyn, Johanna and White, Rob: *Rethinking Youth*, Sage, London, 1997, p. 72.

[3] Clarke, Gary: 'Defending Ski-Jumpers: A Critique of Theories of Youth Subcultures', in Frith, S. and Goodwin, P. (eds): *On Record: Rock Pop and the Written Word*, Routledge, London, 1989. Andes, Linda: 'Growing Up Punk', in Epstein, J.P.: *Youth Culture, Identity and the Postmodern World*, Blackwell, Oxford, 1998. Thornton, Sarah: *Club Cultures: Music, Media and Subcultural Capital*, Polity, Cambridge, 1995.

[4] For a more details of these events see: Bugge, Christian: *The End of Youth Subculture? Dance Culture and Youth Marketing 1988–2000*, unpublished PhD. thesis, Kingston University, 2002.

[5] Miles, Steve: *Youth Lifestyles in a Changing World*, Open University Press, Buckingham, 2000, p. 101.

[6] Interview with author, 27 November 2000.

[7] Marwick, Arthur: *The Sixties*, Oxford University Press, Oxford, 1998, p. 57.

[8] *New Left Review*, vol. 43 (May-June 1967), p. 3.

[9] Childs, David: *Britain Since 1945: A Political History*, Routledge, London, 1997, p. 105.

[10] Childs, *Britain Since 1945*, op. cit., p. 100.

[11] Fowler, David: *The First Teenagers: The Lifestyle of Young Wage-earners in Interwar Britain*, Woburn Press, London, 1995.

[12] Marwick, *The Sixties*, op. cit., p. 57.

[13] *The Times*, 4 September 1957 reported: 'At the weekends the villagers [of Castleton in the Lake District] are accustomed to seeing gangs of youths and Teddy boys, with their girls, arriving from such towns as Sheffield, Leeds and Manchester ... For many of these visitors a good time consists in beating the daylight out of local property if not the population.'

[14] For further discussion on the rise of the teenager see: Marwick, *The Sixties*, op. cit.; and Osgerby, Bill: *Youth in Britain Since 1945*, Blackwell, Oxford, 1998.

[15] Abrams, Mark: *The Teenage Consumer*, London Press Exchange, London, 1959, pp. 7, 9.

[16] Abrams, *Teenage Consumer*, op. cit., p. 9.

[17] The introduction to Abrams's report notes that the *Oxford English Dictionary* describes a 'teenager' as aged 13–19. Abrams however, produced a new categorisation defined as 15–25, and refined this group further by including only those wage earners that had left school and were not yet married.

[18] Ministry of Education, *The Youth Services of England and Wales* (The Albemarle Report), Cmnd. 929 (1960).

[19] Albemarle Report, op. cit., Section 1.

[20] Albemarle Report, op. cit., Section 96.

[21] Hollander, Stanley C. and Germain, Richard: *Was There a Pepsi Generation Before Pepsi Invented It?*, NTC Publishing Group, Chicago, 1992.

[22] Frank, Thomas: *The Conquest of Cool*, University of Chicago Press, Chicago, 1997, p. 229.

[23] Ibid.

24   At the time Collet Dickinson held the Ford account.
25   Bulger, J.: 'Selling the Golden Calf', *New Society*, 17 October 1968, pp. 556, 559.
26   Green, Jonathon: *Days in the Life, Voices from the English Underground*, Pimlico, London, 1998, p. 86.
27   Quant, Mary: *Quant by Quant*, Cassell, London, 1966 in A. Marwick: *The Sixties*, op. cit., p. 67.
28   Negus, Richard in *The Advertising Quarterly*, no. 12 (Summer 1967), p. 41.
29   Molyneux, Maxine: 'Affluent Aspirations', *The Advertising Quarterly*, no. 26 (Winter 1970–71), p. 52.
30   Kelly, Douglas: 'Profit by design', *The Advertising Quarterly*, no. 10 (Winter 1966–67), p. 39.
31   Marwick, *The Sixties*, op. cit., pp. 71–72.
32   Nathan Philip: 'The Teenage Enigma', *Advertising Quarterly*, no. 10, (Winter 1966–67), p. 48.
33   'Poor Times for Advertising', *European Journal of Marketing*, vol. 5, no. 2 (1971).
34   Knowles, Adam: 'The Theory of Residual Imagery', *Advertising Quarterly*, no. 29 (Autumn 1971), p. 20.
35   Restall, Christine: 'Teenagers in the Market', *Advertising*, no. 60, (Summer 1979), p. 30.
36   Shay, Paul: 'The New Consumer Values', *Advertising*, no. 56, (Summer 1978), pp. 15–18.
37   Nixon, Sean: *Hard Looks: Masculinities, Spectators and Contemporary Consumption*, UCL Press, London, 1996.
38   Hegarty, John: *Marketing Week*, 3 March 1989, p. 42. Nixon, *Hard Looks*, op. cit., p. 86.
39   Nixon, *Hard Looks*, op. cit., p. 89.
40   'Blue Print for a New Consumer', *Campaign*, 11 September 1987, p. 55. Quoted in Mort, Frank: *Cultures of Consumption: Masculinities and Social Space in the Late Twentieth Century*, Routledge, London, 1996, p. 96.
41   Mort, *Cultures of Consumption*, op. cit., p. 96.
42   Seabrook, John: *Nobrow: The Culture of Marketing the Marketing of Culture*, Methuen, London, 2001, p. 66.
43   Miles, *Youth Lifestyles*, op. cit., p. 112.
44   'Rebels with Bad Pores', *Marketing Week*, 20 August 1993, p. 36.
45   Ibid., p. 37.
46   Seabrook, *Nobrow*, op. cit., p. 101.
47   Ibid., p. 13. M. Ratcliff, interviewed in *The Daily Telegraph*, 18 July 1994, p. 13.
48   Lee, Martin J.: *Consumer Culture Reborn: The Cultural Politics of Consumption*, Routledge, London, 1993. Osgerby, Bill, in Cobley, P. and Briggs, A (eds): *Introduction to the Media*, Longman, London, 1997.
49   Lee, *Consumer Culture Reborn*, op. cit., p. ix.
50   Ibid., p. xi.
51   Pavitt, Jane: *Brand.New*, V&A, London, 2000, p. 17.
52   Giddens, Anthony: *Modernity and Self Identity: Self and Society in the Late Modern Age*, Polity Press, Oxford, 1991, p. 198.
53   Tomlinson, Alan (ed): *Consumption, Identity and Style: Marketing, Meanings, and the Packaging of Pleasure*, Routledge, London, p. 27.
54   Frith, Hannah and Gleeson, Kate: 'Identity: An Equal Resource?' (unpublished paper presented at the 'Global Youth' conference, September 2001, University of Plymouth). 'Although theories of identity construction emphasise diversity and access to a cornucopia of different styles, images and identities, young people interviewed about clothing and identity describe the selection of particular looks as a compromise between

personal choice, identification and financial resources. The post-modern fetishisation of identity is potentially politicized in a context where identities are not equally accessible and easily inter-changeable.'

55 Miles, Steve: *Youth Lifestyles*, op. cit., p. 120.
56 Wallace, Claire and Kovatcheva, Sijka: *Youth in Society,* Macmillan, Basingstoke, 1998, pp. 183–4.
57 Frank, Thomas: *One Market Under God: Extreme Capitalism, Market Populism and the End of Economic Democracy*, Secker and Warburg, London, 2001, p. 282.
58 Nava has commented that consumerism: 'has already generated new grass-roots constituencies – constituencies of the market place – and has enfranchised modern citizens in new ways, making possible a new and quite different economic, political and personal and creative participation in society.' Nava, Micha: 'Consumption reconsidered: buying and power', *Cultural Studies*, vol. 5 (1991), p. 173, quoted in S. Miles: *Social Theory in the Real World*, Sage, London, 2001, p. 76.
59 Bauman, Zygmunt: *Freedom*, Open University Press, Milton Keynes, 1988.

CHAPTER 12

Losing The Peace: Germany, Japan, America and the Shaping of British National Identity in the Age of Affluence

Richard Weight

'That blasted Common Market', Lord Beaverbrook told Harold Macmillan in 1962, 'is an American device to put us alongside Germany. As our power was broken and lost by two world wars, it is very hard on us now to be asked to align ourselves with those villains.'[1] Beaverbrook's dislike of European integration, and of West Germany in particular, was shared by most Britons in the high period of affluence between 1950 and 1970. However, resentment of American influence was almost entirely a preoccupation of the nation's elites. The British people viewed affluence and the Americanizing effect it had on their culture more enthusiastically and this constituted a key division between rulers and ruled. Yet, in the long run, it was Americanization that brought the British closer to Germany and Japan, because, whatever their views of each other, they were all transformed by it.

Germany

By the end of the Second World War, the British political establishment had learnt the lessons of Versailles. Coupled with the need to counter Soviet power in Europe, this created a consensus for nurturing German democracy through financial aid to the Western Zone rather than undermining it with financial penalties. John Maynard Keynes was a leading advocate of the policy. Even the arch Germanophobe, Lord Vansittart, who had previously damned Keynes as an appeaser, found himself in agreement over reconstruction with his former contemporary at Eton, writing 'we must provide Germany with a regulated prosperity, so ordered as not again to land her and us in war, but to give her opportunity for the joint boons of freedom and prosperity.'[2]

The British people were not so minded. According to a Gallup survey in September 1944, 90 per cent wanted their soon-to-be defeated enemy to pay reparations for war damage, and two-thirds wanted the Ruhr and Rhineland to be turned into an international zone to help do so. Most thought that German men should be drafted en masse to help repair physical destruction to town and country with their own hands (the retention of thousands of prisoners-of-war until 1948 and their use as slave labour in Britain partly satisfied that desire). There was also unanimous support for permanent disarmament and 56 per cent wanted the country split into smaller states so as to reverse the course of German history set in motion by Bismarck.[3]

Not surprisingly, therefore, while the British were grateful for Marshall Aid when it arrived in 1948, they were against the Germans getting a share of it, and thought the Americans were being naïve for being, as they saw it, charitable. The novelist Vita Sackville-West was utterly in tune with popular sentiment when she opined 'the reconstruction of Germany [means] shaking hands with blood-stained murderers who would start it up again if they had the chance.'[4] Visiting Berlin in the autumn of 1948, her husband, Harold Nicolson, wrote to remind her of the economic hardships that even the most prosperous Germans were enduring:

> A deep unhappy helplessness seems to brood over these ruins. My main impression so far is one of utter bewilderment … They drove me to a large villa in the Grunewald where there is a Press club. It is pretty bleak, I assure you. Only one bulb in a chandelier, and of course no heating. The food was all British rations … There is a sense of living in a dugout. It is far, far worse than I expected. One seems to be in a moon landscape across which figures flit. What a deeply unsettling experience it is. How deeply compassionate I feel for these people. Real aching sympathy.[5]

But he too thought that the Germans were a deviant people, a plain fact which their return to prosperity would not alter. Shortly before T.S. Eliot set off on a lecture tour of the British Zone, he asked Nicolson for advice on what 'message' to give the Germans: 'I said the only thing to do was to treat them as ordinary members of cultured society, much as one would treat a dipsomaniac' (Eliot took the advice).[6]

The Soviet blockade of west Berlin kindled some sympathy for the city's people. But it was based largely on anti-Communist sentiment and was not extended to the German people as a whole. Indeed, throughout the Cold War, the British saw little moral difference between citizens of the Federal Republic [FDR] and those of the Democratic Republic [GDR], created in 1949 and 1950 respectively. This was highlighted by the persistent hostility towards NATO plans to rearm West Germany. Nye Bevan's slogan 'No guns for the huns' and the high number of Britons who believed there was a serious prospect of the Nazis returning to power were examples of such Germanophobia.[7] Few were interested in the fact that the young West Germans who mobbed Private Elvis Presley when he arrived in their country in 1958, saw him as an escape from their parents' values and not as the member of a foreign military occupation.[8]

When the British did distinguish between the two countries, it was as a result of West Germany's economic success. Between 1950 and 1960, the FDR's annual growth rate for manufactured exports was 15 per cent (7.8 per cent overall), compared to the UK's 1.8 per cent (2.7 overall).[9] In the 20 years up to 1970, the average disposable income of German households grew by 400 per cent, almost double that of Britain.[10] However, the phenomenon caused so much resentment that it only served to reinforce the image of all Germans as ruthlessly efficient automatons.

The *Wirtschaftswunder* ('economic miracle') that got under way in the early 1950s was observed with alarm in Britain as its share of world markets fell as sharply as that of the Federal Republic rose. Industrialists and civil servants were in no doubt that the German character, and not simply American aid, was responsible. The car industry became a particular source of concern after West German vehicle exports overtook those of Britain in 1956. Contesting the idea that German cars were better quality, the beleaguered executives of Rootes claimed that the company was failing to sell to motorists in the FDR because of 'the intensity of German Nationalism which has been drummed into them over the past seventy years, and particularly by Dr. Goebbels, that they must buy German, and this they are certainly doing'.[11] In May 1956, a working party of Treasury officials reported that Germany's success 'cannot be explained, as could to some extent the expansion which occurred before 1953, by the low level from which she started … If this country fails to meet the German export challenge, it could fall into second place behind Germany as the leading export country in Europe, with all that this implies.'[12]

Two months later, as the Suez Crisis was beginning to rumble, Chancellor of the Exchequer Harold Macmillan was even blunter:

> The government's position is very bad at present. Nothing has gone well. In the M. East we are still teased by Nasser and Co; the Colonial Empire is breaking up … At home taxation is very high; the inflation has not been mastered … Meanwhile, we see Germany – free of debt, and making little contribution to defence – seizing the trade of the world from under our noses.[13]

A more visible sign of Teutonic affluence in this period was the number of German holiday makers that British tourists encountered abroad. They were not popular. Long before the sun bed became a battlefield in the era of cut-price package holidays, the Foreign Office was reporting that Britons resented their recent enemy being affluent enough to travel. One official observed that the phenomenon had 'reactivated the aggressive and tactless characteristics of many Germans', concluding, 'it is hardly surprising that the vast hordes pouring into foreign countries [on holiday] should cause some ill-feeling, particularly in those countries which were occupied by Germany.'[14]

There was a sneaking admiration for the way that an enemy so utterly crushed had picked itself up in such a short space of time. Earlier in the decade, when Harold Macmillan had been Minister of Housing, he had impressed his party and country by getting half a million homes built. But when he visited West Germany on a fact-finding mission, he had been amazed at how much harder the Germans worked than their British counterparts, and he marvelled at their ingenuity in recycling precious building materials from the rubble left by the RAF. His diary records:

> These people are at once formidable and extremely childish. There lies the danger. They like being 'told'. They like a leader … [Yet] we could not have been received with greater courtesy and often, I felt, greater pleasure. There

is a very good side to these people. It is our job to see that Dr. Jekyll remains in possession.[15]

But admiration soon gave way to jealousy. Instead of trying to learn from the Germans, the British mocked them, inverting a series of wartime stereotypes to explain their competitor's success and justify their own failures.

Industrial growth, the British convinced themselves, was only a step away from military aggression; demanding bosses were simply 'Little Hitlers'; time and motion studies and productivity targets merely a shop floor version of the methods used in concentration camps. Hence, the 'stop-go' nature of the UK economy was not a symptom of complacent mismanagement but of Britain's democratic spirit; muddling through was a testament to the democratic national character that had saved civilization. It did not go unnoticed that the term *Wirtschaftswunder* had originally been coined in the 1930s to describe the economic success of the Third Reich (as a result of which, the architect of the Federal Republic's success, Finance Minister Ludwig Erhard, did not like it to be used).[16]

The link between wartime nationalism and peacetime productivity contained other contradictions. As women's presence in the workplace increased, the comics, films, memoirs, memorials and toys through which the British glorified their 'finest hour' became more gendered. Like the violent Western romances of white America, they celebrated the pioneering, martial spirit of the male. In doing, so they catered for a more domesticated generation of men who felt emasculated by the female independence that affluence created and upon which the feminist movement built its foundations. War culture, excluding as it did the contribution to victory made by over three million 'coloured' British subjects, also comforted those who were threatened by the challenge to conventional narratives of nationhood posed by black immigration and civil rights movements. However, like Westerns, there were crossover points that united the sexes, at least, around a national legend.

A prime example is Britain's most popular situation comedy *Dad's Army* (BBC, 1968–77). Enjoyed by men and women, its success rested on its ability to poke fun at class and generational divisions while reasserting the existence of a common culture based on a clearly defined national character. The 1971 film version of the series begins by juxtaposing German invasion plans with the Home Guard's defences. The Germans have a large HQ and elaborate charts, while Captain Mainwaring makes do with the village hall and an AA road map. The German general states that three panzer divisions are ready to spearhead the attack; Mainwaring explains that the platoon must defend the promenade from the Novelty Rock Emporium to Stone's Amusement Arcade. The German general says divisional commanders will communicate with him via short-wave radio; Mainwaring says he will give orders by Boy Scout runners. Finally, a German sergeant tells his commanding officer that Hitler wishes to see the invasion plans; Godfrey, meanwhile, arrives to tell Mainwaring his wife wants him to bring home a pound of sprouts.[17] Released in the middle of acute industrial unrest, the film not only appealed to those longing for social unity. More specifically, its celebration of muddling through in the face of German might appealed to those keen to justify the UK's failure economically to capitalize on military victory.

Therefore, the potency of British mythologies of the Second World sprang as much from a sense of failure as from a sense of triumph. Yet, claiming a moral victory was also problematic because British decency had its limits too. The West German system of *Marktwirtschaft* (social free enterprise) managed to spread affluence while maintaining a better welfare state than that of the UK (even the National Health Service – that great benchmark of British liberalism – was less effective than its German counterpart).[18] As a consequence, West German labour relations were better than the UK's.[19] Film and TV drama dealing with British labour relations sometimes lauded Teutonic methods. An example is the Bryan Forbes/Richard Attenborough feature *The Angry Silence* (1960), described by critic Alexander Walker as 'an attack on union abuses that up to then had never been so scathingly stated in a British film.'[20] Set in an engineering factory, its owner, Mr Martindale, appeals to union activists to consider German industrial superiority and asks them to consider whether, as a result of their wildcat strikes, Britain has really won the last war. Few films actually explored life in West Germany. Cold War spy thrillers – from Bond to the more intelligent 'Harry Palmer' features like *Funeral in Berlin* (1966) – displayed a grim world of Checkpoint Charlie, Communist officers barely distinguishable from the Nazis who staffed mainstream war films, ruling over an East German people imprisoned in a world where consumer choice meant having or not having a Trabant.

Despite their achievements, the Germans were not, as the British liked to imagine them, an arrogant people. Asked by pollsters in 1951 'When in this century have Germans had it best?' only 2 per cent of them answered 'today'. By 1959, the number had risen to 42 per cent and by 1970 to 81 per cent, a figure that held up over the next decade. Yet, when asked if they felt pride in being German, in 1971 only 42 per cent replied 'yes' and by 1981 it had fallen to 35 per cent, while around 40 per cent of young people eligible for national service classified their army as 'potential murderers'. On being elected the Federal Republic's third President, in 1969, Gustav Heinemann was asked whether he loved his country. 'I love my wife', he replied.[21]

Unrepentant Nazis did play a prominent part in the reconstruction of West and (to a lesser extent) East Germany.[22] There was a more overt surge of far right activity in the 1960s largely, as in Britain, targeting immigration – in Germany's case from Turkey. But the revival peaked electorally in 1968 (a decade before it did in England) when the National Democratic Party [NPD] won 9.8 per cent of the vote in the Land election in Baden-Wurttemburg.[23] German conservatives had learnt not to flirt with fascism, and the process of coming to terms with the nation's past was so extensive that the Germans even invented a word to describe it: *Vergangenheitsbewaltigung*. The other reason why the Federal Republic did not produce a racist demagogue like Enoch Powell with mass cross-party appeal, still less another fascist dictator like Hitler, was that affluence mollified discontent with capitalism as an economic system. More positively, it offered an urgently needed alternative definition of what being German meant. German national identity, such as it was in the tortured era of partition and war guilt, was based on a quietistic satisfaction in economic recovery, particularly in the Federal Republic where growth was most spectacular. The Germans were still swayed by national fictions. In cinema, *Heimatfilme* (home films) like *Green Is The Heath* (1955), which presented a sentimental vision of domestic life in rural Germany, were as popular during the 1950s as war films were in the UK. Before the more cosmopolitan work of the New German Cinema led by Rainer Fassbinder gripped critics in the 1960s, *Heimatfilme* provided an alternative to Erhard's technocratic identity. But they were not a direct reaction to it, stemming as they did from a pastoral ideal that stretched back as far as the eighteenth century. And in the end, trade statistics proving the depth of *Wirtschaftswunder* mattered more to West Germans – more even than the restoration of *Deutschland Uuber Alles* as the national anthem in 1952 or Adenauer's triumphant visit to Moscow in 1955 during which he secured the release of German prisoners of war still held by the Soviet Union.

The reverse was true of the British. They became increasingly discontented with their standard of living, especially in comparison to West Germany's, while at the same time remaining intensely proud of being British, primarily as a consequence of their victory over the Third Reich. Even during the high period of UK growth, between 1955 and 1965, when the standard of living doubled, affluence did not shape British national identity in the way that it did in West Germany. As Prime Minister, Macmillan gave growth a patriotic catch-phrase that still defines the era for Britons who remember it, just as Erhard defined it for his people with the words 'today's luxuries are tomorrow's utilities'.[24] But 'most of our people have never had it so good' did not resonate in the UK to the same extent.

Partly, this was because economic growth was geographically less evenly spread in the UK. Whereas in the FDR, citizens from Hamburg to Munich enjoyed similar levels of prosperity, in Britain the main beneficiaries were those living in the south and midlands of England. The decline of heavy industry in Scotland, Wales and the north of England meant that standards of living rose more slowly there, a trend that underpinned the rise of Scottish and Welsh nationalism in the post-war era. Consequently, affluence was a less reliable, even dangerous, way of defining Britishness. Macmillan himself recognized this, as a result of which the speeches he made in Scotland and Wales concentrated on the potential of their unique national characters to effect economic recovery and share in England's prosperity.[25] But whether Britons were enjoying the full fruits of growth or lamenting the fact that they were not, they perceived its historical development in a quite different way to the Germans. For the British as a whole, affluence was seen as a just and necessary reward for the sacrifices they had made to defeat the Nazis. Both as a social reality and as an ideological construct, affluence was a direct continuation of victory in war and not, as in Germany, a way of escaping the memory of the Third Reich and the catastrophe it had led to.

This explains why, at precisely the moment when Britain was enjoying unprecedented prosperity, victory over Germany became embedded in national culture. It also helps to explain why that legend remained so central to Britishness into the 1970s and beyond when growth turned to 'stagflation'. Concern that Britain was losing the peace – whether through trade union militancy or the snobbery of 'the Establishment', depending on your political outlook – underpinned the vain cosmology of moral superiority over the Germans that both Left and Right indulged in at one time or another. Theories about the British economy being hampered by cultural tropes are dubious in any context. But if they should carry any weight here, it was not the pastoral, paternalistic strand of Englishness that generated 'gentlemanly capitalists'. Rather, it was the xenophobic and hubristic legacy of VE Day that prevented British management and workers alike learning economic lessons from post-war Germany.

Japan

Another former enemy, Japan, was also seizing the trade of the world from under the British nose and, indeed, from the Americans who had so heavily subsidized its reconstruction. Although the Japanese economic miracle did not begin until the premiership of Ikeda Hayato (1960–64), it was even more spectacular than that of West Germany. In the decade to 1970, the country enjoyed an annual growth rate of 13.2 per cent, and it survived the oil crisis that hit Britain so badly (Japanese exports grew from $19.3 billion in 1970 to $174 billion in 1985, a rise of 800 per cent).[26] Having not carried out systematic genocide, the Japanese were less burdened with war guilt than the Germans. In 1975, their Prime Ministers began annual visits to the Yasukuni shrine to the war dead and from 1982 school textbooks unashamedly glossed over the most militaristic part of the Showa era.

However, like the Germans, the Japanese developed a quietistic identity that was based primarily on affluence. Hayato and his successors encouraged their people to see television sets, fridges and washing machines as the 'three sacred treasures of the household.' This was a deliberate play on the 'sacred treasures' of mirror, sword and jewel that traditionally symbolized the God-like authority of the Japanese Emperors.[27] The fact that in 1946 Hirohito had been forced by the United States to renounce his divinity, added further symbolic weight to the transfer of national identity from militarism to affluence that the catch phrase denoted.

The centrality of affluence to Japanese identity was demonstrated when the new constitutional monarchy had its first field day in 1959 at the wedding of Hirohito's son, Crown Prince Akihito, Like the coronation of Elizabeth II in 1953, it was the first major royal event to be televised, and like that of Britain's Queen, it stimulated demand for TV sets. But, whereas in the UK, technology was primarily seen to be the conduit for a display of immutable national tradition, Akihito's wedding was about technology and its role in fostering national pride through prosperity. Akihito's bride, Michiko Shoda, was the daughter of a wealthy businessman, and what the press dubbed the 'Michy boom' referred as much to the mass purchase of consumer goods in the years immediately after the wedding as it did to the modernization of the Japanese monarchy.

The novelist Kenzaburo Oe summed up these trends: 'There were', he writes, 'a series of movements to create a new sense of identity and impose it on the Japanese people ... not exactly going back to the pre-war period, but getting them to sing the national anthem, respect the flag and think of the Emperor as part of a wonderful Japanese tradition'. What Oe calls 'the Silent Generation' who had lived through the war took another course:

> They didn't emphasise their own sense of identity or speak up for themselves, either within Japan or abroad. They were the heads of families who got on with their work in silence ... That generation was the backbone of Japan's post-war economic advance.[28]

But the nuances of post-war Japanese identity were as lost on the British people as those of West Germany.

Public dislike of the Japanese, and the national stereotypes it perpetuated, often mirrored that of the Germans. Indeed, 'Japophobia', if we may call it that, was sometimes more intense than Germanophobia. This was because Japan's successful invasion of South East Asia had humiliated the British Empire and, arguably, hastened its collapse more than Hitler's invasion of continental Europe had done. Consequently, those aggrieved by decolonization felt an especial animus towards them, one exacerbated by shame that such humiliation should have been visited on the British by a non-European colonial power. Japophobia therefore had racist overtones. For all the Germans' crimes against humanity, they were still regarded as racial relatives who were troubled with some serious character flaws. The Japanese, on the other hand, were portrayed (especially in boy's comics) as buck-toothed little yellow men with a speech defect – a physiognomic caricature no different in its cultural impact to the caricatures once employed by the British to demean the black people over whom they ruled.

Despite public awareness of the Holocaust, the Japanese were also thought to be a more cruel people than the Germans. In a Gallup survey of 1967, the Germans were most commonly defined as 'hard-working' (35 per cent), 'practical' (15) 'intelligent' (13), 'arrogant' and 'progressive' (12 per cent each). The Japanese were described as 'hard-working' (30 per cent), 'progressive' (18) but also 'cruel' (13), 'warlike' (11) and 'treacherous' (10).[29] Even in films like David Lean's Oscar-winning *Bridge On The River Kwai* (1957), which was implicitly critical of the British officer class, the enemy are portrayed as brutally authoritarian with little or no human compassion. It was the most popular British film for two years running, in 1958 and 1959 and remains a Christmas TV favourite. 'The Men From Camp Z', a series in the *Victor* comic, based one story on that of *Kwai* in 1964. In it, a camp full of starving, exhausted prisoners of war working on a fictional railway in 'the Jap-infested Thailand jungle' break out of captivity with the assistance of Australian commandos. 'Speedo! Speedo!' cry the guards, kicking and rifle-butting the prisoners. 'Speedo yourself, you yellow drongo!' replies one, producing a knife to slit the throat of his tormentor. 'Nice work, lads. Now let's get the Nips outside!' says another, before they set off to destroy the bridge they have slaved to build for the Japanese.[30] Germans on the other hand, are sometimes seen to possess gentlemanly traits. The camp Kommandants in escape dramas like *The Colditz Story* (1955) are a prime example. Removed from the front line (because, we are encouraged to believe, they are not committed Nazis) they observe the

Geneva Convention and are shown to be fair, for all their stiff-necked Prussian humourlessness.

The Germans are also seen to observe social hierarchies more intently than the Japanese, treating British officers with respect commensurate with their superior breeding and education. In *Bridge On The River Kwai*, the conflict between Colonel Saito (Sessue Hayakawa) and Colonel Nicolson (Alec Guinness) begins when the latter refuses to allow his officers to perform manual labour on the bridge. Instead, he offers to make sure the troops do the job with proper concern for the tradition of British craftsmanship so that the structure will last. He then activates a peacetime hierarchy ranging from architects and engineers to carpenters and labourers that corresponds to their military ranks. Saito's attempt to (symbolically at least) blur class boundaries in order to inspire more efficient 'team' working practices may be read, even in this perverse context, as a metaphor for the mass production techniques that the Japanese borrowed from the Americans and then honed after the war. It is doubly symbolic that the bridge of which Nicolson is so proud is destroyed by a Commando task force led by an American, played by William Holden (not, as in the *Victor's* version by an Australian, because the film's producers needed Hollywood financing and so could not afford to downgrade the US contribution to victory in World War Two).

Despite absenting himself and his fellow officers from back-breaking work that will assist the Japanese war machine, Nicolson unites his men through a very particular appeal to patriotism. The triumphant construction of the bridge on his terms, may be seen as a re-assertion of the value, not just of class distinctions (a common theme in 1950s war films), but also of the methods of production on which the British industrial revolution was erroneously thought to have been based. Whatever the case, Saito's approach was echoed in Japanese corporate management techniques. When, during the 1980s, the custom of managers and workers exercising together in the morning was exported to Britain by the car manufacturer Nissan and adopted by many of the 200 Japanese companies operating there, it was ridiculed as a foreign idea which the slovenly, bolshy British worker and his snobbish, uptight boss would reject (correctly, as it turned out, since few non-Japanese companies followed suit).

It is worth noting briefly that the only narrative of the war in which the Japanese were seen to possess attributes that correspond to those of the British was the legend of the Kamikaze. Their suicidal devotion to Japan exerted a strange hold on the British, not only because fanaticism is fascinating, but also because they reminded them of 'The Few'. An elite corps of pilots, the red-bandanaed Samurai of the air may have killed hundreds of sailors when they plunged into Allied battleships; yet they were seen to have waged war more cleanly, and more bravely, than those who tortured soldiers in the jungles of south east Asia. However, this is an exception that proves the rule about the way Japan was screened by Anglo-American filmmakers.

The notorious Japanese treatment of British prisoners of war gave credence to the generally uncompromising portrayal of them in mid-century popular culture and explains its acceptance by the British public. It also explains why the campaign for an apology and compensation by veterans of the conflict in the Far East continued long after the idea of obtaining redress from Germany had ceased to be an issue. State visits to and from Japan were not resumed until the 1970s, and then only because the British economy was in such a dire condition that national sentiment was ditched in favour of trade agreements, a process that culminated with firms like Nissan being induced by desperate governments, and even more desperate unions, to set up shop in Development Areas. Emperor Hirohito made his first post-war visit to Britain in 1971, a full 13 years after the first German state visit, by President Heuss, in 1958, and the Queen did not got to Japan until 1974, nine years after her first trip to Germany. Although Huess got a cool reception, his visit did not garner the hostility of Hirohito's, during which there were noisy demonstrations and colourful articles in the press re-running every aspect of Japan's war record.[31]

This was partly, of course, because Hirohito had been Emperor during the war and was therefore a direct link with the militaristic regime against which Britain fought, in a way that Heuss (an opponent of Nazism) was not. But it was also because the treatment of POWs in the Far East impacted more on British lives than the Holocaust. Perhaps the most telling comparison lies in the British reaction to the dropping of atomic bombs on Nagasaki and Hiroshima in 1945. They were greeted with shock and awe, but there was no more public opposition to the American's action than there had been to Bomber Command's destruction of German cities, most agreeing with the *Daily Mirror*'s verdict that the 'yellow peril' had at last been vanquished.[32] 'VJ Day' (15 August) was almost as rapturously celebrated as VE Day had been and when, a year later, the Cabinet, the British Legion and the Churches considered how best to commemorate the 1939–45 war, the anniversary of victory in Japan was as serious a contender as that of the Battle of Britain.

The 1964 Tokyo Olympics (postponed from 1940) confirmed Japan's rebirth, according to many at the time, including Yoshinori Sakai. A 19-year-old athlete born in Hiroshima on the day of its destruction, Sakai lit the Olympic flame before joining a Japanese squad that came fourth in the medals table after the United States, Soviet Union and West Germany,[33] The event barely impinged on the British consciousness. Despite growing awareness of the full after effects of nuclear fission thanks to the Campaign For Nuclear Disarmament, most Britons continued to regard what happened at Nagasaki and Hiroshima as a necessary part of the defeat of foreign tyrants who had started the war in the first place.

Of course, this did not stop the British consuming Japanese goods on a huge scale. Cheap but reliable cars, motorbikes, television sets, radios and a host of smaller gadgets all bore the imprint of a small group of islands that in the space of a generation became and (despite China's adventure in state capitalism) remains the only country to challenge the West's economic hegemony. Youth culture was recognized by its critics and champions alike as a product of affluence in the 1950s and 60s. Yet, by the 1970s, the machines on which young Britons played their Anglo-American pop music were usually made in the Far East. This culminated with the UK's biggest electronic retail chain, Dixons, naming its own brand Matsui, in the correct belief that in order to sell their products they would have to pretend to be Japanese.[34] The video recorder – invented in 1959 by Norikazu

Sawasaki of the Toshiba Corporation – even changed British leisure patterns after its launch as a consumer product in 1981, undermining both cinema and television by giving people more choice of what they watched and when they watched it.

The difference between the impact on Britishness of German and Japanese economic success is this: although Japanese affluence was built partly on its skill in undermining key areas of British manufacturing, it did not generate the same sense of having lost the peace to a defeated enemy. The legends of the Second World War on which the increasingly fragile British identity was based, were almost entirely located in the war against Germany, particularly that fought on the Home Front between 1940 and 1941. In contrast, the United States' war, from Pearl Harbor to Okinawa, was primarily located in its conflict with the nation that had attacked without warning on 7 December 1941. Moreover, under the regime of General MacArthur between 1945 and 1950, the Americans had taken complete control of the political and economic reconstitution of Japan, moulding it (as they thought) in their own image in a way that even the British had not attempted during their 're-education' programmes in Occupied Germany. Thus, when the Japanese started to threaten American markets, residual anger towards Japan for having dragged the US into war was compounded by bitterness that a pupil had learnt its lesson in liberal capitalist democracy so well that it was now biting the hand which had fed it. In short, although detestation and mockery of the Japanese in the UK strengthened the British idea of themselves as decent, fair-minded people, they continued primarily to define themselves against the Germans.

Europe

The xenophobic fall out from two world wars was compounded by the steady creation of the European Union. The Francophobia that followed De Gaulle's vetoes of the British application to the Common Market in 1963 and 1967 was based on the wounded pride of a spurned suitor. What really drove popular hostility to European integration was the fear that it would restore German power in Europe. A message from Lord Montgomery of Alamein appeared in a full page spread in national newspapers, paid for by Beaverbrook. Warning that membership of the Common Market would mean a German general giving orders to a British one, Monty said 'Germany has disturbed the peace of the world twice during the past 48 years, in 1914 and 1940. Are we to put up with all this again? Never!'[35]

Shortly after the death of Winston Churchill in 1965, Elizabeth II became the first British monarch to visit Germany since 1913. Diplomatically, it was a success. In Hanover, the Queen was taken to the state archives where she was shown the letter written in 1714 by Whig grandees to her ancestor, George, Elector of Hanover inviting him to assume the British throne. But the symbolism of eighteenth century Protestant unity was lost on an increasingly secular nation. Moreover, the British were simply not ready to forget the War. The Queen's visit was part of Harold Wilson's strategy of courting the Federal Republic in order to exert pressure on De Gaulle. But it was a dangerous one and the Labour

Government knew it. On her return, Foreign Secretary Michael Stewart told the Cabinet:

> Two world wars and the horrors of Nazism have left such a legacy of
> bitterness that we cannot be sure Anglo-German reconciliation will last
> unless we for our part make it do so ... We ought to develop Ministerial
> contacts, technological collaboration and cultural and youth exchanges ... If
> we try to encourage the British people to think of contemporary Germany in
> a more friendly way, all the indications are that the Germans will be happy
> to come more than half way to meet us and that this, in turn, will be the best
> possible insurance against a return to atavism. They feel a particular need for
> reconciliation with the British people and this is an asset which we can turn
> to good account. Anglo-German friendship is all the more desirable because
> stability in Germany is a tender growth ... If we rebuff the Germans they are
> that much more likely to conclude that striking independent nationalistic
> attitudes may be the best way of seeking their objectives.[36]

A year later, England's victory in the World Cup Final of 1966 cemented, in England at least, the prevailing view of Germany as an old enemy rather than a new friend. On the day of the final, the *Daily Mail* declared 'If Germany beat us at Wembley this afternoon at our national sport, we can always point out to them that we have recently beaten them twice at theirs,'[37] a comment that provoked complaints about British militarism from the West Germans. The spontaneous celebrations following the victory were widely compared to VE Day. The *Sunday Express* concluded:

> A blaze of Union Jacks waved, as people unashamedly gripped by emotion
> and patriotism danced, wept and hugged each other ... What they will tell
> their grandchildren in years to come is that it was English nerve and English
> stamina which finally overcame the tenacious resistance of [the Germans] ...
> No one who saw this historic World Cup final can deny England their 'finest
> hour'.[38]

The victory came in the middle of the Labour Government's ultimately unsuccessful attempt to avert a sterling crisis: 40 days after Harold Wilson had condemned striking seamen's leaders as 'a tightly knit group of politically motivated men', and 11 days after he had announced a statutory wage freeze. By seeming to pull victory out of the jaws of defeat, the event echoed the way in which Britain had done so during the Second World War and this helped it to become a central part of Anglo-British identity even for those who cared little about football, The narratives of war and deliverance that peppered the reaction to England's victory not only show the extent to which Germany was the prime 'other' by which British national identity was shaped in the twentieth century. They also reveal that unease about the post-war fragility of the UK economy was freighted with resentment of West German affluence. Hence the widely-expressed belief that somehow the result would inspire capital and labour to repeat the victory of Alf Ramsey's men on trading floors, boardrooms and production lines. Richard Crossman (one of Labour's leading Eurosceptics) believed that it 'could be a decisive factor in strengthening sterling.' 'It was', he concluded, 'a tremendous, gallant fight that England won. Our men showed real guts and the bankers, I suspect, will be influenced by this, and the position of the government correspondingly strengthened.'[39] Lord Harewood, the Chairman of the Football Association and a cousin of the Queen, declared that it had:

> raised our prestige throughout the world ... It is indeed one of the few bright
> spots in the sombre economic situation which faces the country this summer.
> We feel sure that many of our export industries will derive a welcome boost
> from this success. The players who have made it possible worked hard and
> made many sacrifices. They have set an example of devotion and loyalty to
> the country which many others would do well to follow.[40]

Unfortunately, Bobby Moore could not stop the devaluation of sterling in 1967. But long after England's footballers failed to make the British work harder and strike less, the West German example was paraded in an attempt to do so. Pro-Marketeers also used it to sell membership of the Common Market, arguing that if the British wanted the FDR's standard of living, they would have to surrender some of their national sovereignty to the European community. Appealing to material aspirations had the added advantage of distracting voters from the long-term constitutional implications of membership and of smothering the more erroneous claims that national identity would be dissipated by it. This tactic formed the basis of the three government-sponsored campaigns for entry between 1961 and 1972 and for the referendum on membership that took place in 1975. It continued to carry some weight until the German economy began to falter as a result of the cost of reunification in 1990.

British envy of their new European partner was such that from the mid-1970s, German companies began to emphasize their nationality in UK adverts, and they often did so by cleverly playing on British caricatures, The legend of Teutonic efficiency and modernity in engineering reached a bizarre apogee in the Audi car company slogan 'Vorsprung durch technik' – to which, in TV commercials, the laconically sarcastic voice of actor Geoffrey Palmer added '... as they say in Germany,' The slogan, which meant 'progress through technology', could have been coined by Erhard himself. In fact it was invented by a British advertising agency and was never used on the Continent. Consumers in the UK were encouraged to desire an Audi by admiring the outlook of its makers while laughing at the humourless obsessiveness which supposedly underpinned that outlook. Therefore, after the British had inverted wartime stereotypes of the Germans to explain how their enemy had won the peace, the Germans bounced those stereotypes back to help secure that victory. A more cruel irony was to come.

America

To the dismay of anti-Marketeers, the United States was in favour of Britain joining a united Europe, believing that it would help to prevent further European wars and costly American intervention. Soon after the Messina conference that formed the basis of the Treaty of Rome, Chancellor of the Exchequer Peter Thorneycroft told Prime Minister Anthony Eden 'I am convinced that the Americans are in a fool's paradise about Messina and ... you should seek to bring home to President Eisenhower the gravity of the dangerous situation which is rapidly developing against the interests of both our countries ... Our businessmen would be ousted from the European markets in favour of their German competitors.'[41]

In fact, more American consumer goods flooded Britain than German or Japanese ones and their impact on British life had been apparent since Thorneycroft was a boy. Coca-Cola was first exported to Britain in the year of Queen Victoria's death and Henry Ford opened his first UK factory at Manchester in 1911, to name just two developments. But it was the arrival of mass affluence that accelerated the trend, especially after the easing of exchange controls and the abolition of hire purchase restrictions in 1958, which enabled US investors to gain a firmer bridgehead. 'Need alliance involve occupation?' asked Francis Williams, author of *The American Invasion* in 1962, 'Must we become Americans to save Western civilisation?'[42] It is worth reminding ourselves of the extent of the revolution that prompted such polemics.

Between 1958 and 1963, 1,000 US companies set up operations in the UK with a total value of $6 billion, almost twice the amount invested by them in West Germany.[43] By 1966, two years after the 'British invasion' of America by the Beatles, there were 1,600 American owned subsidiaries in the UK producing 10 per cent of all the goods made in British factories, including half the cars, office machinery, domestic appliances and cosmetics, plus half the drugs used by the NHS. American companies like Esso, Ford, Woolworth's, Hoover, Heinz and Kodak were household names.[44] Among the British companies taken over by American ones in this period was Rootes Motors which, after all its fretting about the threat from Germany, was subsumed by Chrysler in 1967. US inventions, like the tampon, pop-up toaster, Sellotape, denim jeans, t-shirts, tea bags, caravans, hamburgers, barbecues and emulsion paint, were ubiquitous, and they were sold more conveniently thanks to an American-led retail revolution which transformed the sociology of shopping. That process, already under way in the 1920s, accelerated after Sainsbury's opened Britain's first supermarket at Croydon in 1950 and again after the country's first shopping centre opened at Birmingham in 1965.

More than Britain's other rivals, American national identity was based on the gaining of affluence, although it was defined in a less communitarian way than in Germany or Japan. That difference reflected not only the power of American conservatism but also the difficulty of uniting such a polyglot nation around a collective ideal that did not reference an alien 'other' from which some of its citizens originated, and with which they might feel some residual affinity. As far as affluence itself is concerned, the difference between the economic success of America and that of Germany and Japan was that, to a far greater extent, the former exported a culture to go with its material goods, and it was this which spread the debate about 'Americanization' beyond Whitehall, the City and the CBI.

The simultaneous supplanting of Britain as the superpower of the West intensified concern, drawing in those who were otherwise Atlanticists – like Harold Nicolson. Five years after his visit to Germany, he turned his mind to the US, writing that Anti-American feeling was 'a dangerous and quite useless state of mind'. But, he lamented, 'gradually they are ousting us out of all world authority. I mind this, as I feel it is humiliating and insidious ... they are decent folk in every way but they tread on tradition in a way that hurts.'[45] Since the 1920s, the prime conduits of American culture – Hollywood and the music industry – had been castigated by left and right alike for destroying the British way of life with vulgar fripperies. Commercial television was a major addition to those media in 1955. It led to an expansion of the advertising industry and the associated professions of public relations, market research and polling, all of which helped to stimulate consumption.

The debate surrounding the introduction of ITV revealed the full extent of opposition to Americanization. It also showed how much the wider debate over affluence revolved around the relationship between the individual, society and the state, and how much it was framed in turn by fear of the Soviet Union. Leading Labour Party opposition to ITV in the House of Commons, Herbert Morrison said that it was 'totally against the British temperament, the British way of life and the best or even reasonably good British traditions', and he warned that upon the outcome of the vote depended 'the future of our country, the thinking of our people and the standard of culture of the people.'[46] In reply, the Conservative spokesman, David Gammans, said:

> The critics do not trust their fellow human beings with the freedom of a television knob ... One of the worst changes [in recent years] is the way in which governments all over the world are arrogating to themselves the right to decide what their subjects shall read, see, believe and think ... perhaps it is as well that we got freedom of the press when we did because there are many people who would put up arguments against it now.[47]

He also reminded opponents that the British were among those in Europe who owed some of their current good fortune to post-war American aid. 'Whatever may be said about the Americans ... we might sometimes remember that American prosperity is the highest in the world and that it has produced an over-spill which has helped us and a great part of the free world to live'.[48]

Gammans' view was shared by the majority of Britons. Resistance to Americanization, whether it took the form of intellectual diatribe or government legislation (such as the limitations imposed on broadcast advertising by the 1954 Television Act) was largely confined to the left-leaning middle classes. That was the case even in the immediate aftermath of the Suez Crisis and at the height of the Vietnam war when American neo-imperialism became more blatant. The 1967 Gallup survey of national stereotypes discovered that the British view of the United States had not deteriorated since Mass Observation studied it in 1945, MO had found that 'energy, enterprise, generosity and efficiency' were the characteristics most ascribed to Americans, with 'boastfulness' about their success being the main complaint rather than any intrinsic dislike of their way of life.[49] A generation later, Gallup reported that Americans were most commonly seen to be 'progressive' (24 per cent), 'conceited' (16), 'intelligent', 'generous' (15 per cent each) and 'hard-working' (14).[50]

The public debate on the 'Brain Drain' of engineers and scientists to the United States – at its height when a government enquiry reported in 1967 – showed how highly the British regarded the US. The Americans were not blamed for seducing professionals with higher salaries and status; nor were those who left seen as traitors. Instead, people blamed Britain's less meritocratic society and its weaker economy, whether or not they believed Harold Wilson's claim that the former was to blame for the latter. 'Brains on the whole are like hearts', commented US Defense Secretary Robert McNamara, 'they go where they are appreciated,' Oral testimony suggests that the hearts of such migrants remained in Britain and some were disillusioned with what one called the 'cultural wilderness' of North America.[51]

Still, the key point about the relationship between affluence and identity is this: the British believed that the individualism they prized as the foundation of their national character, was being amplified by mass consumption and not eroded by it. The negative wartime caricatures of the Germans and Japanese – fossilized by post-war resentment of their economic success – remained the paradigms of totalitarian power against which most defined their Britishness. In contrast, the positive view of Americans (for all the envy attached to it) was *re-inforced* by the United States' global supremacy. This was partly because the US had been a vital ally in two World Wars. It was partly also because the process of decolonization which the US encouraged and benefited from did not vex ordinary Britons, whose national identity had ceased to be underpinned by the Empire since the 1940s. Ultimately, however, the idea that Britain had lost the peace to America gained no currency because the British continued to regard the Americans as a more modern and successful version of themselves.

The attempt by politicians and business leaders to persuade the British to admire and emulate the German economic miracle won the European community some grudging support in the 1970s. But it failed to shake the popular view of America as the model of a more affluent, less class-bound and freer society. Hence the fact that whenever the US enlisted the UK in bomb-bay diplomacy, it was seen by the British as evidence of the 'special relationship' that protected their liberties. Meanwhile, every stage of European integration was seen as an attempt by the continent, and Germany in particular, to erode those liberties and erase the national character of an island, even though it was patently becoming more Americanized with every passing generation.

Conclusions

When the magazine *Encounter* asked leading intellectuals for their opinion on European integration in 1963, the response of W.H. Auden was the most perceptive. He reminded readers that, however much the project was ultimately a political and not merely an economic one, whether you were for or against was based on cultural matters that were closely related to social class:

> One will never understand the current debate about England joining the Common Market if one thinks of it as merely a clash between different economic interests. Beneath the arguments Pro and Con lie passionate prejudices and the eternal feud between the High-Brow and the Low-Brow. Instinctively I am Pro. I know Europe first hand, and as a writer I cannot conceive of my life without the influence of its literature, music and art.

On the other hand America and, to a lesser extent, the Commonwealth, appealed to the Low-Brows:

> They are inhabited by their relatives and people like themselves, speaking English, eating English food, wearing English clothes and playing English games, whereas 'abroad' is inhabited by immoral strangers and an Englishman who goes there often still worse, decides to live there, is probably up to no good.[52]

The impact of Continental popular culture on Britain has been underestimated, partly because of xenophobic hostility to European integration, but also because of the tendency to regard the 1970s as the decade in which post-war affluence stalled. Yet it was during this time that foreign package holidays first became affordable to the working classes. Cheap foreign travel enhanced individual freedom as much as the purchase of cars in the period that is commonly associated with affluence. Tourism also began an unprecedented peacetime engagement with the rest of Europe, with a commensurate effect on Britishness that urgently requires further research.[53]

Equally, the reach of America can be exaggerated, especially where 'English games' were concerned. Football was Britain's most successful export. For all the old enmities that the sport replayed it was also a source of affinity between the British, Germans and, eventually, the Japanese; and it was one, moreover, that Americans did not share. Television drove the globalization of football. In 1958, the same year that US investors were given a free hand by the Treasury, the World Cup was comprehensively televised for the first time in Western Europe, and watched by several hundred million people, thanks to their ability to purchase a television set.

Critics also underestimated the extent to which American culture was naturalized after it crossed the Atlantic or the Pacific. British popular music became a fulcrum of national identity in the UK following the 'Beat' explosion of the 1960s, while the same occurred in Germany a generation later with 'Techno'. In Japan, the films of Akira Kurosawa influenced Hollywood directors, the prime example being *Seven Samurai* (1954), which revived the Western genre that Kurosawa had himself been influenced by. The Disney Corporation was forced to adapt Tokyo Disneyland to domestic conditions following its launch in 1983, 28 years after Disney's original theme park opened in California. 'We took the foreignness out of it', remarked one Japanese professor, 'people in Japan were enjoying not the American dream, but their own Japanese dream.'[54]

But it was still a dream, and in their waking hours, neither East nor West could deny that affluence had been the Trojan horse of Americanization. Bernard Harris' *The American Take-over of Britain*, published in 1968, concluded 'From the moment an English baby is weaned on American-owned baby food, until he is carted away in an American-owned funeral car, he is to that extent American-oriented from the cradle to the grave.'[55] Ironically, as a consequence the British way of life resembled that of Germany and Japan far more than it had done before the Second World War. For all the profound cultural differences that continued to divide the world's economic powers, to an unprecedented degree they shared a common culture based on that of America – a culture driven by capital, accelerated by information technology and oiled by the English language.

When Sherpa Tensing arrived in the UK after conquering Mount Everest with Edmund Hillary, the press noticed that he wore two wrist watches in case one malfunctioned. This was seen as primitive naivety about Western technology which evidenced Britain's cultural superiority and, for some, justified the continuation of its civilizing mission to the world.[56] When Emperor Hirohito first went to America in 1975, after meeting John Wayne he visited Disneyland and for the rest of his life liked to wear his souvenir Mickey Mouse wrist watch. There is here a symbolic counterpoint between the confidence of late imperial Britain and the realities of post-imperial Britain. In the long age of affluence, it became harder for the UK to claim moral or material superiority over other nations or even, given the cultural impact of the US, to distinguish itself from them. Announcing the surrender of Japan to the United States in 1945, Hirohito said: 'the war is not necessarily progressing to Japan's advantage'.[57] The peace did not progress entirely to the UK's advantage and, thanks to the hegemony of their biggest ally the British now had more in common with former enemies than it was comfortable for them to admit.

Notes

[1]　Chisolm, Anne and Davie, Michael: *Lord Beaverbrook: A Life*, Hutchinson, London, 1992, p. 517.

[2]　Mander, John: *Our German Cousins: Anglo-German Relations in the 19th and 20th Centuries*, John Murray, London, 1974, p. 262.

[3]　Wybrow, Robert J. (ed): *Britain Speaks Out, 1937–87: A Social History as Seen Through the Gallup Data*, Macmillan, London, 1989, p. 16.

[4]　Nicolson, Nigel (ed): *Harold Nicolson: Diaries and Letters 1945–62*, Collins, London, 1968, p. 265, Sackville-West to Nicolson, 14 September 1954.

[5]　Ibid., p. 150, Nicolson to Sackville-West, 26 September 1948.

[6]　Ibid., p. 174, diary entry, 7 September 1949.

[7]　When Bevan launched his attack on German re-armament in 1954, polls found that around 60 per cent were opposed to a European Defence Community, 40 per cent of whom believed that the Nazis might return to power. See Watt D.C.: *Britain Looks to*

Germany: A Study of British Opinion and Policy Towards Germany Since 1945, Wolff, London, 1965, pp. 147–51.

8 See Pells, Richard: *Not Like Us: How Europeans Have Loved, Hated and Transformed American Culture Since World War II*, Harper Collins, New York, 1997, pp. 240–41.

9 Young, Hugo: *This Blessed Plot: Britain and Europe From Churchill to Blair*, Macmillan, London, 1998, p. 106.

10 Fulbrook, Mary: *Germany 1918–1990: The Divided Nation*, Fontana, London, 1991, p. 183.

11 Barnett, Corelli: *The Verdict of Peace*, Macmillan, London, 2001, p. 393.

12 Ibid., 398.

13 Catterall, Peter (ed): *The Macmillan Diaries: The Cabinet Years, 1950–1957*, Macmillan, London, 2003, p. 576.

14 PRO: FO 371/109713, F. Barnes to F. Warner, 17 July 1954.

15 Catterall, *The Macmillan Diaries*, op. cit., p. 318.

16 The career of Ludwig Erhard (1897–1977) had been checked as a result of his refusal to join the Nazi Party. Immediately after the war he was appointed Professor of Economics at the University of Munich where he devised the *Marktwirtschaft* system. His career in politics began in 1949 when he was elected to the Bundestag as a Christian Democrat, joining Adenauer's administration as Finance Minister, in which post he remained until he succeeded Adenauer as Chancellor (1963–66). A blip in the West German economy forced his premature resignation.

17 I am grateful to Dr Mark Connelly for this insight from his forthcoming study *We Can Take It!: Britain and the Memory of the Second World War*, Routledge, London, 2004.

18 West Germany spent around 2 per cent more of its GDP on healthcare than the UK and patients endured fewer bottlenecks.

19 In 1969, for example, the number of working days lost to strike action per 1,000 workers was 510 in the UK, compared to only 20 in West Germany and 200 in Japan.

20 Shaw, Tony: *British Cinema and the Cold War: The State, Propaganda and Consensus*, I..B. Tauris, London, 2001, p. 163.

21 Schoenbaum, David and Pond, Elizabeth (eds): *The German Question and Other German Questions*, Macmillan, London, 1986, pp. 1, 13, 7.

22 This was partly thanks to Hans Globke, Adenauer's State Secretary for the Interior from 1953 to 1963 and his advisor on government appointments, who had previously helped to frame the Nuremburg Laws banning Jews from public life. By 1958, two-thirds of the FDR's Foreign Ministry staff were ex-Nazis, while the GDR, despite exposing Globke, had 75 ex-Nazis in leading government positions. See Kaufman, David: 'The Nazi Legacy: Coming to Terms With the Past', in James, Peter, (ed): *Modern Germany: Politics, Society and Culture*, Routledge, London, 1998, pp. 125–7.

23 Ibid., pp. 133–5. Despite the rising number of attacks on ethnic minorities by neo-Nazi groups since re-unification, the NPD (formed in 1964) has not yet repeated the success it had in the late 1960s, polling no more than 5 per cent of the vote.

24 James, Harold: *A German Identity 1770–1990*, Weidenfeld and Nicolson, London, 1989, p. 187.

25 See, for example, Macmillan's speeches in Cardiff on 8 July 1960, in PRO: BD 25/5.

26 Beasley, W.G.: *The Rise of Modern Japan: Political, Economic and Social Change Since 1850*, Weidenfeld, London, 2nd ed, 1995, p. 251.

27 Horsely, William and Buckley, Roger: *Nippon New Superpower: Japan Since 1945*, BBC, London, 1990, p. 71.

28 Ibid., pp. 83–4.

29 Wybrow, *Britain Speaks Out*, op. cit., p. 84.

[30] *The Victor*, no. 157, 22 February 1964.

[31] See for example, *Daily Express*, *Daily Mirror* and *Daily Mail*, 6 June 1971. A year later, Edward Heath became the first British Prime Minister to visit Japan.

[32] *Daily Mirror*, 10 August 1945.

[33] Horsely and Buckley, *Nippon New Superpower*, op. cit., p. 72.

[34] Leonard, Mark: *Britain: Renewing Our Identity*, Demos, London, 1997, p. 30.

[35] *Daily Mirror*, 4 June 1962.

[36] PRO: CAB 129/122, C(65)119, 'Policy Towards Germany', memorandum by the Foreign Secretary, 5 August 1965.

[37] *Daily Mail*, 30 July 1966.

[38] *Sunday Express*, 31 July 1966.

[39] Crossman, Richard: *The Diaries of a Cabinet Minister. Vol. 1, Minister of Housing, 1964–66*, Jonathan Cape, London, 1975, p. 594, entry for 31 July 1966.

[40] *FA News*, vol. 16, no. 2, September 1966.

[41] PRO: FO 371/122022/11, Thorneycroft to Eden, 20 January 1956.

[42] Williams, Francis: *The American Invasion*, Anthony Blond, London, 1962, p. 11.

[43] Pells, *Not Like Us,* op. cit., p. 190.

[44] Dimbleby, David and Reynolds, David: *An Ocean Apart: The Relationship Between Britain and America in the Twentieth Century*, BBC/Hodder and Stoughton, London, 1988, pp. 275–6.

[45] Nicolson, Nigel (ed): *Harold Nicolson*, p. 245, diary entry 28 September 1953.

[46] *Parliamentary Debates (Commons)*, vol. 522, col. 65, 14 December 1953.

[47] Ibid.

[48] Ibid., col. 47.

[49] Mass Observation also detected a dislike of American 'immaturity, materialism and immorality.' But that view was predominantly held by older, middle-class respondents, see Reynolds, David: *Rich Relations: The American Occupation of Britain 1942–1945*, Harper Collins, London, 1995, pp. 434–5.

[50] Wybrow, *Britain Speaks Out*, op. cit., p. 84.

[51] *The Times*, 27 February 1967. See also *The Brain Drain: Report of the Working Group on Migration*, Cmnd., 3417, 1967.

[52] *Encounter*, vol. 20, no. 1, January 1963.

[53] For a further discussion of this theme, see Weight, Richard: *Patriots: National Identity in Britain 1940–2000*, Macmillan, London, 2002, pp. 485–510, 643–57.

[54] Pells, *Not Like Us*, op. cit., p. 308.

[55] Macmillan, James and Harris, Bernard: *The American Take-Over of Britain*, Leslie Frewin, London, 1968, p. 6.

[56] See Stewart, Gordon T.: 'Tensing's Two Wrist Watches: The Conquest of Everest and Late Imperial Culture, 1921–1953', *Past and Present*, no. 149, November 1995.

[57] Horsely and Buckley: *Nippon New Superpower*, Op.cit., p. 12.

Bibliography

Primary Sources

The National Archive of the UK: Public Record Office (PRO), Kew

The Cabinet (CAB)
CAB 128: Cabinet Minutes.
CAB 129: Cabinet Memoranda.
CAB 130: Cabinet Minutes.
CAB 134: Minutes and Papers of Miscellaneous Committees.

The Prime Minister's Office (PREM)
PREM 8: Papers of Clement Attlee's private office.
PREM 11: Correspondence and Papers, 1951–1964.

Treasury (T)
T 171: Budget records.
T 227: Records of the Social Services Division.
T 229: Central Economic Planning Staff, and Treasury, Central Economic Planning Section: Registered Files.
T 230: Records of the Economic Section.
T 233: Records of the Home Finance Division.
T 267: Treasury Historical Memoranda.
T 291: Records of the Committee of Enquiry on the Control of Public Expenditure (Plowden Committee).
T 298: Registered Files of the National Resources Division.
T 311: Records of the National Economy Group.
T 320: Registered Files of the Public Income/Outlay Division.
T 325: Papers of Sir R.W.B. Clarke.

Foreign Office (FO)
FO 1059975: Economic Problems of Western Europe.
FO 371/109713: Behaviour of German tourists abroad, 1954.
FO 371/122022/11: Visit to Washington by UK Prime Minister: comments by Peter Thorneycroft, president of Board of Trade, on FO official integration brief, 1956.

Welsh Office (BD)
BD 25/5: Visit of Prime Minister to Cardiff on 8 July 1960 to unveil statue of David Lloyd George.

Eisenhower Presidential Library, Abilene, Kansas

Ann Whitman Administrative Series

Arthur Burns Papers
Campaign Series
Cabinet Series
Gabriel Hauge Papers

Papers of Other Organizations

Birmingham Consumers' Group material in private papers of Matthew Hilton.
Conservative Party Archive, Bodleian Library, University of Oxford.
Consumers' Association Archive, London.
Design Council Archive, Design History Research Centre, University of Brighton.
Papers of the Fabian Society, British Library of Political and Economic Science, London.
Labour Party Archive, National Museum of Labour History, Manchester.
Records of the British Employers' Confederation, University of Warwick, Modern Records Centre.

Private Papers

Papers of Mark Abrams, Churchill College, Cambridge.
Papers of Baron Butler of Saffron Walden, Trinity College, Cambridge.
Papers of Lord Boyle of Handsworth, Brotherton Library, University of Leeds.
Papers of C.A.R. Crosland, British Library of Political and Economic Science, London.
Papers of Hugh Dalton, British Library of Political and Economic Science, London.
Papers of Hugh Gaitskell, University College, London.
Papers of Lord Woolton, Bodleian Library, University of Oxford.

Newspapers, Journals, Comics

Advertising
The Advertising Quarterly
The Alfred Herbert News
Birmingham Consumer
Birmingham Evening Mail
Bristol Evening Post
Campaign
Conservative Agents Journal
Consumer News
Crossbow
Daily Mail
Daily Mirror
Daily Telegraph
Design
Encounter
The Economist
European Journal of Marketing
Football Association News
Financial Times
Focus
Forward

Good Food Guide
Guardian
Harpers
Impact
The Listener
London Evening News
Marketing Week
New Left Review
New Society
New Statesman/New Statesman and Nation
News Chronicle
New Home
The Observer
Queen
Sunday Express
Sunday Times
Swinton College Journal
The Times
The Times Literary Supplement
Tribune
Twentieth Century
The Victor

Contemporary Writing

Abel-Smith, Brian and Townsend, Peter: *The Poor and the Poorest*, Bell, London, 1965.

Abramovitz, Moses: 'Economics of Growth', in Haley, B.F. (ed): *A Survey of Contemporary Economics*, R.D. Irwin, Homewood, IL, 1952, vol. II.

Abrams, Mark, Rose, Richard and Hinden, Rita: *Must Labour Lose?*, Penguin, Harmondsworth, 1960.

Abrams, Mark: *The Teenage Consumer*, London Press Exchange, London, 1959.

Balogh, Thomas: 'The Apotheosis of the Dilettante: The Establishment of Mandarins', in Thomas, H. (ed): *The Establishment*, Anthony Blond, London, 1959 (reprinted, Ace Books, London, 1962).

Barker, Paul and Hanvey, John: 'Facing Two Ways: Between the 60s and 70s', *New Society*, 27 November 1969, pp. 847–50.

Barraclough, Geoffrey: *An Introduction to Contemporary History*, Penguin, Harmondsworth, 1967 (original edition C.A. Watts, London, 1964).

Bell, Daniel: *The End of Ideology: On the Exhaustion of Political Ideas in the Fifties*, Free Press, New York, 1962.

Birch, Alan: *Small Town Politics*, Oxford University Press, Oxford 1959.

Booker, Christopher, *The Neophiliacs: a Study of the Revolution in English Life in the Fifties and Sixties*, Fontana, London, 1970.

Borrie G. and Diamond, A.L.: *The Consumer, Society and the Law*, Penguin, Harmondsworth, 1973.

Braine, John: *Room at the Top*, Eyre and Spottiswoode, London, [1957] 1971.

Brittan, Samuel: *The Treasury Under the Tories, 1951-1964*, Penguin, Harmondsworth, 1964.

Brittan, Samuel: *Steering the Economy: the Role of the Treasury*, Secker and Warburg, London, 1969 (paperback edition, Pelican, Harmondsworth, 1971).

Brittan, Samuel: *Is There an Economic Consensus?: An Attitude Survey*, Macmillan, London, 1973.

Buchanan, William and Cantril, Hadley: *How Nations See Each Other: A Study in Public Opinion*, Greenwood Press, Westport, Connecticut, 1972, (reprinted from original 1953 edition).

Butler, David: *The British General Election of 1955*, Frank Cass, London, 1969.

Butler, David and King, Anthony: *The British General Election of 1964*, Macmillan, London, 1965.

Cairncross, Alec: *Essays in Economic Management*, George Allen and Unwin, London, 1971.

Carless, R. and Brewster, Pat: *Patronage and the Arts*, Bow Group, Conservative Political Centre Series no. 205, London, 1959.

Catlin, G.E.G. (ed): *New Trends in Socialism*, Lovat Dickson and Thompson Ltd, London, 1935.

Clark, Colin: *Growthmanship: A Study in the Mythology of Investment*, IEA, London, 1961.

Conservative Party: *This is the Road*, London, 1950.

Conservative Party: *The Election Manifesto*, London, 1951.

Conservative Party: *Prosperity with a Purpose*, London, 1964.

Cooke, Margaret: 'Impressions of America', *Swinton College Journal;* vol. 3, no. 2 (1954).

Co-Operative Independent Commission Report: Co-op Union, Manchester, 1958.

Co-Op: *Press Power for the People*, Co-Op Union, Manchester, 1962.

Council of Industrial Design: *Furnishing to Fit the Family*, HMSO, London, 1947.

Council of Industrial Design: *Ideas for Your Home*, HMSO, London, 1950.

Crosland, C.A.R.: *Britain's Economic Problem*, Jonathan Cape, London, 1953.

Crosland, C.A.R.: *The Future of Socialism*, Jonathan Cape, London, 1956.

Crosland, C.A.R.: *Can Labour Win?*, Fabian Tract no. 324, Fabian Society, London, 1960.

Crosland, C.A.R.: *The Future of the Left and Other Political Commentaries*, Encounter, London, 1961.

Crosland, C.A.R.: *The Conservative Enemy: A Programme of Radical Reform for the 1960s*, Jonathan Cape, London, 1962.

Crosland, C.A.R.: *The Future of Socialism*, revised edition, Schocken, New York, 1963.

Crosland, C.A.R.: *Socialists in a Dangerous World*, Socialist Commentary Supplement (November 1968).

Crosland, C.A.R.: *A Social Democratic Britain*, Fabian Tract no. 404, Fabian Society, London, 1971.

Crosland, C.A.R.: *A Critical Commentary on Co-operative Progress*, Co-op Party, Manchester 1971.

Crosland, C.A.R.: *Socialism Now*, Jonathan Cape, London, 1973.

Crossman, R.H.S.: *Socialist Values in a Changing Civilisation*, Fabian Tract no. 286, Fabian Society, London, 1951.

Crossman, R.H.S (ed): *New Fabian Essays*, Turnstile Press, London, 1952.

Crossman, R.H.S.: *Labour in the Affluent Society*, Fabian Tract no. 325, Fabian Society, London, 1960.

Crossman, R.H.S.: *Planning for Freedom*, Hamish Hamilton, London, 1965.

Darling, George: *Advertising and the Labour Government*, Institute of Practitioners in Advertising, London, 1964.

Denison, Edward: *Why Growth Rates Differ?*, Brookings Institution, Washington, DC, 1967.

Domar, Evsey: 'Capital Expansion, Rate of Growth and Employment', *Econometrica*, vol. 14, no. 2 (1946), pp. 137–47.

Dow, J.C.R.: *The Management of the British Economy, 1945-1960*, Cambridge University Press, Cambridge, 1964.

Drucker, Peter: 'Politics for a New Generation', *Harper's* (June 1960).

Dunne, M: *Telephones and the Private Subscriber*, International Organisation of Consumer Unions, London, 1967.

Durbin, Evan: *The Politics of Democratic Socialism*, George Routledge and Sons, London, 1940.

Fairbairn, David: 'An Approach to Leisure: Conservatism in a Post-Industrial Society' in Bow Group: *Principles in Practice*, Conservative Political Centre, London, 1961.

Friedman, Milton: 'Have Monetary Policies Failed?', *American Economic Review*, vol. 62, no. 2 (1972), pp. 11–18.

Frisby, Terence: *The Subtopians*, Samuel French, London, 1964.

Fryer, Peter: *Mrs Grundy: Studies in English Prudery*, Corgi, London, 1965.

Fuller, Reginald H, and Rice, Brian K.: *Christianity and the Affluent Society*, Hodder and Stoughton, London, 1966.

Gaitskell, Hugh: *The Challenge of Co-existence*, Methuen, London, 1957.

Galbraith, J.K.: *The Affluent Society*, Penguin, Harmondsworth, 1962.

Gilbert, Milton and Kravis, Irving B: *An International Comparison of National Products and the Purchasing Power of Currencies*, OEEC, Paris, 1954.

Gloag, John: *The Missing Technician in Industrial Production*, George Allen and Unwin, London, 1944.

Goldman, Peter: *Some Principles of Conservatism*, Conservative Political Centre, London, 1961.

Goldthorpe, John, Lockwood, David, Bechofer, Frank and Platt, Jennifer: *The Affluent Worker*, 3 vols, Cambridge University Press, Cambridge 1968-9.

Goldthorpe, John, and Lockwood, David, 'Not So Bourgeois After All', *New Society*, 18 October 1962, pp. 18–19.

Gorse, D.H.: 'The growth of consumer groups' in *New Outlook: A Liberal Magazine*, no. 21 (July 1963).

Griffin, Clare E.: 'Britain: A Case Study for Americans', *Michigan Business Studies* vol. X, no. 3 (June 1950).

Gundrey, Elizabeth: *Your Money's Worth: A Handbook for Consumers*, Penguin, Harmondsworth, 1962.

Gundrey, Elizabeth: *At Your Service: A Consumer's Guide to the Service Trades and Professions*, Penguin, Harmondsworth, 1964.

Gundrey, Elizabeth: *A Foot in the Door: An Exposé of High Pressure Sales Methods*, Frederick Muller, London, 1965.

Gundrey, Elizabeth.: *Help!*, Zenith Books, London, 1967.

Halsey, A.H. and Ostergaard, G.N: *Power in Co-operatives: The Internal Politics of British Retail Societies*, Blackwell, Oxford, 1965.

Hamilton, Richard F.: *Affluence and the French Worker in the Fourth Republic*, Princeton University Press, Princeton 1967.

Harbury, C.D.: *Efficiency and the Consumer*, Fabian Society, London, 1958.

Harrington, Michael: *The Other America*, Penguin, Harmondsworth, 1963.

Harris, Ralph and Seldon, Arthur: *Advertising in a Free Society*, IEA, London, 1959.

Hartley, Anthony: *A State of England*, Hutchinson, London, 1963.

Haynes, M: *Advertising on Trial: The Case for the Consumer*, Bow Group, London, 1961.

Hoggart, Richard: *The Uses of Literacy*, Penguin, Harmondsworth, 1958.

Hopkins, Harry: *The New Look: Social History of the Forties and Fifties in Britain*, Secker and Warburg, London, 1963.

Hutchison, Terrence: *Economics and Economic Policy in Britain, 1946-1966*, George Allen and Unwin, London, 1968.

Jackson, Brian: *Working Class Community*, Routledge and Kegan Paul, London, 1968.

Jay, Douglas: *The Socialist Case*, Faber and Faber, London, 1937.

Jay, Douglas: 'Beyond state monopoly', in *Where?*, Fabian Tract 320, 1959.

Jay, Douglas: *Socialism in the New Society*, Longman, London, 1962.

Jenkins, Roy: *The Labour Case*, Penguin, Harmondsworth, 1959.

Jewkes, John: 'The Perils of Planning', *Three Banks Review*, no. 66 (June 1965), pp. 3–14.

Johnson, Harry: 'The Man Who Turned Economics into Commonsense', *The Times*, 9 March 1976.

Kerr, Madeline: *The People of Ship Street*, Routledge and Kegan Paul, London, 1958.

Labour Party: *The Old World and the New Society*, London, 1942.

Labour Party: *Labour Believes in Britain*, London, 1949.

Labour Party: *Labour and the New Society*, London, 1950.

Labour Party: *The Welfare State*, Discussion Pamphlet no. 4, London, 1952.

Labour Party: *Challenge to Britain*, London, 1953.

Labour Party: *Your Guide to the Future Labour Offers You*, London, 1958.

Labour Party: *Annual Conference Report 1959*, Labour Party, London, 1959.

Labour Party: *Fair Deal for the Shopper*, London, 1961.

Labour Party: *First Things Last?*, London, 1961.

Labour Party: *Look Forward: The Labour Party,* London, 1961.

Labour Party: *Signposts for the Sixties*, London, 1961.

Labour Party: *Brighter Party Premises*, London, 1962.

Labour Party: *Crime – A Challenge to Us All*, London, 1964.

Labour Party: *Let's Go with Labour for the New Britain*, London, 1964.

Labour Party: *Labour Women's Conference Report*, Labour Party, London, 1964.

Labour Party: *Report of a Commission of Enquiry into Advertising*, London, 1966.

Labour Party: *Labour Women's Conference Report*, Labour Party, London, 1970.

Labour Party: *Advertising – Green Paper* (March 1972).

Laski, Marghanita: 'Sacred and Profane', *Twentieth Century* (February 1959).

Leven, Maurice, Moulton, Harold G., and Warburton, Clark: *America's Capacity to Consume*, Brookings, Washington, DC, 1934.

Levin, Bernard: *The Pendulum Years: Britain in the Sixties*, Cape, London, 1970.

Luetkens, Charlotte: *Women and a New Society*, Nicholson and Watson, London, 1946.

MacDougall, Douglas: 'Does Productivity Rise Faster in the United States?', *Review of Economics and Statistics*, vol. 38, no. 2 (1956), pp. 155–76.

Macmillan, James and Harris, Bernard: *The American Take-Over of Britain*, Leslie Frewin, London, 1968.

Macrae, Norman: *Sunshades in October*, Allen and Unwin, London, 1963.

Maddison, Angus: *Economic Growth in the West: Comparative Experience in Europe and North America*, George Allen and Unwin, London, 1964.

Malik, Rex: *What's Wrong with British Industry?*, Penguin, Harmondsworth, 1964.

Marcuse, Herbert: *One Dimensional Man: Studies in the Ideology of Advanced Industrial Society*, Routledge, London, 1964.

Martin, John and Smith, George: *The Consumer Interest*, Pall Mall Press, London, 1968.

Mitchell, B.R. and Deane. P.: *Abstract of British Historical Statistics*, Cambridge University Press, Cambridge, 1962.

Millar, Robert: *The Affluent Sheep: A Profile of the British Consumer*, Longman, London, 1963.

Montgomery, John: *The Fifties*, Allen and Unwin, London, 1966.

Myrdal, Gunnar: *Challenge to Affluence*, Gollancz, London, 1963.

Nairn, Ian: *Outrage*, Architectural Press, London 1955.

Nairn, Ian: *Counter-Attack Against Subtopia*, Architectural Press, London, 1957.

Northcott, Jim: *Why Labour?*, Penguin, Harmondsworth, 1964.

Opie, Roger: 'Economic Planning and Growth', in W. Beckerman (ed): *The Labour Government's Economic Record, 1964-1970*, Duckworth, London, 1972.

Packard, Vance: *The Hidden Persuaders*, Penguin, Harmondsworth, 1960 (first published 1957).

Packard, Vance: *The Waste Makers*, David Mackay, New York, 1960.

Packard, Vance: *The Status Seekers*, Penguin, Harmondsworth, 1961.

Paish, Frank: *Studies in an Inflationary Economy: the United Kingdom 1948-1961*, Macmillan, London, 1962.

Pearson, John and Turner, Graham: *The Persuasion Industry*, Eyre and Spottiswoode, London, 1965.

Pevsner, Nikolaus: *Enquiry into Industrial Art in England*, Cambridge University Press, Cambridge, 1937.

Phillips, Morgan: *Labour in the Sixties*, Labour Party, London, 1960.

Phillips, Robert: 'After Affluence?', *Twentieth Century,* nos. 1039, 1040 (double issue, 1968–9), p. 42.

Postan, Michael: 'A Plague of Economists?: On Some Current Myths, Errors and Fallacies', *Encounter*, vol. 30, no. 1 (1968), pp. 42–7.

Potter, Dennis: *The Glittering Coffin*, Gollancz, London, 1960.

Priestley, J.B.: *An English Journey: Being a Rambling but Truthful Account of what One Man Saw,* Heinemann, London, [1934] 1968.

Pringle, Robin: *The Growth Merchants: Economic Consequences of Wishful Thinking*, CPS, London, 1977.

Proudfoot, Mary: *British Politics and Government, 1951-1970: A Study of an Affluent Society*, Faber and Faber, London, 1972.

Quant, Mary: *Quant by Quant*, Cassell, London, 1966.

Research Institute for Consumer Affairs: *British Co-Operatives*, Research Institute for Consumer Affairs, London, 1964.

Research Institute for Consumer Affairs: *Town Planning – The Consumer's Environment*, Research Institute for Consumer Affairs, London, 1965.

Riesman, David *Abundance for What?*, Doubleday, New York, 1964.

Rodgers, W.T. (ed): *Hugh Gaitskell*, Thames and Hudson, London, 1964.

Rostow, Walt: *The Stages of Economic Growth: A Non-Communist Manifesto*, Cambridge University Press, Cambridge, 1960.

Rubner, Alex: *Three Sacred Cows of Economics*, MacGibbon and Kee, London, 1970.

Sampson, Anthony: *Anatomy of Britain*, Hodder and Stoughton, London, 1962.

Samuel, Raphael: 'The Quality of Life' in *Where?*, Fabian Tract 320, Fabian Society, London, 1959.

Shanks, Michael: *The Stagnant Society: A Warning*, Penguin, London, 1961.

Shone, Robert: 'Problems of Planning for Economic Growth in a Mixed Economy', *Economic Journal*, vol. 75, no. 1 (1965), pp. 1–19.

Shonfield, Andrew: *British Economic Policy Since the War*, Penguin, Harmondsworth, 1958.

Shonfield, Andrew: *Modern Capitalism: The Changing Balance of Public and Private Power*, Oxford University Press, Oxford, 1965.

Shore, Peter: *The Real Nature of Conservatism*, Labour Party Educational Series no. 3, London, 1952.

Silburn, Richard and Coates, Ken: *Poverty: The Forgotten Englishmen*, Penguin, Harmondsworth, 1970.

Sillitoe, Alan: *Saturday Night and Sunday Morning*, Pan, London, 1960.

Sillitoe, Alan: *Loneliness of the Long-Distance Runner*, Longman, London, 1966.

Sinclair, Peter: 'The Economy: A Study in Failure' in McKie, D. and Cooks, C. (eds): *The Decade of Disillusion: British Politics in the Sixties*, Macmillan, London, 1972.

Sissons, Michael and French, Phillip (eds): *Age of Austerity, 1945-51*, Penguin, Harmondsworth, 1964.

Socialist International: *Report of the Conference on the Situation in Western Europe, Part 2*, Socialist International, Amsterdam, 1959.

Socialist Union: *Twentieth Century Socialism*, Penguin, Harmondsworth, 1956.

Southworth, June: 'The Wastemakers', *Focus* (UK Consumer Council, April 1970), pp. 2–7.

Stacey, Margaret: *Tradition and Change: A Study of Banbury*, Oxford University Press, Oxford 1960.

Strachey, John: *Contemporary Capitalism*, Victor Gollancz, London, 1956.

Tawney, R.H.: *The Webbs in Perspective*, Athlone Press, London, 1953.

Tobin, James: 'Economic Growth as an Objective of Government Policy', *American Economic Review*, vol. 54, no. 3 (1964), pp. 1–20.

Trenaman, Joseph and McQuail, Denis: *Television and the Political Image*, Methuen, London, 1961.

Tunstall, Jeremy: *The Advertising Man in London Advertising Agencies*, Chapman and Hall, London, 1964.

Utley, T.E., *Enoch Powell; The Man and His Thinking*, William Kimber, London, 1968.

Vandeberg,, Arthur H. Jr.: *The Private Papers of Senator Vandeberg*, Greenwood Press, Westport, Conn, 1974 (reprint of 1952 original).

Watt D.C.: *Britain Looks to Germany: A Study of British Opinion and Policy Towards Germany Since 1945*, Wolff, London, 1965.

Wigham, Eric. L.: *What's Wrong with the Unions?*, Penguin, Harmondsworth, 1961.

Wight, R.: *The Day the Pigs Refused to be Driven to Market: Advertising and the Consumer Revolution*, Hart-Davis, MacGibbon, London, 1972.

Wilkins, Nancy: 'Anything Goes', *Impact* (February 1965), pp. 26–7.

Williams, Lord Francis: *The Twilight of Empire*, Barnes, New York, 1961.

Williams, Lord Francis: *The American Invasion*, Anthony Blond, London, 1962.

Williams, Raymond: *The Long Revolution*, Columbia University Press, New York, 1961.

Wilmott, Peter and Young, Michael, *Family and Kinship in East London*, Penguin, Harmondsworth, 1962.

Wilson, H.H.: *Pressure Group*, Rutgers University Press, New Brunswick, NJ, 1961.

Wootton, Barbara: *Contemporary Britain*, Allen and Unwin, London, 1971.

Worswick, G.D.N. and Ady, P.H.: *The British Economy in the Nineteen-fifties*, Oxford University Press, Oxford, 1962.

Young, Michael: *The Chipped White Cups of Dover: A Discussion of the Possibility of a New Progressive Party*, Unit 2, London, 1960.

Zweig, Ferdynand: *The Worker in an Affluent Society: Family Life and Industry*, Heinemann, London, 1961.

Official Publications

Council of Industrial Design: *First Annual Report: 1945/46*, HMSO, London, 1946.

Council of Industrial Design: *Twentieth Annual Report, 1964/65*, HMSO, London, 1965.

Department of Economic Affairs, *The National Plan*, Cmnd. 2764, HMSO, London, 1965.

Ministry of Education, *The Youth Services of England and Wales* (The Albermarle Report), Cmnd. 929 (1960).

National Bureau of Economic Research: *Recent Economic Changes in the United States, 2* vols., New York, NBER, 1929.

National Economic Development Council: *Growth of the United Kingdom Economy to 1966*, HMSO, London, 1963.

National Economic Development Council: *Conditions Favourable to Faster Growth*, HMSO, London, 1963.

Parliamentary Debates (House of Commons).

Office for National Statistics, *Living in Britain – the 2001 General Household Survey*, Office for National Statistics, London, 2002 (http://www.statistics.gov.uk/lib).

Office of Fair Trading: *Annual Report, 1986*, Office of Fair Trading, London, 1987.

Working Group on Migration, *The Brain Drain: Report of the Working Group on Migration*, Cmnd., 3417, 1967.

Memoirs and Published Diaries

Benn, Tony: *Years of Hope: Diaries Papers and Letters 1940-1962*, Hutchinson, London, 1994.

Cairncross, Alec: *The Wilson Years: A Treasury Diary, 1964-1969*, Historian's Press, London, 1997.

Cairncross, Alec: *Diaries of Sir Alec Cairncross: the Radcliffe Committee/Economic Adviser to HMG, 1961-64*, Institute of Contemporary British History, London, 1999.

Catterall, Peter (ed): *The Macmillan Diaries: The Cabinet Years, 1950-1957*, Macmillan, London, 2003.

Crossman, Richard: *The Diaries of a Cabinet Minister. Vol. 1, Minister of Housing, 1964-66*, Jonathan Cape, London, 1975.

Dalton, Hugh: *The Fateful Years: Memoirs 1931-1945*, Frederick Muller Ltd, London, 1957.

Davenport, Nicholas: *Memoirs of a City Radical*, Weidenfeld and Nicolson, London, 1974.

Galbraith, John Kenneth: *A Life in Our Times*, Houghton Mifflin, Boston, 1981.

Gould, Philip: *The Unfinished Revolution: How the Modernisers Saved the Labour Party*, Little, Brown and Company, London, 1998.

Hall, Robert: *The Robert Hall Diaries, 1954-1961* (edited by A. Cairncross), Unwin Hyman, London, 1991.

Hobsbawm, Eric: *Interesting Times: A Twentieth Century Life*, Allen Lane, London, 2002.

Hodgkinson, George: *Sent to Coventry*, Pergamon, Oxford, 1970.

Institute of Contemporary British History: 'Witness Seminar: The Campaign for Democratic Socialism 1960-64', *Contemporary Record*, vol. 7, no. 2 (Autumn 1993), pp. 363–85.

Jay, Douglas: *Change and Fortune: A Political Record*, London, Hutchinson, 1980.

MacDougall, Douglas: *Don and Mandarin: Memoirs of an Economist*, John Murray, London, 1987.

Macmillan, Harold: *At the End of the Day, 1961-1963*, Macmillan, London, 1973.

Mikardo, Ian: *Back-Bencher*, Weidenfeld and Nicolson, London, 1988.

Morgan, Janet (ed): *The Backbench Diaries of Richard Crossman*, Book Club Associates, London, 1981.

Nicolson, Nigel (ed): *Harold Nicolson: Diaries and Letters 1945-62*, Collins, London, 1968.

Pimlott, Ben (ed): *The Political Diary of Hugh Dalton, 1918-40, 1945-60*, Jonathan Cape, London, 1986.

Rodgers, Bill: *Fourth Among Equals*, Politico's, London, 2000.

Williams, Lord Francis: *Nothing so Strange*, Cassell, London, 1970.

Published works

Addison, Paul: 'Churchill and the Price of Victory: 1939-45' in Tiratsoo, Nick (ed): *From Blitz to Blair: A New History of Britain Since 1939*, Weidenfeld and Nicolson, London, 1997.

Ambrose, Stephen: *Eisenhower: The President*, Simon and Schuster, New York, 1984.

Anderson, Perry: *English Questions*, Verso, London, 1992.

Andes, Linda: 'Growing Up Punk', in Epstein, J.P.: *Youth Culture, Identity and the Postmodern World*, Blackwell, Oxford, 1998.

Andrews, Maggie and Talbot, Mary M (eds): *All the World and Her Husband: Women in Twentieth-Century Consumer Culture*, Cassell, London, 2000.

Annan, Noel: *Our Age: Portrait of a Generation*, HarperCollins, London, 1990.

Arndt, Heinz: *The Rise and Fall of Economic Growth*, University of Chicago Press, Chicago, 1978.

Backhouse, Roger and Middleton, Roger (eds): *Exemplary Economists*, Edward Elgar, Cheltenham, 2000.

Backhouse, Roger: *A History of Modern Economic Analysis*, Basil Blackwell, Oxford, 1985.

Baldwin, Peter: *The Politics of Social Solidarity: Class Bases of the European Welfare State*, Cambridge University Press, Cambridge, 1990.

Barnett, Corelli: *The Audit of War: The Illusion and Reality of Britain as a Great Nation*, Macmillan, London, 1986.

Barnett, Corelli: *The Verdict of Peace*, Macmillan, London, 2001.

Barr, Nicholas: *The Economics of the Welfare State*, Oxford University Press, Oxford, 1993.

Barro, Robert: *Determinants of Economic Growth*, MIT Press, Cambridge MA, 1997.

Bauman, Zygmunt: *Freedom*, Open University Press, Milton Keynes, 1988.

Beasley, W.G,: *The Rise of Modern Japan: Political, Economic and Social Change Since 1850*, Weidenfeld, London, 2nd edn, 1995.

Benson, Susan Porter: 'Gender, Generation, and Consumption in the United States: Working Class Families in the Interwar Period' in Strasser, Susan, McGovern, Charles and Judt, Matthias (eds): *Getting and Spending: European and American Consumer Societies in the Twentieth Century*, Cambridge University Press, Cambridge, 1998.

Berg, Maxine and Clifford, Helen (eds): *Consumers and Luxury: Consumer Culture in Europe 1650-1850*, Manchester University Press, Manchester, 1999.

Berghahn, Volker R: 'Recasting Bourgeois Germany' in Schissler, Hanna (ed): *The Miracle Years: A Cultural History of West Germany 1949-1968*, Princeton University Press, Princeton, NJ, 2001.

Berry, Christopher J.: *The Idea of Luxury*, Cambridge University Press, Cambridge, 1994.

Bewes, Timothy and Gilbert, Jeremy (eds): *Cultural Capitalism: Politics after New Labour*, Lawrence and Wishart, London, 2000.

Black, Amy and Stephen Brooke: 'The Labour Party, Women and the Problem of Gender, 1951-1966', *Journal of British Studies*, vol. 36, no. 4 (1997), pp. 419–52.

Black, Lawrence: *The Political Culture of the Left in Affluent Britain, 1951-64: Old Labour, New Britain?*, Palgrave, Basingstoke, 2003.

Black, Lawrence: '*Which?*craft in Post-war Britain: The Consumers' Association and Politics of Affluence', *Albion*, vol. 36, no. 1 (2004).

Black, Peter, *The Mirror in the Corner: People' Television*, Hutchinson, London 1972.

Bogdanor, Vernon and Skidelsky, Robert (eds): *The Age of Affluence, 1951-1964*, Macmillan, London, 1970.

Bonner, Arnold: *British Co-Operation*, Co-op Union, Manchester, 1970.

Booth, Alan: 'Britain in the 1950s: a "Keynesian" Managed Economy?', *History of Political Economy*, vol. 33, no. 2 (2001), pp. 287–88.

Booth, Alan: 'New Revisionists and the Keynesian Era in British Economic Policy', *Economic History Review*, vol. LIV, no. 2 (2001), pp. 346–66.

Borrie, G.: *The Development of Consumer Law and Policy,* Stevens and Sons, London, 1984.

Bourdieu, P.: *Distinction: A Social Critique of the Judgement of Taste*, Routledge and Kegan Paul, London, 1986.

Bourdieu, P.: *The Logic of Practice*, Polity Press, Cambridge, 1990.

Brake, Mike: *The Sociology of Youth Culture and Youth Subcultures: Sex and Drugs and Rock 'n' Roll?* Routledge and Keegan Paul, London, 1980.

Breward, Christopher: *The Hidden Consumer: Masculinities, Fashion and City Life 1860-1914*, Manchester University Press, Manchester, 1999.

Brinkly, Alan: 'The Problem of American Conservatism', *American Historical Review*, vol. 99, no. 2 (April 1994), pp. 409–29.

Brivati, Brian: *Hugh Gaitskell*, Richard Cohen Books, London, 1996.

Broadberry, S.N. and Crafts, N.F.R.: 'British Economic Policy and Industrial Performance in the Early Post-war Period', *Business History*, vol. 39, no. 4 (1996), pp. 65–91.

Broadberry, S.N. and Crafts, N.F.R.: 'The Post-war Settlement: Not Such a Good Bargain After All', *Business History*, vol. 40, no. 2 (1998), pp. 73–9.

Brooke, Stephen: 'Labour and the "nation" after 1945', in Lawrence, Jon and Taylor, Miles (eds), *Party, State and Society: Electoral Behaviour in Britain Since 1820*, Scolar, Aldershot, 1997.

Brooke, Stephen: 'Memory and Modernity', *Journal of British Studies*, vol. 42, no. 1 (2003), pp. 123–39.

Brown, Callum: *The Death of Christian Britain: Understanding Secularisation 1800-2000*, Routledge, New York, 2001.

Browne, Jen: 'Decisions in DIY: Women, Home Improvements and Advertising in Post-war Britain' in Andrews, Maggie and Talbot Mary M.: *All the World and Her Husband: Women in Twentieth-Century Consumer Culture*, Cassell, London, 2000.

Cairncross, Alec: 'Academics and Policy Makers', in Cairncross, F. (ed): *Changing Perceptions of Economic Policy: Essays in Honour of the Seventieth Birthday of Sir Alec Cairncross*, Methuen, London, 1981.

Cairncross, Alec: *The British Economy Since 1945* (2nd edn), Blackwell, Oxford, 1995.

Cairncross, Alec: *Managing the British Economy in the 1960s*, Macmillan, London, 1996.

Callaghan, John: 'The Left and the "Unfinished Revolution": Bevanites and Soviet Russia in the 1950s', *Contemporary British History*, vol. 15, no. 3. (2001), pp. 63–82.

Cannadine, David: *Britain in "Decline"?*, Markham Press Fund, Waco TX, 1998.

Catterall, Peter: 'Roles and Relationships: Dean Acheson, 'British "Decline" and Post-War Anglo-American Relations' in Capet, Antoine and Sy-Wonyu, Aissatou (eds): *The 'Special Relationship'*, University of Rouen Press, Rouen, 2003.

Childs, David: *Britain Since 1945: A Political History*, Routledge, London, 1997.

Chisolm, Anne and Davie, Michael: *Lord Beaverbrook: A Life*, Hutchinson, London, 1992.

Clapson, Mark: *Invincible Green Suburbs, Brave New Towns: Social Change and Urban Dispersal in Post-war England*, Manchester University Press, Manchester, 1998.

Clapson, Mark: 'Suburbia and Party Politics', *History Today* (September 2001).

Clarke, Gary: 'Defending Ski-Jumpers': A critique of Theories of Youth Subcultures', in Frith, S. and Goodwin, P. (eds): *On Record: Rock Pop and the Written Word*, Routledge, London, 1989.

Cliff, Dallas 'Religion, Morality and the Middle Class' in King, Roger and Nugent, Neill (eds): *Respectable Rebels: Middle Class Campaigns in Britain in the 1970s*, Hodder and Stoughton, London, 1979.

Coates, David: *Models of Capitalism*, Polity Press, Cambridge, 2000.

Cobley, P. and Briggs, A (eds): *Introduction to the Media,* Longman, London, 1997.

Cohen, Lizabeth: 'The New Deal State and the Making of Citizen Consumers' in Strasser, Susan, McGovern, Charles and Judt, Matthias (eds): *Getting and Spending: European and American Consumer Societies in the Twentieth Century*, Cambridge University Press, Cambridge, 1998.

Cohen, Lizabeth, *A Consumers' Republic: The Politics of Mass Consumption in Post-war America*, Knopf, New York, 2002.

Conekin, Becky: *The Autobiography of a Nation: The 1951 Festival of Britain*, Manchester University Press, Manchester, 2003.

Conekin, Becky, Mort, Frank and Waters, Chris (eds): *Moments of Modernity: Reconstructing Britain, 1945-1964*, Rivers Oram, London, 1999.

Connelly, Mark: *We Can Take It!: Britain and the Memory of the Second World War*, Routledge, London, forthcoming, 2004.

Conservative Party: *Manifesto 1979*, Conservative Central Office, London, 1979.

Consumers' Association, *Thirty Years of Which? 1957-1987*, Consumers' Association, London, 1987.

Crafts, N.F.R.: '"Post-neoclassical Endogenous Growth Theory": What are its Policy Implications?', *Oxford Review of Economic Policy*, vol. 12, no. 2 (1996), pp. 30–47.

Craig, F.W.S. (ed): *British General Election Manifestos, 1918-1974*, Macmillan, London, 1975.

Craig, F.W.S.: *British General Election Manifestos, 1959-1987*, Dartmouth, Aldershot, 1990.

Croham, Lord: 'Were the Instruments of Control for Domestic Economic Policy Adequate?', in Cairncross, F. and Cairncross, A. (eds): *The Legacy of the Golden Age*, Routledge, London, 1992.

Crosland, Susan: *Tony Crosland*, Jonathan Cape, London, 1982.

Cross, Gary: *Time and Money: The Making of Consumer Culture*, Routledge, London, 1993.

Curtis, H. and Sanderson, M.: *A Review of the National Federation of Consumer Groups*, Consumers' Association, London, 1992.

Daunton, Martin and Hilton, Matthew (eds): *The Politics of Consumption: Material Culture and Citizenship in Europe and America*, Berg, Oxford, 2001.

Denison, Edward: 'Growth Accounting' in Eatwell, J. *et al.* (eds): *The New Palgrave Dictionary of Economics*, vol. II, Macmillan, London, 1987.

Dimbleby, David and Reynolds, David: *An Ocean Apart: The Relationship Between Britain and America in the Twentieth Century*, BBC/Hodder and Stoughton, London, 1988.

Dintenfass, Michael: 'Converging accounts, misleading metaphors and persistent doubts: Reflections on the Historiography of Britain's "Decline"' in Dintenfass, Michael and Dormois, Jean-Pierre (eds): *The British Industrial Decline*, Routledge, London, 1999.

Dorfman, Gerald A.: *Wage Politics in Britain, 1945-1967*, Charles Knight, London, 1974.

Ellis, Catherine: 'The Younger Generation: The Labour Party and the 1959 Youth Commission', *Journal of British Studies*, vol. 41, no. 2 (2002), pp. 199–231.

Ellwood, David: *Rebuilding Europe: Western Europe, America and Post-war Reconstruction*, Longman, London, 1992.

English, Richard and Kenny, Michael, (eds): *Rethinking British Decline*, Macmillan, Basingstoke, 1999.

Evans, Timothy: *Conservative Radicalism: A Sociology of Conservative Party Youth Structures and Libertarianism, 1970-92*, Berghahn, Oxford, 1996.

Favretto, Ilaria: '"Wilsonism" Reconsidered: Labour Party Revisionism 1952-64', *Contemporary British History*, vol. 14 no. 4 (Winter 2000), pp. 54–80.

Feinstein, Charles: 'Structural Change in Developed Countries During the Twentieth Century', *Oxford Review of Economic Policy, vol. 15*, no. 4 (1999), pp. 35–55.

Fielding Steven, Thompson, Peter and Tiratsoo, Nick: *England Arise!: The Labour Party and Popular Politics in 1940s Britain*, Manchester University Press, Manchester, 1995.

Fielding, Steven: 'Activists Against "Affluence": Labour Party Culture During the "Golden Age", circa 1950-1970', *Journal of British Studies*, vol. 40, no. 2 (2001), pp. 241–67.

Fielding, Steven: *The Labour Party: Continuity and Change in the Making of 'New' Labour*, Palgrave, Basingstoke, 2003.

Findley, Richard: 'The Conservative Party and Defeat: the Significance of Resale Price Maintenance for the General Election of 1964', *Twentieth Century British History*, vol. 12 no. 3 (2001), pp. 327–53.

Finegold, David and Soskice, David W.: 'The failure of training in Britain: analysis and prescription', *Oxford Review of Economic Policy*, vol. 4, no. 3 (1988), pp. 21–53.

Fishbein, Warren H.: *Wage Restraint by Consensus: Britain's Search for an Incomes Policy Agreement, 1965-79*, Routledge and Kegan Paul, London, 1984.

Fitzgerald, Rona and Girvin, Brian: 'Political culture, growth and the conditions for success in the Irish economy' in Nolan, Brian, O'Connell, Philip J., and Whelan, Christopher T. (eds): *Bust to Boom? The Irish Experience of Growth and Inequality*, Institute for Public Administration, Dublin, 2000.

Foot, Michael: *Aneurin Bevan: A Biography*, vol. 2, Davis-Poynter, London, 1973.

Fowler, David: *The First Teenagers: Young Wage-earners in Inter-War Britain*, Woburn Press, London, 1995.

Francis, Martin: 'Tears, Tantrums, and Bared Teeth: The Emotional Economy of Three Conservative Prime Ministers, 1951-1963, *Journal of British Studies* vol. 41 no. 3 (2002), pp. 354–87 .

Frank, Thomas: *The Conquest of Cool,* University of Chicago Press, Chicago, 1997

Frank, Thomas: *One Market Under God: Extreme Capitalism, Market Populism and the End of Economic Democracy*, Secker and Warburg, London, 2001.

Fulbrook, Mary: *Germany 1918-1990: The Divided Nation*, Fontana, London, 1991.

Gallup, George (ed): *The Gallup Poll: Public Opinion 1935-1971*, Random House, New York, 1972.

Gamble, Andrew: 'Theories of British Politics', *Political Studies*, vol. 38, no. 3 (1990), pp. 404–20.

Gamble, Andrew: 'Theories and Explanations of British Decline' in English, R. and Kenny, M. (eds), *Rethinking British Decline*, Macmillan, London, 2000.

George, Vic and Howards, Irving: *Poverty Amidst Affluence: Britain and the United States*, Edward Elgar, Aldershot, 1991.

George, Vic and Page, Robert (eds): *Modern Thinkers on Welfare*, Prentice Hall/Harvester Wheatsheaf, London, 1995.

Giddens, Anthony: *Modernity and Self Identity: Self and Society in the Late Modern Age*, Polity Press, Oxford, 1991.

Gilmour, Ian and Garnett, Mark: *Whatever Happened to the Tories?* Fourth Estate, London 1997.

Giordan, M.: *The Consumer Jungle*, Fontana/Collins, London, 1974.

Girvin, Brian: *The Right in the Twentieth Century: Conservatism and Democracy*, Pinter, London, 1994.

Girvin, Brian: 'The Political Culture of Secularisation: European Trends and Comparative Perspectives' in Broughton, David and Napel, Hans-Martien ten Napel: (eds): *Religion and Mass Electoral Behaviour in Europe*, Routledge, London, 2000.

Girvin, Brian: *From Union to Union: Democracy, Religion and Nationalism from the Act of Union to the European Union*, Gill and Macmillan, Dublin, 2002.

Glancey, Jonathan: *Douglas Scott*, Design Council, London, 1988.

Glynn, Sean and Booth, Alan: *Modern Britain: An Economic and Social History*, Routledge, London, 1996.

Goff, Brian and Fleischer, Arthur A. III: *Spoiled Rotten: Affluence, Anxiety and Social Decay in America*, Westview Press, Boulder, CO, 1999.

Gorst, Anthony, Johnman Lewis and Lucas, W. Scott (eds): *Contemporary British History 1931-61: Politics and the Limits of Policy*, Pinter Publishers, London, 1991.

Grant, Matthew: 'Historians, the Penguin Specials and the State-of-the-Nation Literature, 1958-64', *Contemporary British History*, vol. 17, no. 3 (2003, in press).

Green, Jonathon: *Days in the Life, Voices from the English Underground*, Pimlico, London, 1998.

Greenstein, Fred I.: *The Hidden-Hand Presidency*, Basic Books, New York, 1982.

Griffith, Robert: 'Why They Liked Ike', *Reviews in American History*, vol. 7, no. 4 (1979), pp. 577–83.

Griffiths, R.T. and Tachibanki, T. (eds): *From Austerity to Affluence: The Transformation of the Socio-economic Structure of Western Europe and Japan*, Macmillan, London, 2000.

Hall, Stuart and Jefferson, Tony (eds): *Resistance Through Rituals, Youth Subcultures in Post-war Britain*, Hutchinson, London, 1976.

Halpern, Rick and Morris, Jonathan (eds): *American Exceptionalism? US Working-Class Formation in an International Context*, Macmillan, London, 1997.

Ham, A: *Treasury Rules: Recurrent Themes in British Economic Policy*, Quartet, London, 1981.

Hansen, Randall: *Immigration and Citizenship in Post-war Britain*, Oxford University Press, Oxford, 2000.

Harper, Sue and Porter, Vincent: 'Throbbing Hearts and Smart Repartee: The Reception of American Films in 1950s Britain', *Media History*, vol. 4, no. 2 (1998), pp. 175–94.

Harris, Howell John: *The Right to Manage: Industrial Relations Policies of American Business in the 1940s*, University of Wisconsin Press, Madison, WI, 1982.

Harris, Jose: *Private Lives, Public Spirits*, Oxford University Press, Oxford, 1993.

Hebdige, Dick: *Subculture: The Meaning of Style*, Methuen, London, 1979.

Heffer, Simon: *Like a Roman: The Life of Enoch Powell*, Phoenix, London, 1999.

Henderson, P. David: *Innocence and Design: The Influence of Economic Ideas on Policy*, Basil Blackwell, Oxford, 1986.

Hennessy, Peter *et al.*: 'Symposium: Fulton, 20 Years On', *Contemporary Record*, vol. 2, no. 2 (1988), pp. 44–51.

Herman, Arthur: *The Idea of Decline in Western History*, Free Press, New York, 1997.

Hibbs, Douglas A. Jr.: 'Political Parties and Macroeconomic Policy', *American Political Science Review*, vol. 71, no. 4 (1977), pp. 1467–87.

Hilton, Matthew: 'The Female Consumer and the Politics of Consumption in Twentieth-Century Britain', *Historical Journal*, vol. 45, no. 1 (2002) pp. 103–28.

Hilton, Matthew: 'The Fable of the Sheep, or, Private Virtues, Public Vices: The Consumer Revolution of the Twentieth Century', *Past and Present*, vol. 176 (2002), pp. 222–56.

Hilton, Matthew: *Consumerism in Twentieth-Century Britain: The Search for a Historical Movement*, Cambridge University Press, Cambridge, 2003.

Hinton, James: 'Militant Housewives: The British Housewives' League and the Attlee Government', *History Workshop Journal* no. 38 (1994), pp. 129–56.

Hirsch, Fred and Gordon, David: *Newspaper Money: Fleet Street and the Search for the Affluent Reader*, Hutchinson, London, 1975.

Hobsbawn, Eric: *Age of Extremes: The Short Twentieth Century, 1914-1992*, Michael Joseph, London, 1994.

Hobsbawm, Eric: *Interesting Times: A Twentieth Century Life*, Allen Lane, London, 2002.

Hollander, Stanley C. and Germain, Richard: *Was There a Pepsi Generation Before Pepsi Invented It?*, NTC Publishing Group, Chicago, IL, 1992.

Holroyd-Doveton, John: *Young Conservatives*, Pentland, Bishop Auckland, 1996.

Horowitz, Daniel: *Vance Packard and American Social Criticism*, University of North Carolina Press, Chapel Hill, 1994.

Horne, Alistair: *Macmillan, 1957-1986*, Macmillan, London, 1989.

Horsely, William and Buckley, Roger: *Nippon New Superpower: Japan Since 1945*, BBC, London, 1990.

Hutton, Will: *The State We're In*, Jonathan Cape, London, 1995.

Institute of Historical Research, University of London: *Victoria History of the Counties of England Volume VIII*, Oxford University Press, Oxford, 1969.

Jacobs, Meg: 'The Politics of Plenty in the 20th Century United States' in Daunton, Martin and Hilton, Matthew (eds): *The Politics of Consumption*, Berg, Oxford, 2001.

James, Harold: *A German Identity 1770-1990*, Weidenfeld and Nicolson, London, 1989.

Jefferys, Kevin: *Retreat From New Jerusalem: British Politics, 1951-64*, Macmillan, Basingstoke, 1997.

Jefferys, Kevin: *Anthony Crosland: A New Biography*, Richard Cohen Books, London, 1999.

Johnson, Paul (ed): *Twentieth-Century Britain: Economic, Social and Cultural Change*, Longman, London, 1994.

Jones, Harriet and Kandiah, Michael (eds): *The Myth of Consensus: New Views on British History, 1945-1964*, Macmillan, Basingstoke, 1996.

Kaufman, David: 'The Nazi Legacy: Coming to Terms With the Past', in James, Peter, (ed): *Modern Germany: Politics, Society and Culture*, Routledge, London, 1998.

Keegan, William and Pennant-Rea, Rupert: *Who Runs the Economy?*, Maurice Temple Smith, London, 1997.

Kersbergen, Kaas van: *Social Capitalism: A Study of Christian Democracy and the Welfare State*, Routledge, London, 1995.

King, Desmond: *Actively Seeking Work? The Politics of Unemployment and Welfare Policy in the United States and Great Britain*, University of Chicago Press, Chicago, 1995.

Klein, Daniel: *What Do Economists Contribute?*, Macmillan, London, 1999.

Kramnick, Issac (ed): *Is Britain Dying? Perspectives on the Current Crisis*, Cornell University Press, Ithaca, NY, 1978.

Laing, Stuart: *Representations of Working-class Life, 1957-64*, Macmillan, Basingstoke, 1986.

Lancaster, Bill and Mason, Anthony (eds): *Life and Labour in a Twentieth Century City: The Experience of Coventry*, Cryfield Press, Coventry, 1986.

Landau, Ralph; Taylor, Timothy; and Wright, Gavin (eds): *The Mosaic of Economic Growth*, Stanford University Press, Stanford, CA, 1996.

Lee, Martin J.: *Consumer Culture Reborn: The Cultural Politics of Consumption*, Routledge, London, 1993.

Leonard, Dick (ed): *Socialism Now and Other Essays*, Jonathan Cape, London, 1974.

Leonard, Mark: *Britain: Renewing Our Identity*, Demos, London, 1997.

Leruez, Jacques: *Economic Planning and Politics in Britain*, Martin Robertson, London, 1975.

Levy, Frank: *Dollars and Dreams: The Changing American Income Distribution*, Norton, New York, 1988.

Lewis, Peter: *The 50s*, Book Club Associates, London, 1978.

Lipset, Seymour Martin and Marks, Gary: *It Didn't Happen Here: Why Socialism Failed in the United States*, W.W. Norton, New York, 1999.

Lodge, David: *Changing Places*, Penguin, Harmondsworth, 1978.

Lowe, Rodney: 'Resignation at the Treasury: The Social Services Committee and the Failure to Reform the Welfare State, 1955-57' *Journal of Social Policy*, vol. 18. no. 4 (1989), pp. 505–26.

Lowe, Rodney: 'Milestone or Millstone? The 1959-1961 Plowden Committee and its Impact on British Welfare Policy', *Historical Journal*, vol. 40, no. 2 (1997), pp. 463–91.

Lowe, Rodney: 'The Core Executive, Modernization and the Creation of PESC, 1960-64', *Public Administration*, vol. 75, no. 4 (1997), pp. 601–15.

Lowe, Rodney and Rollings, Neil: 'Modernising Britain, 1957-64: A Classic Case of Centralisation and Fragmentation?', in Rhodes, R.A.W. (ed): *Transforming British Government*, vol. I, Macmillan, London, 2000.

McCormack, Gavan: *The Emptiness of Japanese Affluence*, M.E. Sharpe, Armonk, NY, 2001.

Maddison, Angus, *Dynamic Forces in Capitalist Development: A Long-run Comparative View*, Oxford University Press, Oxford, 1991.

Maddison, Angus: *The World Economy*, OECD, Paris, 2001.

Maguire, Paddy: 'Designs on Reconstruction: British Business, Market Structures and the Role of Design in Post-War Recovery', *Journal of Design History*, vol. 4, no. 1 (1991), pp. 15–30.

Maguire, Paddy: 'Craft Capitalism and the Projection of British Industry in the 1950s and 1960s', *Journal of Design History*, vol. 6, no. 2 (1993), pp. 97–112.

Malsberger, John W: 'The Transformation of Republican Conservatism: The U.S. Senate, 1938-1952', *Congress and the Presidency* vol. 14, no. 1 (Spring 1987), pp. 17–31.

Mander, John: *Our German Cousins: Anglo-German Relations in the 19th and 20th Centuries*, John Murray, London, 1974.

Mandler, Peter: 'Two Cultures – One – Or Many?', in Burk, Katherine (ed): *The British Isles Since 1945*, Oxford University Press, Oxford, 2003.

Marwick, Arthur: *British Society Since 1945*, Penguin, Harmondsworth, 1996.

Marwick, Arthur: *The Sixties: Cultural Revolution in Britain, France, Italy and the United States c.1958–c.1974*, Oxford University Press, Oxford, 1998.

Matthews, Robin, Feinstein, Charles and Odling-Smee, John: *British Economic Growth, 1856-1973*, Clarendon Press, Oxford, 1982.

May, Elaine Tyler: *Homeward Bound: American Families in the Cold War Era*, Basic Books, New York, 1988.

McKellar, Susie, '"The Beauty of Stark Utility": Rational Consumption in America – "Consumer Reports" 1936-54', in Attfield, Judy, (ed): *Utility Reassessed: The Role of Ethics in the Practice of Design*, Manchester University Press, Manchester, 1999.

Mercer, Helen: *Constructing a Competitive Order: The Hidden History of British Antitrust Policies*, Cambridge University Press, Cambridge, 1995.

Middleton, Roger: *Government Versus the Market*, Edward Elgar, Cheltenham, 1996.

Middleton, Roger: *Charlatans or Saviours?: Economists and the British Economy from Marshall to Meade*, Edward Elgar, Cheltenham, 1998.

Middleton, Roger: *The British Economy Since 1945: Engaging with the Debate*, Macmillan, London, 2000.

Middleton, Roger: 'Struggling with the Impossible: Sterling, the Balance of Payments and British Economic Policy, 1949-72', in Arnon, A. and Young, W.L. (eds): *The Open Economy Macromodel: Past, Present and Future*, Kluwer Academic Press, Boston, MA, 2002.

Miles, Michael W.: *The Odyssey of the American Right*, Oxford University Press, New York, 1980.

Miles, Steve: *Youth Lifestyles in a Changing World*, Open University Press, Buckingham, 2000.

Miles, Steven: *Social Theory in the Real World*, Sage, London, 2001.

Mohan, John: *Planning, Markets and Hospitals*, Routledge, London, 2002.

Mort, Frank: *Cultures of Consumption: Masculinities and Social Space in Late Twentieth-Century Britain*, Routledge, London, 1996.

Mueller, Denis C. (ed): *The Political Economy of Growth*, Yale University Press, New Haven, 1983.

Nairn, Tom: *The Break-up of Britain: Crisis and Neo-nationalism*, New Left Books, London, 1977.

Nau, Henry R.: *The Myth of American Decline*, Oxford University Press, New York, 1990.

Nava, Micha, 'Consumption reconsidered: buying and power', *Cultural Studies*, 5 (1991).

Nixon, Sean: *Hard Looks: Masculinities, Spectators and Contemporary Consumption*, UCL Press, London, 1996.

O'Brien, Denis: 'The Emphasis on Market Economics', in Seldon, A. (ed): *The Emerging Consensus?: Essays on the Interplay between Ideas, Interests and Circumstances in the First 25 years of the IEA*, IEA, London, 1981.

O'Sullivan, Tim: 'TV Memories and Cultures of Viewing, 1950-65' in Corner, John (ed): *Popular Television in Britain: Studies in Cultural History*, BFI, London, 1991.

Obelkevich, James: 'Consumption' in Catterall, Peter and Obelkevich, James (eds): *Understanding Post-War British Society*, Routledge, London, 1994.

Offer, Avner: 'The Mask of Intimacy: Advertising and the Quality of Life' in Offer, Avner (ed): *In Pursuit of the Quality of Life*, Oxford University Press, Oxford, 1996.

Orwell, G.: *The Lion and the Unicorn*, Penguin, Harmondsworth, 1982 (first published 1941).

Osgerby, Bill: *Youth in Britain Since 1945*, Blackwell, Oxford, 1998.

Oswald, Andrew: 'Happiness and Economic Performance', *Economic Journal*, vol. 107, no. 445 (1997), pp. 1815–31.

Parsons, D. Wayne: *The Power of the Financial Press*, Edward Elgar, Aldershot, 1989.

Pavitt, Jane: *Brand.New*, V&A, London, 2000.

Peden, George: *The Treasury and British Public Policy, 1906-1959*, Oxford University Press, Oxford, 2000.

Pells, Richard: *Not Like Us: How Europeans Have Loved, Hated and Transformed American Culture Since World War II*, Harper Collins, New York, 1997.

Pemberton, Hugh: 'Policy Networks and Policy Learning: UK Economic Policy in the 1960s and 1970s', *Public Administration*, vol. 78, no. 4 (2000), pp. 771–92.

Pemberton, Hugh: 'A Taxing Task: Combating Britain's Relative Decline in the 1960s', *Twentieth Century British History*, vol. 12, no. 3 (2001), pp. 354–75.

Pemberton, Hugh: 'Learning, Governance and Economic Policy', *British Journal of Politics and International Relations* (2003, in press).

Pemberton, Hugh: *Policy Learning and British Governance in the 1960s*, Palgrave, London, forthcoming 2004.

Perkin, H.: *The Rise of Professional Society: England Since 1880*, Routledge, London, 1990.

Pimlott, Ben (ed): *Fabian Essays in Socialist Thought*, Heinemann, London, 1984.

Pimlott, Ben: *Harold Wilson*, HarperCollins, London, 1992.

Plant, Raymond: 'Democratic Socialism and Equality', in Fawcett, Helen and Lowe, Rodney (eds), *Welfare Policy in Britain: The Road from 1945*, Macmillan, Basingstoke, 1999.

Pollard, Stephen: *The Wasting of the British Economy: British Economic Policy 1945 to the Present*, Croom Helm, London, 1984.

Pommerin, Reiner (ed): *The American Impact on Post-war Germany*, Berghahn, Providence, RI, 1993.

Procter, Ian: 'The Privatisation of Working-Class Life: A Dissenting View', *British Journal of Sociology*, vol. 41 no. 2 (1990), pp. 157–80.

Proudfoot, Mary: *British Politics and Government, 1951-70: A Study of an Affluent Society*, Faber and Faber, London, 1970.

Putnam, Robert D.: *Bowling Alone: The Collapse and Revival of American Community*, Simon and Schuster, New York, 2000.

Ramsden, John: *The Making of Conservative Party Policy: The Conservative Party Research Department Since 1929*, Longman, London, 1980.

Reisman, David: 'Crosland's *Future*: The Missing Chapter on Burnham's *Managerial Revolution*', *Research in the History of Economic Thought and Methodology*, Archival Supplement no. 6 (1997), pp. 207–27.

Reisman, David: *Crosland's Future: Opportunity and Outcome*, Macmillan, Basingstoke, 1997.

Reynolds, David: *Rich Relations: The American Occupation of Britain 1942-1945*, Harper Collins, London, 1995.

Richardson, Kenneth: *Twentieth-Century Coventry*, City of Coventry, Coventry, 1972.

Richardson, William: *The Co-Operative Wholesale Society in War and Peace 1938-76*, CWS, Manchester, 1977.

Ringe, Astrid and Rollings, Neil: 'Responding to Relative Decline: The Creation of the National Economic Development Council', *Economic History Review*, vol. 53, no. 2 (2000), pp. 331–53.

Ringe, Astrid, Rollings, Neil and Middleton, Roger: *Economic Policy Under the Conservatives, 1951-64: A Guide to Documents in the National Archives of the UK*, IHR, London, 2004.

Rodgers, W.T. (ed): *Hugh Gaitskell*, Thames and Hudson, London, 1964.

Rowbotham, Sheila: *A Century of Women: The History of Women in Britain and the United States*, Penguin, London, 1999.

Rubinstein, W.D.: *The Very Wealthy in Britain Since the Industrial Revolution*, Croom Helm, London, 1981.

Rule, John: 'Time, Affluence and Private Leisure: The British Working Class in the 1950s and 1960s', *Labour History Review*, vol. 66, no. 2 (2001), pp. 223–42.

Samuel, Raphael: 'The Lost World of British Communism I', *New Left Review*, no. 154 (1985), p. 10.

Samuel, Raphael: *Theatres of Memory: Past and Present in Contemporary Culture*, Verso, London, 1994.

Schoenbaum, David and Pond, Elizabeth (eds): *The German Question and Other German Questions*, Macmillan, London, 1986.

Scott, Rosemary: *The Female Consumer*, Halsted Press, London, 1976.

Seabrook, John: *Nobrow: The Culture of Marketing the Marketing of Culture*, Methuen, London, 2001.

Seldon, Anthony: *Churchill's Indian Summer: The Conservative Government 1951-1955*, Hodder and Stoughton, London, 1981.

Shanks, Michael: *Planning and Politics: the British Experience, 1960-1976*, George Allen and Unwin (for Political and Economic Planning), London, 1977.

Shaw, Tony: *British Cinema and the Cold War: The State, Propaganda and Consensus*, I..B. Tauris, London, 2001.

Sheldrake, Sarah and Vickerstaff, John: *The History of Industrial Training in Britain*, Gower Publishing, Aldershot, 1987.

Shepherd, Robert: *Iain Macleod*, Hutchinson, London, 1994.

Sim, F.G.: *IOCU on Record: A Documentary History of the International Organisation of Consumers Unions, 1960-1990*, Consumers' Union, New York, 1991.

Singer, Otto: 'Knowledge and Politics in Economic Policy-making: Official Economic Advisers in the USA, Britain and Germany', in Peters, B.G. and Barker, A. (eds): *Advising West European Governments: Inquiries, Expertise and Public Policy*, Edinburgh University Press, Edinburgh, 1993.

Sloan, John W.: *Eisenhower and the Management of Prosperity*, University of Kansas Press, Lawrence, KS, 1991.

Smith, G.: *The Consumer Interest*, Gollancz, London, 1982.

Snowman, Daniel: *Britain and America: An Interpretation of their Culture, 1945-75*, Harper and Row, New York, 1977.

Solow, Robert: 'Growth Theory and After', *American Economic Review*, vol. 78, no. 3 (1988), pp. 307–17.

Solow, Robert: 'Perspectives on Growth Theory', *Journal of Economic Perspectives*, vol. 8, no. 1 (1994), pp. 45–54.

Stapleton, Julia: *Political Intellectuals and Public Identities in Britain Since 1850*, Manchester University Press, Manchester, 2001.

Stewart, Gordon T.: 'Tensing's Two Wrist Watches: The Conquest of Everest and Late Imperial Culture, 1921-1953', *Past and Present*, no. 149 (November 1995).

Stewart, Michael: *The Jekyll and Hyde Years: Politics and Economic Policy Since 1964*, J.M. Dent, London, 1977.

Stigler, George: *The Economist as Preacher*, University of Chicago Press, Chicago, 1982.

Sundquist, James L.: *The Dynamics of the Party System*, Brookings Institution, Washington, DC, 1983.

Supple, Barry: 'Fear of Failing: Economic History and the Decline of Britain', *Economic History Review*, vol. 47, no. 3 (1994), pp. 441–58.

Swagler, R: 'Evolution and applications of the term consumerism: themes and variations', *Journal of Consumer Affairs*, vol. 28, no. 2 (1994), pp. 347–60.

Tanner, Duncan, Thane, Pat and Tiratsoo, Nick (eds): *Labour's First Century*, Cambridge University Press, Cambridge, 2000.

Taylor, A.J. (ed): *The Standard of Living in Britain in the Industrial Revolution*, Methuen, London, 1975.

Taylor, Andrew: 'Speaking to Democracy: The Conservative Party and Mass Opinion from the 1920s to 1950s' in Ball, Stuart and Holliday, Ian (eds): *Mass Conservatism: The Conservatives and the Public Since the 1880s*, Frank Cass, London, 2002.

Thompson, Noel: 'Social Opulence, Private Asceticism: Ideas of Consumption in Early Socialist Thought', in Daunton, Martin and Hilton, Matthew (eds), *The Politics of Consumption*, Berg, Oxford, 2001.

Thompson, Paul: 'Playing at Being Skilled Men: Factory Culture and Pride in Work Skills Among Coventry Car Workers', *Social History*, vol. 13, no. 1 (1988), pp. 45–69.

Thompson, Peter: '"Labour's Gannex Conscience?": Politics and Popular Attitudes in the Permissive Society', in Coopey, Richard, Fielding, Steve and Tiratsoo, Nick (eds): *The Wilson Governments, 1964-70*, Pinter, London, 1993.

Thoms D.W. and Donnelly T: 'Coventry's Industrial Economy, 1880-1980' in Lancaster B. and Mason T.: *Life and Labour in a Twentieth Century City: The Experience of Coventry*, Cryfield Press, Coventry ND [1986?].

Thornton, Sarah: *Club Cultures: Music, Media and Subcultural Capital*, Polity, Cambridge, 1995.

Tiratsoo, Nick: 'Popular Politics, Affluence and the Labour Party in the 1950s', in Gorst, Anthony, Johnman, Lewis and Lucas, W. Scott (eds): *Contemporary British History, 1931-1961: Politics and the Limits of Policy*, Pinter, London, 1991.

Tiratsoo, Nick: *Reconstruction, Affluence and Labour Politics: Coventry 1945-60*, Routledge, London, 1990.

Tiratsoo, Nick (ed): *From Blitz to Blair: A New History of Britain Since 1939*, Weidenfeld and Nicolson, London, 1997.

Tiratsoo, Nick: 'The American Quality Gospel in Britain and Japan, 1950-1970', in Sahlin-Andersson, K. and Engwall, L. (eds): *The Expansion of Management Knowledge: Carriers, Flows and Sources*, Stanford University Press, Stanford, CA, 2002.

Tivey, L.: 'The Politics of the Consumer', in Kimber R. and Richardson, J.J.: *Pressure Groups in Britain: A Reader*, Dent, London, 1974.

Tivey, L.: 'Quasi-government for Consumers', in Barker A. (ed): *Quangos in Britain: Government and the Networks of Public Policy Making*, Macmillan, Basingstoke, 1982.

Tomlinson, Alan (ed): *Consumption, Identity and Style: Marketing, Meanings, and the Packaging of Pleasure*, Routledge, London, 1990.

Tomlinson, Jim: 'Inventing "Decline": The Falling Behind of the British Economy in the Post-war Years', *Economic History Review*, vol. 49, no. 4 (1996), pp. 731–57.

Tomlinson, Jim: *The Politics of Decline: Understanding Post-War Britain*, Longman, London, 2001.

Tomlinson, Jim: 'Economic Policy' in Floud, Roderick and Johnson, Paul: *The Cambridge Economic History of Modern Britain, Volume 3: Structural Change 1939-2000*, Cambridge University Press, Cambridge, in press.

Tomlinson, Jim: *Modernising Britain? The Economic Policies of the Wilson Government, 1964-70*, Manchester University Press, Manchester, in press.

Toye, Richard: 'The "Gentleman in Whitehall" Reconsidered: The Evolution of Douglas Jay's View on Economic Planning and Consumer Choice, 1937-1947', *Labour History Review*, vol. 67, no. 2 (August 2002), pp. 187–204.

Turner, John: 'A Land Fit for Tories To Live In: The Political Ecology of the British Conservative Party, 1944-94', *Contemporary European History*, vol. 4 no. 2 (1995), pp. 189–208.

Veit-Wilson, John: 'The National Assistance Board and the "Rediscovery" of Poverty' in Fawcett, Helen and Lowe, Rodney (eds), *Welfare Policy in Britain: The Road from 1945*, Macmillan, Basingstoke, 1999.

Veldman, Meredith: *Fantasy, the Bomb and Greening of Britain, 1945-80*, Cambridge University Press, Cambridge, 1994.

Vinen, Richard: *A History in Fragments: Europe in the Twentieth Century*, Little, Brown: London, 2000.

Wallace, Claire and Kovatcheva, Sijka: *Youth in Society*, Macmillan, Basingstoke, 1998.

Waters, Chris: 'Representations of Everyday Life: LS Lowry and the Landscape of Memory in Post-war Britain', *Representations* no. 65 (Winter 1999), p. 121–50.

Wattenberg, Ben J.: *The Statistical History of the United States: From Colonial Times to the Present*, Basic Books, New York, 1976.

Waterhouse, R.: 'New Frontiers for Consumerism', *RSA Journal*, vol. 136, no. 5383 (June 1988).

Weight, Richard: '"Building a New British Culture": The Arts Centre Movement, 1943-53' in Weight, Richard, and Beach, Abigail: *The Right to Belong: Citizenship and National Identity in Britain, 1930-1960*, IB Taurus, London, 1998.

Weight, Richard: *Patriots: British National Identity, 1940-2000*, Macmillan, London, 2002.

Whiting, Richard: *The Labour Party and Taxation: Party Identity and Political Purpose in Twentieth-Century Britain*, Cambridge University Press, Cambridge, 2000.

Whitworth, Lesley: 'Shop and Shopfloor: Men's Sense of Belonging in 1930s Coventry', in Putnam, Tim, Facey, Ruth and Swales, Valerie (eds): *Making and Unmaking: Creative and Critical Practice in a Designed World*, Design History Society/University of Portsmouth, Portsmouth, 2000.

Whitworth, Lesley: 'Fear and Loathing in West Germany? Contested Claims for Consumer Identities on Either Side of the Second World War', in Playdon, Peter (ed): *Proceedings of the Living in a Material World Conference*, Coventry University, Coventry, 1999.

Wiener, Martin: *English Culture and the Decline of the Industrial Spirit, 1850-1980*, Cambridge University Press, Cambridge, 1981.

Wilensky, Harold L. and Turner, Lowell: *Democratic Corporatism and Policy Linkages: The Interdependence of Industrial, Labor-market, Incomes and Social Policies in Eight Countries*, Institute of International Studies, University of California, Berkeley, CA, 1987.

Wilson, Elizabeth: 'All the Rage', *New Socialist* (November/December 1983).

Woodham, Jonathan M.*: The Industrial Designer and the Public*, Pembridge, London, 1983.

Woodham, Jonathan M. and Maguire, Patrick J.: *Design and Cultural Politics in Post-War Britain: The Britain Can Make It Exhibition of 1946*, Leicester University Press, London, 1997.

Wraith, R.: *The Consumer Cause: A Short Account of its Organisation, Power and Importance,* Royal Institute of Public Administration, London, 1976.

Wybrow, Robert J. (ed): *Britain Speaks Out, 1937-87: A Social History as Seen Through the Gallup Data*, Macmillan, London, 1989.

Wyn, Johanna and White, Rob: *Rethinking Youth*, Sage, London, 1997.

Young, Hugo: *This Blessed Plot: Britain and Europe From Churchill to Blair*, Macmillan, London, 1998.

Young, Ken: 'Orpington and the "Liberal Revival"' in Cook, Chris and Ramsden, John (eds): *By-Elections in British Politics*, UCL Press, London, 1997.

Zakaria, Fareed: *The Future of Freedom: Illiberal Democracy at Home and Abroad*, W.W. Norton, New York, 2003.

Zweiniger-Bargielowska, Ina: 'Rationing, Austerity and the Conservative Party Recovery after 1945', *Historical Journal*, vol. 37, no. 1 (1994), pp. 173–97.

Zweiniger-Bargielowska, Ina: *Austerity in Britain: Rationing, Controls and Consumption, 1939-1955*, Oxford University Press, Oxford, 2000.

Zweiniger-Bargielowska, Ina: 'Living Standards and Consumption' in Addison, Paul and Jones, Harriet: *The Blackwell Companion to Contemporary Britain, 1939-2000*, Blackwell, Oxford, in press.

Unpublished Material

Black, Lawrence: 'Coming to Terms with Affluence? Socialism and Social Change in 1950s Britain', paper to 'Consensus or Coercion?' conference, University College London, March 1999.

Brivati, Brian: 'The End of Decline: The Blair-Brown Governments and Contemporary British History', inaugural lecture, Kingston University, March 2003.

Bugge, Christian: 'The End of Youth Subculture? Dance Culture and Youth Marketing 1988-2000', Ph.D. dissertation, Kingston University, 2002.

Cairncross, Alec: 'Writing the History of Recent Economic Policy', unpublished paper, 1970.

Dworkin, Dennis: 'Cultural Marxism Revisited: The New Left and British Decline', paper to the North American Conference on British Studies, Baltimore, November 2002.

Frith, Hannah and Gleeson, Kate: 'Identity: An Equal Resource?' paper to the 'Global Youth' conference, University of Plymouth, September 2001.

Pemberton, Hugh: 'The Keynesian-plus Experiment: A Study of Social Learning in the UK Core Executive, 1960-1966', Ph.D. dissertation, University of Bristol, 2001.

Prosser, R: 'Coventry: A Study in Urban Continuity', MA dissertation, University of Birmingham, 1955.

Rollings, Neil and Middleton, Roger: 'British Economic Policy in the 1950s and 1960', paper to the Economic History Society Annual Conference, University of Birmingham, April 2002.

Index

Abel-Smith, Brian 7, 46
Abortion 73
Abrams, Mark 5, 91, 99, 188, 192
Ackroyd, Elizabeth 155
Acts of Parliament
    See Legislation
Adams, Mary 155
Advertising 7-8, 90, 93, 99, 150, Ch. 11
Advertising Quarterly 190, 192
Agriculture 113
Akihito, Prince 209
Albemarle Report
    See Official Reports
Alfred Herbert News, The 169
Amateurism
    Of consumer activists 157, 162
    Of Whitehall 118-9
    And the British economy 2-3, 64,
        118-9, 209
Angry Silence, The (1960) 207
Annan, Noel 74
Anti-ugly Group 88
Architectural Review and 'subtopia' 88
Attlee, Clement 54-5, 72, 74, 76, 81
Auden, W.H. 219
Audi 215
Austerity 5-7, 25-6, 47, 56-8, 69-72,
    74-6, 171

Balance of payments 58, 75, 116-17,
    139, 142-3, 192
Balogh, Thomas 113, 137, 143
Barber, Antony ('Barber boom') 131
Beatles, The 98, 191, 216
Beaverbrook, Lord 203, 213
Bell, Daniel 190
Benn, Tony 60
Betting 61, 63
Bevan, Aneurin 78, 91, 94
Beveridge Report (1942)
    See Official Reports
Birmingham Consumers' Group Ch. 8
Blair, Tony 4, 53, 64

Board of Trade 116, 120, 169
Bond, James 207
Booker, Christopher 36, 49
Borrie, Gordon 152, 156-7
Bourdieu, Pierre – 'habitus' 162
Bow Group
    See Conservative Party
Boyle, Edward 47
Braine, John – *Room at the Top* 91, 94
Bridge Over the River Kwai (1957)
    210-11
Bristol Consumers' Group 87
Britain Can Make It exhibition (1946)
    171, 178
British Commonwealth 210, 219
British empire:
    See British Commonwealth
British Market Research Bureau 178
British national identity Ch. 12
British Standards Institute 177-8
Brittan, Samuel 36, 49, 141
Brown, George 142-3
Butler, R.A.B. 21, 24, 26-8, 37, 40, 42,
    91, 94, 131

Cabinet Social Services Committee 43
Calder, Nicholas 56, 134, 137
Callaghan, James 37, 142
Campaign for Nuclear Disarmament
    (CND) 88, 212
Campania (Festival of Britain) 173
Cars
    See Consumer Durables
Castle, Barbara 89
Christian democracy 19
Churchill, Winston 24, 26-7, 57, 70,
    213
Cinema 6, 88, 207-8, 220
Citizens Advice Bureau 154
Civil Service, modernisation of 42, 49,
    113, 129
Civil society 85, 157
Clark, Kenneth 95

Clarke, Sir Richard ('Otto') 43-5, 115
Class identities 77
'Clean-up TV' campaign 87
Clore, Charles 61
Coca-Cola 216
Cold War 6, 15, 19, 28, 58
Cole, G.D.H. 54
Comics, gendering of content 206, 210
Computers 18
Consensus 85, 129
Conservatism Ch. 2
Conservative Party 2, 6, Ch. 3, 99
    Attitudes to affluence 93
    Bow Group 95
    Committee on the Future of the
        Social Services 39
    One-nation tradition 40, 46
    Recreation, Arts and Sport
        committee 96
    Research Department 26, 36, 39-40,
        45-9
    Thatcherism 40
Conservative voters 28, 92
Consumer complaints 154
Consumer Council 93, 155-6, 159, 177
Consumer durables 2, 7, 16, 149
    Motor cars/cycles 16, 18-19, 23, 85,
        97, 110, 168, 212
    Radios 18, 168, 212
    Refrigerators 86-7, 92
    Washing machines 16, 23, 85-7, 89,
        92, 110
    See also Television
Consumer services 153
Consumer, The 40, 154
    Youth market Ch. 11
Consumerism/consumption 4, 56, 63,
    70-75, 79, 85, 90-91, 93, 108, 109
    (Figure 7.2), 110, 117, Ch. 9, Ch. 10,
    209
Consumers' Association 6, 88, 91, 94-
    6, Ch. 9, 177
    Membership of 158
        Gender of Ch. 9
    See also Which?
Co-Operative movement 94, 96-7, 149
Coronation Street 91, 99
Council of Industrial Design 96, 155,
    Ch. 10
Counter-culture 7, 185, 189
Cousins, Frank 92

Coventry 93, 167, 178
Coventry City Council 93
Credit, consumer 23-24, 61, 85-6, 96,
    149
Crime 87
Cripps, Stafford 55, 57, 71
Crosland, Tony 53, 55, Ch. 5, 90, 95-6
Crossman, Richard 55-6, 61, 72, 74, 78,
    79-80, 96
Cultural industries Ch. 11
Cultural Studies 185, 199
Culture 72-3, 78-9
Curran, Charles 91

Dad's Army 206
Daily Herald 54
    Post-War Homes Exhibition (1945)
        172
Daily Mail 214
Daily Mirror 212
Dalton, Hugh 54-5, 169-71
Darling, George 93
Davenport, Nicholas 55, 59
De Gaulle, Charles 64, 213
Decline 86
Decline, relative 1-5, 58, Ch. 7, 129,
    131
Declinism 1-4, 107, 116, 122, 129,
    131-2
Demand management 109, 114
Democratic Party (USA)
    See United States of America
Denmark 16
Department of Economic Affairs (DEA)
    113, 120, 129, 136, 141
Design 174, 176-7
Design centre (and index) 172-3
Design fairs/weeks 173-4
Diamond, Aubrey 152, 155
Disney 220
Divorce 73
DIY 90
Domar, Evsey 142
Dress sense:
    See Fashion
Durbin, Evan 53, 76

Eccles, David 47
Economic knowledge 130, 136
Economic Planning Board 115
Economist, The 26, 54, 60, 91

Economists Ch. 8
  Political naivety of 140-41
Eden, Anthony 27, 57, 216
Education:
  Independent 40
  State 40-2, 187-8
Eisenhower, President 15, 21-24, 28,
  216
Eliot, T.S. 204
Elizabeth II 213
Encounter 77, 219
Equality 70
Erhard, Ludwig 206, 208
European Economic Community 20,
  48, 55, 63, 95, 203, 218
  British perceptions of 213-15
Experts/expert knowledge:
  See Management and professional
    elites
Export performance 111-12, 114, 168,
  170, 204-5, 209

Fabian Society, The 56, 71, 73, 76-7,
  151
Fashion 100, 188, 190, 216
Fassbinder, Reiner 208
Federation of British Industry (FBI)
  115, 121
Feminism 16
Festival of Britain (1951) 171
Fiscal policy 119
Fleet Street 99, 136
Flexible labour market 117
Focus 159
Football 62, 86, 214-5, 219
Ford 216
Forward 53, 55, 64
France 15, 91, 112, 160
Frankfurt School 'mass culture' 199
Fraser, Michael 26, 40-1
Friedman, Milton 140
Full employment 7, 53, 70, 107
Fulton Report
  See Official Reports
Funeral in Berlin 207

Gaitskell, Hugh 35, 53-4, 59-60, 62, 78,
  90, 94
Galbraith, J.K. 8, 44
  The Affluent Society 6, 24, 54, 58,
    80, 86

Gallup 23, 28, 86, 203, 210, 218
Gammans, David 217
Gardening 86, 90, 97, 175
Gender and consumers Ch. 10
General Agreement on Trade and Tariffs
  (GATT) 110
General Elections:
  (1951) 69
  (1955) 5, 69, 74
  (1959) 2, 28, 53, 69, 79
  (1964) 80, 98, 119, 140
  (1966) 99
  (1970) 142
Germany, West:
  British perceptions of 203-9
  Bundestag election (1957) 28
  Christian Democratic Union (CDU)
    28, 49
  Social Democratic Party of Germany
    (SPD) 28
  Wirtschaftswunder 15, 28, 112,
    204-5
Giddens, Anthony 197
Gloag, John 174-5, 178
'Golden age' 107, 130
Goldman, Peter 92-3, 96
Goldwater, Barry 22
Good Food Guide 88, 153
Gould, Philip 53
Government, central
  Technical co-operation between
    departments 47
  Expenditure by 37-8
  Growth of 35
  Modernisation of Ch. 3
Government, local 381
  Local Government Operational
    Research Unit 87
Greece 19
Green is the Heath (1955) 208
Growth, economic 108, 112, 118, Ch.
  7, Ch. 8, 130 (Figure 8.1)
  'Intoxication by integers' 131
  Political uses of 142
  See also Stop-go
Guardian, The 94-5
Gundrey, Elizabeth 177

Hailsham, Lord 47
Hall, Sir Robert 115, 136
Hanging 63

Happiness 17, 36, 75-6, 79, 88
Harbury, Colin 151, 157
Harrington, Michael 89
Harris, Bernard, *The American Takeover of Britain* (1968) 220
Harrod, Sir Roy 116, 133
Hartley, Anthony 3
Hauge, Gabrial 22-23
Hayato, Ikeda 209
Hayek, F.A. von 138
Heath, Edward 159
Hegarty, John 194
Heinemann, Gustav 207
Heritage 7
Heuss, President 212
Hillary, Edmund 220
Hire purchase
    See Credit, consumer
Hirohito, Emperor 209, 212, 220
Hoggart, Richard 5, 86
Holidays, increase in 107, 205, 219
Hollywood 217
Homosexuality 63, 95
    See also Official Reports
Hoover 216
Housing 6, 26, 38
Howe, Geoffrey 159

Immigration 95, 207
Incomes policies 115, 117, 118, 120
    Pay pause (1961) 118
Incomes, rise in 6, 107, 187-8
Industrial Production 110 (Figure 7.3)
Industrial Training Boards 121
Industrial Training Council 121
Inflation 6-7, 95, 108-9, 114-5, 122, 192
Institute of Economic Affairs (IEA) 37, 47, 93, 139, 141
    Choice in Welfare 44
International Monetary Fund (IMF) 44, 110
International Organisation of Consumers Unions 160
Ireland, Republic of 19-20
Italy 15

J. Walter Thompson 99
Japan 16-17, 112
    British perceptions of 209-13
Jay, Douglas Ch. 4

Jay, Douglas – 'The Gentleman in Whitehall' 61
Jenkins, Roy 55, 71, 78, 95
Joseph, Keith 38, 98

Kamikaze pilots 211
'Keep Britain Tidy' campaign 87
Kennedy, J.F. 24, 28
Keynes, J.M. 63, 136, 138, 203
Keynesianism 7, 24, 108, 122, 133, 142
Keynesian-plus Ch. 7, 129, 135
Khrushchev, Nikita 6
Kodak 216
Korean War 22, 109
Kurosawa, Akira 220

Labelling (of consumer goods) 150, 176
Labour Party 2, 6, 20-21, 24, Ch. 4, Ch. 5
    1964 Women's Conference 92
    Attitudes to affluence 64, 69, 75, 78, 97
    Debate over Clause 4 59-60
    Finance and Economic Policy Committee 59
    Revisionism in Ch. 4, 63, Ch. 5, 95, 158
Lee, Sir Frank 114, 120
Legislation:
    Children and Young Persons Act (1963) 38
    Commercial Television Act (1954) 217
    Consumer Credit Act (1974) 159
    Consumer Safety Act (1978) 159
    Contracts of Employment Act (1963) 39
    Education Act (1944) 187
    Fair Trading Act (1973) 159
    Industrial Training Act (1964) 39, 121
    Redundancy Payment Bill (1962) 39
    Rent Act (1957) 38
    Resale Price Maintenance Act (1964) 48, 110
    Restrictive Trade Practices Act (1977) 159
    Trades Descriptions Act (1968) 96, 155, 159
Leisure 75, 95, 154, 187
Leslie, S.C. 169

Liberal Party 24
  1906-1914 reforms 35
  Orpington by-election (1962) 93
Listener, The 61
Lloyd, Selwyn 116-9, 134, 140
Luxury 18

MacArthur, General 213
MacDougall, Donald 136, 140-41
Macleod, Iain 28, 35, 37, 42-3, 46, 98
Macmillan, Harold 2, 20-21, 26-8, 35,
  37-9, 57, 94, 100, 118, 120, 143,
  187, 203, 205, 208
  'Never had it so good' speech 2, 6
Macnamara, Robert 218
Man in the White Suit, The 149
Management and professional elites 72,
  Ch. 7, 149, 154, 158, 162, Ch. 10
Manufacturers (and COID) 170-71
Marketing Ch. 11
Marks and Spencer 96
Marshall Aid 203
Mass Observation 178, 218
Matsui (Dixon's) 212
Maudling, Reginald 44, 47, 134, 140,
  142
Mayhew, Christopher 55
Michy Boom 209
Middle class 28, 45, 92, 96, 151, 161
Midland Industrial Designers
  Association 174
Mikardo, Ian 78
Millar, Robert, *The Affluent Sheep*
  (1960) 156
Ministry of Labour 116, 120
Molony Report
  See Official Reports
Monetarism 143
Montomery, Lord 213
Moore, Bobby 215
Morrison, Herbert 217
Motor cars/cycles
  See Consumer Durables
Mouse, Mickey 220
'Mr Designer' 172, (Plate 4)
Myrdal, Gunnar 89

NAAFI 85
Nader, Ralph 89, 157
National Assistance Board 38, 46

National Board for Prices and Incomes
  (NBPI) 122
National Consumer Council (NCC)
  151-52, 160
National Economic Development
  Council (NEDC) 39, 48, 118-9,
  121-22, 130, 138, 140
  *Conditions Favourable to Economic
  Growth* (1963) 39
National Economic Development Office
  (NEDO) 39, 136
National Enterprise Board (NEB) 60
National Federation of Consumer
  Groups 152, 155, 158
National Health Service, waiting times
  153
National Incomes Commission 122
National Insurance regulator
  See Tax Regulators
National Institute for Economic and
  Social Research (NIESR) 115
National Joint Advisory Council (NJAC)
  115
National Plan (1965) 119, 129-31, 140-41
National Production Advisory Council
  (NPAC) 115
National Service (military conscription)
  86, 187
National Viewers and Listeners'
  Association 87
Nationalisation 53, 56, 59, Ch. 5
Nationalism 7, 208
Neild, Robert 137
Netherlands, The 15-16
New Deal (USA) 21
New Labour 7, 54
New Left 95, 185
New Left Review 3
New Right/Thatcherism 3, 142, 186,
  195
New Society 95
New Statesman, The 61, 64
News of the World 64
Nicolson, Harold 204, 217
Nissan 212
Nixon, Richard 6, 22-24
Nylons, polyesters 149, 162, 168

Organisation for Economic Cooperation
  and Development (OECD) 17-18,
  131

Organisation for European Economic
    Co-operation (OEEC) 110
Off licences 6
Office of Fair Trading 151, 154, 156
Official reports:
    Albemarle Report (*The Youth
        Services of England and Wales*,
        1960) 189
    Beveridge report (*Social Insurance
        and Allied Services*, 1942) 35,
        37
    Fulton Report (*The Civil Service*,
        1968) 137
    Molony Report (*Report of the
        Committee on Consumer
        Protection*, 1962) 159
    Pilkington Report (*Report of the
        Committee on Broadcasting*,
        1962) 93
    Plowden Report (*Control of Public
        Expenditure*, 1961) 43
    Robbins Report (*Higher Education*,
        1963) 38, 135
    Wolfenden Report (*Report of the
        Committee on Homosexual
        Offences and Prostitution*, 1957)
        62
Opinion polling 45
Organization of Petroleum Exporting
    Countries (OPEC) 5, 109
Orwell, George 162
Oxfam 98
Oxford Consumers' Group 152

Packard, Vance 89, 155
Padmore, Sir Thomas 114
Parliament, Acts of:
    See Legislation
Pay pause (1961)
    See Incomes Policy
Payroll regulator
    See Tax Regulators
Penguin Books 2
Pensions, old age 38-9, 41
Permissive society/'permissiveness' 7,
    29, 76, 87, 95, 98
Phillips curve 109, 142
Phillips, Morgan 71, 80
Pilkington Report
    See Official Reports
Planning 56-7, 63, 72, 77, 118, 130

Plowden Report
    See Official Reports
Political and Economic Planning (PEP)
    115, 152
Politicians, economic naivety of 140-41
Politics, culture of Ch. 6
Politics, professionalization of 99-100
Population growth 133, 187
Portugal 19
Post Office Savings Bank
    See Trustee Savings Bank
Post-neoclassical endogenous growth
    theory 118, 134
Potter, Dennis – *The Glittering Coffin*
    (1960) 61, 90
Poverty line 38
Poverty, rediscovery of 46
Powell, Enoch 35, 37, 42, 45, 100, 207
Premium Bonds 61, 92, 94
Presley, Elvis 204
Priestley, J.B. 88, 149, 168
Prisoners-of-war 203
Productivity 108, 111 (Table 7.1), 132
Profumo scandal 64, 99
Public Expenditure Survey Committee
    (PESC) 43, 45, 119
    See also 'Plowden Report, 1961'
        under Official Reports
Public houses, licensing of 73
Public lavatories 153
Public vs. private sphere 71, 90, 190

Quant, Mary 190-1
Queen 86

Radio 98
    See also Consumer Durables
Ramsey, Alf 214
Rationing 5, 15, 27, 74
Reconstruction, post-war 108, 116, 122
Refuse collection/disposal 87, 153
Republican Party (USA)
    See United States of America
Resale Price Maintenance 93, 117, 149
Restaurants:
    See *Good Food Guide*
Retail Price Index, calculation of 85
Riesman, David 89
Robbins Report
    See Official Reports
Robinson, Joan 134

Rock and roll 94, 188
Rodgers, Bill 55
Rostow, Walter 132
Russell, Gordon 175

Saatchi and Saatchi 193
Sackville-West, Vita 204
Sainsbury's 216
Sampson, Anthony 3, 137
Scandinavia 19, 160
Second World War, cultural legacy,
    myths of 206-7, 210
Secularisation 16, 87
Selective Employment Tax 137
Self-liberation:
    See Happiness
Shanks, Michael 3, 137
    The Stagnant Society 64
Shone, Sir Robert 133
Shonfield, Andrew 137
Shop opening hours 117
Shopper's Guide 177
Sillitoe, Alan – *Saturday Night and
    Sunday Morning* 86
Social policy Ch. 3
Spain 19
Sport 86
Sputnik 64
State Participation Unit Trust 59
State, relationship of individuals with
    72-3, 80, 179
Statistical revolution 132
Sterling, fixed exchange
    rates/devaluation of 114, 119, 143,
    214-15
Stewart, Michael 214
Stop-go 57, 114, 138-9, 206
Suburbs/suburbanisation 6, 89, 149,
    151, 162
Suez crisis 205, 217
Sunday trading 63
Supermarkets 96, 216
Supply-side policy changes 117
Sutton Coldfield Consumers' Group
    157
Sweden 49, 121

Tariff protections, proposed abolition of
    117
Tate Gallery 62
Tawney, R.H. 72, 75

Taxation 19, 23, 26-7, 42-4, 48-9, 53,
    56, 117, 119-21, 137, 205
Teddy Boys 188
Teenager, category of 188
Telephone 8, 85, 168
Television 6, 16-17, 23, 45, 61-2, 88,
    90, 94, 97, 110, 212, 217, 219
Tensing, Sherpa 220
Thatcher, Margaret 49
    See also Conservative Party
    See also New Right
Thompson, E.P 88, 185
Thorneycroft, Peter 27, 44, 216
Time 190
Times, The 54, 61, 161
Times Literary Supplement 61
Titmuss, Richard 46
Tivey, Leonard 152, 156-7
Tokyo Olympics (1964) 212
Tomlinson, Jim 1, 2, 58, 112-3
Toshiba 213
Townsend, Peter 7, 46, 72
Trade Unions 27-8, 45, 118, 121-2
Treasury, The 15, 27-8, 36, 39, 43, 45,
    48-9, Ch. 7, 205
    Report on 'Economic Growth and
        National Efficiency' (1961) 44,
        48-9, 116-8
Tribune 56, 60, 64
Truman, Harry 20
Trustee Savings Bank 59

Unemployment 7
Union of Soviet Socialist Republics
    (USSR) 17, 57-8, 74, 78, 203
United Nations 110
    UNESCO 15
United States of America 6, Ch. 2, 58,
    64, 80, 86, 89, 112, 132, 160, 216
    British perceptions of 216-18
    Consumers Union 160, 176
    Democratic Party 23, 28, 64
    New deal 21
    Presidential election (1948) 21, 25
    Presidential election (1956) 28
    Republican Party 21, 23-4, 28
University of Birmingham 151-3
    Centre for Contemporary Cultural
        Studies 185-6

Vansittart, Lord 203

Victor 210
Video 212-13
Voluntary Service Overseas (VSO) 47,
    93

Walker, Patrick Gordon 78
Washing machines
    See Consumer Durables
Waterhouse, Rachel 152, 156-7, 161
Wayne, John 220
Webb, Beatrice and Sidney 71, 73
Welfare state 2, 16, 19-20, Ch. 3
Which? 95, 154, 162, 177
Whitehouse, Mary 87-8
Williams, Francis 8, 99, 216
Williams, Raymond 5, 8
Williams, William Emrys 174
Wilmott, Peter 5, 86, 89
Wilson, Harold 3, 55, 80, 143, 213, 218

'White heat of technology' /
    modernisation of Britain 64
Wolfenden Report
    See Official Reports
Woman 172
Woolton, Lord 27
Wootton, Barbara 87
Working class 71, 86
Worswick, David 56

Xenophobia 219

Young Conservatives 87, 93, 97-9
Young, Michael 86, 89, 93, 95-6, 158,
    160
Youth/young people 154, Ch. 11, 212-13
    Youth sub-cultures Ch. 11

Zweig, Ferdynand 5, 178